WESTMAR COLLEGE

W9-BVH-198

Martin E. Marty is Professor of Modern Church History at the University of Chicago as well as Associate Dean of the Divinity School there. Associate Editor of *The Christian Century* and author-editor of a fortnightly newsletter, *Context,* he is also the author of *The Search for a Usable Future, The Modern Schism, A Short History of Christianity, Righteous Empire: The Protestant Experience in America, The New Shape of American Religion,* and *Varieties of Unbelief.* Dr. Marty is Vice-President of the Lutheran Commission on Social Concerns, a Fellow of the American Academy of Arts and Sciences, and editor of the University of Chicago Religion in America series.

HISTORY OF RELIGION

Protestantism

Protestantism

MARTIN E. MARTY

Professor of Modern Church History
University of Chicago

HISTORY OF RELIGION SERIES

General Editor: E. O. James

Holt, Rinehart and Winston
New York   Chicago   San Francisco

280.4
A388

BX
4811
.M347

Copyright © 1972 by Martin E. Marty
All rights reserved, including the right to reproduce
this book or portions thereof in any form.

Published simultaneously in Canada by Holt, Rinehart
and Winston of Canada, Limited.

ISBN: 0-03-091353-5

Library of Congress Catalog Card Number: 76-182759

First Edition

Printed in the United States of America

87081

To Alfred P. Klausler and John Strietelemeier

CONTENTS

FOREWORD

Books in this "History of Religion" series may accent either history or religion. As an historian I have seen no need for another general history of Protestantism and particularly not of its sixteenth century origins. For that reason the stress falls here on religion. This book is an historically informed, theologically interested phenomenological study of Protestantism as a religion. No attempt is made to provide a full chronological accounting in narrative form of Protestant origins and development. This topical approach is phenomenological in the sense that it deals with the data and phenomena of Protestant churches and cultures, combining concerns for ritual, doctrine, ethos, and expression. It strives to display an awareness of the cultural conditioning of Protestant experience and is content to describe rather than to defend it or to seek to be normative about the subject.

One could pursue such a study in a variety of ways. Most tempting, most simple, and most distracting for readers would be to attempt a catalog of the varieties of Protestantism through a sequence of denominational references, or to write a kind of comparative study of the various breeds of Protestantism. Without for a moment understating the case for the heterogeneity displayed through the history of evangelical churches and Protestant culture, this essay concentrates on the convergences and coherences that have also been manifest. Equal attention is paid to the Protestant churches and Protestant culture.

Perhaps the reader can best locate this book if the author will provide here the answer he has given when during the past three years people would ask, "What are you working on these days?" The answer would go something like this: "I have been asked to prepare a volume for a series on the History of Religion which is being published in Great Britain and the United States. Some of the volumes deal with primitive or ancient religions, such as those of Scandinavia and pre-Columbian America, or with Manichaeism. Others have to do with earlier phases of living religions; one on the early Christian Church is typical. A few volumes are to deal comprehensively with the history and present manifestations of

ix

living faiths; a book on Islam and one on Roman Catholicism have already appeared. Mine has to do with world Protestantism. Rather than write an apology for it or a theological defense, I am to look at it from a great distance, as it were; from that vantage the assignment calls for me to describe how Protestantism came to be what it is and to interpret its life today."

Rather than devote much of the book to the insoluble problems of defining the subject matter, it seemed best to be rather matter-of-fact and to reach for the *Oxford English Dictionary*, which defines Protestant as "the Christian churches or bodies which repudiated the papal authority, and separated or were severed from the Roman communion in the Reformation of the sixteenth century, and generally any of the bodies of Christians descended from them; hence in general language applied to any Western Christian or member of a Christian church outside the Roman communion." If a phenomenon belongs to Eastern Christianity, Roman Catholicism, or recent schisms from either, it does not belong properly in this book. If it does not fall into those categories, it may very well be implied here, however marginally.

One way to solve the problem of definition would be to rest content with description and to refrain entirely from judgment; in that approach anyone who wants to be considered Protestant is considered Protestant. We were able to go quite far with such a point of view except that it was necessary to include some churches which do not always see themselves as Protestant. Among these are high Anglicanism and similar versions of Lutheranism, on one hand, or some of the heirs of nineteenth century primitive Gospel movements which argue that their ties are only to the first and never to the sixteenth century, on the other. Common usage and social pressure seem to push these groups into the Protestant camp and they certainly share what is predominant in this book's emphases, life in a Protestant culture.

No worries are here expressed about the negative sound of the word "Protestant" or about a definition which is similarly negative, concentrating as it does on that part of Western Christianity which "repudiated papal authority." The positive features of Protestantism will be evident throughout the book; "What's in a name?" might be the natural question when these are discussed. On the other hand many Protestants believe that the "Protestant principle of prophetic protest" is such a vital contribution to the history of religion that it deserves separate treatment and one need not be ashamed of its presence or the sound of its name.

This principle defines Protestantism more than many of its adherents might care to believe. Rejection of the papacy, in Oscar Cullmann's argument, is the all-encompassing overt mark of Protestantism's belief that the eschatological tension between present and future, between "already fulfilled" and "not yet finished" has not been removed in the life of the Christian Church. Hence infallibility as consolidated in the papal office is denied by all Protestants. Catholics, on the other hand, believe that the tension has been partially removed through the infallible teaching office as guaranteed through the papacy. The attitude toward the papacy colors Protestant philosophies of history and is to be apparent among the movements discussed in the present work.[1]

Such a definition also suggests that the author has not been able to find other completely consistent elements in the definition of Protestantism. The conventionally supplied answers urge that Protestants are united in their teaching on divine grace and biblical authority, but honest phenomenological inquiry suggests that that is not and never has been the case. Some Protestants and some other Christians have had and continue to have more in common with each other than do all Protestants with each other on these admittedly central teachings.

Unless the immediate context makes clear that something else is meant, evangelicalism is frequently equated with Protestantism. The exceptions will refer to parties in nineteenth century Anglicanism and nineteenth and twentieth century American Protestantism. No one has found adequate words to describe sectarian, radical, or left-wing Protestant traditions (as opposed to establishmentarian, conservative, or magisterial Protestantism), so we have employed those terms without embarrassment, apology, or pejorative interests. The sons and daughters of those traditions have begun to accept those terms and to deal proudly with them, and they will be able to see that nothing judgmental is implied when they are used here.

Because of the geographical provenance of the work, the author has been aware of the possibility that the Anglo-American nexus might receive too much attention and has consciously set out to balance this by reference to the continental Reformation and its heritage.

So far as reference materials are concerned, the authors of this series have shown signs of having wrestled with the problem in differing ways. In the case of ancient Scandinavia, for example, Professor Turville-Petre found it necessary to provide reference to

extremely inaccessible, remote, and obscure materials of the kind
to which only a few scholars around the world would normally have
access. But a book dealing with an expansive and accessible faith
such as Protestantism, and one which includes such a broad level
of generalization as this comprehensive accounting must, would
serve few readers well were it merely to suggest sources in the
writings of a few familiar Protestant shapers and founders as background for summary statements.

Instead, the editors and author determined that the most useful
thing to do would be to provide an extensive bibliographical set
of notes for further reading and inquiry. These references follow
numerals which appear in a continuity at the end of paragraphs
throughout the eighteen chapters and appear in essay form at the
back of the book. I thank Father James Connelly, C.S.C., for his
part in helping me organize these titles and Mrs. Rehova Arthur
for preparing this manuscript as she has done with two earlier
books of mine. Mrs. Delores Smith and Miss Richelle Session were
also helpful in various stages of manuscript preparation. Dean
Joseph M. Kitagawa of the University of Chicago Divinity School
has given numerous kinds of encouragement for the research and
writing and I thank him as well as the students at Chicago in whose
presence many of the paragraphs which follow took original shape
and were tested. Finally I should acknowledge the contributions of
numerous audiences made up of Protestants, non-Protestants, and
anti-Protestants who during the past score of years have by their
support and criticism helped me forge the definitions and scrutinize the approaches which follow. They have used the Protestant
principle of prophetic protest on me enough to remind me that
this book is anything but the last word on its subjects. The book
is dedicated to two friends who over twenty-five years ago began
to give encouragement by publishing my first writing efforts. It is
about time I acknowledged my enduring debt to them.

Martin E. Marty

Chicago, Illinois
January 1972

I. Protestantism in Space and Time

1. THE NON-PROTESTANT WORLD

Religious forces occupy space. They both shape their environments and are shaped by them. The locations of Protestantism, therefore, reveal much about its inner life and its intentions. It has been officially established and culturally dominant largely in north central Europe and North America. Fortunately for Protestant expansionists, this locale was the scene of a worldwide movement of commerce, trade, and political force, at least during the nineteenth century. As a result of that Euro-American development, and in part because it inspired the expansion, Protestantism was carried to beachheads and outposts all around the world.

Protestantism gives its adherents the impression of being at home almost everywhere because of these nineteenth century moves. To the majority of the world's people, however, this impression of the West is not borne out in reality. Most people of the world live where Protestants are not, and most Protestants live where the world's majorities are not. A fruitful way, then, to discuss an atlas of Protestantism is to try to perceive this faith's cultural outreaches through the eyes of the non-Protestant world.[2]

In a world of colored people, Protestantism often looks like a white religion. In a neo-nationalist world and in an anticolonialist era, it is remembered by many as an expression of Western nationalisms and colonialism. In an age of Christian ecumenical striving, it is perceived as the legacy of countless independent and competitive missionary efforts. On Buddhist, Islamic, or Hindu soil it is sometimes recalled as an expression of political, military, or commercial endeavors more than as a religion.

Where other religions have been dominant, Protestantism has seemed to be the invader or the intruder. Sometimes it was propagated by people who were insensitive to other cultures or who were eager to extirpate such cultures along with the religions that were bonded to them. The fate of Protestantism in the non-Protestant world, then, is tied very much to social and political realities over which Protestant leadership today has almost no control.[3]

Not that all images and artifacts of Protestantism are negative. On countless coasts and even inland, the Protestant outreach has left clusters of charitable institutions, manned by obviously self-sacrificing, humble, and devoted people. An anti-Westerner may find it difficult to send a card of thanks to religionists from outside his culture, yet he may recognize that many clinics or hospitals in his part of the world were begun by and often still are operated by Protestants who have no desire to exploit him.

Many institutions of education, from preelementary through postgraduate, were initiated and supported by Western Protestants who were positively interested in the development of people elsewhere. Some of the most vehemently anti-Western leaders of the Third World were educated at such schools, and their habits and outlooks reveal both salutary and negative features of that experience. On many occasions when tragedy overtakes people, Protestant distribution agencies are ready in emergency to make possible an outpouring of relief supplies "with no strings attached." These gestures and institutions are among the most attractive features in an ambiguous heritage.

The agent of Protestantism—how is he or she seen or remembered? Here it is difficult to generalize. Many a Third World leader has commented on the graves of Europeans and Americans in his own nation. These are often the graves of people who gave themselves for their beliefs and for other people, without making demands for return or seeking glory. But others had the experience of contact with Protestants who brought the Bible in one hand and the sword or flag in the other; these were men and women who treated non-Caucasians as a kind of white man's burden.

As a result of the work of both kinds of missionaries, in many of the non-Western nations Protestantism became sufficiently established that indigenous leadership could be developed, and what came to be called Younger Churches were organized. Where that is the case, Protestantism has come to look like a native growth and seems less to be an exotic or condescending import. Instead, it seems to be a partner in the development of people in Asia, Africa, and Latin America.

The forms and genius of Protestantism look different in nations where it was never well established. Almost inevitably, the faith of missionaries tends to accent personal evangelism; after all, evangelists are sent out to witness to Christ and to win others to Him. (In many parts of the West, where populations were almost unanimously, if often only nominally, Protestant or Christian, little man-to-man witness had ever been evident.) Evangelistic religion will tend to be emotional, revivalistic, and pietistic, a warm and inviting faith to those attracted, but an angry and judgmental religion to those repelled, to those threatened with the wrath of God for their unwillingness to accept Christ.

This evangelism provides a notable contrast to the often more passive and taken-for-granted mood and tone of Protestantism where it has been the force of a settled majority. The missionary spread literacy and was visibly involved in translating, publishing, and distributing the Bible and other written materials. He tended to be either a lonely pioneer in new territory or a resident of an enclave, out of touch with other Protestants in his field. Competition was most visible in missionary areas, since agents were sent from many Western nations and denominations; in the West, except for North America, there was usually a single dominant Protestant group in each territory.

The limits of Protestant expansion can best be seen when one glances at the example of the world's largest nation and the home of one-fourth of its people, China. So far as can be known, Protestantism is a force that has come and virtually gone from this part of the world. A few church buildings exist and, say occasional Western visitors, are kept open—perhaps as showcases for such tourists. No one outside China is able, of course, to measure how many Chinese have held on to their faith, either as a kind of subversive and secret expression, or so transformed that citizens can live simultaneously with both it and an anti-Western regime.

Officially China opposes every trace of Western religion, and not long after the Communists came to power in the middle of the twentieth century all representatives of the churches from the West were forbidden new entrance, forced to leave, harassed, persecuted, or martyred. Chinese church leaders for a brief time remained in contact with non-Chinese, but these ties were rather quickly broken and little is known about the question of the survival of Protestantism there.

Certainly there is no public presence; today's Chinese youth, who have no personal memory of the missions, have heard of Protestantism if at all as an extension of imperialism. Yet even these negative references give some indication of the part the churches played in the development of modern China for at least a century and a half. While Catholics had carried on work as early as the Middle Ages, the first Protestant to enter was Robert Morrison, as late as 1807. He and those who followed him were surrounded by millions of Buddhist, Taoist, and Confucian adherents.

The Protestant fortune rose and fell at various times with the differing degrees of acceptance tendered Western influences in the vagaries of Chinese policy development. In the Boxer uprising at the turn of the century, 189 Protestant missionaries were killed in the most aggressive single action taken against Europeans and Americans before the Communist revolution. On the other hand, some Chinese leaders, among them Sun Yat-sen and Chiang Kai-shek, were counted among the Protestants during the next half century. This fact only counted against the faith at midcentury when the Nationalist lineage was supplanted by the Maoist Communists. Protestantism evokes only negative connotations in recent Chinese history.[4]

In Asia there were also nations now Communist where Protestantism has not come and gone simply because it had never come. Not that there were no people at the Western missionary-sending centers who would have liked to enter Tibet or Mongolia. Many evangelistic Christians believed that Christ's second coming would be delayed until His Gospel had been preached to the uttermost parts of the earth and until men everywhere had had the opportunity to decide for or against the message. But these Buddhist and Lamaist strongholds were physically difficult to reach because of mountains, climate, and desert. Even such obstacles were not responsible for hindering hardy generations of missionaries. Rather, Tibet and Mongolia were among the nations which were virtually entirely closed to Western religious influence, and where missionaries were simply unwelcome and forbidden. The *World Christian Handbook* sometimes has listed the presence of several hundred Moravians in Tibet, and efforts by Bible translators have been noted, but both there and in Mongolia there has been no positive Protestant cultural influence.

In some parts of Asia, on the other hand, the Protestant presence was felt and it endures. For example, when Chiang Kai-shek took his government into exile on Taiwan, or Formosa, after Communists prevailed on the mainland, he moved to an island where the missions were active. Being Protestant and because he encouraged anti-Communist forces, he gave backing to their extension. The crowded island's culture has been shaped largely by tribal, Buddhist, Taoist, and Confucian influences, but since the early eighteenth century when the Dutch controlled it and when Dutch missionaries came with the traders, there has been mission work on Formosa. English Presbyterians came around 1865 and most major denominations have since been represented. Because many of the world's Protestants have tried to keep some ties with Communist China and because they sustain some hope for China's future reopening, the Formosan Protestants have progressively cut themselves off in protest from much of ecumenical Protestantism.[5]

Efforts by Protestant churches to penetrate and have an influence in Korea were always more successful. A Buddhist and Shinto nation, it came to be known as the most Protestant part of Asia, having become hospitable to missionaries late in the nineteenth century after long having held the reputation of being the "Hermit Kingdom." The missionaries were largely Anglo-American, arriving from the usual sources but also from Australia after 1887. Many of those hundreds of thousands of Korean Protestants have taken their postconversion life seriously and have become known for their tenacity and for their internal divisions.

A kind of Puritan tinge colors much of Korean witness. While little is known of Protestant survival in Communist North Korea, in the South the church people are rather widely known by their neighbors as disciplined, Lord's Day-keeping, Bible-reading, strict, conversion-minded respondents, whose more moderate fellow believers have taken an interest in higher education and built institutions for its support.[6]

The most complicated history of Protestantism in an Asian nation belongs to Japan, which was the most tightly sealed-off of the Pacific nations until its opening in the middle of the nineteenth century. Eager and heroic missionaries there found traces of Christian communities that dated from Catholic penetrations in the sixteenth century, but they seldom built on these remains. At their peak, Christians numbered 3 or 4 per cent of the population on the islands of Japan, and, of course, not all of these were Protestant. Their stock inevitably rose and fell with various changes in Japanese attitudes toward the West, but even during World War II, when two imperial powers were clashing, Protestantism was not completely proscribed.

The churches were encouraged to form and were then forced into the Kyodan, a United Church of Christ which survived on a voluntary basis after the war. Protestantism has been developing in the face of Buddhist and Shinto revivals and in the presence of hundreds of postwar "new religions" including the energetic and militant "value-creating society," *Soka gakkai,*

In Japanese eyes, Protestantism assumes its traditional missionary character, with a few additions. There has been the usual denominational competition, along with the conventional evangelism, worship, and hospital work. But Japan has developed a number of native leaders who had a worldwide impact on Protestantism. One thinks immediately of Toyohiko Kagawa, who often spoke for Japanese Christian life in the middle years of the twentieth century. Through people like Kagawa, whose books were read around the world and who often represented Japanese Protestantism at missionary and ecumenical gatherings, the Japanese began to reinfluence the sending churches.

The world's most literate nation has also taken a literate view of Christianity, and has accented the intellectual dimensions of faith more than did most Asians. After World War II the Japanese were often uncommonly interested in European thought, and the writings of Martin Luther, Søren Kierkegaard, and Karl Barth were sometimes best sellers. While much Japanese thought has been derivative of European existentialist Christianity, more recent thinkers have tried to fuse Asiatic religious motifs with characteristically Western dogmatic concerns. For all these energies, however, there is no danger that anyone would ever mistake Japan for a Protestant nation.[7]

Further west in Asia is India, the second most populous nation and one which was particularly attractive to Protestants, especially during the long decades of British imperial dominance which ended in 1947. Since that date Indian Christians have been innovative in their attempts to form transconfessional churches which unite people of different traditions and polities, notably in the Church of South India. While the government increasingly inhibits outside missionary intrusions, there is a sufficiently strong indigenous church. It has produced leaders of the stature of D. T. Niles and scores of others. Still, Indian Protestantism is unknown in tens of thousands of villages, is a tiny minority presence in the cities, and is surrounded by a sea of adherents to warring Hindu, Muslim, and Buddhist religions. A somewhat similar case applies in Pakistan, the largely Muslim territory which had been a part of India through most of the missionary period.

Continental Protestantism had entered India very early in the eighteenth century and the British, led by William Carey, began work there at the end of that century. Carey had the best of things because of the British governance, though inevitably English missionaries were readily typed as agents of the crown. India more than anywhere else illustrates the complicated story of tensions and ties between commercial forces (the East India Company, for example) and their chaplains or the missionaries who came with them to take advantage of commerce at some times or to judge it at others. Medical, educational, publishing, and charitable enterprises were set up to propagate Protestantism. Few nations provided such a range of stories of missionary heroism and success as did India, and Anglo-American congregations in the West became well acquainted with the Indian story. Today Protestantism remains a durable but small force among India's hundreds of millions of people.[8]

Burma provides a classic case of misunderstanding between cultures. When the British and the Americans, the latter led by the popular Adoniram Judson, entered early in the nineteenth century, they were unprepared for the cultural shock of a hitherto-closed Buddhist nation. The missionaries immediately received negative impressions, which were reinforced when communications soon broke down and Judson and others were imprisoned. The wives of these prisoners reported back about the terrors of Burmese prisons.

The first narratives about the superstition and bondage that went with Buddhism were enlarged upon in letters and reports from returnees. The negative attitudes brought to Burma by subsequent missionaries were, of course, reciprocated. The Burmese characteristically came to see Protestantism as an intrusion; they have remained largely aloof.[9]

"Indo-China," including Vietnam, was long under French and thus Catholic dominance, and only a few small Protestant groups had much success there before the Communist triumph in the north and the protracted unsettled military situation in the south complicated the picture of missionary development. Indo-China, it is safe to say, is culturally almost untouched by a Protestant ethos or effort.

Finally, so far as the Pacific nations are concerned, the islands include areas (such as New Guinea) which were not really encountered by Protestants until well into the twentieth century. Some of the last contacts with what amount to Stone Age cultures developed in the islands. But there are also places like Sumatra, where the Batak people, especially during the years of Dutch influence, were uncommonly open to Protestantism and where 100,000-member-strong churches developed styles of their own. The Indonesian Protestants remain small minority voices in the mid-twentieth century, and later have battled Muslims, Hindus, secularizing forces, and Communists.

The Philippines are the most Christianized islands, but since their change came during Spanish rule, their Christian history is heavily Catholic, and Protestants were not welcomed until 1898, after the end of the Spanish-American War. Since that time numbers of competitive Protestant churches have carried on reasonably effective work, but have been able to do little to shape the public life or mores of the Philippines.

Australia and New Zealand represent the great Pacific exceptions and can be compared to the early United States and Canada as outposts of British evangelicalism. As such they belong to the Protestant world and can often be inferred when terms like "Anglo-American" are employed.[10]

In Asia, Protestantism was rarely excluded before the middle of the nineteenth century. On the other hand, it was never dominant on a national scale, even though it had localized impacts. Depending upon the degree of quiescence or resurgence of the longer-established religions of the people, this Western expression was encouraged or inhibited. Almost everywhere, including in the nations where it has been ecclesiastically or educationally productive (as in Korea or Japan), Protestants remain a small minority.

Everywhere evangelicalism was seen to be a latecomer to cultures that were conscious of their long traditions, of histories much older than Europe's and certainly than America's. While they produced some native personalities of note in the whole Protestant world, most of these Asian churches were seen by their neighbors to be dependent, divided and competing outposts of various Western intrusive and imperial powers. Millions of Protestants are in Asia, but Asia is in no sense ecclesiastically and in few senses culturally Protestant.

Africa represents an equally vivid chapter in Western Protestant missionary history. From the viewpoint of the African genius, it includes a similarly interesting history of cultural development. In most of Asia, where Protestantism has met setbacks it has been almost totally repudiated. In Africa, however, what has come to be called a post-Christian or post-Protestant epoch has taken on a different appearance.

In Africa literally thousands of post-Christian sects are emerging. They creatively fuse some elements of the religion they learned from missionaries with native growths, and occasionally add fresh revelations from charismatic leaders. Couple this with the vision of many Westerners that a large share of the Christian future may belong to Africa where new forms of church life are developing, while the West undergoes increasing secularization, and something of the complex drama of Africa is manifest.[11]

In such a huge, culturally pluralistic continent, representing at least as many varieties as does Asia, it is difficult to generalize about Protestantism. Christian developments are occurring almost everywhere in northern Africa in the presence of very assertive Muslim missionary activity. In southernmost Africa a special problem appears because Protestantism is the highly visible and public expression of white ruling minorities in largely black nations.

Africans are leaders in the worldwide "revolution of color," and the long imperialist ties on the part of many missionaries almost certainly calls into question further invasions on the part of white missionaries in some nations. Only a small minority of Protestant missionaries had ever publicly condemned colonialism in Africa. Many were even more culturally imperialistic than were their Asian counterparts—in part because of the subliterary and animistic character of the indigenous religions they encountered. Missionaries have been remembered as having supported white ruling forces and of having tried to impose their own ethos, including, for instance, antipolygamous and nuclear familial patterns which were often disruptive of African tribal life.[12]

The comment that Protestantism has had almost no shaping influence in some parts of the world certainly applies to almost all of northern Africa which has been a Muslim area for well over a millennium. The seat of many distinguished leaders of early Christianity (Tertullian, Cyprian, Augustine), northern Africa has seen the disappearance of most Christian traces by the time of the rise of Protestantism in the sixteenth century.

A glance at almanacs of Protestant population reveals the impenetrability of the Muslim nations. Algeria, Morocco, Somalia, Tunisia, and Zanzibar, for instance, include fewer than 2,000 Protestant representatives each, and there are almost no other Christians there, either. Many of these are members of field staffs of Western agencies. If a Protestant presence has been ruled out by a long tradition of Islamic exclusion, it is further complicated today by much Western and particularly American support of the state of Israel, whose continued presence has been one of the few uniting symbols in the Arab world. The future of Protestant expansion in such a period would look dim, indeed.

In part because it has been more involved with European nations than others, Egypt has had more exposure to Protestants than has its neighbors. Some Western-based educational missionary schools were founded and survive there as enclaves of an outside, non-Arab culture. The numbers of Protestants are not too impressive, but there are about 50,000 Egyptians related to American Presbyterian missions and about 75,000 members of the Evangelical Church in Egypt, Synod of the Nile. No other Protestant group claims 15,000 members.

Ethiopia, a Christian (Coptic) exception in North Africa, does include a 125,000-member Protestant group, the Sudan Interior Mission, and Sudan itself has a rather strong Anglican (80,000-member) diocese. Protestantism, then, is better represented in that part of northern Africa which borders on the Red Sea than in the central and western portions of northern Africa.[13]

If Protestants had little taste or opportunity for northern African expansion, this was not the case for Central Africa, where dramatic stories of missionary heroism in an inhospitable climate had great impact on the adventure-hungry West. Here, too, there were more significant Protestant successes. In Central Africa, because there was less competition against a literary culture than there had been in Islamic lands, Protestantism had a more decisive role in shaping the governmental and educational life of emerging nations for a century.

Anglicans are strong in Uganda, an African nation whose lore is well known in Europe particularly, because of Roman Catholic interest in martyrs there. Tanganyika (now Tanzania) exhibits the heritage of missionary activity by northern Europeans, particularly by Germans. When one speaks of Protestant cultural influence, he is likely to be concentrating on modern cities like Kampala, Uganda, or Nairobi, Kenya, or any place where institutions of learning have had social consequence. Less is known of the tribal territories, where development of major institutions has been more difficult.[14]

West Africa represents a special problem because of the history of Protestantism's part in slavery. While it is well known that many black West Africans were complicitors in the slave trade, and while Arabs were the greatest slave traders in earlier centuries, in the Protestant era the British, the Dutch, and eventually the Americans acquired the worst reputation for exploiting, enslaving, and killing West Africans. Where the legacy of slavery has not produced negative images, the Catholic imperial residues in Portuguese colonies in West Africa have been inhibitors against a Protestant presence.

The best record for Protestants came whenever their missionaries opposed slavery in earlier centuries or whenever they countered Catholic-national colonialists in the recent past. In any case, where Christianity shows up on demographers' charts, it is Catholic (on the islands of the Azores, Cape Verde, or Madeira) or "mixed" in Nigeria (against tribal and Muslim competition) and in Liberia, where well-meaning Westerners set up a colony for returning blacks in the nineteenth century.[15]

South Africa is the notable exception in the Protestant atlas. Here is one of the few territories outside central or northern Europe and Anglo-America where Protestantism does show up on population charts. Here large elements of the population are adherents of black or white evangelical churches, and governmental, educational, and cultural institutions are often in Protestant hands.

The ethos of a kind of puritanical Protestantism is highly visible, for example, in the Republic of South Africa, where Dutch Reformed Christians are both fervent believers in and ready applicants of religious sanctions to their policies of apartheid, or absolute racial separation. The white minority that led Rhodesia in its move of independence from Great Britain also made explicit reference to Protestant norms in support of its racial policies. Eighty-five per cent of South Africa's 2,500,000 Europeans are Protestant. In these nations the colonial heritage lives on longest; here the black nationalist surge has been least free to develop.[16]

Returning to the nations where Protestant efforts have been largely met with indifference or hostility, the Near East provides another example of Protestantism as a tiny minority. Afghanistan has been closed to Protestantism. Iran numbers at most 8,000 and Iraq fewer than 2,000 evangelicals, and there can obviously be almost no positive cultural impact in such circumstances. In large but lightly populated Saudi Arabia fewer than 1,000 Protestants could be found, and a Protestant population would be virtually nonexistent in Yemen.

The nations bordering the Mediterranean have had exposure to Christian and Protestant influences for a variety of reasons, many of them having to do with bonds to biblical lands and their neighbors. While Eastern Christians were able to adapt and survive during the years of Muslim imperial rule, Protestants were not present until the nineteenth century. Even today only a few enterprising evangelicals have had successes in the largely Muslim population. There are fewer than 10,000 Protestants in Jordan, but Jordan is aware of Protestantism because of its involvement with international issues and various religious rationales relating to its neighbor and enemy, Israel.[17]

Syria and Lebanon are special cases. Eastern rite Catholic Christians and the Orthodox are well represented. As a result of nine-teenth century efforts, Protestants are at home there too, having established some notable higher educational institutions. The largest of the Syrian groups is related to American Presbyterians. A group of similar size, the largest element among Lebanese Prot-estants, also has Presbyterian ties. These nations' religious history in relation to the West has also been rendered complex by the changing attitudes that people in Anglo-America and Europe show to their enemy to the south, Israel. In any case, Syria and Lebanon are much involved with Western political history in our time, and Protestantism is not unknown.

Israel is in every sense a special instance in the Christian world. Many fundamentalistic Protestant groups, because of their millen-nial views, interpret certain biblical passages as commending them to be represented in Israel as a sign of efforts anticipating Christ's return. Others have sentimental and emotional ties committing them to sustaining at least some kind of work. Still others have kept some sort of ministry open because of the cosmopolitan character of Israel, as a means of serving travelers and diplomatic or com-mercial representatives during their stay in Israel.

Because so much of Israel's population came from nations where Protestantism was strong (including Germany, where the memories are naturally almost entirely negative, so far as Chris-tianity is concerned), Israelis are highly aware of and reasonably interested in world Protestantism. Despite these contacts, the ac-tual Protestant population is extremely small. Many boards or agencies are represented without a single Israeli adherent, and the more successful ones number membership in the thousands. Israel is officially a Jewish state, with a strong Muslim and a smaller Uniate and Orthodox Christian representation. There is a certain Protestant presence, but the positive shaping of the culture is entirely in other hands.

If the reader is beginning to come to the conclusion that "world Protestantism" is really a rather provincial North Atlantic affair, a survey of the situation in largely Orthodox or Roman Catholic religious populations will only underscore the impression. This survey has been accenting other religious forces surrounding Prot-estants in the fields they once regarded as missionary outposts. It has paid less attention to antireligious or postreligious entities. In many parts of the world these are far more significant competitors than are non-Protestant religions. In few places is this more true than in what might be called the Orthodox orbit, that part of the world where Eastern Christians predominate in the Christian community but where Christianity itself has been surrounded or displaced by generally hostile forces—in particular, in this case, the Communist states of Eastern Europe.[18]

The Orthodox orbit includes some of the Muslim nations already discussed, Greece and its neighbor islands, and Eastern Europe "behind the Iron Curtain," as Westerners like to locate it. Greece, which withstood a Communist surge in the 1950s and vacillates between democratic and repressive right-wing regimes, has never been hospitable soil for Protestant work, and except for the 15,000-member Greek Evangelical Church, is touched by only a few hundred conservative converts of missionaries. In Cyprus, fundamentalistic Protestants alone are present, and they number only a few hundred adherents. More significant, obviously, is the question of Protestantism in Eastern Europe.

Russia, after a half century of Soviet discouragement and even persecution of religious forces, has scores of sects operating at the edges of the Russian Orthodox Church. At their side are numbers of small Protestant groups. In the nineteenth century Lutherans were represented among German minority communities. These have virtually disappeared and the only well-known remaining Protestant groups are Russian Baptists. Some are evangelicals of native growth and some are the result of earlier formal missionary enterprises.

Religious yearbooks give the number of these evangelicals as around 3,000,000, but it is difficult to get accurate statistics or gain a clear picture of the character and witness of their churches. Generally exemplifying a rather strong, sometimes naïve kind of faith, they are often anti-Orthodox, in part because many of them have themselves repudiated Orthodoxy and in part because by their standards they do not see a vital kind of faith among the Orthodox adherents.

Their attitudes toward the government are ambiguous. Many of them support the Communist leadership because their literal reading of the Bible tells them to support the powers that be, whether these are congenial to Christianity or not. Others find no difficulty compartmentalizing their "secular" life in the public and political realm from their highly personal and private faith. Still others may have no difficulty showing allegiance to both systems, as many Orthodox do. Some may use their individualistic kind of Protestantism as a means of quiet resistance to the governmental ideology. We do know, however, that Russian evangelical educational institutions have been largely eliminated. They are not free to advertise services or erect churches, but worship is tolerated.[19]

Less possibility for Protestant existence is present in what have often been called satellite nations, or in pro-Chinese Albania, where Protestantism had been hardly represented. Some Protestant communities survive under severe limitations in Romania, Bulgaria, and Yugoslavia. None of these has ever belonged to "the Protestant world," and conditions for Protestant expansion and survival are not considered favorable in the Cold War era.

Passing over the Baltic areas which were heavily Lutheran and over Poland, Czechoslovakia, and Hungary, the central European nations where Protestantism had some historic role (since these will be discussed in the chapter which surveys the atlas of Protestant nations), this leaves those parts of the world where Roman Catholicism dominated even after the rise of Protestantism: the Mediterranean nations and Central and South America.

Sixteenth century Protestantism made almost all its expansive gains to national dominance within several decades, and efforts to bring reform Protestant-style to southern Europe failed. There were notable reformers and some of these had small followings, particularly in intellectual circles. But no well-organized churches resulted from their efforts. In the nineteenth century missionary period and since, some efforts have been made to establish Protestant churches, but for the most part only small enclaves resulted. Sometimes these evangelical efforts were formally prevented from being furthered. Just as frequently their spokesmen came upon populations that were Catholic, secular, or anticlerical. In none of these cases were people in a shopping mood for Protestant offerings.[20]

Except for an occasional stray guest in this ecumenical era, Protestantism is of course unrepresented in southern Europe's smallest state, the Vatican. Surrounding Italy includes members of the aggressive Assemblies of God in the tens of thousands, and a few thousand Baptists, Methodists, Lutherans, and Seventh-day Adventists, but these are considered to be peculiarities on the Italian scene. The only Protestant church with deep roots is the small Waldensian community, which perpetuates a lineage of medieval, pre-Reformation churchmanship.

Portugal and Spain have remained virtually untouched by Protestant culture or churches since the sixteenth century, when they had stood as Catholic strongholds. In recent times some evangelicals have known successes in Portugal, and figures as high as

100,000 adherents have been claimed, the vast majority of them being listed under *Missionaria e Educational.*

While in 1966 Spain enacted a religious liberty measure that has made Protestant existence there more bearable, Spain has always been one of the two or three most militantly anti-Protestant countries in the Christian world. Still, without major educational institutions or other agencies which could help them become well known, somewhere around 50,000 Protestants are listed on church rolls. These belong chiefly to conservative evangelistic groups, and they claim to be growing.

More mixed is the record in France, where many of the major events of the Reformation occurred. France is considered a Catholic (and secular) society, but from the sixteenth century to the present it has not lacked fairly strong Protestant churches. One of the strongest of these is the Lutheran church in Alsace-Lorraine, bordering on Germany. The most important for all of France is the Église Réformée de France, with over a third of a million members. Because of the considerable Protestant impact there, France will be included also at the edges of the Protestant world. In northwest Europe and the British Isles, Belgium, Luxembourg, and Ireland remained heavily Catholic and are exceptions to the generalizations about Protestantism's sweep of north central Europe and the British Isles.

"Latin America," Central and South America, has for almost half a millennium harbored native Indian, Catholic, and secular forces, all without much Protestant influence. All Central American populations—in Mexico, Guatemala, British Honduras, Honduras, El Salvador, Nicaragua, and Costa Rica—are listed simply as Roman Catholic. A partial exception is Panama and the Canal Zone as a result of United States influence over the canal area. There Protestantism counts over 40,000 members.

All the Andean nations of western South America are reckoned as overwhelmingly Catholic populations. The same is the case with eastern South America, particularly the large nations of Argentina, Brazil, Paraguay, and Uruguay.

The vagaries of Dutch and British colonial history cause Surinam and British Guiana (now Guayana) to be the South American exceptions, for populations there include more Protestants than Catholics. For similar reasons of British or United States dominance, there are several Protestant exceptions in the Caribbean Islands: Jamaica, the Virgin Islands, Leeward Islands, Windward Islands, the Bahamas, and to some extent Trinidad and Tobago.

But the larger Christian populations were Catholic in Cuba, Haiti, the Dominican Republic, and Puerto Rico.

While there is no such thing as a Protestant culture or a strong Protestant cultural stamp in Central or South America, there are millions of Protestants as the result of missionary efforts, migrations from Europe (e.g., of Germans to Brazil and Argentina), and the inevitable contacts that are corollaries of trade and intercultural commuting. These Protestant endeavors take on a different coloration on Catholic soil from what they do where only non-Christians have been encountered, or where there was a simultaneous intrusion of Catholics and Protestants, as in most of Asia and Africa.

While Protestants have done some work among the Indians who had never accepted Catholicism, most of their evangelism was attempted among people who had been nominal Catholics and who had grown up in South America's peculiar Catholic climate. This meant that they either had drifted from or repudiated Catholicism. As a result, until the very recent past most Latin American Protestantism has been markedly anti-Catholic.

In the nineteenth century the earlier efforts for Protestant representation were made by continental, British, and North American "mainline" groups—those which have now found each other in ecumenical organizations like the World Council of Churches. They remain, but for the most part they carry on quiet educational or charitable work, worshiping through traditional forms and appearing to many to be quite passive.

In the twentieth century the real gains are being made by Pentecostal and other fundamentalist groups, "faith-missions" or "spirit-filled" churches which often stress speaking in tongues, intense personal evangelism, Bible transmission, and rigid moral standards. These groups, often out of contact with each other and always beyond the range of the ecumenical Protestants in North America, have begun to be open to common work in Latin America. They have sometimes even begun to take a more congenial attitude to an increasingly more tolerant Catholic leadership. While their efforts have by no means begun to fill some South American spiritual vacuums or to cause the population to feel a Protestant cultural impact as a whole, they do help constitute an entity sometimes called Third Force Protestantism, which will receive separate treatment.[21]

What is left? The religious demographic charts tend to confine themselves to nations like the following when they list the countries that make up much of the Protestant world: Norway, Sweden, Denmark, and Finland; the former Baltic nations; Switzerland and the Netherlands of the original Reformed thrust; Germany; England, Scotland, and Northern Ireland; the United States and Canada, Australia and New Zealand. These, plus an occasional reference to central Europe, South Africa, or missionary churches will make up the locale for most of the ensuing story.

While Protestantism in the non-Protestant world may not often be felt and experienced by the majorities which are out of contact with it, these younger churches have played an ever larger role in the development of ecumenical Protestantism in recent times, and they will also often be implied throughout the book. For example, future discussions of Protestant attitudes to the family can hardly progress without reference to the challenges to those attitudes in the areas of Africa where missionaries encountered polygamy. And Third Force Protestantism, Pentecostal in character, is influencing all of evangelicalism—chiefly out of its Latin American base.

The era of rapid transportation and instant mass communication, then, has served to make the Protestant world both smaller and larger. Smaller: its power is dwindling in the presence of a secularizing tendency that has seemed to accompany technology in the West and elsewhere. It meets political setback on many fronts in its old homeland. And larger: the ecumenical era has made it possible for all Protestants to profit from the experiences of each other, as they could not have done even in the headier and more optimistic atmosphere that accompanied the endeavors of missionaries in the nineteenth century. The result has been the beginnings of the breakdown of Western parochialism in the Protestant churches, as their leaders learn that the evangelical faith can find witness in many kinds of cultures.

One question remains: if Protestantism expanded in the sixteenth and nineteenth centuries, will it now settle for its existing place in the world? Will the Protestant atlas in the future look much as it looks now? Efforts to expand Protestant influence and church life have not died. More missionaries are on the scene late in the twentieth century than were in a day when a higher premium was placed on missionary endeavor.

There are changes. For one thing, there has been an Americanization of Protestant mission work. In 1958, almost 28,000 out of 43,000 Protestant missionaries were from the United States. Second, whereas the earlier missionaries came from the ecumenical churches, today's new majorities are from "faith-missions," which

are independent, often militantly fundamentalist and loosely structured Pentecostal and holiness groups. This means, among other
things, that they often carry not only a negative view of the world's
other religions and of Catholicism, but also of historic Protestantism.

   While it would be foolish to try to estimate in advance the degree
and measure of their successes, it seems clear that if there is to be
Protestant expansion in the future, it will take on a character different from that known during the past century and a half of missions
—and the world around such new Protestant communities will
have an opportunity to take a second look at new styles of being
Protestant.

2. THE FORMATION OF THE PROTESTANT WORLD

The schism in the Western churches, beginning early in the sixteenth century, forbode the eventual end of the entity commonly called Christendom. Christendom represented the peculiar bond of Christianity with European culture, united under pope and emperor. As a result of the Constantinian settlements in the fourth century, this Christian world included a Catholic political resolution. It also implied a culture whose art, philosophy, literature, and common life were infused with Christian themes, attitudes, intentions, and influences.[22]

The term "Christendom," of course, has been applied also to post-sixteenth century Christian culture, since Protestants and Catholics alike are Christian and because the old cultural bonds did not break at once. But a new term is needed for the new kinds of relationship between faith, territory, and culture after evangelicalism began to make its way. "Protestantdom" could refer to the dominion where Protestantism had influence, to the connection between land and church, to the milieu shaped by non-Roman Catholic churchmen of the West. A more elegant term is "the Protestant world."[23]

The formation of the Protestant world occurred suddenly, and its general borders were reached within decades. One might say that while the Christian Church is twenty centuries old, only twenty to fifty years of these ages were given over to development of the new Christian atlas within the Western churches.

Many sons and daughters of the Reformation have reached some sort of consensus by which they agree to celebrate the rise of the Reformation as dating from 1517, when Luther's Ninety-five Theses signaled the beginnings of the challenge to Rome. Antecedents of the Protestant movement had, of course, been on the scene for two centuries, and signs of Luther's own break came earlier than 1517. Provisionally we may accept this symbolic date for the genesis of Protestantism. Twelve years later the movement received its name at the Diet of Speyer, when the "Protestant"

parties were so labeled. By the end of still another decade most of
Western Europe, except for much of France, had been reached by
Protestantism and whole populations had converted along with
their leaders. After a third of a century, by the time of the Peace
of Augsburg of 1555, the new continental map had been drawn,
and the Anglican settlement in the British Isles was in view.[24]

Given the importance for world history of the British Isles,
France and Germany, the Low Countries and Switzerland, Scandinavia and east central Europe, one is instinctively curious about
a movement that could win its way so rapidly. From the viewpoint
of world population in the twentieth century an opposite observation comes to mind: how small the empire of Protestants!

After the middle of the sixteenth century only North America,
Australia, and New Zealand, as transplants of the original northwest European culture, and the fringe of outposts of Protestantdom as a result of the nineteenth century missionary enterprises,
occasioned the altering of contours of the earliest Protestant maps.
While from one point of view, then, Protestantism has world-
historical significance, from another, one can reduce it to scale by
reference to Alfred North Whitehead's remark that it represented
a domestic quarrel of northwest European people. It was ignored
by the Eastern church and eclipsed by the concurrent and emerging scientific and secular worlds and world-views.[25]

Except for the American transplants, the colonization of Australia and New Zealand and the missionary beachheads, the actions
after the middle of the sixteenth century were largely internal. The
historian can observe how on Anglican soil Methodist, Congregational, or Baptist churches were formed. He is interested to learn
of Pietist and Puritan movements in various Protestant areas. He
can take note of the countless new sects as results of schisms in the
existing churches. But few of these basically change the maps he
could draw dividing the world of Western Christianity—itself a
circumscribed territory—as early as the 1550s.

The student of the Protestant churches as a church, of Protestantism as a movement, and of the culture of evangelicalism as a
culture is forced to make decisions and to generalize. He can treat
the Protestant atlas as the scene of innumerable fascinating movements, the breeding ground of exotic species. He can concentrate,
as many have, on the exceptional occasions and the curiosities
within Protestantdom. He can hold readers' attention by describing the curiosity-inspiring exceptions such as the Latter-day Saints,
the Christian Scientists, or the Jehovah's Witnesses, all of whom

are somehow related to forces that were turned loose in the sixteenth century.[26]

The proportion of books devoted to such churches or groups
as opposed to those which concentrate on the "mainline"
churches in recent times has grown disproportionately large.
But such an approach distorts the larger reality, does an injustice to the often undramatic, prosaic, and more powerful
majority situation. To make sense of Protestantism as a whole,
then, this book will concentrate on the main outlines of Protestantism in an analysis that will rely more than a little on statistical and territorial configurations, at the expense of the often
overtreated mutations or marginal groups.

Given such a basis for determining proportions of space to
be devoted to various subjects, many easier decisions follow.
For example, no matter how inaccurate statistics of world religions may be, and no matter how indeterminate the standards
of membership are (should one count nominal or practicing
members, children along with adults, etc.?), it is clear that Lutheranism has made up by far the largest block of Protestants
through the centuries and down into the late twentieth century.
Figures of world Lutheranism usually run to around 80,000,-
000. Lutheranism also claims some place for priority, though
here one should be more careful, because other Protestant
movements like Moravianism can claim continuities with medieval movements many decades older than that; Waldensian enclaves in Italian Protestantism are also older. Still, Lutheranism
was early. Given the almost mythical status granted Martin Luther by secular historians and folklorists alike, one legitimately
turns first to the Lutheran movement for some insights into the
nature of Protestantism.[27]

Despite the drama, the color, the vigor, and the theological
forthrightness of Lutheranism, however, not for a moment dare
there be a hint that it represents anything like "normative"
Protestantism. Most other Protestants do not recognize themselves in the Lutheran ecclesiastical portrait. It is possible to
put together various coalitions or coalescences of other Protestant subcultures into majorities that would dwarf Lutheranism.
Lutheranism represents one side of the conservative Reformation, retains a continental stamp, has lacked the decisive concern of other Protestants for matters of polity, and adheres to
minority Protestant views of the whole sacramental universe. In
this book, then, Lutheranism may sometimes be given space

early in the discussion of a topic, but almost always it will be regarded only as one pole in a polarity, one part of a complex whole.

The next two combinations, when placed together as one may legitimately locate them on many issues, represent a whole somewhat larger than Lutheranism. By themselves each is only slightly more than half as large as the continental movement. These are the Reformed-Presbyterian complex and the Anglican Communion. "Reformed" generally refers to the churches of continental provenance that grew out of efforts by John Calvin, Huldreich Zwingli, Theodore de Beza, and other Swiss and German or Netherlandish theologians and reformers.

"Presbyterian" is the name often given these movements if they derive from Scotland or England, and in this form they became larger in America than did their Reformed cousins who were continental transplantations. While some early reformers in this tradition paid due respect to Luther's initiative, from the very beginning there were basic disagreements. It only introduces confusion if one overstresses lineage from Lutherans in the Reformed-Presbyterian world.[28]

Because of the systematic abilities of John Calvin and his followers, men who were capable of stating their positions with clarity and logic, the religious point of view growing out of Reformed Protestantism has had decisive influences on all later evangelical theology. Because of the freedom Reformed parties experienced as they established their own styles of theocracy in Switzerland, Scotland, the Netherlands, and Massachusetts Bay, one is given opportunity to study Protestant political alternatives to Lutheranism's generally Erastian and often passive views of civil society. Reformed Christianity's theocentrism is often in tension with and at other times complements Lutheranism's Christocentrism. The Reformed churches were often more eager to assert themselves in the public realm, setting out to transform it by reference to Christ's Kingdom, while Lutheranism often allowed for autonomous secular orders to develop around it.

The Anglican Communion, as it came to be called in the nineteenth century, represents parallel but distinct developments. The parallels came about because the Reformation in England was more Reformed than Lutheran. Before the movement took shape, Henry VIII had condemned Lutheranism. Thomas More, who never quite fitted into either old Catholic or new Protestant England, knew for sure that he did not want to fit into Lutheranism and engaged in bitter polemics against the Lutheran position. There were students from Wittenberg and other German universities on the British scene during the years of England's religious change, but they were out-numbered by the continental travelers from Reformed territories. And when English Protestants were exiled during moments of Catholic monarchical backlash, they frequently became refugees in Switzerland or Holland, there to be influenced by Reformed positions which they took back to England.[29]

While early Anglicanism was to be influenced then by Calvinist points of view, and later by Arminianism—a deviation from within on Calvinist soil—it would be unfair to see it as a dependent force. Anglicanism may have a Reformed theology, but it also has an "Anglican" tone, developed under native British auspices. The external settlement may have been political in character, but through it all men of genius like William Tyndale, Thomas Cranmer, and Richard Hooker were providing guidance for the shape of the post-Roman church in England. Concerns for polity, liturgy, and fresh models of relation to the civil realm gave a kind of autonomous character to this third version of the conservative Reformation.

Most of the thirteen American colonies were founded during years of English supremacy; some American churches have often had an Anglican stamp even when they were not united with the Anglican Communion. And the nineteenth century missionary movement coincided with the growth of England's empire, so Anglicanism became truly catholic in the sense of its universality. Forty million people (most of them numbered in England) are not many to spread around the world. But there is a thin dispersal of influential Anglican people in both Americas, Australia, much of southern and eastern Africa, and southern and southeast Asia—almost everywhere in the Christian world but where Eastern Orthodoxy is the majority faith.

If, on topic after topic, after reference to Luther and the Lutherans and then to Calvin or Zwingli and the Reformed, we move on to allusions to Anglicanism, these will not mislead the reader. At times the Methodist churches will also be implied along with Anglicanism. From one point of view, they are eighteenth century extensions of the conservative Reformation. John Wesley and many of his closest associates tried desperately to remain in the parent Church of England. Much of Methodist theology derived from Anglicanism, as did its sacramental position, liturgy, and many elements of polity. At other times distinctive and innovative Methodist positions will receive attention, for from other points of view Methodism can be seen as perhaps the most creative and successful post-sixteenth century movement in Protestantism, and it deserves some separate attention.[30]

Among the reasons for notice given Methodism is the fact of its size, spread, representativeness, and energy. If there are approximately 80,000,000 Lutherans and 40,000,000 each of Anglicans and the Presbyterian-Reformed, there are over 30,000,000 Methodists in the Protestant world. In the nineteenth century, as an Anglo-American force with a missionary theology, Methodism was also free to be successful, as indeed it was, in becoming a worldwide creed, however marginal its colonies were in Asian and African cultures.

Approximately equal in size to the Methodist churches if taken separately are the members of the Baptist complex. But if these are united with Congregationalism, the 35,000,000- plus 5,000,000-member combination ranks the "independent" or "free churches" with Presbyterian-Reformed and Anglican communions. The Baptists are, like the Methodists, largely a derivation from Anglo-American established churches. Their stress on disciplined membership and on "believers' baptism" led them to separate organization, but much of their ethos as heirs of the English churches remains apparent. The same is the case with Congregationalists, who insisted with the Baptists on the independence of each local gathering, but did not ordinarily make the move toward adult baptism. Congregationalism is almost entirely Anglo-American in its provenance.[31]

Mention of the Baptists, however, should at least call to mind the continental roots of Anabaptism and sectarian Protestantism in general. ("Sectarian" is never used pejoratively in this book.) These radical groups began to take shape within the first Protestant decade and appeared as a counterforce virtually wherever established Protestants came to power. It is difficult to trace all the lineages from continental Anabaptism, just as one cannot always point to clear lines between English Puritanism and its sundry heirs.[32]

For understandable reasons the churches which came from antiestablished sects, the offshoots of exiled, refugee, and persecuted Protestant movements, are harder to see in combinations than are the huge Lutheran, Anglican, and Presbyterian-Reformed families. But even though they make up no large statistical bloc, they have always had influence beyond their numbers, and when taken together form the heritage of "radical Protestantism," which deserves treatment of almost equal space to that accorded, say, Lutheranism.

Throughout this book, sectarian, free, radical "believers' churches" will again and again be posed or poised as an opposite pole and an authentic representative of Protestantism over against the conservative or established forms.

An approach which determines accents and proportions on the basis of the Protestant atlas can do justice to Protestant culture and the main families of its theology and polity. It cannot and does not pretend, then, to be engaged in enumeration of every Protestant variation or possibility. Often these other groups can be included by implication wherever they have ties to the larger and older groups, though they may be mentioned only when they hold exceptional points of view. Only such a method of treatment would make possible any kind of reference to scores of groups in the United States, that breeding ground of the largest variety of Protestants. A glance at its churchly alphabet will illustrate what commitment to this approach means.[33]

The Adventist bodies, important for their adherence to some Old Testament laws or to Sabbath observance, and for missionary activity, include up to a half million Protestants. They are of particular interest when premillennial views of the future arise.[34]

The Assemblies of God bear some resemblances to historic sectarianism, derive some "holiness" positions from Methodism, and are of noteworthy interest when modern pentecostal movements are discussed. They and the Pentecostal Assemblies make up each about half-million-member clusters, both of which are highly evangelistic and are growing rapidly.[35]

The Brethren, a quarter of a million strong, are in the lineage of continental Anabaptism, even though the name has changed, as are the slightly smaller Mennonite groups. The Disciples of Christ and Christian Churches, three or four million strong, range across the conservative to liberal spectrum, but often as cognates of Baptist and Presbyterian churches. They deserve mention chiefly when attempts to restore pure and primitive Christianity are taken up. The Churches of God bear family resemblances to numerous Methodist, Pentecostal, and revivalist churches, and their half million members are not treated separately.[36]

Some once-independent groups like the Evangelical United Brethren have helped simplify the analysts' tasks in this ecumenical century by merging with other and larger groups like the Methodist churches. The Friends, or Quakers, are now quite small; they share treatment accorded Independency but will be referred to on several occasions where their distinctive views of politics or the sacraments set them apart.[37]

The Latter-day Saints, almost 2,000,000 strong after little more than a century, would regard themselves as being at the edge of conventional Protestantism, which most of them decisively repudiate. Therefore there need be no responsibility to regard them as representative. Nevertheless, they often took over more than they knew of New England and New York theocratic views and in some respects are a "typically American" church. They will rarely show up on these pages.[38]

Unitarians and Universalists are statistically small; they share much with the independent Protestant traditions and can often be taken up with them. Yet their distinctive views on the doctrine of God and man call for occasional separate treatment, particularly because they derive from some first-generation Protestant impulses. Yet they are statistically small and geographically rather isolated on the Protestant map.[39]

What this necessarily brief run over the American Protestant range has suggested is this: if even in the "dry tree" of denominational separation one can reduce the outlines of Protestantism to a half dozen families, then in the "green tree" of general unity in established-church nations it is even more realistic to make the attempt. Perhaps nine out of ten people called Protestant can trace something of their lineage to the parties implied on these pages by terms like "Lutheran," "Presbyterian-Reformed," "Anglican," "Methodist," "Baptist," "Congregational," and "radical-sectarian," and for that reason these designations will receive at least nine-tenths of the attention.

Those who seek catalogs of Protestant varieties are well advised to consult studies of comparative doctrine or ecclesiology. The purpose of this book is to outline Protestantism as a whole, with its largest centerings of distinctiveness and tension, and to try to discern the elements of a Protestant culture. Without further apology, then, it is possible to set the stage for what follows by a short recall of how Protestantism did spread in its first generation or two, to provide the map which has predestined Protestantism to the shape it has taken ever since.

Lutheranism, the faith of the majority of Protestants in Germany and Scandinavia, swept those areas almost instantly and was never again to grow beyond them except through transplantation to America and, in a smaller way, through establishment of small Lutheran missionary colonies elsewhere after the eighteenth century. The Germanic and Scandinavian stamp has remained strong throughout. Martin Luther, an Augustinian monk who could no longer "find a gracious God" in the Roman Church of his childhood, took his scriptural and theological training with him as he was excommunicated from the papal church. He began his activity at the University of Wittenberg, one of a number of university centers where he and his colleagues were to establish their intellectual bases.[40]

Germany at that time was anything but a nation; it was a congeries of petty principalities, most of whose princes had in common a developing sense of Germanness, a hope for a German destiny, and a resentment against papal exploitation of their resources. It would be unfair to reduce Luther's reformation to a mere nationalistic impulse, but it would be false to overlook the congruity between his direction and the interests of princes and people in Germany.

The Lutheran rise took place in what is today called East Germany, and much of Lutheranism is today, as Westerners would say, "behind the Iron Curtain." Yet it did spread to West Germany, sharing more space with the Reformed movement the closer it came to Switzerland and France. Lutheranism did not even win all of central, northern, and eastern German lands, but had to settle for life in a situation of everpresent enduring Catholicism.

Luther was not particularly missionary-minded, and made few provisions for formal extension of his Gospel through established patterns. He did, of course, expect his preaching and teaching to have secondary effects beyond the people in close range of the pulpit or the Wittenberg classroom. He was a genius at the use of the new communications media of his day, the printing press being of particular aid in the propagation of a reformist Gospel. Yet he did not know how to envisage a single alternative to Catholicism and was reluctant to be made the head of such a movement; his church was named Lutheran against his wishes.

As a result of his printed works and of guest scholarship at Wittenberg on the part of a number of Scandinavians, the people of the north adopted the Lutheran version of Protestant Christianity at the time they made a politico-spiritual move, dictated in part by economic concerns, outside the papal range. In fact, with the movement of whole populations to Lutheranism, Scandinavia be-

came at least nominally even more Lutheran than Germany, and
has remained so until modern times. Only there did Lutheranism
become a mass movement. Gustavus Vasa in Sweden and Christian
II of Denmark and Norway followed in the footsteps of German
princes in seeking to limit Roman possessions and powers, and
around 1523 all three major parts of Scandinavia converted.[41]

Since the transition was made so easily, almost without effective
opposition, the churches there retained much of the character
earlier associated with Roman church life, and some reverence for
saints and shrines endured along with many Catholic liturgical
usages. Leaders there were and are called bishops.

Lutheranism made its way to a lesser extent also in Hungary and
Austria, but the majority there remained Catholic and many Reformed Protestants also made their home at the southeastern
edges of the Protestant domain. They found themselves next to
where "the Turk" held sway, to frustrate further southeastward
moves. The Counter Reformation cut down greatly the size of the
Lutheran family in Hungary, after some startling early successes.[42]

The basic Lutheran map, one might say, was established within
six years of the circulation of the Ninety-five Theses, and it did not
have to be redrawn until heirs of the people Lutheranized during
those years moved to the United States of America in the eighteenth and nineteenth centuries. The Reformed situation was
more varied, more fluid. Although Zwingli participated in the earliest Swiss movements and came up with his own statement of faith
by 1523, which was also within that six-year period of Lutheran
spread, the Zwinglian accents were picked up more by radical
Protestantism.

The much greater influence on subsequent Reformed-Pres-
byterianism came in the 1530s from John Calvin, the French-
educated reformer beckoned by native Swiss to aid them in reform
at Geneva and elsewhere in Switzerland. He fled to Geneva in 1536
from France, and quietly but firmly began to develop the theocracy
on Reformed lines. As a refugee center, Switzerland was well
poised to develop leadership for second-generation Protestantism.[43]

Before long it was Calvinist Protestantism that began to be accepted in "Huguenot" France. There Marguerite d'Angoulême of
Navarre did what she could to support and protect Calvinists.
Some Lutherans and Reformed Protestants came to have considerable influence in Catholic France, but they were harassed and
persecuted, and their domain was highly limited.[44]

Reformed Protestantism, instead, made its way to Dutch territories, where Calvinism was to provide much of the incentive for William of Orange's opposition to the Spanish exploiters of the Dutch. This occurred shortly before the rise of a Dutch empire, and helped Reformed churches make their way to many other parts of the world, however small their home base may have been in the Netherlands. Dutch Calvinism was soon to be shaken by internal dispute. Jakob Arminius, who questioned rigid predestination doctrines, was head of the other party. Various versions of Arminianism were to be reincarnated in later Unitarianism and, in a more orthodox way, in Methodism.[45]

While Lutheranism had smaller impact in the Netherlands, these territories were also the home of numerous Anabaptist parties, particularly those named after Menno Simons, a pacifist who led some of the persecuted groups. Still the majority in the Netherlands, as in Switzerland and southwest Germany, was never to become Anabaptist but remained Calvinist Reformed.

The other great geographical expansion of Reformed Protestantism on roughly Calvinist lines was the Presbyterian formation of Scotland. John Knox was the leader of this dramatic reformation. He was a preacher who could rely on the anti-Catholicism of the common people. A man who knew little etiquette and even less fear, he courageously confronted nobles and even Mary Queen of Scots, who desired to marry a Spanish prince and to keep Scotland in the Roman fold. A man of authoritarian personality and democratic tendency, he found in Calvinism the theological system that spoke to his heart and his needs.[46]

Knox's movement came to be known as Presbyterianism, because of its distinctive polity. It was built around the idea of government by elders or presbyters, organized in a synodical fashion. Knox had learned his doctrine while exiled in Geneva, and carried it back to Scotland in 1559, where by 1560 Parliament accepted his resolution and in effect set up the pattern that was to prevail despite ongoing bloody encounters with Catholicism. Presbyterianism later made its way with Scots settled in northern Ireland, an island which otherwise remained the Catholic outpost in the British Isles. The Scottish solution came at the end of the second Protestant generation.

The Protestantization of England began to occur within the first two decades of the Protestant movement. The Church in England had been Roman, but after a number of swings of the pendulum which followed monarchical fortunes and preferences, it became

Protestant. Many Anglicans do not like the name, because it seems to play down the catholic intentions of their church. Henry VIII licensed some monastery burning and pillaging, and there were some persecutions, but for the most part the original Church of England kept what it could from the past.[47]

The story is complicated because of the history of those catholic retentions, the vagaries based on ties to monarchical history, and the complexity and vagueness of theological expression in that period. As is well known, some of the change from Roman Catholicism came as the result of Henry VIII's changing marital fortunes. Most of the dramatic parts of the Tudor struggle occurred in the middle of the 1530s; by the time of his death in 1547 Henry had moderated in his Protestantism and some quasi-Catholic practices were returning. The Apostolic Succession in episcopacy, a distinctive mark of the Church of England, was never interrupted.

In ensuing decades, Edward VI (reigned 1547–1553) favored a kind of Lutheran Calvinism; his successor and half-sister, Mary, wanted to restore Catholicism (1554–1558), but another half-sister, Elizabeth I (1558–1603), held to a moderate Protestant position and cultivated ecclesiastical leaders of a generally Calvinist point of view. The result was an Elizabethan Settlement which allowed for comprehension, the inclusion of a rather wide variety of styles of theology and churchmanship.

The mark of Anglicanism's expression was the Book of Common Prayer, developed under the auspices of England's liturgical genius, Thomas Cranmer, a sometime vacillator under Henry VIII who suffered death under the Catholic Mary in 1556. Numerous deaths for which Mary was responsible (e.g., those of bishops Nicholas Ridley and Hugh Latimer) deprived the Church of England of some competent leadership. They also provided subsequent Protestantism with the lore on which much of its anti-Catholicism was based.

While Anglicanism predominated, it did not long have England to itself. Roman Catholics were generally forced into hiding until at least the Glorious Revolution of 1688, but Anglicanism was challenged "from the left" as it were, by the Puritan party, who were sometimes allied with Presbyterians. The Puritans belong to a later generation, coming to prominence in their opposition to James I (under whom the King James Bible appeared in 1611), and culminating in a Puritan Revolution in the 1640s, after a century of Protestantism. The Methodist movement was to rise as still another element for internal reform a century later.[48]

Puritanism and Methodism, for all their distinctiveness, must share the Protestant map with their parent Anglicanism, within whose confines they tried to stay. The radical party in Puritanism was Separatist, and, led by Robert Browne, became antecedent to Independency or Congregationalism, which lived on in England and has had decisive impact beyond its numbers in American history. English Baptists also grew out of these factions. One can date the rise of Congregationalism from around 1560 and the Baptists (under John Smyth) around 1606. A still more radical movement, the Quakers, dates from 1647. But these were later variants; the actual Protestantization of England took place between 1534 and the late 1550s.[49]

What will often here be styled radical or sectarian is distinctly a first-generation Protestant movement and deserves to be treated as a counterpart to established evangelicalism almost everywhere on the Protestant map. The Congregationalist-Baptist-Quaker nexus in England is certainly part of it, but it is later than the Swiss and German versions. Anabaptism in Switzerland was on the scene as early as 1521, four years after the symbolic beginning of the Reformation. The Mennonites were visible in the Low Countries around 1536. They spread from Switzerland, Germany, and Holland into parts of Eastern Europe. When the middle colonies of America opened up for settlement, many of these persecuted groups found their way there. It is difficult to point to the radical-sectarian "place on the map," because by definition these parties usually neither sought nor accepted privileged status. They were designed to oppose existing bonds between civil and religious society, and the concept of a Christian or a Protestant culture would have seemed idolatrous to them. They were a pilgrim people, "not seeking a continuing city." Yet if they were nowhere on the Protestant map, they were also almost everywhere on it, and their voice was heard through Protestant history as it will be in these pages.[50]

3. THE PHASES OF PROTESTANT THOUGHT

The conception of a history of doctrine would make little sense in many religious cultures, since they rarely define themselves around the consolidation of teachings. Yet Christian history conventionally accents the cognitive dimensions of belief. The faithful not only believe in God but they believe that this or that teaching is true. For that reason, over a period of many centuries there were definitions of dogma, and hence historians of dogma had a subject matter. The Protestant churches, carrying over as many of them did the heritage of the ancient ecumenical councils (Nicaea, Chalcedon, and the like) thus inherited a history of doctrine and a substantive field for historians. The first volume of any two-volume work on the history of the cognitive and definitional elements of Christianity, the volume leading up to the Reformation, can carry virtually the same chapter headings in both Protestant and Catholic works.[51]

Beginning with the second volume, which would cover the sixteenth to the twentieth centuries, however, the chapter headings, subject matter, and even modes of expression and styles of curiosity begin to change radically. Protestantism lacks an official and embracing magisterium, or teaching authority, and even insofar as Protestants set out now and then to be magisterial, they lack the ability to enforce articles of faith in the way that official Catholicism can under and through its papal office. So, while Protestantism can at least share the widely held suggestion that the whole church was represented in the ancient ecumenical councils, where so much dogmatic definition went on, it explicitly rejects the modern councils, such as those held at Trent in the sixteenth century and at the Vatican in the nineteenth and twentieth centuries. The first two of these were exclusively Roman Catholic affairs and the third, though it breathed a new spirit of positive accommodation to secular, religious, and Protestant tendencies, still is the history of non-Protestants and belongs only obliquely and accidentally in Protestant histories.

Two options remain, then, for Protestant analysts and historians. The first has superficial attractions but it tells less about the

Protestant thought world than it may seem to at first glance. This route commits the chronicler to a kind of denominational and then comparative writing of the history of formulation in the many different Protestant churches. For, although Protestants have had neither unity nor papacy, they have not always rejected the efforts to formulate in official ways.[52]

The Anglicans in their Thirty-nine Articles, the Lutherans in their Formula of Concord, and the Reformed in their expressions at Dort, Heidelberg, and Westminster, were certainly setting out to do what their fathers at ecumenical councils had done. They wanted to expound the Christian faith in terms appropriate for their day; to define and formulate the teachings necessary for salvation; to rule out negative and heretical features.

On the basis of these efforts they then set out to organize their parties, to separate from others, and to purify the internal life of their own churches by purging them of heterodox teachers and teachings and by sanctioning approved teachers. Where one lacked the coercive papacy, he could still set out to persuade, to use social and communal pressure, or just to make life uncomfortable for the deviant or maverick who was being frozen out of the fellowship.[53]

Were this a history of the Protestant churches, such an approach to the writing of the record would make sense, but it would be disintegrative to the plot of anything that seeks to discern lineaments of Protestant consensus and wholeness or synthesis. As a simple statement of fact: almost no Anabaptists, Brethren, Mennonites, or Dunkers ever read themselves into the history set forth by the authors of the Augsburg Confession or the Helvetian Confession in official Lutheran and Reformed churches in Germany and Switzerland. The Lutherans never expressed more than mild curiosity about the Anglican Thirty-nine Articles; they certainly did not regard them as appropriate definitions for their own church life.

To carry the story into modern times: the Barmen Declaration, written by Lutheran and Reformed churchmen in Nazi Germany, may have been regarded with awe and favor by non-Germans, but even though it was ecumenical it did not speak for, and did not try to speak to, the situation of African and Asian churchmen—as Catholicism's documents in Vatican Council II determined to do. Protestant history of dogma thus disintegrates into separate and often mutually exclusive histories, even though these may individually be informative and even though one can write them fairly easily, since he need do little more than exegete the documents in question.[54]

Another method, which sets out to accomplish something similar, though without simply satisfying the demands that historians of dogma impose upon themselves, is to deal with the much less formal kind of teaching on which the parties of the church never necessarily vote. It is possible to write histories of Protestant thought or theology in such ways that the reader can begin to acquire a vision that transcends national, confessional, and denominational lines.[55]

The differences between such a venture and the writing of the history of comparative dogmas are obvious and deep. The theologian may not have the same magisterial status that a council of the church, a pope, or a formal dogmatician may have—or may think he has. The theologian may be responsible to the whole life of the church; he may self-consciously set out to speak faithfully for the whole tradition; he may be charged by a constituency to serve a quasi-official capacity. But in the end he speaks for himself, and his thought is reckoned with by many contemporaries and by all of posterity only for its own sake, judged by the intellectual power and creativity which it manifests.[56]

In the Protestant era the location of the theologian took on a special significance, and it tended to limit and condition his language and his impact. In some previous centuries most theology had been written first by bishops and later by monks; both of them were safely within the ecclesiastical culture. Beginning with the reformers, Protestant thought has been developed primarily in the academy and the university. Even where the churches have set up seminaries of their own, these draw on paradigms from the secular university. Professional Christian thinkers have been housed in the universities and they have been particularly responsive to various currents of thought that style or give shape to various ages in Protestant history.

The theologians may withstand the substantive force of much secular teaching by their contemporaries, but they tend to be uncommonly reflective of the existing climates of opinion—even in what they reject. As one example, when Darwinism, scientific evolution, or evolutionary ideology arose in the nineteenth century academy, Protestant thinkers wittingly and unwittingly found themselves relating to developmental, progressive, and evolutionary modes—even when they opposed them.

The very brief survey of the history of Protestant thought in a

book like this—a book which does not profess to be a library on
the varieties of Protestant dogma, doctrine, and opinion—can
serve only a modest purpose. With broad strokes of the brush it
can indicate something of the transitions in kinds of Protestant
thinking. The base for understanding consensus or synthesis in
different epochs can begin to be outlined. In such a discussion of
international and transconfessional thought worlds or contexts
one can begin to grasp some sense of Protestant consensus, if only
in the choice of problems that the churches accepted for their
agenda in a particular age and in the choice of modes of thinking
used to address them.

Not for a moment should the theological part be confused with
the ecclesiastical-cultural whole. Theologians obviously do not
speak *to* everybody and, though they may not always like to be
reminded of it, they do not speak *for* everybody. They are often
lonely, isolated figures, sometimes divorced from the day-to-day
religious life of many in the churches. Yet their influence should
also not be underestimated, since they do represent life at the
crossroads between church and world in the realm of intellect.
Their books and their students serve to propagate their representations. Looking back, it is possible to see that most changes in the
thought worlds of theologians were reflected in the liturgy, the
piety, and the practical expression of great numbers of the faithful.

A study of the various stages along the Protestant way, then, will
provide an opportunity to see how continuities in the substance
(the same symbols: God, Christ, Spirit, sacrament, book) are transformed by changes in the modes of expression. No claim is made
that every corner of the Protestant world, in Europe, Britain, the
Americas, and later Asia and Africa, moved on quite the same
schedule in intellectual life or that they all embraced the successive
modes and addresses with equal fervor and intellectual clarity. Yet
it is not unfair to point to various movements and styles as being
sufficiently expressive of broad Protestant modalities. Some of
these left such deep marks that they have to be reckoned with in
most subsequent Protestant life.

Japanese Protestants often sound more like continental existentialists than do heirs of latter-day continental existentialism. Not
a few African Protestants, in the simplest of circumstances and with
only minimal literary resources, may sound like pure-form seventeenth century scholastics because of their education by missionaries who derived from Reformed orthodox traditions. Protestant
thought is expressive of its ages, and at various moments has

helped shape the general intellectual currents. A survey of these
moments illumines more of Protestantism than only the dark and
shadowy corners of gray institutions called seminaries or cultural
pockets called theologians' studies.

The first generation of theological thought almost anywhere in
Protestantism was characterized by *ferment*, experiment, and free-
form expression. Such characterizations are predictable. It would
be difficult for an historian of religion to picture the explosion of
a new religious emphasis without such chaos at its heart. New
leaders and prophets appear on a scene, depicting to people some
sense of their plight, evoking symbols which impart dignity and
hope, and invoking courses of action to bring about change in the
world.

Ordinarily it is a vision more than a system which moves such
leaders and their followers. They make do with whatever tools and
instruments are at hand. They do not always fashion a complete,
intact, integral ordering of thought and then try to fit the world
into their mold. They improvise, make false starts, borrow, probe,
jab, retreat, re-embark. Protestantism was born in this fashion, just
as other social movements came into being.[57]

Nowhere is this characteristic more clear than in the radical
forces of the Protestant left, the leaders who wanted to carry on
the most comprehensive attacks on inherited Catholicism. From
these Anabaptists and other radicals has come very little in the way
of systematic theology. Most of them had been trained in the
Catholic thought of their day, and they fused this learning with
their new prophecies.

We picture them less in the study and more in the pulpit or on
horseback or seeking refuge. They knew what they did not want:
the Catholic sacramental-hierarchical system with its authority.
They began to know what they did want, but no simple system
satisfied. Many of them were futuristic in their outlook, promising
a Kingdom to come, yet using the language of the agitator or the
poet and not that of the reflective thinker.[58]

Most Protestant histories begin with Martin Luther, who belonged much more to the university than did his radical counterparts and who was soon to lead a new and counterestablishment.
He knew something of the issues that separated realists from nominalists, followers of Thomas Aquinas from William of Occam. He
was born in an age when the scholastic verities were slipping away,
and yet few knew how to replace them. He shared the Nominalists'
love of the empirical and their rejection of speculation, though he

was anything but an orthodox member of their school. To his formal training in the writings of Augustine or Peter Lombard he joined his doctoral interests in the exegesis of Scripture.

Scripture was not a neat document that could easily and lightly be reduced to formula. Given all the pressures and attractions of his external world and the polarities within his personality, it is no wonder that Luther resorted to dialectical modes of thinking. He was able to live with apparently contradictory extremes, with logical paradoxes, broken symbols, loose ends. This characteristic provides something of the vitality that attracts some people to Luther's thought, just as it has brought frustration to many later followers and scholars. One can make him say almost whatever one wants, and Luther has been used by conservatives and radicals alike. So it is with most founders.[59]

Almost immediately, however, Protestant movements began to turn to a second stage, one of *formulation*, consolidation, and the beginnings of system. Philosophers and historians of religion might be tempted at this point to say that matters were on schedule. It is almost a truism to say that in a second generation religious movements and social forces tend to crystallize, to harden, and sometimes to take on some of the shapes of the forces they first set out to oppose.

More positively, one could say that followers cannot live only by the ecstasy and contradiction that go with ferment. Sooner or later they will quite naturally begin to be reflective and to place matters in perspective. Protestantism was blessed with a number of such formulators, and their influence has remained to the present.

Huldreich Zwingli belongs more to Luther's model of thinking: he, too, was shaped by medieval philosophy, though he was more congenial to Renaissance humanism than was Luther. He differed somewhat in his way of looking at the world, because he rendered sharper than did Luther all distinctions between the spiritual and the material, the divine and the human. He was also more systematic as a political thinker than Luther was. Still, Zwinglian thought is half-formed, ill-formed, in a twilight range between generations.[60]

Philipp Melanchthon and John Calvin among the Lutheran and the Reformed parties serve better to illustrate the formulative generation. Melanchthon was Luther's younger contemporary, on whom Luther relied for many of the statements of their element's position. Melanchthon was a broadly learned humanist, more open to philosophy than was Luther, who often saw in philosophy a kind

of striving speculation which, he felt, would lead man to claim that
he had achieved intellectual union with God on man's own terms.
Melanchthon may have shared Luther's doctrinal point of view,
but he set out to place philosophy back into the service of the faith
in direct and acknowledged ways. His *Loci communes* (1521, later
editions through 1543) gave each doctrine its "locus" or place, and
thus clearly provided the clue that he was working with some of the
scholastic approaches to truth. While he and Luther had some
minor disagreements about teaching, the ability of the two to com-
municate despite such different approaches to theology suggests
an openness toward system in Luther and a refusal to be closed in
by system in Melanchthon.

John Calvin was the supreme systematic thinker among early
Protestants, and his *Institutes of the Christian Religion* have rarely if
ever been challenged for their combination of logical clarity and
inventive thinking in the biblical and Protestant tradition. Trained
as educator, lawyer, and logician, Calvin brought his disciplines
together in such a way that he could order evangelical thought,
keep it in dialogue with the biblical witness, and suggest the logical
import. In the eyes of the less philosophical reformers, his tendencies got him into troubles. Thus his teaching on predestination,
because he carried it to a logical conclusion, led him to what has
been called a double predestinarian view.

Any of the reformers could have said that God foreknew and
foreordained that some people should be saved through Christ;
most of them were reluctant to go as far as Calvin did. He saw that
the logic of a position which stressed that God was absolutely
sovereign would then lead him also to state the opposite: that God
also foreknew and foreordained who should be condemned. In
Calvin such a position was presented with careful qualifications
and with a spirit that could keep his readers away from fatalistic
tendencies.[61]

Most northern European thought followed Luther's pattern for
a couple of decades, and western and central European thinkers (in
France, Switzerland, and the Lowlands) tended to follow Zwinglian
and Calvinist emphases. Protestants in England devoted themselves less frequently to the beginnings of dogmatic formulation.
Under Thomas Cranmer, many in the newly protestantized
Church of England were in close contact with Swiss reformers and
lived in part off their endeavors.[62]

In England formulation had to do more frequently with polity,
liturgy, or devotion, as classically stated in the Book of Common

Prayer of 1549. Even there forty-two articles, later reduced to thirty-nine, served to represent the moment when the Protestant movement began not merely to wave flags ("This we believe!") but also to issue standards ("This you should believe, if you would go with us"). It should be said that the formulations of this transitional period still allowed for contradictory elements and were open-ended toward fresh statement and experiment.

The last half of the sixteenth century and the first quarter of the seventeenth saw the full development of crystallized or second-generational thought. In the main lines of the Reformation (all but the radicals), the Protestant parties had won new space under the sun. While England was vacillating under alternative Protestant and Catholic monarchs, the Protestant future was assured. In most territories in Germany, Switzerland, Scandinavia, and the Netherlands, the Protestants were now in command.

On the principle of *cuius regio, eius religio* Protestant leaders were free to impose a single religious settlement on their territories. This meant that Protestants could no longer be united within a territory by simple opposition to Catholicism. They began to have the leisure to fall out among themselves, and they did. Thus Lutheranism was torn by several doctrinal disputes. Some parties were accused of antinomianism, the idea that because of Christ's gift, no law was to be imposed on Christians. Others were seen as synergists, because they granted too much to men's cooperative powers in the drama of salvation. A dispute over adiaphora suggested that Lutherans did not know where to draw the line between which rites and practices should be imposed and which forms should be voluntarily followed.

Out of this period of infighting came the need to move much further than Melanchthon had in his *Loci communes* or in the broadly accepted ecumenical document of Lutherans, the Augsburg Confession of 1530. Luther and, after his death, some sympathizers, began to write additional confessional statements, culminating in the long, complicated, polemical Formula of Concord of 1577. The systematic dogmatic statements were bound together in the Book of Concord of 1580, which became normative for many Lutherans ever after. Almost every large Protestant group followed suit. Thus the Calvinists at Dordrecht (or Dort) in 1618–1619 came up with a similar document for their position, a piece that was designed to reject the Arminian challenge, which would have softened Calvinism. The

Westminster Confession had similar intentions, and is adhered to by conservative Presbyterians late in the twentieth century.[63]

After the century of ferment and then of formulation by individuals or ecclesiastical parties came a half century of much more rigid philosophical adaptation in a period usually called that of *orthodoxy*. This, too, was ecumenically Protestant, tending to appear all over the evangelicals' maps and across most confessional lines.

In most cases the orthodox dogmaticians combined biblical materials with some elements of tradition (from the church fathers, for example) and blended these with the newly accepted neo-Aristotelian philosophy that was still regnant in the northern European universities in the middle half of the century. Structurally, their multivolume products bore resemblances to the scholastic works that the reformers had left behind.

While few of these systems are studied today, the later orthodox find their approach congenial, just as more liberal Protestants see orthodoxy as the period of a fall, or the time of the introduction of sterility and near-death. These systems combined Aristotelian concepts of knowledge with Protestant insights concerning the character of God and human need. Characteristically, they gave every teaching its "locus," almost always beginning with a locus on Scripture. In Protestant scholastic orthodoxy, novel if rigid doctrines of scriptural inspiration, based on one or two clues in the New Testament and borrowing from Hellenistic Judaism, were enlarged upon. In an uncertain age these systems imparted a sense of authority and served as the foundation for all ecclesiastical expression of Protestant life.[64]

Much of the internal disputes within later Protestantism has followed two lines: one set of spokesmen claims to be representing the prophetic first generation of thinkers over against scholastic and sterile orthodoxy. The other party convokes the orthodox as the natural outgrowth of the original ferment, as the protectors of the founders' rough-cut treasures. But even the most avid defenders of orthodoxy are prepared to look back and see that in all the philosophizing a one-sided intellectualization of Christianity was going on. The heart was being forgotten for the head; the openness of Christian experience was being closed by the passion for accuracy in philosophical formulation. A reaction was destined to set in. This occurred around the eighth decade of the seventeenth century.

Perhaps the most acceptable name for the challenger to and

successor of orthodoxy is *pietism*. First named by its enemies, this emphasis within the various Protestant churches can be viewed in part as a reaction to that intellectualization of Christianity. Positively, it saw itself not as a reactive force but as an authentic reproducer of Christian experience. In their accent on experience and on human response, pietistic elements can be seen as modern and anthropocentric. Philipp Jakob Spener, in *Pia Desideria*, was the first great issuer of pietist appeals. The university at Halle became the center for such thought. At pietism's heart was an epistemology that differed vastly from orthodoxy's objective and object-centered theology. Now knowledge was to grow out of and be experienced in the hearts of the regenerate. While formal pietism was distinguished chiefly in continental Lutheran and Reformed parties, there were counterparts elsewhere.[65]

Thus in England both the earlier Puritan and the later Methodist movements had pietistic tinges. In all these emphases, experience was determinative. People were to know in their hearts that they had been regenerate and then they were to act out the consequences of the new birth in their daily life. Pietism, Puritanism, and Methodism did not see themselves as unorthodox. Indeed, most of their spokesmen would have been content to see themselves as inheritors of orthodoxy, as reproducers of the key teachings of the scholastic generation.[66]

None of the new Protestants wanted to deviate from biblical teaching; they merely wanted to cut through the many centuries of traditional accretions back to the simplicity of the Bible. They did not sever themselves from the established churches of their homelands, though some of them failed in their efforts to stay in and they also failed in their goal, which was to vivify the official churches. Thus the Methodists in America and then in England could not permanently be housed in the mother Church of England.

The reign of pietism was brief. Within decades the pietist emphasis had moved off into devotion and activism, as in the case of the missionary-minded Moravian, Count Ludwig von Zinzendorf. The pietist intellectuals (and their Puritan counterparts) began to move further in their rejection of the importance of cognitive elements in belief. An inevitable erosion of particularity was accompanied by an equally inevitable loss of passion for the separate tenets of the orthodox. Thus the pietist historian Gottfried Arnold in 1699 and 1700 produced a large "non-partisan" church history, in which good was found in many of the heretics who would have

been ruled out by the orthodox fanatics. Such leveling prepared
Protestants for a new age, one which earlier pietists could not have
foreseen and certainly would not have welcomed. All that was still
to come was an epistemological change, and the churches would
be on their way toward the Enlightenment, or rationalistic era.

Enlightenment, or rationalistic, Christianity was ecumenically
Protestant, and thus fits into our international and transconfessional survey with ease. It is important to remind ourselves now
and then that not all followed the new climate of opinion or accepted every detail of each world-view. Many men and women of
simple faith would not have understood rationalistic expressions
of evangelicalism and they would have opposed them had they
comprehended them. Not all the prayer books or liturgies of the
period breathed the Enlightenment spirit. But not only the intellectual centers were imbued with a new spirit. The sermons remaining from the rationalistic age showed that the preachers were
learning the lessons from their theologians, or were developing a
rationalistic witness on their own.[67]

Enlightenment Protestantism may be called Deism in England,
the religion of the *Aufklärung* in German-speaking lands, or republican religion or reasonable Christianity, in America. But some
common elements were present everywhere. The metaphysical
background of scholastic orthodoxy was decisively rejected. There
was an ellision from sometimes thoughtless pietism toward a
thoughtful embrace of the empirical world. Men of the late seventeenth and eighteenth century intellectual orbit were giving themselves to observation of the natural world, in astronomy, geology,
or botany. A man-centered culture like that of the Renaissance
humanists reemerged, and Protestant thinkers shared in it. The
celebration of human reason stood where acceptance of divine
revelation had earlier served as the center of witness and thought.
Ancient views of natural reason or natural law were resuscitated by
men like the legally trained Hugo Grotius or Samuel von Pufen-
dorf. Supernaturalism, or revelation from outside the empirical
order, was regarded with suspicion and eventually despised.

The more formidable intellectual statements of Enlightenment
Christianity came from Germany, in a move that went from "Leibnitz to Lessing." Leibnitz constantly sought universal truths, keys
to classifying all knowledge, "the answer to everything," just as
scholastic orthodox thinkers had done through extensions of revelation. While much of the *Aufklärung* served to move people out of
the church and even into opposition against it (as French rational-

ism did against Catholicism), those who stayed in the church cultivated what might be called a "supernatural rationalism."

They did allow for some minimal intrusion of a transcendent order, but on the basis of the acceptance of the Bible on rationalistic terms. Then they moved to show the simple congruence between revealed and reasonable truth. Jesus Christ became more the exemplar than the savior, and an impersonal view of God began to replace views of him as personal Father. Revelation might complete, fulfill, or certify the order of reason, but it could never be in conflict with it. Preaching turned moralistic and abstract. The poetic dimensions of the faith were minimized. The missionary or activistic spirit of pietism was tempered.

In England, Deism was the characteristic expression of reasonable Protestantism. In the hands of men like Lord Herbert of Cherbury, Joseph Glanvill, or Matthew Tindal, it remained in or near the Church of England, and was proclaimed from many an eighteenth century pulpit and defended in many an episcopal see. The titles of the chief books indicate the direction of Deism: *The Vanity of Dogmatizing, Catholic Charity Recommended, Christianity as Old as Creation*, and *Christianity Not Mysterious* are typical.

Deists were critical of the existing churches for being either too orthodox or obscurantist, on one hand, or blindly pious and emotional, on the other. They attacked "priestcraft," arguing that many clerics stressed supernaturalism as a means of frightening and enslaving followers. They accepted a generally mechanistic view of the universe and along with it a mechanical view of morals. The note of judgment was retained: either now or hereafter men would be judged for their acts. The British Enlightenment in Protestantism was reductionistic: it sought Christian unity on rather simple terms of acceptance of rational Christianity. A generally democratic philosophy in the hands of John Locke can be seen as a kind of synthesis of enlightened Protestant thought.

The Enlightened phase, while it intended to represent permanent natural or reasonable truth, was also culturally conditioned and highly ephemeral. Its lasting legacy in Protestant theology was the critical temper it brought to the study of the documents of Christian history, including the Bible. In the period of the Enlightenment Protestant thinkers began to study the nature of the formation of ancient writings and they were no longer content with the naming, dating, and views of the integrity of the biblical books or with the integrity of the canon itself. In the nineteenth century the critical inquiries were to be resumed, long after the simplism of

Deism or the universalizing tendencies of the *Aufklärung* were forgotten.

The destruction of the Enlightened effort came from within. In England David Hume, while attacking revelation, also pointed to shortcomings in natural religion. Humean philosophy relied on experience rather than revelation and questioned the use of empirical methods to the extent that men were no longer able to move from the observed world to the noumenal, the world of unseen universals beyond it. On the Continent the philosopher Immanuel Kant performed a similar service.

Once again a pendulum was to swing back to the experiential and emotive elements in Protestantism, with a reappearance of Methodism, or *evangelicalism,* in England and America—out of Puritan roots—an evangelical awakening that bore some ties with the older Pietism on the continent. The warmed heart was again elevated over the informed head in the hierarchy of Christian values. The awakenings took many forms from John Wesley in the 1740s through John Newman in the 1840s. The path of the former led out of the Church of England toward a freer expression of faith within a tightly disciplined Methodist polity. The career of the latter led from the Church of England into Anglo-Catholicism and then, beyond the Oxford, or Tractarian, movement, to Roman Catholicism. Between them were many who remained within their confession or denomination but worked for a vital piety, an activistic posture, and a recovery of Christian orthodoxy.[68]

In the hands of the evangelicals there was a new recognition of democratic man, the product of industrial and political revolutions, the man whose intuitions had to be appealed to by effective preaching and through spirited hymns and simple expressions of piety. Among the ecclesiastical romantics there was an attempt to satisfy the minds of the same kind of people by giving them a sense of a tie with an organic, developing Church that transcended the ages and yet bonded in a new way with each. As a result some, among them the German conservatives, called for "back to Luther" movements around 1817, three centuries after the Protestant Reformation had begun. Others engaged in liturgical reform, consciously taking on classic liturgy from the Reformation and even the pre-Reformation era.[69]

In England, devotion to Gothic architecture—rejected in the Enlightenment as mystico-magical leavings from the Middle Ages—reappeared. Almost everywhere there was a new appreciation of the emerging state, and a mystique of the "folk" was associated with neo-conservative Protestantism in Scandinavia, the United States, Prussia, and the expanding British empire. The theology of the period tended to be moderately conservative but it no longer carried orthodoxy's scholastic attachment to philosophy with it, nor the Enlightenment's appeal to reason. Alfred North Whitehead has pointed to the absence of any first-rate intellectual formulations to support the pietist-Methodist age of modern Protestantism, despite its genius in the field of activism.[70]

Concurrent with the rise of evangelicalism was a *historicizing* of Protestantism in a movement that can best be called a response to the crisis of historical consciousness. This occasioned by far the most complex interpretations of Protestant Christianity, and while it held the field in the liberal period ending around World War I, it has never been left completely behind, nor have the problems it raised been fully and effectively addressed. In some respects, this phase simply grew out of the "modern human condition." It is characterized by a skepticism, a relativism, an inability to be content with evasion of a question the Enlightenment posed for Christians: how can eternal and universal truth be based on particular and contingent historical events such as God's revelation in the man Christ Jesus?

The Enlightenment-style criticism of the integrity of biblical texts was carried to new extremes. There was a new appreciation of other religions of the world in "the history of religions" school, even though this robbed Christianity of its sense of exclusiveness and superiority. Classic dogma was seen to be a product of its various epochs and their styles of thought, and did not embody universal and eternal truth, either.[71]

While the historicizing questions were eventually to reach all of Protestantism, the United States, for example, did not experience the depth of the crisis in the first half of the nineteenth century; its time was to come when Darwinian evolution challenged Christian interpretations of history late in the century. The center of the struggle was in Germany, where at the beginning of the century a theological genius who has often been ranked with John Calvin, Friedrich Schleiermacher, a professor at Berlin, frankly began with human experience and human consciousness as he expounded at great length *The Christian Faith*. He seemed rather casual about how the details of his system matched the Bible, and minimized revelation and the supernatural. Yet he paralleled or shadowed most of the classic themes of Protestant thought. After Schleiermacher, the question of consciousness and anthropological concerns in general have tended to dominate in all but the most reactionary Protestant thought.[72]

Far more radical than Schleiermacher were the left-wing followers of the theologian's contemporary at Berlin, the philosopher Georg Friedrich Hegel. The Hegelians began by seeking the current concretions of the absolute Spirit, with the firm belief that their effort would provide a new charter for developmental Christianity. But Hegel's spiritualizing and universalizing were soon turned into a dialectical materialism in the works of Ludwig Feuerbach, who was in some respects a precursor of Karl Marx. The researches of David Friedrich Strauss led, in 1835, to a *Life of Jesus*, which was really an essay on myth and on the impossibility of writing a life of Jesus. Some of the left-wing Hegelians began to doubt Jesus' existence. Others, in the spirit of Feuerbach, who reduced theology to anthropology, made it possible for Karl Marx and Friedrich Nietzsche to bring matters to an end with their social and personal visions of a dead God and the birth of new historical processes.[73]

Another version of the historical pursuit came from the line of the neo-Kantians, an approach that won more adherents in England and, by the end of the century, in the American New Theology and Social Gospel movements. The neo-Kantians picked up both Kant's love for the phenomenal and his accent on the will and on ethics. They began to restore confidence in some of the historical dimensions of Jesus' life and Christian history, and associated these with a philosophy of values that asked men to bring in the Kingdom of God among men. The question now asked had nothing to do with metaphysical truth but rather with the effectiveness and the values and worth of revelation, particularly in the life of Jesus, the exemplar and teacher. The Schleiermacherian subjectivism was carried into a new social dimension by this school, which grew particularly out of the influence of Albrecht Ritschl. The British churchmen who produced *Essays and Reviews* and *Lux Mundi* late in the century breathed a Ritschlian spirit of biblical criticism, confidence in historical inquiry, and progressive hopes about the coming Kingdom.[74]

The reaction to liberalism, whether in Schleiermacherian or Ritschlian forms, came chiefly from Germany, which has been the proverbial home of Protestant theological innovations for two centuries. Often artificially clustered together under the name *neo-orthodox* were the names of certain dialectical thinkers, existentialists, antischolastics, devotees of "crisis theology" or "theology of the word": Karl Barth, Emil Brunner, Paul Tillich, and Rudolf Bultmann on the Continent, the brothers Reinhold and H. Richard Niebuhr in America, or men like Peter Taylor Forsyth in England. They differed vastly from each other. But they shared a root experience in seeing the death of the old humanism and optimism around World War I and were more responsive to the kind of existentialist thought associated with the name of Søren Kierkegaard back in the middle of the nineteenth century. They decried progressivism, and then set out on differing paths of reaction.[75]

Karl Barth, beginning at the end of World War I, forcefully attacked liberalism and man-centered theology in the interests of a new revelationism and transcendental point of view which pointed to God as "the Wholly Other." Rudolf Bultmann took on the Ritschlians through his form-critical scholarship which cast doubt on most historical affirmations about Jesus and Christian origins and then reaffirmed the Protestant teaching of justification by grace through faith by an ingenious application of existentialist categories derived from Martin Heidegger.

Paul Tillich fused a kind of Hegelian-Schellingesque idealism with a Schleiermacher-like love of experience and an existentialist analysis of man, as he set out to correlate philosophy and theology. The Niebuhrs inherited the problems of liberalism as sons of the American Social Gospel, yet they also took on some of the dramatic revelational accents of the Barthians and lived between relativism and biblical prophecy.

Toward the end of the careers of each of these there were new affirmations of one or another of the tenets or attitudes of nineteenth century liberalism. Barth could even write of *The Humanity of God* once again. Their successors have returned to some of the anthropocentric and sometimes optimistic notes of the earlier liberalism.

In none of the above epochs have Protestants come together in councils to affirm or endorse a bond with this or that philosophy. In every age many have been free to ignore the claims of the regnant theologies or to counter them. Never has theology encompassed all of Protestant church life. Yet, remarkably, in every age Protestant leadership has tried to meet the challenges of the secular world or to seize the initiative by fresh formulations of Christian truth.

While through it all Protestantism remained segmented by national and denominational experience, there has been a rather remarkably ecumenical realization of phases. Ferment, formulation, orthodoxy, pietism, enlightenment, awakening, historical crisis and liberalism, existentialist reaction—all of these have been in some degree or other international and interconfessional. In many periods it has seemed less important to ask Protestant thinkers which church they belonged to or what was the country of their origin than to ask where they had studied, to which philosophy they related, or how they regarded the threat and the promise of the secular world. If one did not like the answers he received, he could always wait around a generation or so for reaction to the prevailing opinions, for Protestantism has tried many successive modes of witnessing, and has framed that witness in philosophy and theology.

ing to this doctrinal system or that, it may just as fairly be argued that modernity brought these possibilities to the Protestant scene. Further pluralism was the result.

The contemporary era, informed as it is by mass media of communication and formed by rapid means of transportation, has one further difficulty in understanding Protestant division in the past. The awakened Christian conscience tends to be judgmental about forefathers who lived in eras when the disunity of the Church was not considered to be so offensive. If they wish to comprehend the situation of the past, however, they have to imagine themselves back in a world of considerable isolation. One could and probably would spend his whole life in a valley of Norway or Switzerland, in an isolated village in Hungary or on a prairie in South Dakota, without contact with people of other cultures.

In many places the literacy percentage was low, and the common people could hardly be expected to keep themselves informed about the value systems of remote people with whom they would never come into contact. When one is not aware of a fellow believer who differs slightly, or when he never comes into contact with such people, any yearning for unity is likely to be a more or less abstractly spiritual tendency and it will lack urgency.

Since Protestantism did not kill off the inherited idea that the prince of a region determined the religion of a region, whole populations of territories were converted to a single brand of Protestantism. Other types of evangelical believers were at some distance beyond the range where they could cause scandal.

Yet there were contacts between families and groups of evangelicals; these sometimes served to stimulate appeals to unity. Just as often they were abrasive and led to more disunity or at least to more insistence on the validity of separate forms. For one thing, the Reformation produced Protestant exiles who had to go from place to place to escape repressive and persecutory measures by others who were Protestant. They were both disruptive and evangelizing forces in their new environments. They attracted people to their movement and they inspired backlash against their positions.

Meanwhile, vagaries of governmental changes between Catholic and Protestant powers led to political ostracism, and groups like the Marian exiles served as an internationalizing force. Students from universities which served as centers of the Reformation departed to sites where international influences prevailed, there to propagate their views, views which were often at variance with existing Protestant opinions. International communication, in short, could divide just as much as it could inspire common understanding.

Similarly, serious efforts by theological parties to come to terms with each other did not always lead to unity. The most famous of these earlier contacts was that staged for Martin Luther and Huldreich Zwingli at Marburg Castle in 1529. The purpose was to see whether they could come closer together in their diverging views of the Lord's Supper. Some political motivation was behind the sponsor's efforts, but the religious parties saw good reason to examine each other's position, too. The result was not ecumenical concord but a deeper and more hardened position.

Zwingli was more ready to accept his counterpart despite substantial differences, but Luther's insistence that the Swiss spokesman had a different spirit led him and his followers increasingly to break off contact and to despair of bringing continental Protestantism into a single movement.[77]

Where there might have been theological unities, political and personal differences might often intervene. There were pro-Lutheran forces in Henry VIII's England, but the kingly defender of the faith was so vehement in his attacks against Luther that later when he parted with Roman Catholicism it was difficult for the Church of England to pay much positive attention to the continental voices.[78]

The intensity with which minutiae of doctrine were debated is difficult for moderns to comprehend. In their world, inherited Christian doctrine does not matter that much. Political kingdoms do not rise and fall over views of the Lord's Supper. Whether the inspired Scriptures are inerrant or not may be a disturbing question to people inside church circles, but it seems to have little to do with the way the world is arranged. The vital issues in later times have to do with national boundaries, political ideologies, economic approaches, racial attitudes, and confusions over what morality is.

In the sixteenth and seventeenth centuries, attitudes toward doctrine *did* shape political forces, as in the case of some factors behind the Thirty Years' War. In a more metaphysically minded age the question of how the world was put together did relate to the way the supernatural order was conceived. One has to think of the factionalism within twentieth century leftist student movements, guerrilla forces, or agencies that inspire black leadership, in order to comprehend how emotional were the debates over position in early Protestantism. While the debates eventually cooled, they left hardened and easily inheritable confessional or sectarian patterns behind them.

Given Protestantism's tendencies toward disunity, some advocates decided to make a virtue of necessity. As a result, Protestant divisions have often been exaggerated. When modern political pluralism, as in the United States, permitted the various groups to compete on equal terms and even more particularly when capitalist-competitive ideology was then applied, not a few leaders justified division on individualist grounds. It was reasoned that Protestant division was itself a ratification of evangelical doctrines of freedom. The more varieties, the more evidence of freedom.

Sometimes there were suggestions that a kind of Darwinian survival of the fittest was at stake. Competition was licensed in the sense that the better team would win, the unworthy would not survive, and future generations would be well served. Sometimes a market sense prevailed: competition was a stimulus to activism in service to others; each tried to do better. Or competitiveness made possible a wider variety of options so that more outsiders could be attracted to one or another version of Christianity. At the very least, the divided pattern, when consolidated in the form of denominationalism in a free society, guaranteed the liberty of men to pursue different approaches to God without threat to their life or reputation.

These antiecumenical claims, some of which have survived even down into the period of awakened Christian consciousness over the matter of disunion, led to enhanced views of Protestant division. So did the attacks of outsiders. Roman Catholic historians, for example, have regularly supplied the longest lists of Protestant groups, with the suggestion that to accept the evangelical mode of church life would lead only to factionalism.

The appendices of Catholic works on Protestantism have as a frequent feature reference lists of the varieties. Thus John A. Hardon reached for the tables in the *Yearbook of the American Churches* to document his *The Protestant Churches in America* and came up with colorful and exotic church bodies. The Baptists alone included Duck River (and Kindred) Associations of Baptists, Free Will Baptists, General Six-Principle Baptists, Two-Seed-in-the-Spirit Predestinarian Baptists (16 churches, 201 members in the United States). The implication of such compilations is that Protestants only divide.[79]

Through the centuries of increasing separation and disunity

there were some countertendencies to balance these. Not always were they the result of efforts by church bodies to set their houses in order. One of these tendencies resided in the fact that not all the divided Protestants took their separatist claims too seriously. People could step back a little distance and see that there were coherences, that Protestants were not as divided as they appeared to be.[80]

Some would do this on the basis of polity, and find that important separations occurred on jurisdictional lines: Episcopal, Congregational, Presbyterian, and Methodist. Or the bewildering variety of American denominations (with over 250 groups listed in the *Yearbook*) could be reduced to nine or ten families, whose total made up perhaps nine-tenths of American Protestant membership.

Others saw that the divisions which mattered followed simple two-party lines: ecumenicals versus evangelicals, liberals versus conservatives, pedo-baptists versus Anabaptists, literalists versus critical readers of the Scripture, sacramentarians versus people who understressed the sacrament. The vital divisions were within and not between the denominations or national churches. The denominational form was then a mere survival of tradition, circumstance, and accident.

Still another mitigating factor has been the presence in every Protestant generation of certain ecumenical personalities. Denis de Rougemont, a French-Swiss leader in the middle of the twentieth century, spoke for this old tradition when he remarked that his spirit never could be patient to wait for formal unity negotiations. He found men and women in a number of religious confessions, divided by arbitrary traditional lines, yet already united in their common devotion to Christ and their common vision of the world's need and of some tasks which were before them. These irenic personalities anticipated expressions of unity that became formally licit only much later. Those who came into contact with such people in any generation might find their own divisions judged even as they caught a vision of a unity that could one day be theirs.[81]

The prehistory of modern ecumenism is not so slight as these paragraphs might suggest, however. While it is easy to see the divisions of Protestantism, it is important also to notice that from the beginning there have been organized and conscious efforts to bring evangelicals together, and the story of unitive Protestantism has to be told for the sake of comprehending the meaning of this history.

Most noteworthy is the fact that the Reformation doctrines were ecumenical in intention and that the confessional statements of the Protestant parties were usually comprehensive and inclusive in their outreach. It is easy to look back and note that the unitive impulses were not always much stressed or that the terms for following them were often out of reach of others, but Protestant acceptance of ecumenical ancient creeds, of the term "catholic" (in many cases) for the Church and the declaration of intention to find unity with others have all been elements on which later generations of unity-seekers could build. They could argue and they have argued, then, that the quest for a uniting Church has been no denial of the intentions of the fathers, but has been a working out of these.

A second feature of first-generation Protestantism was the presence in almost every militant group of some irenic spirits, often of humanist orientation. Thus in the Lutheran communion, although Martin Luther usually stood apart as a definer of differences, his closest associate, Philipp Melanchthon, was a man of humanist sympathies who tried, also through his work with the Augsburg Confession, to keep the Reformation parties open to each other.

When any group had internal difficulties, persons such as these irenicists were most often mistrusted and accused, and Melanchthonians could be dismissed with the epithet Crypto-Calvinist. But they also did leave elements in the tradition on which later uniting spirits could draw. Calvinism was by definition more of a mediating force than Lutheranism, and John Calvin wanted to bring together separatists.

In England many leaders of the Reformation were ecumenical spirits, and the Anglican principle of "comprehension" allowed for different nuances of doctrine. But these tendencies were checked by Henry VIII's monarchical policies, which often prevented them from being worked out. Many radical evangelicals were ecumenical in their outreach, too. They sought spiritual unities that would transcend the apparently arbitrary lines imposed by religious establishments.

From the first there were efforts to define ways for Protestants to unite. Sometimes these sought an essence of Christianity, restated ideals of Christian simplicity, or outlined the direction for future unity. The names of some of the surviving documents of the era suggest the seriousness of intentions: the Zurich Consensus, the Wittenberg Concord, the Consensus of Sendomir. Plans for unity were formulated by John Calvin, Thomas Cranmer, Martin

Bucer, John à Lasco—none of them minor figures in the Reformation movements.[82]

Too many factors militated against their efforts. The early Reformation ferment did not allow for much compromise. Protestant movements were tied to too many competing national forces. Men placed higher premiums on other marks of the Church than that it was and should be one. Later generations of Protestantism almost had to begin all over again.

Among the impulses to bring about unity the one least fondly advertised in later generations and the one that was also least spiritually satisfying was on political grounds. From the efforts of Philip of Hesse to bring Luther and Zwingli together down through the Prussian Union of 1817 and into most recent times, as when the Japanese Christians were more or less coerced into the Kyodan, political leaders have sought concord among religious parties. Sometimes this was done to help populations overcome distractions: so long as they were squabbling about doctrine, it was not likely that they could unite on other governmental matters or against common foes.

Just as often there was an imperial design. When Prussia began to rise above some of its neighbors among the 300 territories of early nineteenth century Germany, a united Protestant Church was seen as a great hope for those who looked for a spiritual unity behind the nation. While the old Holy Roman Empire was breaking up over a period of three centuries, continental leaders tried to fill the vacuum with new military or national forces, and they sometimes looked to a united Protestantism to help give birth to a single new Europe.

The same political power that could reach out to encourage or force unity, however, could also be used to perpetuate divisions. On numerous occasions in the seventeenth and eighteenth centuries there were possibilities for the increase of amity between the Church of England and Nonconformity or dissent of various types. Yet the theological or devotional impulses which created the climate of readiness were to be denied because the Church of England was tied to the crown, and the royal leaders or parliamentary officials were not in the mood to give up some of their prerogatives by recognizing dissent or summoning energies to have the established and Nonconforming churches brought together on some new set of terms.

Of broader mass appeals have been the efforts through the whole Protestant era to bring unity based not so much on jurisdictional or doctrinal lines but more on the order of spiritual or devotional expression. There is something about the mystical impulse which is at once highly individualistic and universalistic. Insofar as it is individualistic, it tends to downgrade the importance of the structures of church life entirely.

Most of the debate over polity, organization, and doctrinal formulation seems to the mystic to be a false objectification of the divine spiritual impulse and has to be transcended. At the same time, the mystic in finding his higher unity with God expects to meet others of kindred spirit in that higher unity, and for that reason his vision can also be seen to be universal and encompassing. God who is All is capable of embracing people who have been separated from each other along the arbitrary lines drawn by humans. This mystic or spiritualist approach has been lived out in less intense and more readily available forms in numerous pietist or evangelical tendencies throughout Christian history.

The spiritual approach works both ways, just as the political does. If the governmental leader might both impose unity and, when it suits him, frustrate it, so the spiritual pietist might inspire unity even as he removed men's hunger for it. By his suggestion that church institutions or organizations are of secondary importance, he tends to sap the energies of those who would work to reorganize them. He tends to abandon the people whose spiritual life is inhibited by rigid lines of denominational life. Pietists, for example, made contributions to later hymnbooks; the hymns sung by people in various parts of antiecumenical Protestantism have been the most ecumenical features of their life. But the fact that this lore is available to them even if they could not unite in worship with the authors, were these present in their congregations, tends to be forgotten and little effort has been made to create better channels for common Christian expression.

The third most commonly perceived avenue toward Protestant unity before the twentieth century is usually called the humanist approach. The humanists in the Protestant tradition were not, of course, what humanists are usually considered to be in the twentieth century. Later usage suggests that the humanist is the man-centered, creative, agnostic person, the one who without God seeks the best of what men have tried to affirm in the presence of God.

In the Reformation era the humanists were the men devoted to the humanities, lovers of classical language and learning, university people of humane instinct who had a breadth of knowledge that was not accompanied by a polemical spirit. Similarly, in the Enlightenment era this type of person reemerged, usually to seek simplicities and unities in Christian doctrine and order.

Ideologically, the humanist has tended to see doctrinal and political complexity as a fall from the intended mode of Christian life, recalling both the childlike example of Jesus, the simplifying tendencies of major schools of philosophy, and the historical contingency on which many complex differences were based. Some of the humanists were friendly to Protestantism but remained within Catholicism; Erasmus was the most noted of these. Those who were Protestant were pioneers in formulating approaches to Christian unity.[83]

The humanist, like the politician and the pietist, contributed to unity but was seldom heeded and sometimes was used to stimulate reaction and more disunity. Most humanist simplifications did not do justice to the complex ways in which people adhere to historical religions like Protestant Christianity. Most of the faithful have found that they were to give up what humanists found to be irrelevant because it was the property of their particular party or tradition. But what was given up, in their eyes, was the very matter which made their faith attractive to them.

The humanist-intellectual approach was often impractical, not meeting felt needs and answering unasked questions. The humanist was most vulnerable to the charge that he was ready to compromise on Christian essentials and that he would deny the truth of Christianity. So the most dogmatic partisans could make of him a bogey to frighten people back into ever more divisive schools of religious thought.

A survey of efforts to seek Protestant unity before the twentieth century could well concentrate on the United States, since that nation was best known for the wild pluralism of its evangelical parties. The divisions in America were the result, largely, of two factors. The first of these was the fact that American Christianity inherited the varieties of European Christianity. The early settlers in Virginia were Anglican, and in New England they were Puritan. Some persecuted British Quakers and Baptists soon complicated this dual picture. Between them were the Middle Colonies, where continental emigrants from Lutheran Sweden or Reformed France coexisted in William Penn's empire with Mennonites, Quakers, and various persecuted continental or British groups. To this colonial pattern were added wave after wave of later immigrations, each bringing with it the expression of religion known in separated parts of Europe. Protestants in the United States had no chance to be united.[84]

The second factor in the American pattern was the separation of civil and religious realms that accompanied the formation of a single nation out of numerous colonies, most of which had had competitive religious establishments. The resultant voluntary principle licensed the groups along the eastern seaboard to move to western frontiers to set up daughter churches. As they did so, individualistic types were free to separate from these parent churches and to devise denominations of their own. Before the Civil War almost all disputes of any consequence led to the formation of whole new sects; after that time the process was slowed down and the trend was reversed. Post-Civil War disputes were often carried on within denominations without so easily leading to ruptures. But by then the main damage to the cause of Protestant unity had been done. By 1890 there were already over 140 denominations active on the scene.

The most serious efforts toward unity came in the nineteenth century. One impulse resulted from what have come to be called the primitive gospel, or restorationist, movements. Men and women looked out at the crazy-quilt of denominations and then back to the New Testament. Lacking the critical understanding which has seen many tendencies and factions in the early church there described, they had idealized and romanticized pictures of the simplicity of the earliest group of disciples and the clearly defined order of the apostolic circle. If only men would go back to the patterns outlined there and would refrain from imposing on men's minds and bodies ideas and orders that were not directly prescribed or pictured there, all would be well!

The best known of these movements was that which came to be called the Disciples of Christ, the Church of Christ, or the Christian Church. These were made up of people who wanted to do what they could to transcend denominationalism, avoid ecclesiastical innovation and terminology, and retain scriptural simplicity. While they were reluctant to admit it, they were seen by their neighbors as unsuccessful and turned out sociologically to be just some more items in the proliferating sequence of denominations. The Latter-day Saints, or Mormons, were one of the more colorful bodies born at that time out of distaste for competing revivalist denominations.

Another American pattern foresaw unity on evangelical party lines. That is, facing infidelity, on one hand, and Catholicism, on the other, some Protestant leaders felt that they could best serve Christ by working on what was essential in their inherited patterns of church life. They would compromise where compromise was possible, minimize where differences were inevitable, and accent common purpose in world missions, benevolent or humanitarian endeavors, and theological inquiry.

They had to turn their backs on unorthodox groups like Unitarians and Hicksite Quakers, and often unwittingly concentrated their efforts on the Anglo-Saxon (British) denominations, since the continentals brought over different practices and were smaller minorities. But some Lutherans like Samuel S. S. Schmucker were ready to forget some of the particularities of Lutheran approaches to communion in their eagerness to be at home in the proto-ecumenical organization called the Evangelical Alliance. This agency was formed on international lines in 1846.

The evangelical movement did produce a kind of common ethos, but it was torn apart by issues like slavery, north-south tensions, differing approaches to doctrine, and a surprisingly durable if not actually accelerating spirit of denominationalism.

To these might be added a number of catholic approaches to Protestant unity. One of these grew out of German Reformed circles, most notably at that denomination's small seminary at Mercersburg, Pennsylvania. The nation's most noted church historian of the century, Philip Schaff, taught there for some time. Schaff tried to outline "The Principle of Protestantism" in the most comprehensive terms, seeking to overcome the weaknesses and develop the strengths of both continental and British Protestantism into a new and higher unity. More theological was his colleague John Williamson Nevin, who at midcentury criticized the biblicism of the primitivists and the evangelicals: their appeals to the Bible did not serve to unite them; they should reexplore the church's tradition.[85]

Needless to say, such an approach was a minority voice. It did not, as its enemies argued, lead to the enhancement of Roman Catholicism in such hands any more than it did in high church Episcopalianism as advocated by Bishop John Hobart and some distinguished successors. These traditional and catholic arguments found few followers outside Episcopalianism and, ironically, some of the more catholic or comprehensive appeals were seen to contribute to even more factionalism and party spirit within existing groups.

If the primitive, evangelical, and catholic approaches did not produce theologically satisfying pan-Protestantism in America, this did not mean that Protestantism found no way of asserting its unity. Early in the century a remarkable evangelical empire thrived for some time. It was made up of a network of agencies designed to spread Christian teaching, to engage in foreign missions, to reform the morals of the nation, and to promote charitable activities. Its leadership was lay as often as it was clerical and was thoroughly interdenominational. Out of it grew the American Bible Society, the American Home Missionary Society, the American Board of Commissioners for Foreign Missions, and literally scores or hundreds of similar institutions. For decades these provided outlets for Protestants of unitive sentiment, and many survive to the present. But intersectional rivalry disturbed their peace; bureaucratization slowed them; resurgent denominationalism compromised them.[86]

In England the fact of Anglican establishment made difficult the effecting of unity with dissenters and Nonconformity even if, especially after 1689, dissent experienced ever growing privilege and profited from a new toleration. England always had its tireless workers for Christian unity. John Dury, for instance, is remembered in any recall of ecumenical pioneers. But while the Anglican theory allowed for variety and many Anglican theologicans discerned true ecumenical tendencies in their own doctrine of the church, at home they were not free to unite with others.[87]

In England as elsewhere movements to vivify and revitalize the church often led to further division. The Puritan movement was the first great example. In the middle of the eighteenth century the Wesleyan revival led to the same consequence. John Wesley was in a way a high church Anglican, desperately eager not to be seen as a schismatic. But toward the end of his career he compromised with destiny and undertook acts which recognized his actual status: he was seen as a separatist. Methodism in the middle of the nineteenth century was itself torn by numerous separations and schisms.

By the nineteenth century, then, Independents, Presbyterians (largely Unitarian), Congregationalists, Quakers, and many schools of Methodists coexisted with the Church of England. While there were few efforts to bring about denominational unity, it was possible there as in America for evangelicals to work and worship together across these lines. So it was that many evangelicals in the Church of England felt more at home with Methodists than with their own broad church or high church fellow believers.

The Society for the Promotion of Christian Knowledge as early as 1698 and the London Missionary Society in 1792 were typical of the elements in the missionary-benevolent network of the century, and they inspired many successors. The Young Men's Christian Association in England and in America brought together benevolent evangelicals of many denominations.

Many reform agencies did not follow lines of ecclesiastical jurisdiction. By the late nineteenth century the Anglican Lambeth Conferences had turned men's attention to the claims for wider Christian unity, and in 1888 the famous Lambeth Quadrilateral stated the Church of England's approach to unity. Anglicanism was often described as a bridge church for Christian unity, but the more radical Protestant groups found its keynote, Episcopalian polity in the apostolic succession, to be a stumbling block on the path to unity. Anglicanism did pioneer in twentieth century styles of ecumenism.

We have already looked at some of the earliest continental efforts. After the Reformation era and in the period of dogmatic definition, some humanist theologicans like George Calixtus worked to bring about Lutheran–Reformed reunion as a basis for a common Protestant Christianity. Calixtus worked for unity on grounds which he saw to be common in the first five centuries of Christian history before the church fell. In the process he had to give tradition and the councils more status than many continental Protestants were ready to do. He was accused of being a syncretist, a superficial mixer of doctrines, an impractical dreamer without much following. The noted jurist Hugo Grotius set forth equally detailed plans for Christian unity, but they did not receive much more hearing.

The partially successful trends toward unity came more from the slightly later circles of pietism. Pietism was a reformist movement within the established church late in the seventeenth and early in the eighteenth centuries. In the hands of Philipp Jakob Spener and August Hermann Francke it was doctrinally placid enough not to be permanently divisive, genteel enough not to disrupt the establishment, yet effective at attracting large followings. By accenting the warmed heart instead of the dogmatic head it made possible a new valuation on piety and Christian work. While geographical distance kept Lutheran and Reformed pietist parties apart to some extent, they would meet—as they did on the estate of the Moravian lay leader, Count Ludwig von Zinzendorf, there to forget doctrinal particularities in the interest of a higher unity that would promote world missions.

While the pietist downgrading of doctrine and its accent on simplicity both helped generate and give a place to rationalism (as in universities that had been pietist strongholds), the pietist heritage was not wholly lost. In the nineteenth century it was revived in various movements of confessional and liturgical renewal. Many of these were open to engaging in common missionary enterprises across denominational lines and out of these circles came the leaders of the German, Swiss, and French side of the Evangelical Alliance of 1846. Generally, pietism was doctrinally conservative or moderate, but ecumenically it was often more successful than were the innovative and liberal Protestant schools which seldom won the confidence of large members of continental parishioners.

Between the time of pietist and the later awakenings there occurred the continental Enlightenment, which in France took virulently anticlerical forms, but which in Germany and elsewhere was more conservative about ecclesiastical life and often wanted to transform Christian particularities into new universals. Such a movement, with its accent on natural reason and natural law, was disposed toward the minimizing of doctrinal differences and the purging in Protestantism of what it sought to define as accidental historical accretions.

The best-known example of formal ecumenical endeavor in the German *Aufklärung* was the philosopher Leibnitz, who carried on extensive correspondence, always well intended but often frustrating, with the great French Catholic bishop and historian Bossuet. Leibnitz wanted international and interconfessional concord for the sake of the shaping of a new Christian Europe. It could provide examples for, and overwhelm or attract, the non-Christian, non-believing world. A man audacious enough to look forward to Roman Catholic partnership quite naturally absorbed Protestant differences into his higher synthesis. But his was a rather rarefied intellectual approach and drew few followers.

The radical movements in Protestantism provide the widest variety of ecumenical approaches. When the unitive movement took permanent shape in the early twentieth century, many heirs of these forces were leaders, but the earlier history was more ambiguous. On one hand, the dissenters against Calvinist and Lutheran establishments could unite in their common miseries as exiles from persecutors. At the same time, many of them stressed the unity in the Spirit, a unity which they felt to be denied them by their autocratic persecutors.

On the other hand, many of these left-wing churches and groups lived at such a pitch of intensity that they did not take time to

compare their own visions with those of others. Or they were led
by charismatics who sometimes claimed private revelations or
novel kinds of religious experiences which saw all other Christians
to be heretical. So the sectarian spirit worked both for unity within
radical Protestantism and also for the perpetuation and deepening
of differences.[88]

The modern Protestant unity movement was taking shape late
in the nineteenth century. The Y.M.C.A. and the Y.W.C.A. were
joined in 1895 by the World's Student Christian Federation.
Groups like these gave voice to the adventurous tendencies of
young people who were critical of the scandal of division and were
ready to devote themselves to Christian work if the churches
united. Meanwhile they directly contributed to endeavors to bring
about unity.

They were joined by lay groups, who found their own efforts to
witness or reform the world frustrated by infighting. Missionaries
returned from their fields to report that conversions were sometimes prevented among prospects who were bewildered or
offended by the variety of the Christs who were offered by Norwegian Lutherans, the Church of England, and American Baptists, all
of whom might be working side by side, but not together, on the
same little island somewhere.

All these were joined by some theologians and ecclesiastical
leaders who gathered up various strands of earlier Protestant witness to argue for the advantage of being united. More rapid transportation was creating the effect of a smaller globe, so men could
comprehend a united church. Efficient communications increased
people's awareness of division and the possibility of their discourse to contribute to reunion.

Some of the same forces which produced pan-Protestant unitive
striving were also apparent in the attempts of confessional bodies
to set their own houses in order. Late in the nineteenth and early
in the twentieth centuries Reformed, Congregationalist, Anglican,
Methodist, Baptist, Lutheran, and other geographically widespread groups formed conventions or federations. In one sense
these retarded comprehensive Protestant unity moves, since fellowship with long-forgotten fellow confessors from other lands
came easily and was often immediately emotionally satisfying.
Some energies that could have been directed toward larger unity
were cut off by such satisfactions. On the other hand, intercultural
contacts on confessional lines stimulated the kinds of acquaintance
that led to more hunger for Protestant conversation and unity.

Still another manifestation of moves toward cooperation came in the twentieth century where in nation after nation federations of churches came into existence. Leaders of these rarely tampered with denominational autonomy and asked for and expressed unity only to the degree that the constituent churches permitted. But they did allow for interdenominational theological explorations and the achieving of many effects for reform and benevolence. The Federal Council of Churches was organized in the United States in 1908, and similar bodies were formed also in the nations where pluralism had been less visible as well as in the areas of the Younger Churches which, in the missionary period, had inherited the legacy of division.

The principle of unitive Protestantism began to be realized in a new way as divided churches bearing the same confessional name (Presbyterian in Scotland, Methodist in England, Lutheran in the United States) moved past the sectarian stage and back into the confessional. That is, they tried to overcome differences born of personality conflict, political dispute, or minor partisanship and to cohere along the lines of theological principles set up by the founders of their churches or more in congruence with developmental expressions of their faith.

Once they had gone through the complex negotiations involved in such organic mergers many of them had a taste for interconfessional organization. Thus a United Church of Christ was born in Canada, in the Philippines, and in Japan in the second quarter of the twentieth century, and new groups of that type have been in the process of formation in India, and in the United States after midcentury.[89]

The most widely observed exemplification of Protestant unity strivings was the formation of the World Council of Churches. Three strands, in particular, went into it. Already mentioned was the missionary tendency, which became visible at the Edinburgh Missionary Conference in 1910. This was a largely Anglo-American gathering which gave a foretaste of worldwide interconfessional unity. From this event the modern movement is often dated. The missionaries and spokesmen continued to meet periodically on their own at Jerusalem, Tamburam, and elsewhere, but in New Delhi in 1951 they were integrated into their daughter organization.

A second accent came from the people who had witnessed the ravages of war and foresaw the fruits of a global approach to Christian endeavor. These pioneers began to know "Life and

Work" together long before they were able to overcome theological differences. They met at Stockholm in 1925 and Oxford in 1937.

The third force was made up of people who argued that a satisfying unity could be attained only if "Faith and Order" were taken into consideration. They debated and compared theology and polity at Lausanne in 1927 and Edinburgh in 1937.

After the interruptions of World War II and much quiet planning, the World Council of Churches was formed at Amsterdam in 1948. It has met approximately every six years since. While this agency, headquartered at Geneva, Switzerland, later provided the means of Protestant-Orthodox contacts and was recognized by Roman Catholicism as a base for Protestant-Catholic conversation, it was originally, at least, overwhelmingly Protestant in outlook and interest. The World Council of Churches served at the time of its organization to dramatize the long steps that Protestants had taken. Meanwhile its difficulties—budgetary, bureaucratic, theological, political, generational—also called attention to the difficult path ahead.

The secular world does not consistently pay much heed to religion, so religious unity is not often regarded as one of the world's items of urgency. In the religious world Christian unity represents the aspirations of a small minority of the people. Within Christian circles, Protestantism represents a highly localized third of the people. Therefore its internal life is less dramatic than are Protestant/Catholic, Christian East/Christian West, Christian/Jewish, Judaeo-Christian/other religion, or religious/secular encounters of various sorts. Not many decades after the World Council of Churches had been formed, then, it was eclipsed by new tendencies in the world of religion and had difficulty finding means to support itself or modes of relating to the new realities.

Many relatively conservative Protestants in the north Atlantic sphere found the political expressions of the World Council and similar organizations to be too representative of socialistic or radical sentiments of Christians from the Third World. At the same time, Third World Christians found such originally Western organizations too settled in conventionally developed societies, or incapable of transcending their own complexity and the interests of their nations, to be of much help in the newly formed societies. Radical theology provided a severe test of the biblical and liturgical inquiries that had been characteristic of ecumenical moderates. Many young people, if they were interested in remaining Protestant at all, were bored by or put off by institutionalism, including its ecumenical forms, and they looked for Christian action and thought in more dramatic forms than such organizations could provide.

Therefore, it is uncertain as to the form future efforts at uniting Protestantism will take, but in the twentieth century the principle which placed a high premium on common witness, worship, and work had at least successfully displaced the older enhancement of competition.

Protestant ecumenism has had its opponents, too, both within and outside Protestantism. Some Protestant neo-evangelicals and all fundamentalists have rejected the mainline unitive movements. Each of them has stated that unity is possible only when people have agreed on all terms of theology. In the case of conservative Protestants this claim has not been accompanied only and always by complete isolation. Instead, the neo-evangelicals simply agreed on a different set of essentials. Among these usually were an inerrant Bible and doctrines like the Virgin Birth, the substitutionary atonement of Christ, and the physical resurrection of Christ.[90]

Opponents are less careful than many ecumenical Protestants to insist on agreement concerning baptism or the Lord's Supper, which they may regard as secondary. Curiously, the ecumenical impulse is so strong that even resistant groups ordinarily find it advisable to work together or to unite, as they do in support of evangelistic crusades or in organizations which parallel the World Council of Churches, but with less doctrinal comprehension. "Cooperation without compromise" is the motto of one American group whose slogan implies a judgment on Protestants who, they feel, have compromised truth for the sake of unity.[91]

Secular spokesmen also seem to be of two minds about unitive Protestantism. On one hand, the general good will generated by Christians who have said, "Cease Fire!" is regarded favorably by those who seek concord in the world. Christian division was a scandal preventing outsiders from taking a positive look at the total Christian claim. But many non-Christians have expressed the idea that the unitive movements of Christians are signs of capitulation to the secular and modern spirit. They argue that only people who have lost their nerve, who have a weakened faith, or who are relativist about doctrine will work for religious unity. By their definition the truly religious man stands apart for the purity of his vision, avoids compromise for the sake of the prophetic, and probably has a persecutory spirit.[92]

Such critics of Protestant ecumenism can find plenty of historical warrant for their observation concerning a changed spirit of Protestantism. But Protestants can respond and have responded by pointing to the fact that unity is born at the center of the Christian vision, "that they may all be one," and that they have picked up the most neglected biblical mandate and promise and given it its rightful place in their priorities.

II. God's Ways with Man

5. THE PREOCCUPATION WITH GOD

To the Westerner, it always comes as some sort of surprise to learn that not all religions have had God as an object. In the West, a bond between the religionist and such an object seems automatic. To have a God is to be religious and to be religious is to have a God. Yet some Eastern religions or religious philosophies have not been organized around such a connection; Zen Buddhism is an example. When Westerners speak of a crisis in religion they regularly refer to the problem of dealing with the reality of God; the term itself represents problems. When they write histories of secularization, they tell stories of the ways in which many people have become casual about God and, eventually, godless. By many Western definitions, not to feel that there is an Other or to feel that one is alone in the universe is a mark that one has stopped being religious.[93]

Most Protestants share the view which automatically connects God and religion. When poll-takers reach Europeans who live on historic Protestant soil, or their American counterparts, they learn that from 80 to 97 per cent of the people will respond with a "Yes" to the question, "Do you believe in God?" Given this theistic or deistic foundation, it is only natural that the pages of Protestant history would be devoted to discussions of the Protestant conception of God, and indeed the historian finds that to be the case. However, it is almost impossible to reduce the materials on those pages to a coherent outline. One might say that the history of Protestant thought is a history of differing and not always compatible concepts of God. Certainly on the level of reflection, then, one cannot say that Protestants are to be denominated Protestants because they share a common picture of God.[94]

From one point of view such a situation is startling; from another, it is to be expected. It is startling because one might think that religionists ought to get together on their central theme before they define themselves over against others—others being Roman Catholics, Jews, and various kinds of secularists. Yet Protestants rarely call conferences on the doctrine of God and rarely write books devoted to efforts at rallying people around that theme.

On the other hand, difficulties of this sort should be expected. When they do address themselves seriously to the problem of the many concepts of God that are operative, Protestant thinkers begin by speaking of God in such ways that He is not easily reducible to definition. To utter the syllable "God" is to speak of the unlimited, the unconditioned. In that case, since definitions limit and condition their objects, it is impossible to come up with clear ways of defining who or what God is.

Before attempts will be made to bring some sense of order or coherence to Protestant strivings with the problem of God, it will be useful to illustrate the chaos by citing some of the varieties of definition which have prevailed somewhere or other within Protestantism in recent centuries. Only thus can we render dramatic the thesis that Protestantism has existed and endured without recognizing a consensus about the nature of God. It could almost be demonstrated that virtually every picture of God that could be devised by prophets or philosophers has in fact found numerous advocates among Protestants.

To begin at the most mathematical and mechanistic end of the spectrum: many Protestants have been deists. In the deist conception God is not even described in personal terms, yet in the Enlightenment era many British and American churchmen were near-deist in their outlook. Not a few Anglican bishops at that time devoted themselves to expounding quasi-deistic views of God. They may have qualified their picture of this remote deity by touching some bases in biblical revelation and by allowing that this inaccessible First Cause or Supreme Being was somehow operative in the moral example of Jesus of Nazareth, that something of the eternal order of nature and reason was existent in this model.

The believer was not called upon to address this deistic God but only to adhere to the order of things. No conversion was called for; one had only to recognize nature and reason. The one whom Jesus of Nazareth had called Father was translated from "He" to "It," and was mathematically circumscribed by eighteenth century Protestants. Some deists, of course, moved entirely out of the churches and came to oppose them. Just as many stayed, seeing in their picture of God a legitimate transformation of that object reverenced by their forefathers in the faith.[95]

In the twentieth century the impersonal God shows up again in circles of Protestant theology in the form of various naturalisms or empirical points of view. One thinks here of the theologians who have been influenced by Alfred North Whitehead's philosophy of process, thinkers who see in natural process itself "the source of human good," and ascribe to it many of the attributes once extended to God. Some even go to the point of suggesting that the data of Christian revelation can best be understood by reference to process.[96]

Particularly since the theory of evolution came to be widely accepted in the churches a century ago, many forward-looking religious thinkers have set out to synthesize Christian and scientific themes around naturalistic pictures of God. The presence of some sort of order in the universe is all that is needed to initiate such a concept of God. Anglo-American liberal thinkers for two generations have extrapolated on the basis of this understanding. They part company with the deists because the deists conceive of this order only in remote but somehow objectified terms, while naturalists or process-thinkers see God in the middle of the world. Although this concept of God has drawn few adherents in the churches' pews, it carries considerable weight among some academic philosophers, scientists, and theologians who consider themselves to be Protestant.

A third illustration of the acceptability of completely nonpersonal views of God is pantheism, a view that does raise more problems for Protestantism than do the previous two. Many Protestant mystics and some philosophical idealists have defined God in pantheistic terms: all that there is, is God, and God is all that there is. Rather than carry out these implications crudely, religious thinkers will qualify their assertions by pointing merely to the sense that whatever men mean by God must be all-pervasive and immanent: how can one speak of an unlimited God and then limit this spatially or conceptually? How can anything be outside of God, if God is the necessary essence, substance, and cause of all that there is?

Such a point of view was advocated more seriously in philosophy (Spinoza, Hegel) than in theology, but the Hegelian idealist influence has been strong for over a century in German universities and, in different forms, in British ecclesiastical circles. More recently some American "death-of-God" Protestants have stated that they preach the death of God in order to remove God from limitations and frankly identify themselves as pantheists. Protestantism has trouble with this concept, however, because it insists that "God beyond the gods" judges all our conceptions, and pantheism allows for no such transcendent point of reference.[97]

Still another way to speak of God without immediately introducing the personal note was the route taken by Paul Tillich. While some of his enemies see in his writing a disguised humanistic atheism that simply could not part easily with religious terms, just as many other people name him among the great shapers of mainline Protestant thought in the twentieth century. Tillich, using some categories from Hegel and Schelling, developed an existentialist kind of idealism, in which God could come to man in history. Essence took on the conditions of existence in the New Being in Jesus Christ. At the same time God could be simply "the ground of being" itself.[98]

Although the Bible rarely speaks of God in terms easily translatable to such philosophical categories, Tillich would argue that he was merely abstracting from biblical data or from materials not essentially incongruent with the biblical revelation of God. At one time he defined his work as an effort to overcome the distinction noted by Pascal when that French mathematician-theologian asserted that God the Father of Abraham, Isaac, and Jacob was *not* the God of the philosophers. Protestantism has had thousands of advocates of worship of the Father for every one philosopher-advocate, but Tillich felt that a disservice was done if the two modes and two worlds were not somehow brought together in a single synthesis.

Personal views of God have drawn more adherents than have these generally impersonal approaches. But to have said "personal" is still not to have successfully narrowed or limited the families of ideas or realities signified by Protestants who speak of "God." For some there are sophisticated witnesses to God as "Wholly Other," who has come most near in Jesus Christ. For others, to speak of a personal God is to bring to the fore crude anthropomorphic pictures which finally lead to a widely accepted Protestant view that sees God as a sort of "Man Upstairs." A personal God may be the bearded figure of high art, as in William Blake's etchings, or the creation of the at once ominous and doddering aged figure of Protestant Sunday school art.[99]

Among many Protestants a kind of "Unitarianism of the second person of the Trinity" developed, and they simply equate personal God with Jesus Christ. Still others will say that they cannot expand on their assertion that God is personal, that they must rely on the Holy Spirit to carry on inner testimony to the reality of God.

A canvass of prominent names in Protestant thought provides

whole collections for each category. The mystic Jacob Boehme often spoke in trinitarian terms, but as he related these to his sense of "the abyss" he verged on pantheism. The Arminian liberals and latitudinarians in eighteenth century Anglican pulpits and their counterparts in New England Congregationalism's proto-Unitarianism shared the deistic concepts. Behind their benevolent deity was the watchmaker God who set a process in motion but withdrew from the scene.[100]

The shaper of much of modern theology, Schleiermacher, from some points of view sounded pantheistic as he located God in the awakened human consciousness. The left-wing Hegelians of nineteenth century Germany and some radical theologians in America, England, Holland, and Germany in the twentieth century readily proclaim that "God" is dead—meaning the God of Christian revelation and the anthropomorphic pictures of him. Yet they have often insisted on remaining in the churches and being considered Christian atheists. For Albrecht Ritschl, God sometimes seems to be a personalization of love. Ernst Troeltsch, relativist in outlook, could not begin to confine "God" to something or someone who bore a special relation only to Christianity.[101]

Over against all of these Karl Barth and the neo-orthodox could speak of God as the Other who was "in heaven" while we men are "on earth," reinvoking Kierkegaard's sense of the infinite qualitative difference between God and man. Only in the "humanity of God" in Jesus Christ could men even begin to find and then to speak of God. Gerhard Ebeling and numerous later "theologians of the Word" have resisted ideas of objectifying God as a thing, as a being in a sequence of beings. Gustaf Aulén, a Swedish bishop, preferred to speak of "pictures of God" as a means of making clear that men cannot capture God by definition; they can only witness to some of their apprehensions of him. John Baillie spoke of God as "the Other who is most near."[102]

There have been Protestant Trinitarians, Binitarians, and Unitarians, some of whom have cut themselves out of the churches and others of whom have insisted that *they* were the orthodox. No pope, council, or panel of heresy judges has put them out. It is impossible, clearly, to draw the lines around Protestantism by beginning with the concept of God being propounded by its adherents. It is preferable to say that "God" is the point at which other aspects of one's theology or religious reflection come to focus; from the use of that syllable one can learn much about other details of one's system or his worship.

While the list of options about God could be continued to book length, such an approach may seem to some readers to be an egregious exaggeration of the chaos in Protestantism. All that this shows, says the critic, is the variety of philosophies that have been operative, philosophies that find the concept of God useful for definition.

The more moderate critic may go on to say that all this only illustrates the ingeniousness and innovative spirit of theologians, who take their tradition seriously but who greet changes in the world-view with openness. They constantly try to make the Protestant interpretation of Christianity relevant for people of various periods of history and various cultures. They would prefer to concentrate neither on the varieties of operative philosophies in a half millennium of Western experience, on one hand, nor on the cleverness of adaptive theologians, on the other. They would point to coherences and consensuses rather than to chaos and variety.

Elements of coherence are present in Protestant history, and it is valuable to state what can be said about the ordering of Protestant thought about God. The first ordering principle is this: Protestant witness in the form of preaching, teaching, and conversation of the faithful, has ordinarily been marked by a serious grappling with biblical portraits of God.

From one point of view, this seems to settle little, since one does not have direct access to the biblical materials. They come filtered through the tradition of centuries, and before one confronts the *sola scriptura* (the principle of "Scripture alone") he has normally already encountered or been shaped by a culture and a church in which various attributes of God, most of them of philosophical derivation, have been expounded. He hears that God is omnipotent, omnipresent, ineffable, and then he hears about God in the Bible. And the Bible is really a library of the experiences of many different kinds of people over many centuries. On its pages, too, a variety of pictures are presented: a changeless God; a suffering, experiencing, and thus a changing God; a remote and aloof sovereign; a God who risks all by involving himself with human history, one who creates and destroys, one who promises the overcoming of evil without satisfactorily accounting for the presence of evil.

Despite the problems of access to the Bible in any direct sense and of varieties of witness in the Bible, one has moved far along if he can successfully demonstrate that Protestant witness begins with and generally wants to be measured by the biblical accounts. This means that most of the time, if forced to choose, the evangelical will say that he worships, in Pascal's terms, the Father of Abraham, Isaac, and Jacob and not the God of the philosophers.

In so saying he frankly acknowledges a God in history, a creator, redeemer, and consummator, one who cares about beginnings, middles, and ends of history. Such a God speaks and can be addressed. The records of hundreds of pages in the Bible bear this out. God spoke in the Garden of Eden and from the burning bush. He spoke to Noah and through the judges and prophets. He was addressed by Jesus of Nazareth and revealed himself to Paul on the road to Damascus. His purposes were unfolded in the historical record of a people, the children of Israel, and in a second covenant with a new people of God, the disciples gathered around Jesus of Nazareth and in the presence of the resurrected Lord.

To say historical and personal, then, is also to open the door for the problems of anthropomorphism. Protestants have in their popular piety and preaching been more than ready to take these biblical risks. When they do so, they may be following what philosophers argue is necessary: to deal with ultimate reality in symbolic forms. God does not have hands or a countenance or a holy arm, even though the Bible uses these symbols. But, say the faithful, neither is God the Ground of Being or the Supreme Being or the First Cause. These are all verbal symbols, other instruments for speaking of the final and boundless realities. Given the choice, says the preacher, he will go with the rich imagery of the Bible rather than with the philosophers' abstractions. Then he will face the problems of crudeness in anthropomorphism, risks he prefers to passive or neutral relations to philosophers' concepts.

From the biblical, historical, personal, and anthropomorphic model with which he works, the Protestant proclaimer then legitimately derives other elements of his God-picture. The biblical God as witnessed to in Protestantism is always sovereign. There can be no one higher than He; while there is mystery in His dealings with man, this is the result of His transcendence. He keeps His own counsels and has His own purposes. He remains inscrutable in the depth and riches of His wisdom over against that of finite man.

This note of sovereignty is the first one struck in some Protestant circles, notably those that derive from Calvin. For Luther the counterpart to this sovereignty, a theme never minimized or denied by the Calvinists, came first: God is first of all a God of love, who creates out of love and who in Christ would save all men. He worried little about what such a picture did to the view of sovereignty which allowed that a sovereign God had to have the power and freedom to condemn men. God, said the radical reformers, is first of all Holy and Spirit, speaking where and as He will, and inspiriting men to follow Him and to speak for Him. Virtually all the philosophers' scholastic definitions of God's attributes (His omniscience, omnipresence, etc.) reappear then in the form of various elements of biblical record.[103]

The second great generalization about Protestant doctrines of God is this: almost all Protestants in most periods have inherited and enlarged upon the historic Christian definition of God as Trinity; Father, Son, and Holy Spirit unite in one Godhead. To some, such an inheritance may seem curious: the term "trinity" does not appear in the Bible. It is an invention of the church, embraced at early councils with which some Protestants have had little sympathy, and clothed in philosophical categories (of substance and essence) that have not been living options for most people in the Protestant era. Yet, with the exception of people at the Unitarian edges of Protestantism in the Socinian movement, in English Presbyterianism and in American Unitarianism, even those Protestants who do not regularly use the creedal terms find themselves speaking in generally trinitarian categories.[104]

The terms were taken over into the liturgies of most churches, and the textbook categories from the Middle Ages survived in Protestant dogmatic works. Trinitarian language is designed to protect the monotheism on which all Protestants insist even as it sets out to do justice to the problem of Christology: how does Jesus of Nazareth relate as "divine" to one God, and what shall we do with the biblical witness to the Spirit?

The Catholic-Protestant schism, then, did not occur over a dispute about the doctrine of God as consolidated and summarized in the theme of the Trinity. Many Protestants have rejected their own Unitarian fringes or radical theologians by running for refuge to an otherwise rejected past or an otherwise despised contemporary option: even the Catholics seemed better than these Unitarians! After all, for all their errors, it was noted, they did share the trinitarian saving faith. And if Protestants have had difficulty saying exactly what they meant when they confessed the Holy Trinity, they have not been alone in that—so have Roman Catholics. While Catholicism's magisterium is able to be asserted over against too radical innovations or deviations, and while the quasi-official and then official acceptance of Thomism as a philosophy served as a barrier against complete philosophical confusion of tongues when men and women dealt with the Trinity, Catholicism has seen in

Protestant acceptance of the Trinity—even in varying relations to different philosophies and culture—some regulating principle among these Protestants.

A third way of narrowing the range of Protestant options about God is to take a course implied in the preceding pages: to listen to the witness of the overwhelming majority of the faithful as they speak of God. While such an approach is time-consuming and difficult (especially since we lack many kinds of data about the past, to say nothing of the lack of reliable data from the present), it is rewarding. Important clues can be gained, for example, from the kinds of liturgical language which survive and attract the millions.

Much of the abstract philosophical talk associated with the Athanasian Creed finds little favor in the congregations, even if these congregations assent to creedal orthodoxy and stress the historical importance of such philosophical statements. If this is so of orthodox and creedal philosophy, it is even more true of latter-day philosophical statements. Parodists can point to this problem, and they regularly do when they contrive prayers to "Ultimate Reality" or "Ground of Being" instead of to "Our Father."

The language of hymns is another means of access: the survival of hymns in books of many denominational traditions and cultures is not the mere result of hymnal-committee work but is a testimony to "the survival of the fittest." The favored hymns speak of God in personal, paternal terms.

Add to the liturgies, the hymnals, the popular books of devotion in both liberal and conservative Protestantism, the language of letters, diaries, and recorded common speech, and the evidence will be overwhelming. When popular Protestantism says "God," it ordinarily implies the Father who was addressed by Jesus, a personal deity who involves himself with His people and in the affairs of men, who energizes people through the activities of His Holy Spirit.

If the lay people have not always done well at relating Father, Son, and Spirit; if they have not always properly related Trinity to Incarnation and have verged on Christomonism from time to time; if they have sometimes veered toward inelegant anthropomorphism, on one hand, or cool abstraction, on the other, then it must simply be said that so have the philosophers and the theologians. Both are dealing with something which most of them readily define as a mystery of inexhaustible depths.

To point to the catholic orthodoxy of unreflective Protestants is not to suggest, however, that the function of talk about God has not played a different role in their thinking in different periods. One illustration will suffice: a study of some contrasts between the sixteenth century Protestant use of God-language and the contemporary problem.

Were one to speak of "the problem of God" to the people who responded to the sixteenth century reformers' prophecies, he could build a conversation around themes dealing with how God relates to men. The prime illustration, almost archetypal for Protestantism, had to do with the personal experience of Martin Luther. The twentieth century playwright John Osborne depicted Luther as a twentieth century existentialist who doubted the existence of God and stormed against the silence of the heavens. Had he not done so, he might have produced poor theater, for the audience might not have recognized doubt or agony except in terms applicable to them. But in the process he was historically inaccurate. The death of God was not Luther's problem. His trauma had to do with what he should do with a God who was threateningly near, who could destroy man and indeed would do so unless the human subject could find a way to please God. The problem of God, then, was a problem of how His wrath and love related to each other. Protestantism was born out of a different answer from the ones Catholicism supplied.[105]

Another version of this early Protestant problem could be stated in this way: how can the God who *is* be made available to me? How is He "for me"? Philipp Melanchthon in a famous passage argued that to know Christ was to know His benefits and not to be content with philosophical speculation about Him. Philosophical speculation about God was not revelation. It was not the equivalent of God making himself available with saving purpose. The debates within Protestantism, then, centered around theological issues having to do with His transcendence and His immanence; how He hides and exposes himself; how He is God hidden and revealed.

Here there was an early parting of the way. On the one hand, the Lutherans stressed that the finite was capable of bearing the infinite. Luther enjoyed shocking talk about God suckling at a Virgin's breast, about God dying on the cross. Zwingli and Calvin argued that *finitum non est capax infiniti* and thus spiritualized God more than did the Lutherans and those like-minded. This difference in the ways God was apprehended showed up in sacramental talk, where for Lutherans and other realists the bread and wine in some way were bearers of the infinite while in the Reformed tradition they were described as signs of the infinite realm.[106]

The issues of dealing with the Other who is most near, with a wrathful and loving God, an immanent and transcendent one, have not been settled, nor have they been shelved. Each of them is current both in theology and in practical Protestant Christian living. But they have been put into a new context by events and changes in consciousness in the past two centuries. The first phase of change came with liberal Protestantism after Schleiermacher. In the ensuing century, theology verged on anthropology; so said its enemies (Marx), its one-time friends (Feuerbach), and its formulators (Schleiermacher himself). When Luther said that faith was "the creator of divinity within us," the anthropologists in theology hurried to point out that this made man the controller. For Schleiermacher, God was somehow related to a change in human consciousness. Out of these strivings came a century of theological productivity, a revisitation of all the main Christian themes but from a new point of view. The experience of the twentieth century did not permit theologians or the larger community of Protestants to let the question reside there.

A number of factors led to what contemporaries speak of as a new problem of God. The anthropology of liberalism produced a logically consequent question: if man is the starting point, how do we know that God is anything more than an illusion, a projection of men's social needs (as Marx saw it) or of his psychological necessities (as in Sigmund Freud)?

The rise of modern science found Christians to be in constant retreat. God eventually seemed to become a word to cover the current range of human ignorance. With each new human discovery or conquest, the religionists would retreat further and revise again their picture of the forward boundaries of God's location. Astronomy made old pictures of God's spatial transcendence difficult to sustain. The evolutionary world-views caused similar problems for conventional pictures of temporal transcendence. God was less of a problem, it was surmised, in a small, young universe, world-centered and man-centered as it had been perceived to be. But the new world-picture saw man as a late emergence on a dust fleck in an inconceivably large and complex universe.[107]

The death of the liberal humanists' progressive dreams in twentieth century events in world wars, atomic bombs, concentration camps, and world revolutions served to compromise their revised doctrine of God and to intensify the agony of doubters. The Theater of the Absurd and existentialist literature worked on the assumption that the universe was absurd and asked what man should do now that he knows he is alone in a cosmos without meaning and plot.[108]

Philosophers of language raised questions about the propriety of employing the word God, since its signified object, if there were one at all, eluded empirical verification, and such talk thus was meaningless nonsense. Defenses of the existence of God were accused of "dying the death of a thousand qualifications." Little of substance seemed to be left. As the death-of-God theologians put it, "We are not speaking of the absence of the experience of God, but of the experience of the absence of God."[109]

The twentieth century statements of "the problem of God" had many consequences in Protestantism. For many people there has been a simple crisis of faith and a letting go of the Protestant ecclesiastical tradition. For others, there has come a kind of practical atheism as the result of the adoption of ways of life which turn out to appear to be the same whether or not God exists. Still others have seized the moment as the opportunity for fresh reflection and for the quest for a new kind of religious experience.

Fundamentalists have resisted the problem by a premature acceptance of an authoritarian alternative. Politicians have appealed to these quests for authority by advertising that God is alive in national purpose or in their parties' goals. Some theologians have said, in effect: "Yes, God is dead, but in Jesus Christ we find faith and freedom in all the reality that there is. Let us be Christian atheists." And, let it also be said, for millions of Protestants the death of God or the experience of the absence of God represents no great problem. They have a kind of faith that makes witness to God in Jesus Christ still possible. As for the doubters, they have been assured that the God who can justify that sinner who does not morally deserve His love can also justify the doubter who intellectually has not firmly and clearly apprehended Him.[110]

The Protestant conception of God has not materially differed from the Catholic picture through the past four and a half centuries. Both ecclesiastical groups have struggled to relate the personal, historical, anthropomorphic witness of the Bible to the God of the philosophers. Both have been generally content with the trinitarian momentum in the Christian tradition. They have differed in the ways they have seen God making himself accessible to man. The Protestant when he is thoughtful has more consistently tried to use the symbol of a God-beyond-the-gods for prophetic criticism of his own ecclesiastical, national, social, or personal causes. The doctrine of God is to be employed to smash not only someone else's idols but one's own as well. Whether the Protestant has been more successful at this than has the Catholic, for whom the sacraments and sacramentals, the visual imagery and other symbols can easily become idols, is a question that admits of many different answers.[111]

6. MAN IN HISTORY AND HIS DESTINY

History has purpose. If Protestants have not been able to agree on many assertions, they have converged with remarkable consensus on the idea that men's strivings and sufferings are part of a movement in time, a movement with a beginning, a climax, and an end. Discussions of Providence, progress, and process fill the pages of evangelical writings. So familiar is the theme of ends, goals, and purposes in history that it may seem strange to have to note its presence.[112]

That theme, however, is not universal in religions. Most of the religions or faiths of the ancient world or today's Eastern world differ from the Protestant and Christian ideas of purpose. To use an oversimplification: many of the Greek approaches to life and many contemporary Eastern spiritual modes favor views of history which are cyclical or repetitive, as with the seasons of the year in their apparently endless rhythms. Or a religion may exist in order to aid its adherents in their attempts to be removed from the sphere of history entirely, into some sort of Nirvana, a realm free of time and contingency. Not so with Christianity.

The view that history is full of purpose is not unique with Protestant Christians. The Eastern Orthodox have equally stressed the sense that the drama of salvation, centering in the Resurrection, has touched, transfused, and transfigured all of history. Western Catholicism and early Protestantism also did not fight over the question whether man and history have destinies, but only over the matter of the proper means of appropriating a destiny in history. But if the purposive approach to history was present in Orthodoxy or Catholicism, it was intensified in the Protestant Reformation and ever since, through numerous transformations of the evangelical movements.

When Protestants drew on the Christian past, they were most impressed by the men and the forces which had accented purpose. Thus Augustinianism was popular, for St. Augustine had divided the city of God from the city of man, and had located the goal of history outside history—though men in history found their lives shaped by transcendent destiny. Or Protestants drew on various eschatological or apocalyptic visions from the Middle Ages. Among these were Joachim of Fiore's view that Christians had moved past the age of the Father, through the age of the Son, and were moving to the age of the Spirit. Only a few sectarians took this periodization literally, but the impetus behind that vision was preserved in much of Protestantism.[113]

Protestantism's attachment to purpose in history has been so measurable that even in the secular world Protestantism is credited with or blamed for styles of living which call men to account for their use of every moment. There has been little room for contemplation, daydreaming, or drifting in evangelical history. The reformers popularized the picture of history as a theater, wherein the cosmic drama is being worked out in the smallest details of the lives of great and small men and women. History was God's workshop, and He worked through the men and women who inhabited that sphere. This being the case, men were not free to be idle or apathetic. They were faced with countless decisions, all of them bearing some sort of significance.[114]

History was never "mere" history; it included salvation history, and matters of cosmic concern were bartered in the disturbances and trials of men. History had been created by God, who had placed man in the world for reasons. History had been changed by man's fall into sin and by God's curse upon what was fallen. It had been redeemed or transformed when God was incarnate in the flesh of Jesus Christ, when He suffered and died in the event of Christ's crucifixion. A new creation was begun with Christ's resurrection. Now men were to make good use of the time between Christ's first and his second comings. The language of liturgy, prayer, and hymns is marked by these great strophes which were used to divide and periodize history.[115]

The Protestant Christian acts, then, with the end in view—his personal end as well as the end of the historical process as it is now known. Popular piety reveals how much of a preoccupation this action has been. From the sixteenth century to the present, most conservative Protestants have taken seriously the biblical pictures about heaven and hell. There was little innovation or improvisation on this score after medieval Catholicism's demise. The debate centered on the question of the auspices for getting to heaven or hell; on the matter of security about salvation; on the means of avoiding damnation. But universalism—the idea that God being a God of love would find a way to bring all men into positive relation with Him eternally—was a rather rare idea in Protestantism until the eighteenth century.[116]

Sophisticated theologians might do what they could to minimize mythic elements in the vision of heaven and hell, but preaching and piety seized on the rich if often conflicting imagery derived from biblical apocalypses. At the end of life man died; he then would await the judgment. There was some vagueness or dispute over the question of waiting, over separation of soul and body, and over the meaning of time after one had left history. Judgment condemned unrepentant sinners to eternal damnation, usually associated with fire. Those found to be in Christ passed to an eternal reward in the pleasurable circumstances of heaven.

An alternative or accompaniment to the heaven-versus-hell reading has been the prospect of millennium. Millennial teaching grew out of the book of Daniel in the Hebrew Scriptures and out of some of Jesus' parables and the Apocalypse (book of Revelation) in the New Testament. It has been favored by the sectarians of Protestantism's first generation and has been reborn in almost every movement of world transformation or disaster in subsequent Protestantism. The biblical clues suggest that heaven is not a realm spatially removed from the created order as it is now experienced. Instead, when Christ comes again everything in the old Jerusalem and creation will become fresh and will take on the characteristics of a new Jerusalem, a new city, a new creation. Since the Bible often spoke of a thousand-year reign, Christian sects that have devoted themselves to this approach, whether pre- or post-Reformation, have been classified as millennial.[117]

Protestant millennialists have been divided among themselves, however. The more optimistic or progressive types, like revivalist and theologian Jonathan Edwards in America, believed that Christ would come again after the world was prepared to receive Him. God himself had set the time for that return, but He then imparted to men a sense of cooperation in history and gave them tasks to do. They were to repent, acknowledge the covenant with God, live holy lives, and set forth to preach the Gospel in all the world even as they tried to transform world conditions.

The more negative or cataclysmic types, like another revivalist in America, Dwight Lyman Moody, were basically pessimistic about what they saw in history. They did not believe that human agency cooperating with God could make the world really livable, could help cause the kingdom to come, or transform human life.

They read and expounded the biblical texts that pointed out that Christ's second coming would be associated with dire events: wars, rumors of wars, men's hearts failing them for fear, families falling apart, moral standards declining. The task of the Christian as he awaited such a denouement in history was to help rescue as many people as possible from such consequences while there was still time.

The explicit use of millennial imagery may be relatively rare and the formal distinction between postmillennialism and premillennialism even rarer, if one takes all of Protestant history into consideration. But the attitudes and casts of mind associated with those mythological pictures of how the present world will be changed can be translated to other myths, symbols, or imagery. It has been possible to take a basically positive view of human potential inside Protestantism, so long as one qualifies this by concentrating on the divine initiative.

Just as frequently Christians can take negative views and see man to be essentially impotent, having to turn control of history back to God, who holds destiny in His hand. Where Protestants have not differed is in the idea of destiny itself. It has been inconceivable for reflective Protestants through most of their history to see the human story as merely "one damn thing after another," a treadmill without meaning or purpose or hope. Their vision has motivated the Protestant mission in the world and has been taken over into much of the ethic of productivity in the modern secular world.

More broadly applicable distinctions than those associated with millennialism were condensed some years ago in a typology devised by the American thinker H. Richard Niebuhr. Some of the sectarians carried their view of what Niebuhr called "Christ against culture" to such extremes that they wanted to have little to do with the worlds of politics and commerce. They formed sects simply to turn their backs on the world, to create an approximation of pure community, to keep themselves unspotted from the world. From the 1520s in Germany to the present-century Hutterites of western Canada there have been those for whom oath-taking, serving in the military, adopting the fashions of the outside world, or associating with the unregenerate has meant a denial of destiny.[118]

Within the sect the focus is eschatological: they want to be a people prepared for God's final working out of His purposes. Others may be converted to this way of life, or God may elect some to choose it, but most fulfillment of purpose goes on within that community which is itself already a sign of the world to come.

At the opposite extreme liberal Protestantism of the nineteenth century chose to produce an approach which Niebuhr called the "Christ of culture." In that immanentist and optimistic reading, evil was present in the world, but it was somehow a minor and temporary intrusion on God's plan for His created world. The fall was acknowledged but its impact minimized. The effecting of grace in Christ meant that God had not abandoned His creation, but instead He honored it with a new visitation.

The kingship of Christ over all men was asserted, and a kind of universalism began to be acceptable in history: the cosmic purpose of God could not permanently rule out any of His creatures— especially those who had never had an opportunity to follow His invitations. But what really mattered was the future. Christ was the "end" of the world and of the Church, so the two would converge in a higher unity in Him. The conventional symbol for invoking this kind of future was the Kingdom of God.

British social Christianity, American Social Gospel movements, and continental religious socialism were alike moved by visions of the Kingdom of God as being both present and in the future. But in this picture, evil was often minimized and God's purposes were seen to triumph so simply that in some cases mere worldliness, an unqualified and uncritical embrace of the world process as it was, characterized this brand of Protestantism.[119]

Christian socialism, the Social Gospel, and religious socialism also had their realistic dimensions and factions as well. Niebuhr tended to favor these in his analysis, and for this realistic interpretation he cast the type of "Christ transforming culture." Like the world-embracing liberals, the transformers saw great potential in the historical process. Christ was pulling men toward a triumphant fulfillment in history and beyond it. Again, the Kingdom of God could be a basic symbol of the future that men were to help God effect. Divine initiative was stressed more consistently than it was by the baptizers of the world in the Christ-of-culture group.[120]

What most characterized the transformers was the fact that they began with a profound view of human finitude, error, and sin. Unlike those who concentrated on individual salvation, they did not always accent personal guilt and the historical event of the fall of man. They may have acknowledged these, but their chief purpose was to see how evil was present in the existing structures of human life. Some spoke of "social sin." Then they turned to see what men could do in effecting an order of justice and righteousness and love.

The historical Protestant roots for the world-transforming views of purpose and destiny can be traced back chiefly to John Calvin, the Reformed leaders in general, and those sectarians who held fairly positive views about the potential of the world. The moment these roots are discussed, the frequent charge that transformationists did not take sin seriously is dispelled. Calvin's name is almost proverbially associated with the term "original sin" and even "total depravity." Nor could transformationism be distorted into the idea that man seizes the initiative in history, for no one more than John Calvin or the early Puritans stressed divine sovereignty and initiative in their encompassing monergism.

The fact of divine election and the reality of divine predestination were not preached to reduce men to fatalism or passivity. Instead, men were to certify their sense of election by work in the world, and they were not to leave the world as they had found it when first they had encountered it. While some of the nineteenth century liberals took these Calvinist-Puritan motifs and attached them to progressivistic and optimistic views of man, the original impulse grew out of extremely sober appraisals of what man apart from Christ could do. The entrance of Christ into history and the proclamation of His Kingdom made all the difference.[121]

The most complicated of the Niebuhrian types was "Christ and culture in paradox." There were Augustinian roots for this, but Martin Luther was the prime Protestant advocate of the position. This approach obviously ruled out the utopianism of some of the progressive sects and qualified the faith in what man could do politically in traditional Calvinism. The world was indeed God's workshop or arena. What men did mattered. But inside history complete fulfillment could not begin to come. Man was both justified and a sinner, and in the political or social realm his sin and pride would be so overwhelming that one could hardly speak of a kingdom of love operative among men.

The stress fell, as Paul Tillich observed, on the rejection of all social utopias and metaphysics of progress; on the corruption in all the structures of human existence; on the individual's need for grace and forgiveness. Luther could more properly be accused of carrying on an Augustinian "soteriological anthropocentrism," a concentration on the ego of the person who is in the process of being saved. There was less of a cosmic note, less accent on the ties between nature and grace and on the individual in relation to community. Not that Luther counseled simple world denial or Christian passivity. But he did hold to a paradoxical view that stopped short of the possibility of transforming the present world through Christian symbols and endeavors.[122]

What these four general approaches have in common is not the drama of *what* happens in Christian history but the affirmation that *something* happens. They all concentrate on a divine agency pushing and pulling men and societies, from some sort of originally blessed but now blighted state to some new circumstances, either in this world or in the one which is to come. The prime Protestant symbol or doctrine for such a view of history originally was that of Providence. Protestantism has tended to be providential in its outlook on salvation history.

God may appear to be a capricious Oriental potentate to the man who stands outside the Calvinistic scheme. But to those within it, He is a guiding and purposive leader, whose actions can somehow be counted upon. To the degree that groups assumed political responsibility in theocracies like that of Massachusetts Bay, the more they knew that they had to be able to speak with clarity on a covenant with God. His will had to be discernible in a book or a code, in a tradition or a community, under the interpretive eyes of elders and ministers and magistrates. Perry Miller, student of New England Puritanism, expressed for that entity words that might be used of political Protestantism in general: God was progressively "chained," accountable to man, less mysterious.[123]

The idea of a chained deity seems to be a logical contradiction to the original Calvinist concept of an absolutely free and sovereign God, but not all Protestants began by setting up for themselves such a logical conundrum or paradox. One of the earliest deviants from the Calvinist way of putting the problem was the party that followed Jakob Arminius in Holland. Arminianism was to serve as a title for numerous Protestant movements: it related to some anti-Calvinist factions in the Dutch church, was applied with some accuracy to some continental Unitarian movements, marked the benevolent views of deity described by eighteenth century Anglican latitudinarians, was represented by early American Unitarians, and most of all was used to signify the doctrine of man and history in the Wesleyan and Methodist movements.[124]

Arminianism, it can be seen from this catalog, has meant many things. But at the heart of them all has been the view of a benevolent deity in tandem with a man who is full of potential. The atoning work of Christ was necessary for the nexus, but given that divine agency, God and man were to cooperate for bringing about a blissful change in human circumstance: toward better reason, or personal perfection, or a reformed and holy society. Arminianism, like Calvinism, has been purposive. It has been even more readily interpreted as progressivistic.

The Enlightenment more than any other event put Protestant views of history on the defensive and lead to many adaptations. All across the Protestant world people began to reaffirm some of the humanist themes that had been present already in the Renaissance. The personal God was often reduced to impersonal abstraction, and Providence became at best a term for order and purpose in the universe. More significantly, man was to take simple and sole responsibility for his history. He was to build the earth, be steward of its limited resources, interpret his existence without reference to heaven and hell or the Kingdom of God.

The Enlightenment was an attractive competitor or alternative, for this "heavenly city of the eighteenth century philosophers" shadowed Christian categories or filled them with new substance. Purpose had not disappeared, but Providence had turned into progress. What was more, the Enlightenment view of history seemed to square with the facts, to be empirically verifiable as John Calvin's inscrutable deity and His effects had not been. While the Enlightenment itself came to an end and while its interpretations have been attacked from all sides, it did succeed in helping to change the understanding of the nature of the drama: man on his own became central, and old-style Protestantism never again had the field to itself, even in the parts of the world where it had once dominated.[125]

After the Enlightenment, Marxism appeared in the nineteenth century, to become a pitiless rival on once-Protestant soil. Unlike Protestantism but like its Enlightenment antecedent, Marxism attacked the personal deity who represented Providence in the Protestant scheme. "God is dead." "Religion is the opium of the people." Sentences like these have been used by later generations to help people remember Marxism's antireligious thrusts. But Marxism beguiled men by taking over also something of Protestantism's eschatological vision. The classless society was used to counter claims of the coming Kingdom of God. The revolt of the proletariat included redemptive and salvific purposes of the kind once associated with Christ and His Church. Marxism was called a Christian heresy because of the degree to which it took over or echoed a Protestant proclamation of meaning, purpose, and pattern in history.[126]

Modern nationalism, a third rival eschatology, resembled Pro-

testantism's dualistic appropriation of history. A good god of battles struggled against foreign devils. Christian messianism was
translated into national purpose and manifest destiny. It was inconceivable for the modern nationalists to deny meaning and purpose in history, but the honors once paid a transcendent deity were
now to be exhausted in devotion to the omnicompetent state.
Many Protestants helped give birth to and nurture this great rival
for men's attention and action.[127]

Most Protestants did not intend to help produce such accidental
by-products of their view of historical purpose and did not welcome the competition from rival interpretations of life. It would
simply do an injustice to the professed beliefs of the vast majority
of Protestant theologians, preachers, and common people to suggest that they devoted their prime efforts to building the great
society or transforming the world. The idea that history had purpose and that within it there was a salvific line has been more
regularly asserted to provide the framework for individual salvation and for the life of the Church. That being the case, the study
of human nature and destiny turns next to the question: "Salvation
from what?" What was the character of man that he needed Christ
and the Church to help him?

At this point the name of Protestantism's most offensive inheritance from Catholicism has usually been invoked. Protestants al-
legedly have accented "original sin" with a vengeance. Significantly, when twentieth century movements have been plausibly
denominated neo-orthodox, they have been criticized chiefly for
reintroducing the notion of original sin into their analysis of man's
situation. Reinhold Niebuhr, an American often classified as neo-
orthodox, observed both that original sin was Christianity's only
verifiable doctrine from the empirical point of view—and that he
had made a pedagogical mistake resurrecting this term for modern
application. Not that it was inaccurate; Niebuhr merely noted that
it conveyed false connotations to moderns, and semantic or emotional confusion resulted.[128]

Neo-orthodox and hence, presumably, orthodox Protestantism
has needed some symbol to describe its view of the extensiveness
of man's plight apart from the rescuing work of Christ. "Total
depravity" was even more offensive, chiefly because of the modern
connotations of "depravity," but also because of the confusion
about what was "total": the original intention had been not to
notice the depth of man's evil but the extensiveness of its reach.
Even his spiritual striving, his piety, his good works were blighted.

All that man is and has to offer has to be altered by Christ.

Original sin was not a Protestant invention or coinage, even if evangelicals were most remembered for stressing this Christian theme. It has roots in the Bible, where Adam's sin was regularly pictured as having universal implications. By one man sin entered into the world. All men ever after were conceived in iniquity and born in sin. No one, said the New Testament, escaped the need for Christ's saving work. Even man's best efforts were likely to lead him to pride and thus tempt him away from God. Protestants picked up the codification of this tradition in the Augustinian lineage. Over against the Catholic appropriation, however, they wanted to be more radical. Catholic theology tended to say that the original divine image in man had been obscured or blurred by the historical fall of man.

The Protestants more frequently (though never unanimously) talked of the original image of God as having been shattered. There was little or nothing to build on in unredeemed man. Luther was most strenuous in insisting that the new man in Christ was truly new; that justification was the creation of a New Adam in place of the Old Adam. Therefore, the same Protestants who had spoken so despairingly of human potential apart from Christ could speak extravagantly of the new man. Luther, with his gift for finding the shocking phrase, said that the justified man was to be not merely *as* Christ, but was to be *a* Christ.

Two views have vied for predominance in most of subsequent Protestant history. Luther's own approach has been translated into many other sets of terms, but he stated it with enough clarity that it deserves repetition. Man is *simul justus et peccator,* at the same time justified and a sinner. Viewed from the aspect of his way of life, his own attempts to justify himself and get right with God, he is an utter failure. When he sets out to please God he looks at the revealed law of God and that law turns out not to save him but only to condemn him even more. Thus the law is a tyrant that judges, annihilates, and utterly destroys him.

Viewed from the aspect of his identification with Christ's work, his being found "in Christ" and garbed in the robes of Christ's righteousness, he stands before God wearing and bearing Christ's perfection. God looks with utter favor on this His new creation. Inside history both aspects are operative, and man does not leave his sinful side behind. He wavers, lapses, falls, is neglectful, is prideful, sets out to impress God, and thus is a sinner. But he repents, resorts to his baptism, shares the Lord's Supper, hears the word of the Gospel preached and accepts it, accepts the gift of righteousness in Christ, and has assurance that God loves him and plans a perfect destiny for him.

While this understanding of man allows for both growth in grace and increase in sanctification or holiness, its paradoxical view includes the realism that calls one constantly to stare at the evil that remains in man as he displeases a holy God.

A different Protestant approach is built upon growth in grace and sanctification and has perfection in view. The vision of perfection under the Sermon on the Mount's injunction to "be perfect even as your heavenly Father is perfect" moved many of the radical sectarians. By segregating themselves from participants in the fallen world and the unreconstructed Church they could create a community wherein perfection could be established as an ideal and worked out to a considerable extent in practical life.

A more open view of the perfectionist approach was propagated by John Wesley and the Methodists. The constant effort of the Christian was to rely on Christ's atoning work and to follow His example until the community of the faithful would actually exemplify the marks of perfection in the world. The Wesleyan view was very complex. Methodists were reluctant to consider themselves sinless, knowing the problems of pride that went with this consideration and remaining conscious of their error and sin. But perfectionism was seen as a somehow realizable ideal in the Arminian impulse and community.

Whether man remains at the same time justified and a sinner or whether he begins to rise above this paradoxical view toward perfection, he must find ways to live in light of the end. The best way to do this, according to the majority of Protestant thinkers, was to see his vocation as a dramatic working out of divine purpose. He needed no monastery as a theater of such a calling. The Christian could be teacher or housewife, plowman or peasant or prince. But life between a nature that pulled him down and a destiny that pulled him toward fulfillment in God was to be interpreted as a drama of good and evil, setback and advance, defeat and victory.[129]

No details of life were too insignificant to be interpreted in the light of Providence, and nothing in the cosmos was too great to elude this view of destiny and history. Protestants regularly cautioned about overreading the will of God into their own causes or, worse, overidentifying their causes with God's purposes. They were not at the same time able to grant an autonomy to history, to allow for events to operate outside God's purposive scope.

A sense of mission and messianism, then, is built into Protestant interpretations of history. Every life is supposed to make a difference; nothing is wasted or lost, either for good or for evil purpose. The more clear people have been about what God's purposes for history have been and the more ready they have been to read themselves into the acts of carrying out those purposes, the more likely they have been to engage in crusades or to be fanatics.

Much of modern nationalism's devotion to warfare has been legitimated by evangelical justifications for right causes. Modern revolutions take at least some inspiration from the sectarian impulse to set history right in the name of Christ. And in competitive individualism, Protestants often have justified their advances at the expense of others on the grounds of God's endorsement of their calling. The reading of purpose into history or out of it can be dangerous.[130]

Positive readings of the Protestant views of human nature and destiny are also possible. A realism at the heart of analysis has kept most Protestants from illusions about the human record and purged them of false idealisms or beguiling utopias, so that they could get to work at the tasks before them. Yet the sense of Providence and a coming Kingdom intruded themselves enough to impart a dignity to the daily efforts of common men and women. These helped them endure in the face of otherwise pointless and demeaning factors in their lives. They imparted hope and provided inspiration for people who set out to build a human world, people whose record has not always been negative. And those who clung to the Protestant vision of destiny also have regularly certified that it provided spiritual benefits and solace as they came to terms with doubts, despair, disease, and death.[131]

7. GOD IN RELATION TO MAN

With rare exceptions, religions have been conceived as having the ability to offer their adherents some sort of contact with divine powers. The exceptions include the more philosophical sets of teachings surrounding the name Confucius, or nontheistic faiths like Zen Buddhism. More frequently, however, the term "religious" is reserved for those spheres of life in which some awareness of the pressure of an outside order is experienced or intellectually perceived. Forces work upon a person or community; these are invisible and somehow supernatural. They are also, ordinarily, personalized. Man's role, then, is to respond in such a way that he has favorable arrangements with these divine powers or gods. If he is not alone in the universe, he must somehow try to relate positively to the Other, if he is to find worth and fulfillment of any kind.

These arrangements take various forms. In many religions the quest for harmony with divine powers is central. Man's symbolization of his social life: the location of shrines, paths, and huts; the rites that gave dignity and meaning to the various stages of his life; the ceremonies that follow the rhythms of day and year—all serve to make it possible for him to come to some sense of concord with the ordered universe.

At the center of a religion there may be the sense of appeasement of the gods; man has fallen out of contact or out of harmony, but through certain forms of self-abasement or sacrifice he can bring himself to draw the attention and favor of the forces who control destiny. Religion often assumes that men are capable of apprehending the holy, of having mystical experiences. Or it may offer a satisfying intellectual grasp of realities that elude the uninitiated.

Original Protestantism everywhere and unquestioningly took over historic Christianity's belief that the universe was ordered by one God and that man's relationship to God was mediated through His Son, Jesus Christ. If there were to be positive harmony and meaning, if the wrath of a displeased God were to be turned aside, or if man were to come to proper knowledge, he could do this only if there were contact with God, and man could somehow be assured of a positive relationship. God could be addressed in prayer. God spoke through His Word, in preaching, sacraments, and the written word of Scripture. Having said that, however, it is difficult to bring to the point of least common denomination the nature of the relationships, to find a term that covers what all of Protestantism is and has been about.

While in the twentieth century some theologians have called the term into question, with many qualifications one can say that "salvation" has been at the center of the Protestant quest. The complaints against the term come chiefly from those who have criticized its narrowing into a particular medieval Western mold which was taken over into some Protestantism. For that reason, to speak of Christianity or Protestantism as a member of the family of "religions of salvation" may connote to some only a concentration on one aspect of some Protestants' experience, notably of those who have had a deep sense of personal worthlessness and sin. That sense is then overcome by a recognition that God in Christ has reconciled man to himself. As a result, man has been extricated from the world and preserved for fulfillment only in the life to come. Were that all that salvation had ever signified, the criticism could be in order. More is at stake, however, in that symbolic and embracing term, and some other shades of meaning deserve to be introduced.[132]

In the Old Testament several roots went into the terms translated as "salvation." *Yasha'* is one of these: it suggests the idea of room to breathe, of space given to man for a sense of release and security. The contrary idea had to do with experiencing life "in the narrows," to be anguished, constricted, distressed. Salvation then meant life-giving, an experience of freedom. Another Hebrew root stood behind the concept that salvation meant a redeeming, a ransoming, a liberation (as of a slave) from foreign powers which had held domain over him. Add to these the connotations of deliverance from events and persons for the individual and for the group, a divinely initiated gift that lasts as long as the eternal Giver lives, and one comes closer to the rich dimensions of meaning associated with the Old Testament terms.[133]

In the New Testament the connections are consistently made between God's saving action and the drama enacted in Jesus Christ. Now some Greek meanings are connected with it: "salvation" means being made whole, being given a positive health (which is much more than merely being free of illness), being allowed to feel safety and rescue. Jesus is the savior in these cir-

87081

cumstances. These New Testament ideas signal an actual change in man's situation, and not merely a personal awareness of his possibilities, a goal for his mystical aspiration.

The situation had involved sinfulness, error, guilt, and condemnation. In Jesus Christ there came a new innocence, a kind of knowledge, and pardon, so that man could stand before God. The New Testament more than the Old adds eschatological overtones: man experiences salvation but he also awaits more and hopes for more. There is to be a final judgment, and man must be spared its terrors and assured eternal life.[134]

In promising room to breathe, the overcoming of anxiety, health and wholeness, deliverance and rescue, Protestantism did not innovate. This promise was also a consistent part of medieval Catholicism. The Protestant debate came to be one over the auspices through which salvation came, the means of experience and knowing it, and the question of credit for initiative in the salvational transactions. Here the differences were vast, even though Protestantism drew not only on shared biblical resources but on church fathers who were revered also in Catholicism—Augustine being prime among these.

From the Protestant point of view, salvation had been given only lip-service in the Catholic system. Man was held in bondage to the sacramental system, constricted by legal requirements of the church, enslaved by the sacrament of penance and not liberated by the Mass. He was dependent upon the good will of hierarchical mediators and was kept unsure of his salvation, in part because of the teachings of merit and the recognition that a state called purgatory lay ahead of him after temporal life and before full salvation could be promised.[135]

The original reformers struck at this system from top to bottom; nothing united them more than their polemic against the merits and works demanded by Catholicism. They railed against the indulgences that were here and there being peddled as a means of appeasing and bargaining with the church and with God. They were later to differ with each other over definitions of grace, but they would all have said that theirs was a religion of grace.

The appropriation of grace meant, from man's side, the gift of faith which grasped the activity of God's initiative in Christ and made it one's own. Some reformers took over the biblical and medieval symbolism from the court of law and said that the turn from judgment to grace, from unbelief to faith, came in a divine act called the justification of the sinner.

If one concentrates on the parts instead of the whole, it would be possible to say that Protestantism had been a religion of justification and thus had narrowed the concept of salvation somewhat. However, interpretations of justification varied widely from the first; they meant less in some parts of Protestantism than in others (in Anglicanism less than in Lutheranism or Calvinism, for example). They have often disappeared from view in subsequent Protestantism. Justification is often reduced to footnotes in systematic theology, while the cognates of salvation persist.[136]

Salvation has meant different things in various Protestant cultures and eras. When, as in the case of Martin Luther, there was a deep sense of unworthiness and sin, salvation meant forgiveness. One could argue that this remained the central Protestant definition in its formal doctrines. But it has been qualified, compromised, or surrounded by other meanings elsewhere and at other times.

In other eras, when man saw himself to be in bondage to hostile powers, supernatural or natural, salvation meant rescue and subsequent freedom. This is the appropriation of Protestantism that many radical groups, people who experienced bondage by Catholic and mainline Protestant establishments alike, cherished. A study of the religion of American blacks, both during formal slavery and during the bondage of the subsequent century of merely nominal liberation, shows that freedom is the center of their salvation experience.[137]

More recently, men like Paul Tillich have spoken for wide segments of Protestantism when they have seen that the religious quest is no longer over sin-sickness and bondage but over estrangement and meaninglessness. Salvation in Christ, then, means some sort of reconciliation and the impartation of meaning. All of these experiences may be corollaries of justification by grace through faith, though theologians may not always use the term. Because of historical precedence and predominance, then, the original understandings have to be reexplored and restated.[138]

The idea of salvation involving at its center the recognition of divine initiative and the experience of a gift to man should have stamped Protestantism always and everywhere as a joyful, eucharistic religious system. It is one of the paradoxes of Protestant life that this has not been the case. Not that many individual Protestants were unable to jump for joy or break into song over their sense that "Jesus saves" or that God justifies, and that they are freed from their sin, their bondage, their despair and frustration.

But this personal awareness evidently did not carry over into culture.

When one mentions Protestantism in cultural contexts, the term connotes a legalistic, repressive, demanding, and grim religion—anything but a religion of saving grace. When a Roman Catholic wants to scorn another for being humorless and judgmental, striving and aspiring, he will quite possibly accuse him of Jansenism and then define Jansenism as a kind of Protestant or Calvinist interpretation of Christianity.

The identification of sober Puritanism with Protestantism in the minds of younger twentieth century Protestants shows how within the tradition itself the legalistic and demanding aspects of the faith have been the most visible elements. This may all point to the fact that Protestantism's attention to its central doctrine has often been merely nominal, or it may mean that Protestants have been less than effective in carrying their doctrine into their style of living and their culture.

However graceless Protestantism often appears to be, it is important for students of religion to take seriously the professed central tenets of a faith. Most movements for renewal in Protestantism (pietism, evangelicalism, Methodism, liberalism, neo-orthodoxy) have made their appeal to the graceful character of the original Protestant statements. They then make their way by calling attention to the way cold and lifeless or dogmatic legalists have cut off the flow of grace in the experience of later Protestant generations.

A religion of grace, stressing divine initiative and calling for man's response, is vulnerable in two directions. There may be so much stress on the divine initiative that one can come to the conclusions that the world is admirably arranged and one may sin as he wishes, since God has taken care of things. The result is, in historic terms, either antinomianism or what Dietrich Bonhoeffer in modern terms calls "cheap grace."[139]

On the other hand, there may be so much stress on man's response, on his ability to repent, to have faith, to produce parallel or consequent holiness that a new legalism results and grace is obscured. Between these extremes Protestantism has normally intended to make its way, and it is the normative expression that here demands attention.

In the eyes of the reformers, the Catholic doctrine of grace was entirely "legalistic" and never antinomian. It was depicted as a lapse back from the New Testament to a perversion of the Old

Testament. The result was seen to be a form of legalism represented in Jesus' time in the Gospel pictures by the Pharisees or in Paul's letters by the backward-looking Judaizers who haunted him as he went about forming congregations.

The Catholic system had turned its back on Augustine's teachings on grace and, said Protestants, was now dependent upon scholastic definitions related to Thomas Aquinas' teaching that grace was somehow infused into man but that merits were still demanded. The attack fell less on the concept of infusion and more on the system of merits or works, a system which, Protestants felt, threw everything back to primitive and enslaving concepts of man appeasing God.

If so, they reasoned, why was the expensive sacrifice of Jesus Christ on the cross necessary? What had happened to the biblical assurances that Christ's gift of himself represented the complete fulfillment, was it not true that the Church's sacramental system was enslaving insecure men, who were not sure whether or not they had satisfied God?

Insofar as this attack inspired and remained central to early Protestantism, as it did in the case of Lutheranism and, to a lesser degree, in most of the rest of the continental Reformation and in the major British and Scottish reforms, there came with the teaching of salvation a reversion to something else that went with Augustinianism.

This has been referred to as a Western anthropocentric soteriological individualism. Western: the Eastern Church kept alive more of the corporate experience of man's destiny, as both the Old Testament and the Pauline teachings about the body of Christ had emphasized. Anthropocentric: it separated man from his cosmic destiny; man could be redeemed or saved apart from the rest of nature despite the witness of Romans, chapter 8, the first chapters of the Fourth Gospel, and the letter to the Colossians that all things were involved in the divine drama of salvation in Christ. Soteriological: because all emphases fell on Christ as *soter* or savior, chiefly from sin, at the expense of other biblical connotations. Individualistic: because personal salvation did not necessarily always grow out of the experience of community. Individual confession and forgiveness came to be the accent, even if this meant extrication not only from the world but also from man's community in the world.[140]

In the modern world, troubled as it has been by the effects of competitive individualism and repulsed as its thoughtful people are over a quest for personal and selfish rescue apart from and even at the expense of others, such words can be used to condemn the whole Protestant vision. In a crowded world, full of shattered and disintegrating symbols, there are hungers for identification with community that seem to be denied by the isolated experience of grace. It is important, then, to notice the cultural context in which the original teaching came about.

In western Europe early in the sixteenth century a chaotic pluralism and competitive economic individualism were not seen to be the problems that they became later. Men could still take community as a given and, if they moved from a Catholic era or territory, they went to an evangelical era or territory and were part of an historical movement. It only remained for them to find their place in the order, and individual or personal salvation there could be stressed as it also had been in Pauline times without such a danger of appeals to selfishness, isolation, or atomization as it later would carry.

A religion of salvation sets out to save men from what really troubles them. In the twentieth century individuals may still feel the weight of sin and seek release—and they certainly seem to in many counseling situations or where personal relations have broken down. But as they go about their daily living they give evidence that other problems are more central.

In the sixteenth century the reality of God was unquestioned: God was a pressure on and a presence in the world and the basic question was: how can one find Him to be gracious? In later times the reality of God has come to be questioned, and for millions the urgent way to put the question is not "Is God gracious?" but rather, "Is God?" Salvation in Christ now might mean that men experience worth, find meaning, overcome estrangement, are integrated into an accepting group, come to terms with their environment—and the overcoming of a sense of sin will be only one among many of these gifts of grace.[141]

At the time of the birth of Protestantism as a cultural force, however, many other questions were secondary and that of release or deliverance from sin was prime. This sense was, we might say, chronic among the common people, who had been trained to look at themselves in the light of such hungers and needs. It was acute in the lives of the religious geniuses who became leaders of the Reformation.

It must be remembered, however obvious the point may seem, that first-generation Protestants had not come from agnosticism or secularity or godlessness to evangelical faith. They had all been shaped in Catholicism, and many of them had wanted to remain in it and to claim for their movements continuity with what had been valid in Catholic Christianity. They automatically took over the questions of their time and place, even though the answers they brought were significantly different from those they had learned and had come to find personally unsatisfying. They were aware of the power of God the judge, of His wrath, of their sin; they would find salvation only if He acted graciously toward them.

At this point it is almost inevitable that one must turn to the psychological record of Martin Luther. Perhaps too much can be made of his case as being normative. Historically, however, both the enemies of Protestantism and many non-Lutheran partisans of it have turned to him for a paradigm of the movement from sin to grace, doubt to faith, condemnation to justification. He had given a fair chance to the Catholic system as it was mediated and moderated in an Augustinian order and interpreted gracefully by his confessor, Johannes von Staupitz. But Luther's attachment to a monastery did not help him overcome his personal doubt, temptations, anxiety, and eventual despair.[142]

His turning came, and the birth of that huge sector of Protestantism which derives from his experience occurred, when he began intensive study of St. Paul's letter to the Romans. There grace was accented. In the letter to the Galatians the legalistic Judaizers were being fought off. Luther was a student of the whole Scripture, commenting in what have come to us as dozens of volumes on the Old Testament. He loved the Fourth Gospel and was at home in the synoptic Gospels. But he read the whole Bible as a corollary of the Pauline teachings of justification.

The key passages now came to be those that announced that a man was justified by faith, apart from the deeds of the law. Nothing in the religious system should provide man a basis of merits with which he could boast. God had dealt favorably with man in the "once and for all" sacrifice of His Son, Jesus Christ. Such a position led Luther to identify with the Paul who could say, "I died under the Law." Interestingly, in commenting on Galatians, Luther added to the list of traditional tyrants that beset man—sin, death, and the devil—the phrase "the law of God."

In a sense, one form of God's expression, even, had been overcome in Christ's victory! The law was in no way a path to grace; it tyrannized. In the words of a Lutheran creedal statement: the law of God *always* accused. It drove man to despair and grace; it was not the path or ladder by which he could climb to salvation. All that man had been, not only his sin but his religious striving, had to be annihilated and killed off. There was nothing in man on which God could build. Everything was a gift of a new creation, the formation of a new man.

Instead of waiting until the end of life or time to stand before the bar of judgment, uncertain concerning the outcome of his trial before God, the man of faith could say that the trial was already over. Christ had taken man's place, had taken on himself the curse of sin when He was condemned to the cross and died. He had overcome sin and the wrath of God when He rose from the dead and when God thus revealed that the reconciliation of man to Himself was now complete, that atonement had been effected.

If man seemed to play little part in the whole drama and if Luther could speak so disparagingly of man's effort, this did not mean that the Christian was to be demeaned. No, now Luther could speak in the most extravagant terms. When God looked at the new man in Christ He saw not sin but Christ's righteousness. True, man was "at the same time justified and a sinner," but he knew that God saw the person in Christ's place. He was not otherwise free to work the works of love without knowing insecurities about his status and without a selfish grasping for credit.in a merit system. He could look at the neighbor's need and not at his own record. This was at the heart of the Lutheran proclamation of man's freedom.

A word remains to be said, then, about the part faith plays in the Lutheran version of Protestantism. Man was justified by grace *through faith.* This assertion could seem to be the first wedge in a new doctrine of merit. Did not man bring faith; was it not his achievement (since the absence of faith was, to Paul and to Luther, somehow man's fault)? Luther never addressed this question in completely logical and systematic terms, resorting instead to what was for him the congenial language of paradox.

Yes, man was responsible; yet faith was also a gift. If it were an achievement, then men would be back where they began in the utter uncertainty of the Catholic merit system. Luther was not himself always secure, and he wrote frequently of *Anfechtungen,* temptations that had been sent not by the devil but by God, to create doubt and cause faith to waver. But through baptism and repentance he could overcome these temptations and accept the gift of faith again. Faith was essentially trust, a kind of existential freedom that enabled man to accept God's gift. It was not so much an assent to certain propositions about God—though in later Protestant scholasticism the intellectualistic note was reintroduced.[143]

If Lutheranism became the largest single bloc in Protestantism, it was still a minority among the many expressions. While Luther's witness was regarded congenially by evangelical Protestants ever after, it was not a completely satisfying statement everywhere. Anglicanism would not have disagreed on the basic point of grace, faith, and justification, although it has seldom elevated the metaphors associated with justification to priority or centrality in its piety or theology. From the first, as one might have expected, Protestants debated the character of the salvation that was to be experienced. Not all reformers preserved Luther's paradoxical statements about faith being a pure gift or his witness to the complete breach between law and Gospel, old man and new, old creation and new creation.

Whereas Lutherans separated justification and sanctification, the holy life with its good works, Calvinism connected the two and saw them to be somehow simultaneous acts. Whereas Luther had argued that repentance came first and that faith was a fruit of repentance, the Reformed parties urged that repentance be seen as a consequence or fruit of faith. Thus in Calvin's teaching, repentance and rebirth were added to faith as part of man's response. This does not mean that Calvin wanted to take away the idea of divine initiative; anything but that. Indeed, his whole teaching of justification was colored by another teaching that dominated his thought.

While Luther spoke of a gracious God, Calvin—without denying God's gracious character—began with a view of the power and glory of a sovereign God. Divine initiative was protected in Calvin's prime teaching about divine election. While Luther had kept in mystery the question of divine responsibility for unresponsive man, Calvin was somewhat more systematic, teaching what came to be called double predestination, wherein foreknowledge of and election to both salvation and condemnation were God's activities.[144]

Calvin departed slightly from the Augustinian-Lutheran individualism by reintroducing language about the saved man being "ingrafted into Christ" and made part of the redeemed community thereby. Luther was not less churchly, but he wanted to isolate the act of justification from all contexts and supports, for the sake of the freedom of God. Calvinism joined much of the rest of the Reformation in a more contextual view: the Gospel was seen in a positive relation to law, the individual was warmly related to community in the drama of salvation, justification came with sanctification and not before it, mystical union with Christ came prior to or with justification and not after it, and God's grace was kept as a correlative of His sovereignty and not as a separate dominant note.[145]

In a formula popular at that time, Calvin concentrated more on "Christ in us" and Luther on "Christ for us." Calvin and his colleagues did all this without reintroducing the merit system. In another condensation of Reformation formulae, he agreed with Luther that grace does not find us willing but makes us willing.

Both moderate Anglicanism, on one hand, and radical Protestantism from Zwingli through the Anabaptists, on the other, while they valued Luther's original insight, tended to be closer to Calvin when it came time for systematic formulation. Many of them gave a more positive place to God's law in man's quest for salvation. They were more ready to stress mystical union with Christ. Almost all of them picked up the biblical passages about "the obedience of faith" and stressed obedience in ways that Luther was less likely to favor.

"Christ in us" predominated over "Christ for us" among most of them, perhaps since many of them saw themselves as beginning to stand further than did the ex-monk Luther from the medieval Catholic metaphors. These had been drawn from either the Old Testament sacrificial-satisfaction picture or the New Testament and medieval law-court portrayals. More often, as in the case of the radical leader Caspar Schwenckfeld, there was a sense of urgency to develop an approach which would change the moral life of followers more readily than Lutheranism seemed to do. Inevitably, some measure of the law crept back into the salvation scheme.[146]

The reader who is at home with the sixteenth century documents on the rediscovery of grace will have been at home at once with this whole discussion. If he has been within range of present-day pulpits in conservative Lutheran, Calvinist, or Reformed churches, he has heard the language of justification outlined in terms much like these. But if his nurture has been in Anglicanism, in the Congregational, Baptist, or Methodist traditions, he may wonder just what world it is that has been discussed to this point.

"Justification" may come up only when the preacher or theologian addresses himself to a relatively small number of biblical texts —almost none of them in the Gospels—which are so favored in Protestant witness. Or it may be left behind as an embarrassing

Latin-sounding word that no longer carries fresh meaning to moderns, and is therefore usually translated beyond recognizability. Grace and faith, then appear in different contexts. This perception of Protestantism is largely accurate. It derives both from the fact that not all evangelical traditions made as much of the accent on justification as Luther and Calvin did and, even more, because so much has happened in subsequent Protestantism. Two examples will illuminate.

In Anglo-American Protestantism between the Reformation and the present stands an event of decisive significance: the Wesleyan phase of the evangelical revival. While John Wesley was not alone, he more than any other gave a new stamp to the teaching of grace and faith, the "way of salvation" in much of modern Protestantism. He picked up some themes that had been developed in Arminianism, a modification if not a refutation of original Calvinism from earlier Holland, and gave it his own stamp.

Wesley's may be called a more modern view, for medieval vestiges were progressively left behind and dominant modern themes —including the question of the capability of man and the universality of God's salvation, both of them "democratizing" motifs, came to prominence. Wesley looked back at Luther's justified man and Calvin's obedient man and added to these the concept of perfectible man. For him, the quest for holiness, morality, and sanctification was prominent.[147]

Though Wesley had a positive regard for his evangelical forefathers and was concerned, as they had been, to be Pauline in his teaching, he was to change much of subsequent Protestant accent on the question of the path of salvation, wholeness, health, and freedom. Whereas Calvin had spoken of the limitations of salvation qualified by the doctrine of election and double predestination, Wesley spoke of "universal salvation." Christ's death had been for all and was now offered freely to all. One might translate it: universal salvation-universal opportunity.

This salvation was full, for it led to perfection; man was no longer to be at the same time justified and a sinner, but was to pursue what was available to him, a kind of perfection which in effect left sinfulness behind. Such salvation was sure, for God the Holy Spirit guaranteed it. It was free, for man was a free agent and God was not to be bound by his decrees of election. Wesleyanism and its correlate forms of Anglicanism became strong forces for missionary and benevolent activities and fulfilling faiths for activists. If men were to be agents of decision and holiness, others must bring the message and the means and work out their salvation in this pattern of holiness. Wesley presented these teachings without neglecting the Gospel accent on grace. He did not want to build on a somber and striving merit system.[148]

The other decisive turn in Protestantism came at approximately the same time, at many places and out of many sources. This might be referred to as the whole modern or liberal trend in Protestant theology. Liberal doctrines of grace derived in part from the Enlightenment's downgrading of revelation, of medieval terminology, and of particular salvation. The rationalist period had also laid stress on natural reason, law, and morality in religion. The transactional views of sacrifice, penalty, satisfaction, and justification were seen as bizarre and enslaving supernatural events, whereas Christ's work was to be exemplary in a humane world. Liberal theology in the Unitarian tradition, whether in Anglo-America or, even earlier, in Poland and Transylvania, pioneered in these accents and was never to desert them.[149]

More influential in formal Protestant theology, however, was the reshaping of Christian thought that went on throughout the nineteenth century on the Continent. Schleiermacher and his colleagues and heirs continued to speak of grace and faith, but the whole path of salvation was relocated for them. He assigned its inspiration to consciousness, the locale for religious response.

Though he wrote in a time that had been influenced by the Enlightenment's individualism, Schleiermacher was himself also at home with a romanticism which stressed organic community, and he found salvation in the development of a community of people who had the experience of God. Awareness, insight, intuition, feeling, response, experience—these were the features of consciousness that helped make man a Christian. Almost inevitably there was a universalizing here, too: in the liberal tradition Christ came more frequently to be spoken of as the preeminent example, teacher, or model and not the unique bearer of the whole divine plan for salvation.[150]

Such an expression of Protestant faith had less room for the wrath of God. There was less concentration on the depth of man's sin or the isolation of the experience of justification. Now the love of God as a generally accessible movement in the world was proclaimed. Man's potential was given new attention. The communal character of salvation came to new prominence.

To this experiential adaptation was added another modern variant, sometimes seen to be derived from Immanuel Kant: religious response was also located in man's moral consciousness. The ethical came to a prominence unknown in earlier Reformation thought, where it had been a corollary or consequence of justification. Now it was an independent article. In the modern pluralistic state, churches have had to advertise their contributions to morality, and the ethical note has been enhanced. Much of modern Protestantism combines variations of Wesleyan, Schleiermacherian, or Kantian themes—if we may condense whole clusters of historical development around certain symbolic names. Man's will, his capabilities, and his responsibilities often take the place of the earlier witness to God's freedom, His sovereignty, and His gift.

The modern movement has not had the field to itself, however. Not only have conservative evangelicals steadfastly continued to reassert the earlier Protestant witness. In more sophisticated and formal academic theological centers the twentieth century also saw a cluster of criticisms of the nineteenth century liberalism or modernization and a variety of appeals sometimes spoken of as neo-Reformation or neo-orthodox in character.

In the hands of Karl Barth there was a most vehement rejection of the modernizers' notes and a new accent on sovereignty, grace, and justification. In the radical biblical theology which was influenced by Martin Heidegger's existentialism, a man like Rudolf Bultmann could define much of his work as an attempt to present a demythologized version of Paul's and Luther's teaching of justification by grace through faith. And out of a background of idealist philosophy and with more positive apprehension of Schleiermacher's witness, Paul Tillich argued that in an age of estrangement and meaninglessness, God's gift is the New Being in Christ —a contemporary translation or adaptation, averred Tillich, of Luther's teaching on justification. On Anglo-Saxon soil Congregational theologians like Peter Taylor Forsyth and John Oman restored similar concerns for Reformation approaches to grace.[151]

The debate has not ended, and the two accents may have to coexist in Protestantism as they have from the first. Both devote themselves to grace, but the liberal version sees more need to connect grace with the initiative and experience of man. Both devote themselves to faith, but the modern picture tries to remove the scholastic (seventeenth century) period's style of attachment of faith to belief, its stress on the cognitive, on assent to propositions. Some have gone so far as to argue now that one must move "beyond belief" and make faith a kind of objectless consent or assent to Being.[152]

Both groups see Christianity offering freedom, release, peace, wholeness, health, and deliverance, though the constriction or limitation on man is defined in different ways by different parties at different times. If sin is the enemy, let there be forgiveness; if meaninglessness, let there be New Being; if anxiety, let there be wholeness and health; if the bondage of social pressure, heredity, environmental concerns, social habit, or religious law, let there be freedom. These seem to be the messages of Protestants who have never stopped talking about salvation, however they translate the term.

III. Bases of Protestant Life

8. THE BIBLE THE RELIGION OF PROTESTANTS?

Wherever religion exists in a postprimitive, literate society, it survives in no small measure as an extension of texts, Sacred Scriptures, or a particular book. The book may represent the sayings of the founder or may recall the events surrounding his life. Ordinarily it will make claims for its own special and even supernatural origin and inspiration. It may be designed to impart information about another order of being, to give directions for practical living in obedience to the tenets of the religion, or to inspire meditation and devotion. Frequently it will be set aside in a canon or as a code. The religious leaders will then be a caste set aside for determining the degrees of faithfulness or deviation in the community, set against its and their standards of orthodoxy.

Thus the Hindu Scriptures are made up of the canon of the Veda —Vedic hymns, Brahmanic treatises, and the Upanishads. Better known in the West is the obsessive regard shown the Qur'an by Muslims. This book, one-fifth the length of the Christian Scriptures (Old and New Testaments) is said to be the Word of God that is preserved on a tablet in heaven. "Only the purified should touch it." The book itself is a sacred object, just as it is an imparter of teaching. In these and other scriptural traditions there are debates over translations and interpretations; schools and sects differ over exegesis of the texts. Yet it is these Scriptures that give much of the unity to their religions.

Christianity stands with these scriptural religions, and has through the years seen virtually every kind of attitude toward its book which other faiths have taken toward theirs. These range from casual disregard or free interpretation through fanatical devotion to the letter of the text. The early church took over the Hebrew Scriptures, often called the Old Testament, and interpreted these as prophetic background to the faith fulfilled in Christ and the apostles. As time passed, men set down sayings of Jesus, surrounded these with stories of His life and death and resurrection, and passed on messages about the meaning of His act in the form of letters to young congregations in the Near Eastern world. The Christian Church, therefore, existed some time prior to the writing of its own particular and unshared Scriptures (since Judaism continued to regard the Hebrew Scriptures as divine), and to the later historian the story of the preservation and selection of biblical writings in a canon seems almost reckless, casual, or haphazard.[153]

Sometime during the second century, however, a canon did take shape, and the Old and New Testaments entered the Christian tradition. From one point of view, the Bible was highly regarded during the ensuing millennium and a half in both Eastern and Western Catholic Christianity. But it was definitely accompanied by a developing tradition of episcopal authority, martyrology, folklore, theological interpretation, and devotional literature, all of which came to receive virtually comparable status in the minds of many. There was never a determined downgrading of the Scriptures, but in the eyes of later Protestantism there had been an effectual devaluation of its status, because tradition had been elevated. God spoke not only through apostles, prophets, and evangelists in the Scriptures. He also spoke through his vicar, the pope; through the bishops and the mystics. The legalists of the church tradition often spent more time with the developing lore than with the original texts.[154]

The reformers virtually unanimously saw their movement as a recovery of the Bible from the traditions which had obscured it and from the authorities which claimed a monopoly on its interpretation. The simple faith of many subsequent Protestants can be reduced to some suggestion that theirs alone is the religion of the Bible and that the Reformation was the opening of the Bible against the will of Roman Catholic authorities.

In the language of some nineteenth century American Protestant primitive Gospel advocates, they would claim that where the Scriptures speak, these Christians speak; where the Scriptures are silent, they are silent. Protestant folklore is rich in the imagery of a Bible chained to the wall and locked so that the faithful would be denied access—until Luther and his contemporaries or the Wycliffites and Hussites just before them, came along to liberate the book, the Gospel, the people.[155]

Where there have been schisms in Protestantism, they have ordinarily concerned differing interpretations of biblical texts; where efforts at reunion have been made, they as often as not begin by common confrontation of similar texts, with efforts made to find concordance in interpretation. Most Protestants have argued that the Bible is perspicuous, that its meaning will be clear to any conscientious person who lets himself be guided by the Holy Spirit. They have been less successful at convincing others in an intensely divided movement that all can agree on one reading. This is a way of saying that they have not often taken note of the degree to which Bible reading is done in a tradition. [156]

Most Baptists read into or out of the Bible an endorsement of adult baptism by immersion and most Presbyterians find in it a chartering of infant baptism with any form of application of water. Anglicans see episcopacy in the biblical pattern, while Congregationalists read a mandate for their own polity in the same pages. Obviously, people of different communions bring something to their reading of the texts, and what they bring is reinforced (or occasionally unsettled) by what they read there.

Such high regard for the Scriptures suggests that Protestants have always recognized the numinous power of words. Religious scholars regularly reveal such awe. Oaths, curses, imprecations, vows—all these reveal the ways in which believers know that the syllables they evoke are supposed to do something, to invoke the supernatural, to effect change beyond words in the world. The Bible was then seen as the naming document which provides a divine address of blessings and curses. While it discloses little or nothing about what is going on in the supernatural order, it constantly elaborates on the meaning of the temporal order when that order is addressed by Yahweh or visited by God's suffering and risen Son. The Bible therefore deserves its elevated status, and as the defining document it has been used to measure heresy and orthodoxy, moral faithfulness, and immoral lapse. It has served to remind Christians that theirs is an historical faith, that religion touches all the details of common life, that eternal issues are faced in the temporal realm—all themes particularly dear to most Protestants.

The story of the Bible's role in Protestantism can be seen first of all as a battle over authority. The Roman Catholic Church in the sixteenth century claimed that the councils and the pope were the authorities in the church, custodians of the Scriptures and the ensuing tradition. They argued that the Protestant revolt would mean the end of authority in the church and perhaps in the world. Without a formal and (though the term was then not yet official) infallible trusteeship of biblical interpretation, anarchy would result and whirl or chaos would be king. [157]

The Protestants consistently saw such claims to be heteronomous, which means that they considered these to be expressive of
another principle outside of and in competition with the divine
tendency in Scripture itself. The church needed divine authority,
and the Bible was a divine revelation. The pope and the councils
were fallible.

Extrication from the papal authority also forced Protestants to
underplay the role of tradition; they neither saw the Bible to be in
a tradition or tradition to be in the Bible and unwittingly began,
despite their doctrines to the contrary, to play down the human
aspects of biblical revelation, to stress the infallibility of divine
inspiration in the documents.[158]

There were exceptions. While all Protestants refused to accept
papal authority, some of them did accord a relatively high status
to tradition. The Ordinal of 1550 in the Church of England paid
due attention to the church fathers, and the Lutheran and other
confessional or creedal writings of the sixteenth century showed
respect to the writers of the patristic era. There were hints of what
later might have been called a development of doctrine, both
within the biblical canon (from promise to fulfillment) and between it and later ages, when God through His Holy Spirit also saw
to it that He was not left without witness.

If ambivalence about tradition as an authority remained, there
was also controversy over the role of experience. At the radical
edge of English Protestantism the Quakers were to stress the revelation of the inner light, and they carried their mistrust of the static
and the material even to the point of concern over misuse of the
Book. On the Continent, radical reformers also spoke in similar
spiritualistic terms and sometimes claimed for themselves the
power to give forth fresh revelation. But while most Protestants
made much of the "inner testimony of the Holy Spirit," this experiential reference was rarely made at the expense of Scripture, but
usually in conjunction with its authority.[159]

The formal authority of popes and councils, the less formal
authority of tradition, and the informal authority of experience—
all these were rejected or played down while the Bible was set aside
to shape and inform Protestantism. Inevitably, such an attitude
presented new problems in evangelical history. People who rejected other sacred objects and images made a sacred object of the
Bible. The Protestant iconoclastic sense often failed people whose
doctrines contended that the Bible as an object was "only a book,"
but whose piety led them to revere it.[160]

Evangelical literature is full of stories which make quasi-supernatural claims for the Bible as a physical object, as in the case of soldiers who were miraculously saved because an enemy bullet was deterred by a Bible in a breast pocket. Sometimes preachers would open the Bible to any page and preach on the text that fell before them, assuming that each page had equal power to shape and address communities. Magazines, greeting cards, church bulletin covers, and other literature which was produced by people who repudiated sacramentals or visible objects like rosaries or crucifixes regularly showed that the leather-bound, lavish Bible was itself an object of veneration among them. In a religion poor on shared symbols, the Book has often had to serve as one.

The Bible and Protestantism are entwined in a common history after the early sixteenth century. People in revolt against empire and pope, conscious of their new territorialism or nationalism, eager to extricate themselves from Rome but fearing anarchy, needed an authority and found it in the Bible. They needed a sacred symbol and found it in the Book. Most Protestant movements immediately saw the need for the vernacular Scriptures, and reformers had to be linguistic experts, providing a common language for emerging areas or territories.

Printing with movable type in "the age of Gutenberg" was roughly contemporaneous with the early Protestant movement. The evangelical leaders exploited the new invention to propagate their movement by putting out scores of editions of a Book that in a previous age had been denied the laity and many priests for economic reasons if for no other. Dissemination of the Bible, then, was an act of a democratizing spirit and a sign of faith in the ability of people to read and interpret the texts in a faithful and authentic manner. Wycliffe, Tyndale, Coverdale, Luther—these and others were busy translators and publishers of the Bible at the dawn of reform.

The German theologian Gerhard Ebeling once suggested that the history of Christianity is simply the history of the interpretation of the Bible. In some respects this seems to be true of Protestantism. The missionary and benevolent movements were born in part of a rereading of the great commission in Matthew's Gospel, the command to teach and baptize all nations. This was an injunction that had been overlooked in much of Protestantism for most of two and a half centuries. The humanitarian endeavors and the formation of societies for propagating the faith and publishing the Bible grew out of men's rereading of that Book and their fusing of a vision of human need and divine command.[161]

Liberal and modernizing theological movements in the age of the Enlightenment or the nineteenth century were reinterpretations of the Bible, often with its supernatural elements removed or minimized. The ecumenical movement in the twentieth century was based in part on a recovery of biblical language, which made interchurch talk comprehensible, and a rereading of the biblical injunctions to give expression to unity, passages which had often been overlooked.

A consequence of the close bond between Protestantism and the Bible is that they often share a common fate. The destiny of a certain kind of literacy or attitude toward history is tied in with the destiny of Protestantism. In backward-looking ages, when the wisdom of the fathers came with a special sanction to new generations, recourse to the Bible came instinctively.

In times of cultural revolution, when men are uncertain about the lessons from the past or when they set out to repudiate tradition, a faith such as Protestantism which has depended upon consultation of old documents and records, is called into question. The popular philosopher of the media revolution, Marshall McLuhan, in prophesying the end of the kind of approach to learning that went with the age of Gutenberg has tied that end with the impending demise of Protestantism. People form impressions about reality in a new way, it is said, and recourse to the linear sequences of biblical texts becomes obsolete, to the detriment of Protestantism.[162]

Not many Protestants seem to worry about the end of the age of the Book. They are too busy debating the meaning of the text and contending for their views. On the matter of regarding and interpreting the Bible itself (as opposed to interpreting various teachings in it), two basically different attitudes have prevailed. One could draw a line through Protestant churches in various countries and find people on both sides of it. The two attitudes toward the Bible are paralleled by differing attitudes toward faith itself. These two deserve examination; it must be remembered that many subtle variations occur within each general school, but two have prevailed.

The first view we shall call liberal, without thereby wanting to connote all the shadings of theological liberalism. By liberal here is meant a generally rather free approach to interpretation, one which, in the words of its advocates, stresses "not the letter but the Spirit."

In the eyes of its enemies, this approach is a modern innovation—though evidences of battles over it are already present
within the canon, and early fathers like Irenaeus, Justin Martyr,
and Origen could be numbered in its camp. Certainly it has
been present from the first generation of Protestantism. Were it
not for the confusing associations of the word, it could even be
called the traditional view. It retains something of the Catholic
sense that the Bible is to be interpreted in the light of the religious and literary traditions, not radically isolated or segregated from its environment and from the rest of learning, literature, and experience.

The liberal view, its antagonists would say, while it may be
orthodox in other respects, tends to see only a quantitative and
not a qualitative difference between the Scriptures and other
sacred writings. The Bible may be inspired, but to a lesser degree so is great religious poetry or mystical writing. The liberal
interpreter would probably put it a different way. In an approach made famous by H. Richard Niebuhr, the liberal may
see biblical history as having an "outer" and an "inner" aspect.
The external approach sees the Bible as a human book among
human books. It partakes of finitude and contingency, and
seems to be an ordinary literary work. But to the eye of faith,
to the man who is grasped by a vision of God's activity in
Christ, there is an internal dimension which compels a different
kind of vision and assent. From this angle, God the Holy Spirit
quickens people to see that the Book is divine and that it has a
special authority.[163]

This school of interpretation considers itself to be particularly Protestant when it stresses the openness of the biblical
canon. That is, there has never been complete agreement in
the church about which books belong in the Bible. Certain ones
were agreed upon, but there had been protest against others. It
was considered theoretically possible at least that other books
could be discovered which the church would regard as belong-
ing in the canon. After all, the canon was itself the product of
the church, and not vice versa. An open canon, it was argued,
kept people from idolizing the collection of documents, making
a god out of a book, or having an all-purpose code.

At the same time, the liberal always stressed levels of intensity or revelational power within the canon as it came to him.
He resists the idea of a doctrine of inspiration which would call
him to grant equal hearing to, say, a passage from the book of

Esther which has no theological reference and to the Gospel of John. He looks for some divining principle which will throw light on such a varied collection of documents as the Bible is.

The liberal prefers to reproduce the Gospel of John in calling Jesus and not the Bible itself, "the Word of God," though if proper precautions are first asserted, its spokesmen will refer also to the Bible as the Word of God. They do not want a simple equation between the two, since God's Word in Christ is also something more and somehow other than the book. These Protestants might say, then, that the Bible is not the revelation but is the witness to the revelation, the written testimony to God's Word and His mighty acts.

Many liberal interpreters like to claim Martin Luther as the Protestant forefather of this approach. He could speak of the Bible as God's Word without making an exclusive identification between them and without idolizing the Bible. Thus even a conservative evangelical and an enemy of the liberal interpretation, the American theologian Bernard Ramm, tucks away in a footnote the reminder that "Luther had some rather loose views of the Bible and inspiration." Luther's divining principle was the revelation in Christ. The Scripture was the manger in which Christ lay.[164]

While Luther had an awesome regard for biblical authority—he averred that he would listen to no other and was completely and only "under" the Word, as in the Bible—he could point to errors, argue with the author's grammar, complain that St. Paul made mistaken analogies or told confusing allegories. He could stress the open canon, argue with the principle by which some books (like Esther) were included and even at times dismiss the theology of books like the Epistle of James as "an epistle of straw" because it did not stress the theme of grace.

Biblical literalists who like to claim Luther can also find passages in which he speaks of biblical infallibility; he was a paradoxical thinker who seemed to dramatize both sides of many questions. However one finally locates him, it is easy to see why the liberals choose to date their free interpretation to Luther's time.

Luther deferred to none in his desire to have the clear word of Scripture settle matters in the church. When confronted with the demand to recant his teaching, he wanted Scripture or sound reason to be used to counter and refute him. Otherwise he would not respond. In order to have available the clarity of the Bible for common people, this "doctor of Scriptures" translated them into colloquial but dignified German. He generally repudiated the allegorical interpretations by which the Catholic tradition had often found hidden and convenient meanings.

Luther wanted to be, he said, a simple grammatical interpreter, even though he never pretended that grammar pierced all the mysteries of revelation. He and his followers played down the idea of rational proofs for the infallibility and authority of Scripture, depending instead upon the convincing power of the Holy Spirit. If he took liberties with passages in his translation, he explained that he did this to reinforce the central message of the Bible, the word of how God justifies man by grace through faith.

The Reformation produced many biblical scholars to the left of Luther, of course. The radicals who stressed new inspiration, spiritualism, or mysticism, were wont to be rather reckless in their regard for the canon, for a book from the past. Within a generation there were men of Unitarian tendencies like Michael Servetus who brought humanist principles to the interpretation of the Bible. But much of the Reformation movement also held to views to the right of Luther, and stands at the head of a tradition which might be termed not liberal but literal. Here, again, historians must be careful not to prejudice the case by the choice of labels. No terms will be adequate to partisans or enemies of these approaches. Literal need not mean literalistic or legalistic, petty and scribal. Instead, there is an intention only to accent the approach that stresses the letter of the Bible as being set apart by a specific doctrine of infallible inspiration.[165]

Among the major reformers, John Calvin can best be seen as a representative of the literal approach. It would be useless to enter here into a discussion as to whether Luther or Calvin was more evangelical as a result of his doctrine of Scripture, or whether each one's doctrine of Scripture resulted from a specific view of the evangelical interpretation. The difference between the two can be understood better by an analysis of the two kinds of minds. Luther was ready to live with loose ends, with a dramatic sense of the dialectical and the paradoxical. Calvin was a logical thinker, a systematician who had to tie loose ends.[166]

If for Luther the sequence was: first I have come to faith in Christ and then I find the whole Bible compelling, for Calvin the question was: how can I come to faith in Christ, unless first I have faith in the reliability of the only testimony I have to Him as a figure from the past? Therefore a view of the inspiration of Scripture had to come first. Calvin stressed both external and internal rational proofs for the reliability and infallibility of the Book. Its preservation and the perpetuation of a people based on it were among the external proofs. Its history could be certified in secular scholarship. More important, of course, was the internal testimony, the effect produced by the miraculous Book which had been guided and guarded by the Holy Spirit.

Once one held to a foolproof view of the Bible, he could move on to the other Christian doctrines and find them all reinforced by it. In Calvin's view, unlike Luther's, the human element of the Book was understated. True, God adapted himself to man's condition by speaking in the language of men's own times and places and not in a special "Holy Spirit language." He adapted himself to the literary styles and conventions of men of different personalities. It was also true that acceptance of the proofs for a doctrine of biblical inspiration did not necessarily bring man to faith; the witness of the Holy Spirit was crucial for that.

The Holy Spirit led men to find ways to overcome apparent errors or contradictions in the text of the Bible. Contradictions in it would have led to a weakening or the destruction of faith. In its more extreme expressions, this literal view of the Bible was seen to be a kind of mechanical or dictational method. God took such a strong initiative in this act of revelation that he literally gave men word-for-word accounts and they merely acted as secretaries. God cannot err, so the Scripture was also completely reliable.

The literal view has always seen itself to be the higher and more safeguarding version. The Bible does not contain but *is* the Word of God. The Book is not the testimony to a revelation but it is the revelation. The canon is not a partly haphazard collection, but was put together by divine guidance on certain clearly definable lines (e.g., in the New Testament, apostolic authorship). There is a qualitative difference between it and all other literature, and the hermeneutical (interpretive) principles by which one comes to it differ from those which one employs on other great literature. If a book is ascribed to a certain author, he must have written it— even if such an ascription seems to place it outside its own time. If Christ refers to passages from Second Isaiah (Isaiah 40–66) as being "Isaiah," even if they give evidence of having been written 250 years after Isaiah's time, then Isaiah it must be. This is upheld even if it means that a prophet is heard talking in detail in the past tense, and with a different style from what he had earlier used, about events that have not yet occurred. What could it mean for the idea of His divine sonship if Christ called a biblical book by an inaccurate designation, asks the literalist.

The literal approach has always been championed in those circles where Protestant scholasticism, with its sense for logic and sequence and for a substantial (as opposed to existential) view of truth or for a propositional approach to revelation, has been favored. Thus in the seventeenth century period of Protestant dogmatic formulation, when Aristotelian categories that had become familiar in the church through medieval Scholasticism were revived in the service of the church, both Reformed and Lutheran theologians wrote works of dogmatics which located a doctrine of infallible Scriptures as an a priori to other Christian teachings.[167] As this view came to be challenged in the Enlightenment, its adherents became defensive and elaborated it even further. When scientific discoveries seemed to call into question elements of biblical world-views, the scientific order had to be challenged. Some literalists did so by compartmentalizing, by living in one mental setting when they encountered science and then moving into an entirely different one when they read the Scripture. Others tried to harmonize the two worlds. When scientific accounts stressed an old world, the literalist took the young-earth pictures of Genesis and suggested that the writers may have meant that the world was created in six aeons, using the terms of six "days" figuratively.

The literal reader accuses the liberal of adapting the Scripture to contemporary opinion, and thus doing it violence. Only hardness of heart and resistance to the Spirit would lead one, he would contend, to place himself and his literary analysis above the Scriptures and Christ. It is clear here again, as so often in Protestantism, that behind the surface issue two approaches of faith are in question. The liberal stresses a kind of subjective-existentialist coming to faith in Christ, after which the scriptural witness is seen to be inspired and revelational. The literal reader stresses the conviction that faith is produced when one comes to have a belief in the trustworthiness of the Bible.

Accusations fly across these party lines. The liberal calls the literal reader obscurantist, fundamentalist, antimodern, and less than trusting in the power of the Spirit. The literal reader sees the liberal as tampering with holy things, making the Bible say what he wants it to. Both try to forget that their approach does not solve everything: for example, Seventh-day Adventists and conservative

Baptists share a belief in an inerrant Bible, but differ on almost everything in it, including the days of worship, the question of Old Testament legislation's binding effect, and the millennium.

At one point, at least, however, the literal interpreter can make a strong case: those who have not shared his a prioristic view have been more open to passing approaches to the Bible. From the liberal camp came the advocacy of Enlightened or Rationalist attitudes toward the Bible, wherein miraculous and supernatural views were played down, mystery was subordinated to clear reason, and "the reasonableness of Christianity" was accented.[168]

After these views went out of vogue, support for higher critical views of the Bible came from the liberal school. The lower, or textual, criticism was supported by moderates of both camps, men and women who were simply seeking the best text of documents whose original manuscripts have disappeared. But the higher critics worked to relate the books of the Bible, ascertain true authorships behind pseudonyms, find different literary levels, and discern the ways in which the Bible was composed out of various situations of the early church. Julius Wellhausen's school in Germany saw a multiple authorship for "the five books of Moses," and its heirs stressed the ways in which the New Testament grew out of community needs.[169]

Concurrent with the rise of modern literary criticism of the text came drastic theological change. The best-known locale for the change was nineteenth century Germany, in a tradition which began with Schleiermacher. Schleiermacher rejected the heteronomous authority of the biblical documents and based the Protestant religious response on feeling, intuition, experience. The believer's subjective attitude in some ways came to be the certifier of the quality of biblical revelation, and not vice versa.

More dramatic theological change came through the left-wing Hegelians, among them David Friedrich Strauss, who were soon depicting levels of myth and were questioning the possibility of learning much about Christ—or even knowing that he really lived. The tendency of these schools was to see the Bible in the family of literature and to treat it as other books were treated. When moderate versions of such views reached England, there were numerous intense doctrinal debates and the equivalents of heresy trials, as in the case of a higher critical bishop, John William Colenso.[170]

All these turns were part of what might be called a crisis of historical consciousness in the Western Christian world. Men were wrestling with the problem of the particularity of Christian revelation as it relates to universal truths or with the problem of Christian truth in comparison to the truth seen in other men's religions. A new relativism was afflicting many reflective men, and they became unsure of the salvation account that had been isolated from the contingencies of history in the literalists' view of the biblical narrative.

While all this was occurring, the literal interpreter found all the more reason to resist science and modern philosophy, to feel more beleaguered and defensive as he saw theological faculty after faculty and scholar after scholar go over to the liberal view in even its more extreme forms. The result was a reaction that in America was called fundamentalism, in which the literalistic approach was reinforced and made the touchstone of all theology. The fundamentalist view is well known around the world because of the publicity given evangelists who speak in its name and because it has produced great numbers of "faith missionaries," who operate with a certitude about their truth born of adherence to this vision of the Bible.[171]

There have been reconciling attempts and some common meeting grounds for moderates in both camps in the twentieth century —or at least there were in the years when neo-orthodoxy held sway in Protestant theological schools. Neo-orthodoxy meant a restoration of a high view of revelation and biblical authority and a repudiation of many kinds of philosophical presuppositions (even when this required the substitution of others). Many literalists enjoyed the biblical witness of Karl Barth, himself no advocate of modern theories of biblical inerrancy. Yet Barth also chided the liberal interpreters as having not taken seriously the "Thus saith the Lord!" of the Bible.

Both camps have been eager to learn more about the situation out of which biblical books grew; to try to find strands of unity within the Bible; to listen to the *kerygma* or word of proclamation preserved in accounts of New Testament sermons. Both seem more ready to examine the theological presuppositions they bring to their doctrines of Scripture. Many of them have wearied of intra-Protestant infighting and want to seek unity on higher levels.

Still, both camps are wary. The liberal feels that he alone keeps alive the Protestant principle with its resistance to the idolization of the human, the objectification of the spiritual. The literal reader

argues strenuously that the alternative is hopelessly subjective and
arbitrary; that it offers no defense against modernity's acids and
calls into question the reliability of God. If the battle shows no sign
of wearing down, let it at least be noted that when Protestants
fight, they fight about the Scripture. They remain a people of the
Book; both sides read it for reinforcement of their point of view.
They want to settle arguments on its basis. In their own peculiar
ways, then, they give it honor, as their fathers have done for centuries.

9. THE EVANGELICAL COMMUNITY

Protestants, like virtually all other religionists, have constantly given attention to the character of their community. Sometimes this has been done formally through devotion to the doctrine of the church. Just as often it occurs informally through the development of polity and practical arrangements. Discussions of the character of religious community frequently begin by reference to words like those from Alfred North Whitehead: religion is what one does with his solitariness. Then would follow a polemic against such individualism or isolationism as being untrue to the nature of the heart of the religious impulse.

That is as good a place as any to begin discussion of Protestant community, so long as it is remembered that Whitehead knew more about contexts of religion than he put into that sentence. This reference is important in our discussion because Protestant Christianity has often been vulnerable to various individualisms, and some of its advocates as well as some neutral observers have reduced it to a kind of atomizing individualistic faith.[172]

Protestantism has had room for mystics, many of whom would fit Whitehead's picture. The mystic does what he can to attain union with the divine on the divine's level, away from the distractions of temporality and conventional communal concerns. He may come from community, and may report back to it—one pictures the cloistered contemplative—but his moment of mystical union transcends communal concerns. A Jacob Boehme or an Evelyn Underhill may share or account for such moments, but these are exceptions. The very fact that they could be denominated "Protestant mystics" imparts, through use of the adjective, a sense of communal effort to their strivings. Mysticism is theoretically remote from community but is practically dependent upon it. In any case, the mystical tendency has been relatively infrequently seen in Protestantism, and the numbers of mystics who are Protestant but who want nothing to do with other Protestants has been exceptionally rare.[173]

A second assault on the reality of religious community sometimes has come from Protestant existentialists. The existentialist begins with an absurd and disordered world, and in his attempt to summon the courage to be or to find resources for avoiding suicide, he may find his struggle to be private and that he is very much alone. Thus Søren Kierkegaard, the most notable Protestant existentialist, was in quest of the "moment before God." He believed that the task of the disciple was to be "contemporaneous with Christ" and frequently parodied the efforts of those who said that faith was somehow dependent upon a "cloud of witnesses" through space and time. In his *Philosophical Fragments* he spoke disparagingly of "the disciple at second hand," the one who had no contemporaneous experience of Christ and who relied upon the testimony of others for what he then called faith. In the *Attack upon Christendom* the Danish thinker inveighed against what passed for community in the established church of his day, and there and elsewhere gave plausibility to the charges of those who said he lacked a catholic view of the Church and that he wished to lack it. Twentieth century existentialists often stress the lonely agony at the edge of the abyss and picture what Christian affirmation emerges to be that of the desperate response of God's lonely man.[174]

A third and less consistent or less thoughtful attack on the communitarian nature of Protestant experience has come from defenders of the late eighteenth and early nineteenth century versions of Christian individualism. This was allied to the rise of the politically autonomous man at the time of the democratic revolutions. At the same time, the appearance of new forms of capitalism during the early industrial revolution provided the occasion for "the self-made man" or the entrepreneur to make his appearance.

Particularly in America, where a frontier was being tamed and where fortunes could be made in a hurry, the Protestant churches provided ideology for rationalizing a spirit of competition which set man over against man in the quest for material possessions. The political and economic defense of individualism was adduced over against purported "socialistic" interpretations of church and world. Advocates of it base their observations on an inaccurate rendering of history: the frontier pioneers and even the capitalist entrepreneurs, if they were religious at all, were so in relation to extant religious communities. A preacher was always on hand to bless their efforts. Advocates of this kind of individualism counter by saying that the Protestant "right of private judgment" stands at the root of this rather churchless individualism; one did not need to depend on the ministries of others to be or to become right with God.[175]

Protestant pioneers would agree with one element in the mystic's, the existentialist's, and the individualist's contention: each person must believe for himself just as he must die for himself. There must be a personal appropriation of a religious vision. Each person has a horizon, a field of vision, a perceived world, and his grasp is his own. Therefore Protestantism has never discouraged the laity's attempts to strike out on its own to have a personal experience of faith. Fundamentalism has often narrowed the issue of salvation to the question, "Do you accept Jesus Christ as your personal savior?" The language of Protestantism is full of personalized apprehensions and calls for personal decisions. However, these laymen somehow live off the inherited capital of a complex tradition and community and are never successful at cutting their decision off from the setting of community.

The problem of community has, however, been particularly acute in Protestantism. Among all the religions of the world, few have been as torn by various national and confessional divisions, denominational and sectarian distinctions, and individual partisan interpretations. In the midst of such a thicket of reality who can find the community, the church? And this obvious problem was made even more complicated in the nineteenth century when Protestant scholars robbed many of the faithful of the picture that the original Christian community had been pure and undivided.[176]

The net effect of the historical criticism of the Bible and of early Christian records was to show that there had been no golden age from which the later quest for community could be measured. The apostolic church revealed a variety of polities and factions, led by gifted spokesmen as distinguished as Paul and Peter. The idea of restoring a primitive community and using it as a model for later community seemed ever more difficult. Alongside this disintegration of the model was the presentation of alternative paradigms of community: the other world religions were beginning to be viewed appreciatively. A certain relativism tended to grow from the act of observation: men in other communities also seemed to seek and find God. Why bother with Christian sociality?

The historical critics of Christianity as well as the advocates of the "history of religion" school, while they helped complicate the faith of many believers, also helped them refine their analysis. They both contributed to an understanding which saw that the religious impulse was socially based. Add to these the contentions of students of industrialization and urbanization that modern life is inevitably built on complex relationships and that in the modern city "we are members one of another," plus the political contentions for the welfare state and various kinds of socialism, and the background stands out. Whether or not Protestant man was willing to go along with it on his "secular" side, he did belong to a kind of analog to "the body of Christ" and his destiny was socially determined.

During those late nineteenth century years the sociology of religion worked its way into analysis of community, both compromising and supporting historic doctrines of the church in Protestantism. From that time on nontheological factors had to be introduced into any ecumenical discussion; men could write, as Robert Lee did, of *The Social Sources of Church Unity* or as H. Richard Niebuhr before him had of *The Social Sources of Denominationalism.* The sociologist of religion could track the mystic, the existentialist, or the individualist to his lair—and then proceed to provide the tools to help locate each in communities which he may have thought he was rejecting. He could suggest what psycho-social needs in man religion was addressing and could relate "the community of the Holy Spirit" to the other social pole, "the institutions of men in history."[177] The sociologists of religion have also served to demonstrate the ways in which Protestant community is itself shaped by cultural and social forces that were partly secular, partly religious. They were able to demonstrate that there is a social construction of reality which gives man his revelation and nurture, also in Christianity. From Karl Marx they learned how people in groups work to transform the world of nature and matter and to fabricate a history. They glanced backward into Protestant history to see how various left-wing religious forces had participated in such ventures.[178] The social analysts of religion could rely on phenomenologists like Maurice Merleau-Ponty to see "perception as a way to the world." The believing Protestant has already been inserted into a world before his primal concepts of subject and object take form. "My body is wherever there is something to be done"; and my body is not where Tarzan's or Robinson Crusoe's was, away from civilization. Following the language analysts, these social thinkers have taught the churches to see that language itself is social in character. "Language, then, is the form of community life, in the sense that it makes us present to each other, not as separate individuals, but precisely as members to one another," wrote Brian Wicker, with the work of Ludwig Wittgenstein in mind.[179]

The case for sociality based on language is most compelling in Protestantism, dependent as it is on "the Word." As soon as any attempt is made at communicating, one draws on a language shaped in community. The Bible makes no sense at all except in the setting of God's revelation to His people; most of the biblical metaphors for the Church can be translated into some version or other of talk about people in clusters. Images, metaphors, symbols are all conditioned by the experience of community. The word "father," rich in connotations in a stable and creative home, is incomprehensible as a signification of a loving God to some children in a slum where fathers are possibly unknown or unwelcome. Terms such as the "Kingship" or "Lordship" of Christ imply people who are led by a king; the Israel of old and the new community in Christ are prototypes for what follows in the name of Christianity. Where the confessors or theologians were occasionally reluctant to see the out-and-out or top-to-bottom social and communal character of Protestant faith, the philosophers and social analysts have stepped in to help them, and the theology of community can be reappraised in fresh ways today.[180]

Far from being born as an individualistic protest, most of Protestantism inherited ancient doctrines of the church. Reformers did not begin as carefree and casual destroyers of Catholic ecclesiastical symbolism. Many of them first asked whether it could even be that they were possibly wrong and the whole papal church was right—so concerned were they over the ruptures in the church. Yet when they came to the conclusion that they had to leave, or when they were excommunicated, they immediately set out to reconstruct the reality of the Church in their own new situations. Only the radicals believed that there was nothing to retrieve from the medieval church. For the rest, the "one, holy, catholic, and apostolic" Church confessed in the creeds was to be theirs. Yet there was more variety in the applications of the doctrine at the time of the birth of Protestantism. Protestants could retain baptism, the Lord's Supper, the Bible, the doctrine of God, but they had to reject the Catholic version of administering the church.[181]

The most immediate and vivid signal of the change came in the attack on the papacy and with it on the hierarchy. The drama of that act is often lost on later Protestants, who take for granted the ease with which the papal church was left behind. To be a Protestant is to reject the papacy; therefore, it must have been easy to reject it—so goes the thinking. The problem with such thought, however, is that papacy stood at the pinnacle of a structure of beliefs and administration which helped hold together the world of sixteenth century men and women. Who knew what would happen to the universe if it were toppled? Who knew for sure whether saving alternatives could be presented?

The reformers made no mistake about the integrality of the papal issue in Catholic thought. As late as the twentieth century Pius X, in 1906, was able to continue to define the Church as "the mystical Body of Christ . . . a society of men headed by rulers having full and perfect powers of governing, instructing and judging. It follows that this Church is essentially an unequal society . . . a society comprising two categories of persons." And at the head of one category, the clerical-hierarchical, was the pope. The Protestant movement wanted to remove the sense of inequality and the division between the two categories. Striking out at the pope was the biggest step toward doing both.[182]

If after the original trauma it became relatively easy to live without the papacy and to come up with a variety of alternative church orders, this did not solve everything. A second problem immediately came to the surface. The Reformation took root independently in nation after nation under leaders who did not fully agree with each other. From the first it was clear that the disruption would not lead merely to one counter-Church but to a competitive cluster of churches.

What happens then to the reality of the "one, holy, catholic, and apostolic" Church, to which most Protestants were giving much more than lip service? If there was to be an Anabaptist and a Presbyterian, a Calvinist and a Mennonite church what would one do about his profession of a single church? Among the variety of answers there came a set of adaptations of the old Augustinian distinction between the visible and the invisible Church. This distinction was most congenial to Calvin. Luther preferred the language of an inward and an outward Church.

Significantly, none of the reformers wanted to take seriously the invisibility of the Church, if by that was meant only a doctrinal reality, a Platonic entity, an idea in the mind of God that was in no way to be realized in the world. Luther and the Lutheran confessions repeatedly and explicitly repudiated such a concept of the Church. Why? Because the Gospel always convoked a visible and tangible assembly of believers, a congregation of saints, a *communio sanctorum*. Meanwhile, even within the congregations where the Gospel was preached in its purity and the sacraments were properly administered, there could well be hypocrites and faithless people masquerading as believers. All that did not trouble Luther, as one example, doctrinally; the Holy Spirit knew who His own were, and the sorting could come later.[183]

At the same time, even where the Gospel was not being purely preached or the sacraments fully administered according to God's ordinances, the Spirit could be at work, and true believers—thus visible members of the Church even if they were "outwardly" mislocated—could exist. They had existed during the ages of the papal church. The consistent note was this: the Church is people, it is personal, it is a visible "inward" company of believers occasioned by Gospel and sacraments.

The issue for Calvin was similar; invisibility was not to be used to make the Church into a vague idea or ideal. What was invisible about the true Church was not its nature or membership but its boundaries. One could not know how many respondents to the Spirit's inner testimony there were in the papal church or in the other Protestant churches, just as one could not know how many poseurs there were in the Church where the Gospel was properly preached. But in no case could the visible/invisible distinction militate against a favorite metaphor of Calvin's: the Church was the "Mother of the Godly." God ordained this company of believers and made of them a living organism. More than Luther he built into the doctrines of the Church that infused Reformed-Presbyterian circles the suggestion that a test of the Church was the solidarity of the brothers, the need for mutual assistance. And he scaled his version of ecclesiology by reference to the fact that those in the Church were the elect, placed there by God.[184]

In the Church of England the doctrine of the Church was taken over even more intact than on the Continent. In part this may have been made possible by the fact that the monarch and the whole church made a change from papal control at once. While there were to be reversions toward the papacy in the monarchy, the die had been cast and all that had been said about the church could continue to be asserted—except for papal supremacy. Therefore, perhaps not anticipating the rise of Puritanism, Separatism, Quakerism, Congregationalism, and other Nonconformities, the Anglican theologians did not devote themselves so readily to revising the distinctions between the visible and the invisible Church as did their continental counterparts. They retained apostolic succession in episcopacy as of the *esse* of the Church, though no extensive body of theory came into existence at the beginning to clarify the sanctions implied in this inheritance.[185]

The course followed by Anglican, Lutheran, Reformed, and Presbyterian churches led most of them to take the sociological form delineated as "churchly" by Ernst Troeltsch and a host of classifiers in his train. This distinction was posed over against "sectarian" or "mystical" views. In the Troeltschian picture the church type was essentially conservative, as were these groups which wanted to carry over whatever they could in continuity with the church of previous ages. It tended to seek to be coextensive with political boundaries of the empire, the nation, the state, the city. It was presumed that all the people within a given entity were members of "the church," baptized into it as a matter of course and remaining in it until and unless they took steps to exclude themselves.

The church type takes generally positive views of secular authority and, in effect, lets the secular arm then do some of its work. It is more ready than not to be identified with elites and ruling classes; in these cases prince-bishops came to govern Lutheranism, the monarch ruled Anglicanism, and the Calvinists provided leadership in what amounted to a theocracy.[186]

If, except for rejection of papacy and adaptation to the new situation in the matter of the visible and invisible Church these reformers really turned out to be conservative ecclesiologically, the same was not the case with the radical reformers. On few topics was the split within the early Protestant forces more dramatic than on the subject of the nature of the Church. The left-wing Protestants moved on entirely different premises toward dramatically different goals. They would have nothing of the trappings of the sociological "church type," and happily accepted the terms to which Troeltsch could later apply the name "sect-type."[187]

The sect tends to be small, radical, turning its back on the world, demanding high standards of membership, and willing to exclude the half-hearted or deviant. It would count the support of ruling classes a sign that it must have compromised somewhere along the way. Sectarians conceived of themselves as God's people on the march, from the exodus of slavery to Roman Catholics and established Protestants alike, or as exiles in their midst. A sense that they were beleaguered and besieged marked their activities. We speak here of Mennonites, Dunkers, Schwenckfelders, Brethren, Anabaptists, Levellers, Diggers, and other radical reformist groups.

All these might also accept the idea of one, holy, catholic, and apostolic Church, but its realization was quite different for them. Basic to their interpretation was this disagreement with other Protestants. They repudiated many ideas of continuity. There had been no pure church through the medieval or papal centuries. To be sure, some took pains to trace the little sects that withdrew from mainline churchly life during the Middle Ages. But just as many others did not care about finding a thread of the true Church. Instead, they posited the idea of a fall in the Church, perhaps around the fourth century. When under Constantine the civil and religious authority became effectively one and when the church took responsibility for the culture, the original apostolic community was no more. The task of the Reformation was to restore and reinstitute the primitive New Testament community in the form it had held before that fall.

A whole new set of metaphors now came into play. The radicals and sectarians often preferred biblical language about the Kingdom to that associated with the Church. Kingdom imagery was kinetic, bold, promissory while "church-language" in their view was static, staid, and conservative. In place of talk about membership in a semicivil church, the Anabaptists enjoyed the reference to being called to discipleship and to finding communion on its terms. Fellowship was inevitably stressed, for in the sect people were even more conscious of their need for each other than they were in the less well-defined official churches.

Many similes or analogies came from the language of marriage, the family, and friendship. Even though most of these churches were pacifist in outlook, they borrowed military terms to describe the sought-after discipline and spirit of cameraderie. At the heart of their talk was the sense of voluntary participation. One was not simply baptized by birthright. Baptism was a matter of personal decision in response to the calling and inspiring Spirit, an act for believers only. The church was to be governed not by apathetic or tyrannical outsiders but by assenting and committed fellow believers. Much of the drama of the Reformation era and subsequent Protestantism has come in the interplay between the two main types of ecclesiology in the evangelical movements.

There was to be one further elaboration in the church/sect picture, this one occasioned not by theological initiative but by practical adjustments. Denominationalism, which had its roots in Puritan England, rose to nearly normative status in legally secularized and functionally pluralistic societies like that of the United States of America. In nine of the thirteen colonies when America was formed, "church" types had predominated, and Anglicans were established in the south and Congregationalists-Presbyterians in the north. But in the middle colonies and increasingly in the presence of northern and southern establishments many dissenting or sectarian traditions were present.[188]

The eventual result was to work out a national Constitution which was silent on the issue of favoring establishment and the matter was left up to individual states, all of which in about a half century rejected ecclesiastical establishment. But the new mixed situation produced a new ecclesial form and demanded a new term, for which "denomination" imposed itself with an inner logic. The word "denomination" does no more than denominate; it does not rank or favor churches over sects, or vice versa. It seems fair in that it forces all, including those with theological reserve clauses about the problem (including Roman Catholics or Anglo-Catholics) to accept the same terms as other groups do.

The denomination, then, was a tardy Protestant invention for societies where in fact numbers of churches had to coexist and compete. The ground rules of the denominational game assured that no church would be favored by the civil power, nor would any people find sanctions taken against them so long as they remained within a very broad and generally approved consensus. (Extreme groups have found their violations of the consensus inhibiting at times: Jehovah's Witnesses suffered over their beliefs about saluting the flag, Hutterites and Doukhobors over the matter of taxation, Christian Scientists over some health matters, and earlier Mormons in cases involving polygamy.[189])

The denomination also allows for free and fair competition. People may join the church of their choice or reject all churches. Meanwhile, within each group the members have the opportunity to work at keeping the integrity of their private and exclusivistic theological positions. They can even assure themselves that they represent the true visible Church, whether any other true visible churches agree with them or not.

Except for one fundamental distinction between the churches-in-continuity and the sects-after-the-fall, Protestantism, then, developed relatively homogeneous views of the importance of Christian community and invoked widely accepted New Testament sanctions for the courses they had taken. But in the matter of organizing and governing the churches there was less agreement. The Lutheran Church of Sweden and the Church of England retained episcopacy in the apostolic succession as being of the *esse* of the Church. Other Scandinavian and German Lutheran churches and later Methodism provided for bishops, though without the same sanctions.

In much of Protestantism a kind of "presbygational" pattern developed. It derived in part from presbyterial and synodical pat-

terns. Laymen had more say in rule than they did inside episcopacy, and they played a larger part in calling pastors. Even more
innovative was the congregational polity. In this theory local control was basic, though the churches—each of which had the power
to call their ministerial leaders—might band together for common
purposes with others. But in this interpretation, the congregation
was the basic administrative, political, and theological unit of the
New Testament church and this basis was to endure in the church
of later ages.

The library of comparative polity can stretch as large as
could a library of comparative dogma in Protestantism, but it
may not tell too much about the ways in which community is
actually perceived and administered in most churches. A
strange amalgam of the three basic forms has tended to develop in the denominations, blurring the old church/sect lines.
In the modern, interactive, mobile world the congregational
polity does not retain its practical force as once expressed in
the intimacy of village cultures. Too many problems can be
faced only on a transcongregational basis, and when some prior
autonomy of local groups has been surrendered. So congregationalists became "consociational" long ago.[190]

More significantly and more recently they have made a more
secular adaptation. They have acquired a bureaucratic character, one which cancels out much of what was to be defended in
older congregationalism. On the other hand, as modern Protestant denominations, ecumenical forces, and bureaucracies have
moved into ever more controversial spheres of life, many people of nominally episcopal or presbyterian polity have turned
toward a "new localism," in order to assure budgetary and
policy-making control of local levels, to the frustration of the
national.[191]

Thus the politics and administration of Protestant community
have seen both increasing bureaucratization and increasing localism. To both of these has been added a frequent resort to
episcopal or quasi-episcopal styles of leadership among elected
or appointed heads. Wherever personal charisma is present, it
is possible for denominational presidents or jurisdictional heads
to enact many of the features of episcopal life, though without
theological or historical claims for apostolic succession in each
case. Not surprisingly, advocates of the three polities as well as
those working out annual adjustments in the face of exigencies,
tend to unite in one activity: backing up into the New Testa-

ment to prove that the adjustment they made is the one the apostolic Church had in mind all along.

Protestant Christians grasp and appropriate community in countless ways, not all of them routinized theologically or in official polity. Their fellowship, in pluralistic societies, has often and long cut across denominational lines, as they create ad hoc ecumenical cells for Christian conversation, study, prayer, or action. They participate in networks of agencies for good works or for propagating the Gospel. They may initiate cells or in some other way find primary, intimate, face-to-face groups. But most basic for Protestants has been the congregational or parochial unit. For centuries the field of vision of churchgoers has concentrated so much on the local church tower and the area or people that can be seen from it, that it is fair to say that the local reality preempts most of the attention that could theoretically have been given the ecumenical reality.[192]

"Parish" derives from ancient Greek words having to do with sojourning and mobility, and in Christian usage it denoted the band of exiles who gathered in a hostile setting somewhere or other. With Constantinianism and ecclesiastical establishment in the course of centuries it came to be a term applied to the geographical units within which one church was placed, and which implied a single pastoral care and charge. In the modern world, the parish came often to be equated with the congregation and inevitably meant a congregation of a specific denomination, one which might be in competition with the local churches of other denominations.

The face-to-face appeals being strongest in such units, most decisions about religion relied on the environments it created. The pastor of each was basic to value formation in the parish. Here worship, education, social life, and works of charity were carried on. The minister or priest became the chief spiritual leader, administrator, business and civic representative, and educator— though in larger parishes a division of labor was provided when economically feasible or where enough lay volunteers were available.[193]

The modern world has not dealt lightly with the parochial pattern. Ecumenical theology calls into question the competitive character of congregations in easy geographical range but out of confessional distance from each other. The parish does not remain a meaningful social unit in a time of great mobility; it does not reflect the natural boundaries of contemporary urban life. It is too intimate and small for some large tasks which need doing but is often too large to permit people to have a salutary integration into a social group.

While the parish or congregation presents an increasingly secular view of life gained from its environment, it is not free to shape even the basic religious values in an age of mass media and intercultural concepts. Not all congregations provide theologically intact challenges to their people, and members tend then to become unclear about their purposes. Ministers complain of uncertainty in their roles. Much of the activity of congregations has to be designed just to keep the institution going, and not always do they help members to be distinctively Christian in their relations to the world.

Despite the many obvious and demonstrable criticisms, the congregation or parish has not yet yielded its normative status. Because of its flaws, its critics have devoted much attention to alternative "underground-style" patterns. While some of these provide paradigms and parables or have an integrity of their own, none has come close to replacing the obsolescent parish models.[194]

Meanwhile, parishioners are prevented less than before from seeking community among the likeminded in other congregations of the same or other confessional groups, to link up nationally or internationally with fellow adherents of the same denomination, and now and then to share some larger experience of the one, holy, catholic, and apostolic Church. However they go about these tasks, twentieth century Protestants no less than their ancestors reveal their hungers for community and display a variety of attempts to satisfy these hungers.

10. THE LAYMAN AND THE PROFESSIONAL

The question of leadership and followership is among the most urgent in the history of religions. Religious groups like other organized human entities have characteristically been preoccupied with defining the meaning of adherence and the changes of status that go with conversion, initiation, maturation, or sanctity within a prescribed system. At least as much attention has gone into the question of the sanctions of leaders. In most religions some sort of appeal to supernatural claims is made as authorization for the leader's role.

Christianity has been no exception, since almost always after the first generation or two it has made distinctions between laity and clergy and has regularly reappraised the definitions and reexamined the rites and privileges of both. In Catholicism the clerical system was very complicated, with hierarchical ranks of deacons, priests, bishops, and—in a different category—cardinals and popes among the bishops. Protestantism has allowed for different ranks within ministry, but except for episcopacy in the apostolic succession in a few churches, these ranks tend to follow functional and bureaucratic lines, and the fundamental division within Protestantism is simply between laity and clergy.

Protestantism has usually conceived of itself as having made distinctive contributions to the understanding of the laity and, even more, as having provided superior self-images for laymen and laywomen. An examination of both the history and the theology, however, suggests that the Protestant record has been self-contradictory and even paradoxical. Some traditions which stressed high doctrines of the laity have, in practice, been quite clericalized and others which have high doctrines of the clergy have known a vital lay life. Other factors beside doctrinal definition have played a part in these historical developments.[195]

The term "laity" comes from the Greek word *laos,* which means people, as in the "whole people of God." So it was used in the New Testament. A few later scholars have argued, with some warrant, that a distinction between laity and clergy does not appear there, because the early church had only what is today called a clergy and lacked what is now conceived of as laity. That is, all members were somehow explicitly to be active as ministers. By the end of the first century the clergy/lay distinction begins to appear in the writings of Clement of Rome.[196]

Through subsequent centuries, with the professionalization of the ministry, "lay" began to take on connotations of ignorance and vulgarity. One who is a layman in the presence of law or medicine is one who is not expected to be very intelligent about these spheres. So, too, the layman in religion is not assumed to be knowledgeable about what really matters in theology and church-manship.

Thoughtful Christians have always been uneasy about such a situation and have pleaded for a recovery of New Testament realities. They regularly remark that authentic rebirth in the life of the Church comes with the recovery of the laity. But the tendency through Christian history has been to fail to experience the full life of all its ministers, namely, all its people.

The distinction between clergy and laity was heightened through the Catholic centuries, so that by the time of the Reformation the two were clearly set apart on qualitative grounds. The clergyman was not only "more" or "higher" in the scheme of God, but he was also "other" in the plan of salvation. Some definitions of the Catholic Church even went so far as to say that the church was comprised of the clergy: popes, bishops, priests. This body was surrounded by the laity. The sacramental system was dispensed through the clergy. The monastic orders, whether made up of ordained priests or lay brothers and sisters, was also set aside and marked for special regard. Especially when Christians came to rate virginity higher than marital life, celibacy added to the special merits that went with monastic or clerical orders. Implicitly, the status of the laity was thus lower.

The Reformation was seen to be a correction of this situation. The leaders at least gave lip service and, more frequently, offered genuine evidence that they wanted to see laity and clergy related in a new way. Best known among these was Martin Luther, a relatively conservative leader who on this point tried to be radical. There was no separate and special path to salvation for priest or monk. He had no particular route, no higher rank or richer display of merits. In fact, said Luther to reinforce the point, the faithful Christian mother who was washing diapers or scrubbing the floor was serving God more faithfully than the monk who scourged himself and mouthed praises all day long.

The Protestant doctrine of vocation, a sense that all of life was hallowed, was born of such expressions. Many went further than Luther. Some radical reformers even did away with the whole concept of a set-apart and professional clergy, though many of them in their second-generational life joined the most established reformers in retaining a clergy.[197]

The classic Protestant phrase for the new version of the laity was "the priesthood of all believers." The phrase was designed to carry with it rich biblical connotations and was intended not to detract from the priesthood of priests or ministers. Rather, it set out to say that what had been the property of the few was now that of all Christians. Many priestly functions had been removed in the Protestant picture. The professional ordained man no longer served as the only mediator of holy things through the sacramental system. This meant that all believers could share in the enduring works of priests. What were these?

In the case of Luther, they amounted chiefly to intercession. Zwingli tended to join Luther in this affirmation, so that it may be said that there was no laity (because there were no nonpriests) in their conception. In the case of Calvinism it was somewhat different; there, it has been said, there were no priests—all were laymen. Calvin would do away with the connotations of priestliness, preferring alternative terms to "the priesthood of all believers." Priesthood was an honorary title, not a description of function in Calvinism.

Priesthood, then, meant the power to intercede for brother Christians before God's throne of grace; to bear mutual witness; to confess, repent, forgive, and be forgiven. Later advertisers of the degree to which Protestantism enlarged the lay role have argued that out of this sentiment was born a whole charter for modern democracy in the civil realm and participation in the ecclesiastical.[198]

Without question, Protestants have assigned much responsibility to laymen in the administration of their parishes and larger ecclesiastical units. They have seen to it that provision is made for lay determination of fundamental questions in church life. In most groups laymen also take part in the assemblies which debate and formulate theological and doctrinal concerns. It may also be— though this is more difficult to prove—that the lessons learned, for example, in Congregational or Presbyterian churches bred in people the desire to see privilege and rights extended in the governmental realm. Those who are self-determining in one area may very well seek to extend their power in others. The evidence on this score—one thinks of Lutheranism's general sense of servility in the civil realm, despite the doctrine of the priesthood of all believers—is ambiguous.

Despite high doctrines and large roles for the laity, it cannot be said that Protestantism through its history has often realized a fulfilled status for the laity. The roots of the problem are difficult to discern. Two explanations are advanced most frequently. The first has a secular tone to it. By the time Protestantism emerged on the scene, the secular experience had advanced enough that a characteristic feature of complex society, "the division of labor," had set in. This meant not only that the laity were increasingly drawn away from diffuse and ill-defined ways of life that had permitted them to devote themselves to affairs of the church. It also meant that they were not free to develop the kinds of expertise which the modern, technical world demanded. To put it another way, what was everybody's job was nobody's job, and even without scriptural sanction, metaphysical claims, or a tradition to which to appeal, mere professional need provided the foundation for elevated views of the ministry.

The absence of biblical distinctions made it difficult for Protestant theologians to outline exactly what a layman did, given the professionalization of the clergy. The churches that practiced infant baptism allowed for emergency baptism by laymen and women, but this was nothing distinctively Protestant, and almost all churches prescribed that an ordained man ordinarily should baptize. Little, therefore, was implied by that rubric.

In many traditions a layman could assist in the administration of the Lord's Supper, and some service books were sufficiently vague so as to leave unsettled the question as to whether an ordained minister had to be present—hardly the grounds for a high doctrine of the laity in the sacramental life. In theory all Christians could confess to each other and counsel, but the professional minister was set aside for that, and therefore a special prestige went along with pastoral activities. Perhaps the greatest gap was in the matter of preaching.

Hendrik Kraemer, a modern theologian who sided with the laity in the question of church renewal, argued that the undeveloped attitude toward preaching was behind Protestantism's failure to develop its theology of the laity. In principle, all Christians were able to preach because all were to witness to each other, to edify the brothers, and to witness to the outside world—good definitions of preaching. But in the gathered congregation, the mainline reformers at least, and along with them a surprising number of radicals and free-church men, set aside the formal act of preaching. When churches were built, the position and height of the pulpit provided a symbolic authority for the person engaged in the central act of Protestant worship. Universities and seminaries concentrated on preaching.

People were trained to measure the quality of worship on a particular day by assessing the value of the sermon and the competence of the preacher. While it was true that men stressed that the preacher was a mere mortal with fallible thought processes, he was also to assert that when he spoke, it was God's Word that was being uttered. Given all these supports, the act of preaching more than anything else became normative for Protestant delineations of ministerial roles which would replace the old Catholic priestly understanding.

When it came to preaching, however, Dr. Kraemer pointed out that Protestants equivocated in their view of the priesthood of all believers. In the process, they paid respects to their high view of the act of preaching but they downgraded the laity. Those Protestant groups that consistently chartered lay preaching were rare. One was not to preach in the public congregation, it was often said, unless he were "properly called." In theory anyone could be "properly called," but from the beginning to the present, most Protestant churches have certified as qualified only those who had special training in the interpretation of the Bible and the act of preaching.

All this led to a certain intellectualization of the priestly role, and removed from consideration the contributions of simpler laymen. Where there were laymen more qualified to interpret and to speak, this meant that there must be some special sense of calling for a clerical caste, the members of which could speak even though they did not have as good credentials as those laymen who were silenced or silent.

Of course, there have been exceptions. Some of the continental pietists authorized the equivalent of lay preachers. The Wesleyan Methodist movement went further than most others, particularly in England, to provide for lay preachers. But these men were so often selected and trained with such care that they became clericalized laymen. They were the virtual equivalents of ordained men in style and interest, even if they brought the added vantage of their secular employment to their preaching.

With the increased freedom and informality of the modern world, more and more churches have provided, through devices such as "Laymen's Sunday," the opportunity for sermons by non-professionals. These continuances, however, only call attention to the exceptionality of what is going on. When most Protestants hear of preaching, they think of it as the central corporate act of their churches; when they think of preaching they usually think of specially trained, ordained males. When they do, they instinctively see laymen and women as having other, secondary functions.

Despite such handicaps, the Protestant laity has often emerged as a responsible majority in evangelicalism's still-clerical society. While most laymen and laywomen have remained anonymous, as have their counterparts in political, military, and business society, different models of lay leadership present themselves in Christian history. Rarely have these been theological. John Calvin, for instance, was a layman at the time he wrote his great *Institutes of the Christian Religion;* his training was chiefly in law and humanities. But Calvinism has made little of his status at the time the greatest Protestant systematic theology was written, and few members of the Reformed Church are made aware of it. Hendrik Kraemer, mentioned above, is a modern example. The term "theologian" usually connotes to Protestants a seminary- or university-trained man who works in a clerical setting.[199]

Since early Protestantism often progressed by the use of the sword and since so many issues of the time were settled on the battlefield, the military leaders who led Protestant causes were often cited as models of Christian militancy and manhood. Best known of these were Oliver Cromwell in the Puritan revolution in England and Gustavus Adolphus, a pious and noble Swedish ruler who came to the partisan evangelical cause in the time of the Thirty Years' War.

Another area in which Protestants have been conscious of the distinctive contributions of laymen has been in the arts; Bach, Rembrandt, and Milton have been regarded as God's servants. Law is another field of lay expertise; Hugo Grotius is remembered as a paradigm of leadership in this area. In the modern world and in the industrial age, the successful entrepreneur, the business man who professed to live by Protestant principles, was often advertised to young people as a model of Christian success and charity.[200]

One realm in which the talents of laymen have been put to work more readily than in some others is the whole evangelical-missionary enterprise. The Moravian Count Ludwig von Zinzendorf was a layman. His piety, theology, energy, and organizing ability had an intercultural and interconfessional outreach. The Anglo-American age of missions began with the efforts of a shoemaker, William Carey. The lay catechist often was a recognized figure in mission fields, as was his self-sacrificing counterpart, the medical missionary or nurse.

Laymen's abilities were put to work in organizing the network of benevolent agencies: in America, the Tappan brothers provided funds and skill along with inspiration for their "errand of mercy"; in England, Henry Thornton and William Wilberforce, along with others of the Clapham Sect, headquartered near London. They set a style for lay response that was widely copied for scores of years to come. In the rise of the ecumenical movement numbers of laymen, among them John R. Mott and J. H. Oldham, played organizing roles, though it must be said that as the years passed the unitive organizations bore increasingly clericalized casts.[201]

When a woman's name turns up on the pages of the male-dominated books of Protestant history, she will almost always be a lay person. To cite this adds another dimension to Protestantism's sense of caste and, some would say, denial of the priesthood of all believers through its conventional historic limitation of ministry to men. Some of the radical groups allowed for women prophets, and there were women who were founders and shapers of some traditions: Anne Hutchinson in America's first generation of "enthusiasts"; Mother Ann Lee of "the Shakers"; Mary Baker Eddy, at the fringes of late nineteenth century American Protestantism; Ellen White, who did much to establish Seventh-day Adventism; but most of the more established groups did not change on this point until well into the twentieth century, and indeed it can be questioned how much actual change has occurred.

Women were denied ordination and excluded from the act of public preaching largely, it is usually pointed out, because St. Paul, speaking out of the context of his culture, wanted women's role limited. Critics pointed out that Paul was often personally harsh in his treatment of women, and that many of his other opinions on similar subjects were conveniently neglected by later Christians (the matter of covering the head in worship being an example), but his precedent stood. It was reinforced, of course, by the general Protestant perpetuation of cultural imagery which kept women in subordinate roles. The widening concept of the ordination of women may do much to help Protestantism come to terms with the questions of what laymen and ministers are. Until then, the male character of the ministerial office will continue to complicate the attempts of those who want to keep biblical concepts of a single *laos* of God alive.

Denied ordination, women nevertheless have often distinguished themselves. One whole new elite was the long-suffering semiprofessional caste of ministers' wives. The ending of the practice of celibacy throughout early Protestantism meant something new in Western Christianity. Not for centuries had a woman been at the side of the priest as a wife. Now the Protestant parsonage or manse took on a cultural importance. Very often it was the center of learning and instruction; almost always it was watched for the models of family life and morality that were being projected.

In almost any society where Protestantism has long been strong it has been recognized that the lists of people of prominence are inordinately lengthened by the names of sons and daughters of Protestant parsonages. Their mothers are usually given the credit for influencing them. The restoration of the monastic ideal—something that would be theologically permitted in many sectors of Protestantism—has been difficult.[202]

Excluding female monarchs, some of whom did not consider themselves to be lay people in the conventional sense, Protestantism still evidences plenty of examples of women's achievement. Selina, Countess of Huntingdon, provided a center for the expression of evangelical life in the eighteenth century revivals in England. Hannah More of the Clapham Sect distinguished herself. Elizabeth Fry and Florence Nightingale in prison-reform and nursing were often cited as exemplars of evangelical virtues. In the United States women like the Grimké sisters were aggressive abolitionists, and the temperance and moral-reform societies were often led by women. Many of the pioneer suffragettes, women who worked to extend the franchise to their sex, were motivated by their Protestant backgrounds. It must also be said, however, that as often as not they left their evangelicalism in order to free themselves from what they saw to be the restrictive residues of Protestantism's demeaning views of women.

Women were active in the rise of Sunday schools (a factor that retarded acceptance of Sunday schools in some circles). They were set aside as deaconesses in the middle of the nineteenth century, particularly by continental Protestants and American Methodists. The missionary wife, nurse, and teacher inspired others to see the part women could play in church service. But they were rarely permitted to preach, and their confinement in the laity added to the restrictive character of the definitions of laity.[203]

If Protestant laymen and laywomen have been active in the more conservative evangelical causes, liberalizing forces have also made use of their talents. In the rise of British Christian Socialism in the middle of the nineteenth century a layman like J. Malcolm Ludlow played a distinctive role, and in the American Social Gospel Movement, Richard T. Ely was a lay leader. Still, despite the rhetoric of liberalism, laymen did not play a larger part in the sector of Protestantism that was most ready to assign them nominally higher status and broader duties.[204]

When one thinks of the leadership of the Younger Churches in the ecumenical era, he again finds himself most conscious of clerical participants; laymen have rarely been the leaders. The ecumenical movement has had departments on the laity. Books on the emergence of the laity or the renewal of their ministry abound, but after decades of experiment many professionals talked cynically about the rarity of theologically equipped and ecclesiastically subtle laymen.[205]

Virtually all Protestant polities assign a special importance to lay participation in the various church assemblies and governing bodies. Vestries, councils, boards of trustees, deacons, and elders provide power bases for them, and in many church orders meetings of the whole congregation provide a platform for lay expression on policy and doctrine. Congregationalism most of all wanted basic decisions to be in the hands of the whole group of the faithful. Presbyterianism elevated the lay elder to decisive rank; churches with synodical policy, Reformed and Lutheran, expected much of representative laymen. Even Episcopal polity is thoroughly at home with the power of laymen in institutions such as the House of Deputies. In England, in the Houses of Parliament it is laymen who have debated revisions in the Book of Common Prayer and other equally important matters.

Twentieth century Protestantism has seen many experiments with new forms of lay life. On the Continent the Evangelical Lay Academy has been widely advertised as an emerging pattern for ministry. People of various walks of life go there for intensive preparation or discussion to equip them to carry Christ into the world of their work. Centers of renewal in England and America have often been built to enlarge the influence of a layman who held to particular Christian visions, and much of the effort to propagate new styles of Christian living has proceeded through such channels. It must be said, however, that though these experiments have been important as parables and for their own intrinsic worth, they involve only a tiny minority of Protestants. Most church members probably carry in their minds centuries-old stereotypes of lay passivity or circumscribed positions.[206]

The layman has not been alone in uncertain status; the minister's role has also suffered from lack of clarity, since so little attention has been paid to the question of the sanctions for the clergyman's work. The credentials for preaching in the Bible had little to do with educational experience; herdsmen, shepherds, and fishermen were called, often suddenly. Some Protestants, among them certain Baptists and primitive Gospel groups, have kept this memory alive in their approach to the sense of call for ministry. Others demanded an educated ministry made up of men who underwent long and strenuous introductions to theology and pastoral care.[207]

One became a minister by experiencing or recognizing some sort of call. Then he usually underwent special preparation. A confusing link in the chain of his development came at the point of the rite which set him aside and chartered his task. For most Protestants, this has been called ordination. Whereas ordination has been regarded sacramentally in Catholicism, almost no Protestants have been willing to include it in the sacramental category. The nearest one comes to such a concept is in Anglican Orders, where apostolic succession has been retained as being integral to the act of ordination and the effectual character of priestly ministry. The precedents for this were seen in the New Testament story of the laying on of hands of the Seven in the book of Acts; the setting aside of Paul and Barnabas at Antioch; Paul's reference to "overseers" in one of his speeches; his words to Timothy (in a late writing which most scholars do not ascribe to Paul), advising him to regard highly the charisma that came with the laying on of Paul's hands in a kind of ordaining act. Certain spiritual gifts were seen to be conferred to the ordained through these acts.

The Anglicans, then, kept more of the inherited Catholic patterns of priesthood than did many Protestant groups, who saw authority residing more in the charisma of the person than in his office. In the episcopal traditions (operative also in the Church of Sweden and some other Lutheran circles) there was also more readiness to keep the sense of grades of ministry, again on the basis of New Testament claims. Itinerant evangelists, apostolic leaders, teachers, preachers, prophets, bishops, presbyters, pastors, and deacons were mentioned, at least in the New Testament. The baptized mature male candidate, properly trained, presented himself for Orders and was then chartered to carry out the office of ministry. Some Anglo-Catholics see ordination to be a sacrament of a secondary character, but few other non-Roman Catholics in the West do.[208]

Curiously, no matter how limited the role of the individual layman or how high or low the definition of ministerial functions may be, much of Protestantism has tended to be both congregational and episcopal in practice in the modern world. It is congregational in that much of the power lies in the hands of lay assemblies, which usually determine the dominating fiscal policies and, with them, many other decisive matters of church life. It is episcopal in that, no matter how organized, some sort of *primus inter pares*, first among equals, rises to become a pastor to pastors and an overseer of groups of congregations so that certain common tasks can be undertaken. Often there is no theological sanction for this role, except in formally episcopal bodies; mere bureaucratic necessity or personal authority may contribute to such a situation.[209]

Ministerial functions, then, are also surprisingly similar throughout Protestantism, no matter how varied the sanctioning concepts of ordination and polity may be. In more settings one pictures the Protestant minister to be related to a single parish or congregation (though in modern times very large minorities fulfill other roles) and there he is known first of all for preaching. Sociological studies demonstrate that he often conceives of preaching as his most important task and his people usually picture him first as a preacher. Secondarily, he administers the rites of the church, including baptism, confirmation, and the Lord's Supper, along with some rites which are also shared by non-Christians, marriage and burial being preeminent.[210]

The minister plays an important part in shaping congregational policy and, where he is an effective and respected pastoral leader, more often than not will find ready assent on the part of his laity. He may instruct the young for confirmation and will normally take a part in adult education. He is the parson or representative person in the community, and is to take a part (usually noncontroversial) in its affairs. He will often be a counselor. Insofar as he conceives of his task as being prophetic, he will also challenge his followers and the community at large to change their way of life.[211]

The question of the garb of the cleric has been open in Protestantism. In general, the more priestly ministries (which are episcopal, altar-centered, and depend on the charisma of the office) have favored more ceremonial garb in and out of the sanctuary. In modern Anglicanism, Lutheranism, and elsewhere the "Roman" collar—probably an Anglican invention of the 1860s—has many wearers. Those who conceive of their ministry as being more prophetic, depending more on the charisma of the man and his message, and the low-church or free-church ministers in general have worn more subdued or conventional garb in the sanctuary and dressed like the laymen of their time and place outside it.

There have been exceptionally wealthy and well-positioned Protestant ministers. In England, for some generations the third sons of aristocrats took Holy Orders. While they might be third in the familial system, they often inherited comfortable situations. In modern America, the successful metropolitan minister has often been a kind of entrepreneur who gathered a devoted affluent following which took care of his needs. But privilege of that sort has certainly been the exception, not the rule.

The style of living of the Protestant minister has generally not contributed to anticlericalism. Seldom have the charges of fiscal self-seeking been made to stick. More often, the minister lives at or below the economic level of the people he serves, from lower through upper middle class in recent societies. Before that, for example in Germany and England, many were conceived of as lower-rank civil servants, with very little income. In earlier societies members provided not only housing but food and favors to help ministers keep body and soul together. They have, in general, projected portraits of men of modest circumstances with a professional status belying their humble means.

In complex societies, of course, the minister has taken on an ever longer list of duties. In the United States, the theologian H. Richard Niebuhr asked ministers to come to terms with their role and to see themselves as "pastoral directors," and not only as priests or preachers. The pastoral directors had oversight of extremely complicated congregational organizations, and found themselves dispersing and distributing their energies through a variety of administrative tasks that were seldom anticipated in Christian history. In this role they became directors of laymen whose special talents could be better used when they helped create a climate in which their administration and ministry could be free and effective.[212]

While probably an accurate description of the actuality, many ministers rejected the picture as being far from normative or ideal, even if they themselves could not successfully reach back to older priestly or preaching models. The image of ministry remained as confused as that of the laity. Many Protestants have made virtues of these necessities and argue that lack of clear job descriptions for laymen and clergymen will continue to bring them together and make them ready to take on the unanticipated tasks which the world presents.

11. THE MEANINGS OF BAPTISM

Most religions recognize certain symbolic rites which make visible some of the realities that cannot always be easily dealt with verbally. These sacraments, as Westerners are wont to call them, combine the myth or history on which the religion is based with certain needs in the present life of individual adherents. The ritual accompanying them provides symbolic order in an otherwise often apparently random and plotless universe. The participant in the rite becomes part of an experience which somehow transcends ordinary existence.

These sacred acts serve as a kind of transaction point between the sacral and profane worlds. As such, they impart some sort of power and effect a change in the lives of those who share in them. Space and time are somehow overcome, and the divine reality is made present. Words serve to interpret the act or to enhance its value. Protestantism is no exception: it also has such rites, some features of which it shares with other religions.[213]

The family of rites dealing with stages in personal development fulfills several functions in many sacral societies. For one thing, expression must be found for interpreting the juncture of nature and history, for bringing the observed cosmos into relation with the particular meaning incorporated into a myth or a revelation. This natural bond is connected to a temporal or developmental one, for the rite is associated with stages on life's way or with passage at crucial phases (such as birth, coming of age, marriage, and death). Often sexual connotations are also associated with such rites.

Particularly when one becomes a part of a new community either through conversion, as a result of special deeds, or simply because he or she has grown up, he may have a conscious or unconscious desire to mark a new birth. He seeks something which will represent his desire to leave the past behind so that he can make new beginnings in a new context. He may be conscious of a guilt that came with his former way of life and want a definite separation. The physical act of washing can then be transformed into a symbolic or spiritual act. Lustrations are common in the world's religions. The act of washing takes on the function of an initiation rite.

Protestantism, appearing where and when it did in world history, adopted some of these phenomena and rejected or radically transformed others. It was born in repudiation of the Catholic sacramental-hierarchical system, and in reaction played down features which it saw to be magical in Catholic initiation rites. At the same time, the medieval world-view was disappearing. Whereas not long before, sacraments served as transparent sets of symbols, open to another and transcendent order, at the time of Protestantism's birth a certain skepticism had already set in, not about the existence of another order—atheism in its modern form had not yet appeared—but about the ability of elements from the created order serving as the Creator's authentic bearers.[214]

Protestants feared that the symbols could be endowed with so much power and received with so much devotion that the reality behind them would be neglected in favor of the visible and the tangible. A certain intellectualization of religion was also going on, and this led Protestantism to bring new attitudes to initiation rites, which in the Christian case meant baptism.

Protestantism generally created or let develop a break between nature and sacrament. Water symbolism had played a great part in many religions, and the Bible is rich in evoking it. The world was created as a chaos of land and water; Yahweh acted to divide the land and the water. The children of Israel used water as the element for passage from bondage to freedom, leaving behind not only the land of Egypt but the pursuing troops of the Pharaoh. The psalms of the Hebrew Scriptures are rich in descriptions both of the terrors of wild and mysterious water and of the healing effects of sweet and serene waters. In the New Testament, John came to announce the forthcoming Kingdom, transforming Jewish water rites into baptism. Jesus came down to the Jordan, there to be baptized as prototype for those who were to follow Him.

Protestantism retained the use of water and in its sermonic elaborations on baptism often made reference to these historical dimensions of rescue. However, the natural power of the element was not only neglected but often deliberately obscured from recall and significance. The biblical history was reviewed but the natural matrix out of which the history grew was not seen to be pertinent.

With this neglect of the natural there was also an almost complete playing down of sexual symbolism. Whereas in Catholic piety something at least had been made of the water enveloping the creature in the womb, this feature largely disappeared in Protestant expression. Medieval baptism was rich with sexual symbols: not a few interpreters called attention to the womblike character of the font. In the Easter (baptizing season) rites, the large Paschal candle was ceremoniously plunged into the womb of water, and sometimes drippings of the warm wax were ritually dropped into that water. The use of the candle was rarer in Protestantism. If there were any association between womb and font, this passed to the unconscious, for it is rarely referred to after the Reformation.[215]

What survived from the medieval understanding was neither the tie to nature nor to sexuality but, rather, the washing, related to the sin and guilt of the previous life, and the sense of initiation for a new birth or a second start and new opportunity in life. To these survivals Protestantism added new and predictable aspects. Most important was the new power associated with "the Word." The biblical command and promise received prominent attention and the natural element was used chiefly because of this command and not because of any special understanding of water. Thus Martin Luther explained that water without the Word was simple or natural water only—a concept hard to picture in many religions, when either there is no such thing as simple, natural water or it can be transformed into a quasi-magical substance when a part of the sacred ritual.

If the word was now what mattered, the corollary of this was faith. Many Protestant debates centered around the question of how faith was a part of baptism. To this nexus of word and faith was added the importance of the command. Sometimes those who were unwilling to say exactly what baptism did effect or why it was otherwise necessary did resort to claiming that it was done for mysterious reasons since, at least, it was a dominical order, an explicit command by Christ.

The approach which stressed word plus faith plus command should surprise no one who has studied Protestantism; it comes with perfect consistency. Speculation about the power of the water disappeared. The story of the baptisms of John and Jesus was regularly recounted, and the biblical occasions in which Paul or others baptized were carefully scrutinized for clues as to the proper means of administering and interpreting baptism. Protestantism is a Word religion, and even this one of two most sacred rites is not permitted to obscure that feature.[216]

As a result, the use of water came to be a less and less visible feature, from the lavish water of the Jordan River through the cisterns of the early church, past the large medieval fonts, to the small handbowls often in use in churches where the minister took care not to splash so much that an infant's garments would be dampened. Problems were created: one of the chief biblical texts about baptism was from Romans, chapter 6, wherein the believer is "buried" in the water and "rises" with Christ—an association hard to keep vivid when only a few drops of water are used.

Still, for all their debates about baptism, their neglect of water symbolism, their accenting of the word, almost all Protestants have kept some form of baptism. The Quakers, who often scorned external rites, rejected it, and some modern liberal churches like the Unitarian make it unnecessary or optional. On the other hand, some groups made more of baptism, now reinterpreted, than Roman Catholics did, and the name survived in their church names, whether Anabaptist (for baptizing again), or simply, Baptist. Most but not all Protestant groups that practice baptism require it for the member who wishes to live a complete Christian life. Interpretations of what happens to the person who neglects or despises baptism vary.

The relations of community to baptism have differed widely. In European nations where the church was officially established by law, virtually whole populations were baptized, as they had been in the Catholicism which was supplanted there. Even in the twentieth century, after formal church disestablishment, the rite has been continued and almost all children—unless their parents have taken pains to list themselves as dissenters—are brought for baptism, whether or not they ever reappear in church. Words implying that the parents are covenanting to bring up the child under Christian disciplines are usually repeated, but there may be no intention on their part to live up to these. On the other hand, there as well as in parts of the world where the faith has been part of a voluntary pattern in church life, such good intentions may exist and infant baptism be taken seriously.

The administration of baptism as entrance to community has often differed wherever dissent reigns or wherever the community is considered to be sectarian. There adult baptism is a common means of guaranteeing that only faithful respondents will commit themselves or, in the case of infant baptism, that firm pledges will be exacted from the sponsoring parents.[217]

Observers of Protestant baptism would ordinarily see either of the following approaches. In the statistically overwhelming practice of baptism of infants, the ceremony is usually held in the church building. It may occur either in the setting of public worship or as a private adjunct to corporate liturgy. A font, usually a bowl set into a pedestal, is located at a prominent place. In the more liturgically formal churches, it may be at the entrance, as a symbol of baptism's significance as a rite of beginning. More frequently, however, it is in front of the congregation, near an altar or table and a pulpit. In most cases, an ordained minister or other especially set-apart person performs the rite. In some cases parents alone and other sponsors or godparents who speak for the child present that child, who is usually dressed in white. The age of the person may vary from a few days to a few weeks old, though, of course, people may be baptized at any time when they want to become members of the church, or their parents want them to. The minister reads the words of the baptismal liturgy and then applies water by pouring or sprinkling or daubing.[218]

In the case of adult baptism, or believer's baptism as it is sometimes called, the person presents himself or herself. The age may vary anywhere upward from nine or ten years, depending upon the church's judgment as to when people can responsibly take on a commitment of their own. Except in the more rigorous groups where river baptism is still practiced, the event may occur in a large prominent tank, which a minister and the person to be baptized, often both robed, enter. In this case, after the words are read and some pledges or professions have been spoken, the person is completely immersed.

Fundamentally, three versions of baptism have come to predominate in Protestantism. While they have much in common, each tells something about differing attitudes not only toward water or nature or rites of passage and the effectiveness of ritual washings but also about attitudes toward what faith is and does.

Since believer's baptism, usually of adults and by immersion, is the most radical departure from the way baptism is practiced in the Orthodox- and Catholic-majority parts of the Christian world, it should be discussed first. It arose in the sixteenth century, particularly among the dissenting groups who felt that the original reformers were not carrying their protest and changes far enough. The rebels against the reformers were strenuous in their objections to any view of the sacraments which might imply a sense of magic, and felt that infant baptism was just such a case.

What is more, their inquiries led them to the conviction that most of what the New Testament said about baptism applied best in the contexts where people could speak for themselves, could give assurance of their faith, and could promise to make a baptismal covenant. They reasoned that had Christ and the apostles desired infant baptism, with its drastic revision of this context, the Bible would have made the command clear and not left it in uncertainty.

Such an approach seemed at the same time to downgrade and to enhance the meaning of baptism. To the more catholic Christian, believer's baptism was a suggestion that baptism was not vital for man's salvation. Obviously, thousands of young Christians died before they reached the age at which there could be such styles of baptism, yet nowhere in their rhetoric did these groups speak as if they felt such young people died outside the range of God's mercies. Therefore, in their eyes His grace could be and was extended in some way outside a baptismal covenant. This seemed to make baptism a rite of secondary quality.

On the other hand, these early reformers, called Anabaptist because they baptized again (almost everyone presenting himself having been baptized earlier by Catholics or other Protestants), found that they were indeed calling special attention to the importance of baptism. Many of the Anabaptists, Baptists, and Dunkers, came to be named after this particular feature of their witness. They took baptism very seriously and had no difficulty showing that many New Testament values associated with the act could best be performed and fulfilled in the setting of believer's baptism.

The choice to reject infant baptism can be accounted for in two ways. Many Christians, among them the New England separatists in Congregationalism, wanted to raise the standards of church membership. They used baptism as a sign of such a discipline. As a consequence they became Baptist. On the other hand, some read the New Testament, were convinced that infant baptism was wrong, and because of this belief became separatists.

In both cases, elaborate efforts have been made to discern a line of continuity from John the Baptist through the early church and past the medieval sects into Reformation times and, of course, beyond, to show that God had not left himself without witness and that a true Church had always existed even in the eras when a magical form of baptism seemed to predominate.

The existence of "baptized pagans" in modern nations, where people go through the rite but have no intention of following its implications, has led believer's baptizers to continue their more disciplined approach. In the twentieth century some Protestants who have previously baptized infants, now reacting against the trivialization and casualness of the rite, have again argued that—whatever may be lost by the change—much would be gained if all Christians deferred baptism until it could be associated with commitment.

The accent in adult baptism is on a view of faith which assigns a large role to man's decision and will. No effort is made to remove the picture of God's initiative. It is asserted, however, that God's initiative relates to an assertive response by man. Man is converted, he comes to faith, he confesses that faith, and then he desires and receives baptism, ready to follow commands and to be obedient to Christ. In such an approach baptism is not so much an initiation rite for the first passage in life's way as the beginning of responsible participation in the church community.

The concept of regeneration or the idea that the water plus the word actually does something is excluded. It is more a symbol or a sign of a bond that has been effected between man and God rather than the occasion through which God works a new thing. In addition to this rationale, one more feature is sometimes added. The Baptist tradition makes much of freedom and of soul liberty, and feels that baptism of infants deprives them of the liberty to reject or stand apart from Christian community.[219]

The majority of Protestant churches do baptize infants as well as adults, and they practice what might be called reformed baptism because it shows marked changes from the Catholic rite and derives from the Reformed churches' tradition. As with believer's baptism, there seems to be a greater stress on faith in the word than in Catholicism, but a new accent falls on the meaning of the covenanting community out of which the parents come to present the child.

There is great concern that the central Protestant teaching about the forgiveness or remission of sins be associated with the act. The Heidelberg Catechism said that the purpose of baptism was "to have the forgiveness of sins from God, through grace, for the sake of Christ's blood, which He has shed for us in His sacrifice on the Cross, and also to be renewed by the Holy Ghost, and sanctified to be a member of Christ, so that we may more and more die unto sin, and lead a life blessed by God and without blame."

The formula "in Christ" is stressed: the baptized person, conscious or not, is to be found "in Christ." He is "clothed with Christ" or with Christ's righteousness. Whether he knows and feels it or not, he has experienced in baptism what Christ went through in death and resurrection. The new life has begun. It is a thoroughly Christ-centered rite. As the infant grows, he is told of the covenant and nurtured in the church. He returns to the effects of the faith associated with baptism whenever he repents. Baptism is chiefly a sign or a seal of an invisible transaction that has already gone on between God and man in Christ. It puts the seal on a covenant, a promise, a pledge. The command of Christ is what matters; the water is secondary.

Baptism is, then, not an actual effecting of the change in a person's life but, rather, a mark and reminder of the change. As such, it is not an absolute necessity, though it is strongly enjoined upon all. For this reason, most reformed Protestantism does not provide for emergency baptism and the called minister usually baptizes. Regeneration is not an effect of the act; instead, there is the "ingrafting of the child into Christ."

It could be said that reformed baptism is a public sign or profession that God has acted. Baptism assures forgiveness and cleansing, chiefly because of the words which declare the promises of God. One is not baptized to acquire forgiveness but to permit the community to make a profession of its faith in the reality of God's gracious activity. This is all consistent with the reformed effort to purge sacramental rites of any trace of magic, of the idea that they work on their own apart from faith, of the concept that the symbols actually effect the change. With slightly varying emphases, baptism with this understanding is practiced in Anglican, Presbyterian, Congregational, and Reformed Protestantism.[220]

From the viewpoint of the non-Protestant, including the Roman Catholic Christian, the version of Protestant baptism which displays the least change from the Catholic practice was retained by Martin Luther and his followers. The Lutherans were Protestant in their rejection of water mysticism or magic. Apart from the Word of God, the water was simple and natural and without effect. But with the Word of God, baptism did actually effect change. It was described as bringing forgiveness of sins, delivering man from the devil and death, giving eternal salvation to those who believe in the promises of God. The water does not do these things; it is the Word.[221]

The event does accomplish regeneration: this the Lutherans would say as the Calvinists and others would not. Something really happened in the rite. It was not merely symbolic and did not only "sign." It was more than a seal or a pledge. For this reason, the Protestants of this lineage did provide for emergency baptism by midwives or any other believing Christian (though there was no self-baptism). As to the fate of the unbaptized who had good intentions or who were children not brought by neglectful parents, the Lutherans were ambiguous. The Bible said that he who was a believer and was baptized would be saved. The same verse also said only that the one who did not believe would be condemned. Only unbelief (and thus the despising of baptism) was damning.

As was the case in reformed Protestantism, the one who was baptized as an infant returns to baptism in every act of repentance. Daily by his conscious activity, he relives his dying and rising with Christ. A breach between the life of the pre- and post-baptized, pre- and post-repentant one is stressed. The Old Adam is drowned and a New Man comes forth. This idea was consistent with a Lutheran view which made much of a discontinuity as over against a gradual change between what man was under the activity of the Gospel and what he was when viewed as a sinner under the Law.

Along with other Protestants, the Lutherans mentioned that they baptized because of the command and promise and placed strong emphasis on the Word of God, including the repetition of a trinitarian formula, baptizing people "in the name of the Father, and of the Son, and of the Holy Spirit." The view of faith implied in all this was that baptism is a gift, not an achievement. The act of baptism was more than a seal or a symbol; it was the act of liberation. Baptism created faith, it did not wait for faith. Baptism brought forgiveness, it was not a sign of forgiveness.

In the ecumenical age, adherents of the three approaches have grown closer together. While intransigent Baptists in fundamentalist circles are vehement about the exclusive validity of their understanding, other Baptists have been slightly more acceptant of alternatives and, it must be said, sometimes more casual about their own approach. Roman Catholics, at the same time, have paid respects to the seriousness with which advocates of believer's baptism take the act. The middle-of-the-road reformed Christians have sometimes explored the possibility of rejecting infant baptism. Karl Barth, for example, spoke against the practice and at various moments reform movements in the Anglican church have considered moving on from it. Others in this school have been more relaxed in their interest in baptism at all.

The Lutherans have generally stood their ground, but many of their scholars have reexplored the meaning of what other Protestants have meant by symbol and seal and have taken new interest also in these alternatives. Ecumenical Roman Catholics tend to accept all three versions, and it became a truism after Vatican Council II that baptism as practiced in Protestantism was not a major hurdle in the path to Christian unity.[222]

12. THE SACRED MEAL INTERPRETED

The sacred meal plays a central part in the observances of many religions. Coming together for a ritual banquet deepens the fellowship and commitment of the adherents. It sanctifies the common events of life and permits celebration of the uncommon. When a companionable human act carried on in contexts of reasonable intimacy is deepened by ritual, all meals take on a different meaning. Usually such sacred meals are enacted to parallel presumed activities in the life of the gods. What goes on on earth is somehow a shadow or a foretaste of what goes on in unseen realms or a recall of what had happened in the past. The rhythms of the year, the sowing or harvesting of crops, the inducements to fertility can all be recognized to the accompaniment of plate and cup.

Christianity is not unique or even exceptional, then, in having a meal at the center of its rites. In doing so, it again took over some practices of ancient Judaism and transformed them. The Christian sacred meal also began in a world where mystery religions stressed secret rites, and some early meanings of the act are shrouded from simple examination. The Hebrew scriptural bases were more important. The Hebrews held numerous festivals of thanks for Yahweh's blessing on the fields. The most important meal was associated with the Passover, remembered as an event when the angel of death who visited the Egyptian enslavers' homes passed over the houses of the children of Israel, sparing them for their trek out of bondage to freedom and nationhood. The Passover was observed in the spring of every year.

Some of the Gospel accounts depict Jesus reenacting a Passover meal "on the night in which He was betrayed." While some controversy persists concerning the timing or the degree of appropriation of Passover meanings, there is no question but that much of the ritual imagery associated with the regular Christian meal held in continuity with the records of that event perpetuate some elements of Passover practice.[223]

The Gospel stories tell of Jesus in the presence of His disciples. Aware that His earthly course had largely run out and conscious of the sacrifice of his life ahead of Him, He expressed a desire to eat a banquet with his disciples, since He would not eat with them again until they shared life in the eschatological Kingdom. He washed their feet as a mark of humble ministry, discoursed with them, and tested them. After supper He passed bread and a cup, referring in each case to His body and then to His blood, and commanded that the disciples should often do the same in memory of Him. In the case of the cup, one remembered word finds Him offering forgiveness of sins with it. After His death and resurrection a number of early gatherings of disciples were connected with the intimacy of a room and a meal like the one at which they had met.

The book of Acts finds the disciples continuing in table fellowship, with emphasis on the breaking of bread. But the earliest accounts of all give some indication of the degree to which the ceremony was still attached to a regular banquet. St. Paul was obliged to chide the Corinthians for their practice of coming together for a meal which often led to too much eating and drinking on the part of the rich and little or none for the poor. The practices associated with the meal led to drunkenness and abuse, and Paul wanted to regularize matters by separating the sacred meal of the Lord from their mere coming together. The surviving documents from the second century of the Church's life continue their preoccupation with the meal, whether it be Justin Martyr's description, the Didache's prescription, or the rumor-filled words of excluded outsiders who spoke of bacchanalia and cannibalism at the Christians' closed gatherings.

In a long process of transformation through the Middle Ages the meal was at once reduced and magnified. It was reduced in that it seemed to be a meal only in a vestigial sense. The original Upper Room was replaced by chapel, church, or cathedral as the setting. The table around which eaters and drinkers gathered became an altar, at one end of the gathering. The cup eventually was no longer passed, but was drunk only by the priest. The faithful might come forward to participate after fasting and acts of confession, but they received only a bit of bread—hardly enough to make the symbolism of a meal vivid. Formal words and gestures accompanied the sharing. As time passed it became more and more a spectacle which the faithful watched. Here was some sort of sacrificial reenactment of Christ's death, to be observed more than shared. The priest might whisper the words and a rood screen could surround even the visual aspects with the sense of mystery.[224]

Through all these developments some attention was given to doctrinal definition, though, given the importance of the ceremony in the medieval church one is surprised not to learn of more. Particularly at the time of the scholastic synthesis in the high Middle Ages a theory was worked out to explain just how the body and blood of Christ were present in the bread and wine of a later day. Since the scholastics said that the bread and wine underwent a change in substance (though not in the accidents of appearance and chemical makeup), this made Christ present in a physical way, as He could not be present apart from the service.

It is easy to see how with such associations the reduced meal became an enhanced rite and the meal, now called the Mass (probably after the closing words, *Ite, missa est*), was the center and focus for the whole of the Catholic life. The Mass might be celebrated without the congregation present, but it existed for them. The bread might be reserved for taking to the sick, for display in a monstrance on the altar, or to let its miraculous powers shine forth at the head of a procession. The Mass highlighted the daily life of the priests, the weekly celebration of the resurrection of Jesus, and was observed in conjunction with the high feasts and saints' days of the church year. As an exclusive rite it also had political potential, for salvation was tied to it. In the hierarchical episcopal system salvation could be denied the unworthy people who were refused the Mass.

As the meal was vestigial in Catholicism, so the Mass itself came to be vestigial in much of Protestantism. For while almost all Protestants took it over in some revised form, they also tended to reduce the numbers of occasions when it was celebrated from daily to weekly, from weekly to monthly or quarterly and even annually. From the beginning until now the occasional churchgoer who misses an occasional Communion may go months or years without being made aware of this rite.

Given such neglect, it is also surprising to the student of history to see how much ink was spilled in polemics over the Catholic version and how much controversy and infighting ensued between Protestant parties over its meaning. Even twentieth century discussions of intercommunion in the ecumenical movement occur with an intensity not always shared by the faithful in their congregations. It might almost be said that the Lord's Supper (or Mass, or Eucharist, or Holy Communion, or Lord's Table) was more fought over than enjoyed in Protestantism.[225]

The reasons for the original polemic are not hard to understand.

The reformers found it necessary to break the Catholic link at its strongest point. So long as the door of heaven was locked or unlocked in the acts of confession and the Mass, it would continue to have profound psychological and political powers. It was the instrument that kept the hierarchy and priestly castes in control. At the same time, popular piety—often with ecclesiastical encouragement—associated many magical powers with the changing of the bread to body and the wine to blood, and this piety seemed to keep people in superstition.

In an age when doctrinal niceties were taken seriously for their own sake, the reformers were offended at what they saw to be perversions of biblical ordinances themselves. Meanwhile, both in counter-Catholic and intra-Protestant debates, it became evident that other issues connected with the Lord's Supper could best be discussed in connection with it. Among these were the ubiquity or localization of Christ's body, self-examination and confession, the nature of ministry and fellowship, and, perhaps most of all, the character of divine initiative and human response in faith.

Given the frequent neglect of the Lord's Supper, it may seem surprising that debate over it was not neglected. Yet it should not surprise anyone to find these debates complicated, for complexity was built into the inherited Lord's Supper. The meal's origins were partly surrounded by obscurity. The Gospels and Paul do not tell later generations enough about its intentions and meanings to satisfy all curiosities. The overtones of Passover and other Jewish rites combined with the hints of mystery religions in the environment tangled matters further. But most of all, its connections with medieval schools of philosophy (as in the whole matter of transubstantiation) led Protestants to have to try to be more logical, rational, and argumentative about the sacrament than most of them wanted to be. They preferred to speak of it as a mystery and to let it go at that, until they were forced to be more specific about meanings.

For present purposes it is unnecessary to retrace all the debates, to describe Communion doctrine and practice in many of the hundreds of denominations or to outline the rites that have been developed in the books of church order here and there. Instead, only a few families of emphases can be noted, allowing for exceptions and overlappings and overlookings. The sophisticated eucharistic precisionists can always find more subtle ways to describe these families of approach, but there is room also for a common-sense view, an attempt to condense the meaning of the Lord's

Supper to some of the apprehensions and perceptions of the faithful recipients or participants, people for whom overdefinition has meant the death of meaning in the rite.

One way to begin, then, is from the observer's point of view. What will the visitor to Protestant churches see when the Eucharist is being celebrated? In every case, contrary to the medieval experience, the whole congregation is permitted both the bread and the cup, though the cup—particularly in evangelical circles where alcoholic beverages are prohibited—may contain unfermented grape juice. Ordinarily, however, the faithful receive wine and bread, the bread being more often than not a white uncrusted wafer-thin plastic-looking fragment. (In present-day liturgical revivals there is some interest in restoring breadlike bread in richer quantities.)

The sacrament is not regularly shared by very small children, though the age of access may vary widely. In the more liturgical churches, confirmation or some similar form of preparation precedes the licensing of people as they come to Communion. In some churches the presiding ministers (or, in some cases, laymen) bring the elements to people in the pews; in others, people come forward to stand or kneel around or process past a table or an altar. An air of stateliness and sobriety surrounds the proceedings and, despite the connotations of joy, it must be said that sometimes the dignity has a somber cast. In some churches there is open Communion, with all believers invited. In others close Communion calls forth only those who have confessed the faith in a particular denominational pattern.[226]

Before the service, some Protestants may fast as a sign of bodily preparation, an act that is permitted and sometimes encouraged but only in very rare instances enjoined. Some Protestants also retain the rite of private confession of sins, but ordinarily confession is now a corporate act within the same service as the Eucharist. After the service the forgiven Christian is expected to conduct himself in a manner congruent with the Gospel, his life refreshed by participation in the sacrament and his heart ready for works of love.[227]

During the service, in addition to some form of corporate recognition of the communicants' unworthiness, there will usually be a sermon or a homily and a number of elements of the Mass carried over even into many of the low churches: the *Kyrie, Gloria, Credo, Sanctus,* and *Agnus Dei,* in vernacular translation. In the more informal Protestant Communions these may have been replaced by other liturgical features, many of which are designed to perform similar functions of reflection and praise. There may or may not be a eucharistic prayer, but there will be some version of the "words of institution" recalling Jesus' directions at the first Lord's Supper, as recorded in the New Testament.[228]

All of this was or is supposed to accomplish something much different from the functions of the Catholic Mass. The reformers and their heirs have been generally consistent in their opposition to Communion as a sacrifice, at least in the medieval sense. There is to be no sense of appeasing or propitiating God, of winning His favor by fulfillment of a command to obey or somehow reenacting Christ's sacrifice, though we shall see that some other forms of the idea of sacrifice are here and there encouraged. Second, there is to be no idea of transubstantiation, of an actual if invisible change in the elements to body and blood of Christ. To many free-church men, some Anglican and Lutheran formulations seem to come very close to this assertion, but those who adhere to these formulations insist that there are differences.

Third, there is to be no hint of an *ex opere operato* observance, of an enactment that suggests an effect simply because of the objective carrying through of the ordinance, the feature which to Protestants seemed to be the base of magical interpetations in Catholicism. Finally, except for Anglo-Catholic observers, there is no "reserved host," no sense of a continuing localization of Christ's presence in the bread that may be set aside for communicants in sickroom or elsewhere, or for adoration on the altar or in procession.[229]

While it may be easy to describe the negatives and to suggest what it is that almost all Protestants repudiated in their taking over the Mass, it is much more difficult to be fair to the subtleties in their positive descriptions. The first family of these to be discussed may be called the Zwinglian-Reformed, for Huldreich Zwingli was perhaps the most consistent and logical among the Protestant interpreters of the meal and because so many Reformed and free-church Christians follow something of his interpretation.[230]

Let it also be added that Zwingli's view was in some respects the most modern, in that it reflected a postmedieval world-view. It also is the most Protestant, because—whatever it may have lost, in the eyes of its enemies—it most vigorously disallowed a devotion to the material objects of bread and wine and most rigorously protected the spiritual reality apart from identification with the material. In Zwingli's world, the old sacramental bond between the symbol and what it *is* was reduced to the suggestion that a symbol only signs and signifies, that it merely represents another plane of reality without being transparent to it. The finite is not capable of actually bearing the infinite.

The Zwinglian view, then, concentrated on the spiritual meaning of an ordinance that was carried out in response to Christ's command, designed to bring about a sense of communion among participants, and intended to be a memorial feast recalling the events and words of Christ's last night with His disciples and His subsequent death and resurrection. Of all the reformers, Zwingli most stressed the idea of the communion of believer with believer and of all with their Lord, who is only spiritually present. The result was to be a strengthening of faith and a new resolve, even as it was a tokening of God's grace in Christ, here manifested in a somewhat different form.

When Zwingli tied faith to the sacrament he found it necessary to undervalue or give no real religious weight to the bread and wine at all. One has faith only in the spiritual, so he cannot tolerate any suggestion that the bread and wine localize Christ's presence in any way.

If Zwingli's was the most modern and most Protestant view, the historian is tempted to say that Luther's was most medieval and perhaps the most Catholic. Non-Lutherans have often found difficulty in completely separating Luther's view that "in, with, and under" the bread and wine one receives the body and blood of Christ from the view called transubstantiation. Some have even used the word "consubstantiation" to suggest that the substance of the body and blood come along with the substance of the bread and wine.[231]

Many followers of Luther reject that term, however, because it connotes a scholastic philosophy which they find alien to biblical or Lutheran thought. Yet those who do use the word show at least one proper instinct, which is to recognize that Luther attached much more significance to the elements of the bread and wine and localized Christ's presence in them in ways that few Protestants did. Luther saw himself protecting this interpretation from the charge that it could lead to idolatry by accenting the dynamic character of the word associated with the sacrament, and seeing no power in the bread and wine apart from faith in the words of command and promise of Jesus.

Luther, in his own mind, was following his own radical liturgical principle. "The closer any mass approaches to the first of all masses, which Christ celebrated at the supper, the more Christian it is." But his critics pointed out that in most of his writings about the Lord's Supper and his sermons to communicants, Luther reduced the many biblical associations of the sacred meal to one, the forgiveness of sins. Communion was for penitents who were forgiven through the gift of grace; it was, in Luther's mind, less a meal for the thankless who would become thankful, the self-seeking who saw in it the sign of sacrifice, the separated who would experience communion. There was, then, a certain soteriological anthropocentrism in the old Augustinian tradition. Communion often became an individualized act in which the believer received the full impact of the personal words, "Given and shed for you!" in Christ's institution.

In Luther's arguments with Zwinglians, Calvinists, and anyone else who differed from him, more issues than those dealing with the gift of forgiveness were included. Notable among these was his insistence that Christ's real presence was possible because of the ubiquity of Christ's ascended body (as opposed to his antagonists' view that that body was now localized in heaven and could not be shared in a local presence when men communed). Another stress fell on his view of faith, in which he deemphasized man's act of will or spiritual preparation. Instead, the faith in the sacrament was also a gift which was the result of divine initiative.

Luther's approach seemed to some to come close to *ex opere operato* observance because he made so much of Paul's injunctions to examine oneself, since unworthy reception of the sacrament could bring down a divine condemnation. If Zwingli's positive contribution lay in his recognition of the meaning of Communion, Luther's was a substantiation of the sacramental experience of forgiveness.

Between these two stand the mediating position of John Calvin and the comprehensive approach of the Anglicans. Calvin saw values in both Zwingli's and Luther's approaches. With Zwingli, Calvin found it necessary to stress that the finite is not capable of bearing the infinite, so there can be no localization of Christ's presence. This meant that he denied Luther's idea of ubiquity and saw Christ's ascended body to be removed from earth. But along with Luther, Calvin wanted more than a merely spiritual interpretation, and he did not like Zwingli's suggestion that the body and blood were merely represented or signified in the bread and wine.

Calvin's own sacramental view allowed for the fact that God was actually working something through the Lord's Supper. Sacraments are outward signs whereby "God sets forth and declares his good will towards us, to uphold the weakness of our faith." They are seals or marks of God's power. Against Zwingli, Calvin minimizes man's contribution. Those who read the Calvinist tradition as being close to Zwingli do well to hear the Scots Confession of 1560: "We utterly damne the vanitie of thay that affirme Sacramentes to be nothing ellis but naked and baire signs."

In Calvinist Switzerland, the Netherlands, Scotland, and parts of Germany, then, a somewhat higher view of the sacrament prevailed than among the Zwinglians and the radical reformers whose views paralleled Zwingli's or were derived from them. The symbols in the Lord's Supper were not "merely" anything. They were rooted in salvation history, and were not arbitrary signs. The accent then fell on the combination of God's Word and man's faith.[232]

This connection was stressed also in Anglicanism, which is most difficult to describe for a number of reasons. The Anglican genius in sacramental thought, Thomas Cranmer, took more seriously than other reformers the idea of mystery in the sacrament and was less willing to set forth logical, rational, ordered views of the meaning of the meal. He was content to do what he did best, to help produce a magnificent order, or liturgy, for worship. Anglicans have characteristically been more concerned with revisions of their Prayer Book and with the components of the liturgy than with taking on other Protestants to debate precise dogmatic formulations.[233]

In general, the Anglican pattern falls into the Calvinist part of the spectrum. More is pictured as being transacted than in the Zwinglian view, but all except Anglo-Catholics would be nervous with Luther's more material concept. Article XXV of the Thirty-nine Articles of 1571 sees the sacraments as "not only badges or tokens of Christian men's profession, but rather they be certain sure witnesses and effectual signs of grace and God's will towards us, by which he doth work invisibly in us." There was, perhaps, some neglect of the eucharistic features in early Anglicanism, which has been largely overcome in later times. With the Zwinglians, Anglicans were strong in their affirmation of the communal aspects of the Lord's Supper.

Anglicans have worked to express the beauty of the rite. They have discussed polity and auspices more than they have turned metaphysical about the material and spiritual elements. The nineteenth century liturgical revival, particularly that associated with

the Oxford Movement and subsequent Anglo-Catholicism, revealed views more Catholic than Luther did, but this significant
party does not see itself as Protestant, and takes some pride in the
measure of the distance between its own view and that of the rest
of Anglicanism.

Continuity between these original positions and those of
churches bearing the names or standing in the lineages of these
founders are not always clear. High church Swedish Lutherans are
more at home with Anglo-Catholics than they would be with some
Pennsylvania Lutherans, whose use of grape juice and whose understanding of the Lord's Supper may seem closer to that of Methodism—just as that Methodism may have little in common with the
views of its founder, John Wesley, who on this subject could be
described as a kind of high church Anglican! The men and women
in the pew have, through the ages, found it difficult to penetrate
or accept the scholars' definitions and, so far as can be determined,
they tend to accept the gifts of the sacrament with a rather simple
faith.

The ecumenical era has revealed certain tendencies in the understanding and practice of the Lord's Supper among Protestants.
More are intercommuning or coming to open Communion, an act
of acceptance which enlarges Christian fellowship even as it blurs
dogmatic definition or downgrades the necessity for such definition. Many Protestants are trying to follow Luther's idea of com-
muning in the style of "the first Mass" and are experimenting with
forms which gather people seated around tables, using real bread
and richer measures of wine.

More important, they are trying to bring back the whole range
of biblical meanings. Over against the doleful and dour penitential
observances, they stress eucharistic joy. The sign of the eschatological banquet marks their rites. The age of "the people of God"
is moving from individualistic toward new corporate understandings. An age that has problems with the past sees in this rite one
way of making the past present in a commemoration sealed by the
Holy Spirit. Even some hints of sacrifice are reintroduced, so long
as these mean not appeasing acts but the responsive delivery of
one's body and whole being as a commitment that goes with the
gift of grace in the sacrament. Finally, reexplorations of the meaning of signs and symbols permit Protestants to reassert the old
values associated with the mystery of this meal.[234]

IV. Expressions of Protestant Life

13. THE GOOD MAN AND THE GOOD LIFE

What makes a Protestant a good Protestant? Religions characteristically make demands upon their followers. Certain norms are set forth and the adherents of the religious group are measured in the light of these. In the case of Protestantism these norms related both to the question of how members fulfill their obligations of church membership in the ecclesiastical realm and how they are to live as Protestant Christians in the world.

There is an inward, inverted, "churchly" side to the question of what it is to be a good Protestant, and many of the energies of institutions are devoted to spelling this out and to compelling response to what is then called for. There is also an outward-looking, "worldly" side which receives almost equal attention in the sermonic literature, the tractarian corpus, and the conversation or diaries of evangelical Christians. To consider one without the other would do an injustice to the persistent double-sidedness of Protestant self-measurement. To listen only to the preachers might lead one to overlook concerns for "the other six days" and ethics, morality, and behavior. To listen only to academic theorists might lead one to interesting intellectual discussion but require him to overlook the actual energies given to the question of fulfillment within churchly institutions.

Protestant culture has regularly begun to shape the good life by concentrating on the way active church members respond to the calls for formation of personal and intimate life under the auspices of the church. The good Protestant celebrates the rites of passage in connection with the Christian community. However little the formal theologians devote themselves to the topic, the popular literature usually begins with the home. Marriage, whether it has a civil or a sacramental base, is to be consecrated in religious rites. It takes on a special character because the couple professes vows based on the Word of God and leaves the altar with the blessing of Christ. The partners are to honor each other as "one flesh" in an indissoluble union. It is expected that procreative acts be included in marriage, though through the years companionship and sexual fulfillment have played larger and more complementary roles. The good Christian home will make provision for prayer and worship within its confines. Morning and evening prayer are encouraged in the literature of Protestant piety, and a "table grace" over food was long virtually taken for granted. Anniversaries of weddings are regularly observed as part of the measurement of God's blessings on the union.[235]

The next emphasis falls on child-rearing. Generally lacking in a literature supportive of the monastic ideal, evangelicals have rarely concentrated on an ethic for the unmarried or the childless. The sermons seem to assume that the nuclear family is normative and that the people being addressed will have, do have, or have had children in the home. The good Protestant arranges for the baptism of his child soon after birth, or, in the churches with traditions of believers' baptism, he will try to set up the circumstances wherein the maturing young person will have occasion to decide for Christian discipleship.

It must be said that much of the familial literature in Protestant societies has been thoroughly bourgeois in character. This literature has asked for the development of virtues which will help children adapt to the surrounding competitive cultures, and then will set standards for generosity and moral decision within them.

The parents teach the children to pray, bring them to ecclesiastical institutions for religious education, read the Bible to them, supervise their moral development, and counsel them. Whether or not this picture is congruent with the actual situation of the Protestant home in the modern world, the ideal is still regularly expressed.[236]

Beginning with adolescence and young adulthood, the developmental stages in which the sexual instinct is strong, Protestantism intervenes in the person's life and seeks to bring Christian counsel to bear on questions of sexuality. This may include the concern that the Protestant young person avoid religiously mixed marriage, sometimes on biblical grounds and more often as a part of sage advice for the preservation of faith in the person and strength in the religious community. Marriage to a Roman Catholic, for example, used to lead to forced commitments to raise children in the Catholic Church. Marriage to unbelievers has been regularly pictured as a threat to one's values and to the integrity of one's belief.

There has been great concern for bodily expressions of the sexual character, with general prohibition of extra- or pre-marital coitus. At various times, Protestants have been observed proscribing dancing because of the association of erotic or sexually stimulating gestures or postures with it. The good Protestant avoided stimuli which would awaken sexual impulses outside the marital bond.

An extensive literature on the art of dying rounds out the interests of popular Protestantism in the realm of intimate familial living and concern for rites of passage. The good Protestant prepares for holy dying. He lives in such a way that he will not be afraid to be taken suddenly. Considerable expression exists about deathbed conversions and the high risk involved in postponement of decisions to believe in Christ and to lead a moral life. The fulfilled Protestant is not necessarily taught to welcome death, but he is not to fear it, since the situation of life in Christ and under grace removes from him the fear of condemnation.[237]

Even within the types of Reformed faith where election and predestination are propounded as doctrines or bases for the plot of life, a literature of assurance and consolation has grown up. Old age has been honored, more or less on biblical lines, and sermons often reflected the preacher's awareness that much of his congregation might well be made up of people who are nearing the end of life. "Christian burial" was sought at a time and in places where burial in honored rites and in sacred soil was reserved for those who led manifestly active and reasonably holy lives in the church. The secularization of burial rites and beliefs has led more and more Protestants to minimize this concern about disposal of the body in recent decades.

When the measurement of "good Protestantism" moves beyond the circle of the family or the stages on life's way it is concentrated in the realization of obligations of church membership. Protestant counsels on this subject vary depending in part upon the context. In what the sociologists call churchly Protestantism, where membership lists of churches are roughly correspondent to the population rolls of society itself, the idea of turning one's back on secular culture is more rarely expressed. There is or has been more freedom to discuss the obligations of citizenship in conjunction with those who are inactive in churches.

In historic sectarian Protestantism, where discipleship and high standards of personal decision and commitment were prerequisites for membership, much more attention has been given to the distinctiveness of the Christian way. Again, where the churches were established by law and their support was more or less guaranteed by the civil society, injunctions differ from those in societies where religious support, including especially the fiscal aspects, is dependent upon regular and voluntary participation and donation.

Regular attendance at the hours set aside for worship is taken for granted. Even to write such a sentence may seem like a gratuitous act in Protestant church circles, until it is recalled that such attendance is not automatically a part of all religions. Protestants have a conception in which their "religion of the Word" occurs when the congregation is gathered. True, the individual reads his Bible, holds his own devotions, and prays, but to absent himself from the public worship deprives him of a sense of participation in the forward movement of the people of God. Not to attend implies a neglect or a despising of God's Holy Word, the setting up of a block against God's creative and shaping activity.

In voluntary societies, attendance also can be used as one of the marks of response, and is regularly advertised as a sign that the Gospel is effective. The worshiping Protestant is also more likely to be an almsgiver and a financial participant in the support of the institution, so in societies where churches have been disestablished, the very existence of the churches depends in no small degree on the regular and enthusiastic participation of worshipers.[238]

In the overwhelming majority of cases the Protestant worshiper and attendant is expected to help provide for the service of God in His place. This may mean to aid fiscally or personally in building and caring for a house of God, in support of a divinely called and set-apart minister of the Gospel, and in the program of the churches. In the past two centuries this program has moved from the more simple kinds of charities and almsgiving to a complex of benevolent, humanitarian, eleemosynary, educational, and missionary organizations. The good Protestant of the nineteenth century in particular was to give money so that missionaries could be sent abroad. Then and later his goodness was noted also in proportion to the degree he supported hospitals, orphanages, and reform movements.

The tendency in modern centuries has been for most Protestants to link these appeals to more secular ones, and to minimize the line between the service of God through the churches and through other voluntary societies. The more radical Protestants have also grown increasingly weary and wary of institutional appeals, and large minorities like to speak of a future Christianity unburdened by expensive buildings, complex institutional appeals, and the burden of extensive church programs.

Implied in these two sets of canons has been a third: the good

Protestant prays. By prayer here is meant the whole construct of responses to God's person both within the gathered fellowship and at home and in private. Whereas some religions tend to restrict the prayerful response to corporate activities, Protestantism has consistently called upon its faithful to speak for themselves to God. In some traditions missals, breviaries, and prayer books are provided for virtually every contingency of life. In others, free or spontaneous prayer following certain biblical and historical models is projected as the ideal.[239]

While prayer is revered for its intrinsic values, the connection between prayer and fulfillment of the rest of Christian life, as in morality or ethics, is what concerns us at the moment. The praying Protestant is likely to set his mind on other than merely selfish concerns. For this reason intercessory prayer, which has been described as "loving one's neighbor on one's knees" is frequently enjoined. The man who prays for the good of the other is supposed to work for the other's good. The man who intercedes for victims of war in a warring world is expected also to work for peace. The man who prays for a sick neighbor is also expected to develop a sense of responsibility for medical advance and the provision of hospitals.

The concern for intercession has never ruled out personal petitionary prayer. Despite its frequently selfish sound, prayer that asks has been justified on the basis of Jesus' endorsement of it. It is expected that the petitioning church member will be extraordinarily aware of God's creative and redeeming activity and concerned about holiness. Prayer is not, then, a separate activity; it gives shape to the rest of the Protestant's life as he walks in the presence of a personal and holy God.

The behavior that is encouraged on the basis of familial, ecclesiastical, and prayer life more often than not alludes to models of virtue and vice over which the individual has considerable control. Pietism and evangelicalism in particular and conservative Protestantism in general have often tended to confine their moral preachments to just these narrowed areas of life. As the modern world saw the development of autonomous political, social, and economic realms, conservative Protestantism often relied on vestiges of medieval Christian synthesis to carry out God's purpose for society. Or these realms were simply written off, as being the devil's arena where the Christian would be tainted.

The conservative evangelical has argued that if he does well at preparing individual Christians to make conscientious personal decisions as a citizen or worker in his vocation, the world will be improved. As a result, conservatism tends to reject statements or proclamations by the churches on moral situations in the larger political world. The exceptions tend to be about political decisions which relate closely to individual vices: gambling, prostitution, the use of alcoholic beverages.

The rise of liberal Protestantism in the nineteenth century saw theologians repudiating this paradigm. They argued that no political forces should be regarded as beyond the scope of God's coming Kingdom and thus beyond the range of the church's corporate witness. Without necessarily relinquishing interest in the questions whether Protestants should use profane language, overindulge in consumption of alcoholic beverages, gamble their funds away, or engage in lapses from approved norms of sexual conduct, they did try to find ways to relate personal to public morality. Social evils and social good were as important as personal vices and virtues. The issue of how one invested his money or dealt with people of other races was, to the liberal at least, as important as were the issues of gambling and dancing.

Whether conservative or liberal, individualist or social in outlook, both kinds of Protestants have had to reckon with some of the same fundamental questions of Christian ethics, moral theology, and theological foundations for behavior.[240]

A paradox lies at the heart of the appropriation of Christian ethics in Protestant histories. Certainly the majority of the historians and the theorists would describe the Protestant grasp of ethics as one which concentrates on love, on Christian liberty, on spontaneous concern for the neighbor. Yet the picture Protestants have given to observers of their churches and cultures has been related to moralism and legalism in ethics. They are portrayed as defensive, negative, often ascetic people who build morality into every area of life and make moral demands on the basis chiefly of what they take to be divine commands and obligations. Perhaps Protestant ethical talk on the basis of love and its demands is simply destined to have difficulty finding incarnations; the reasons for the frustration of ethics concern us less here than does the attempt to discern what reflective Protestants have claimed their moral basis to be.

The first of the sources of Protestantism's bases of morality and ethics has often been natural law, though it must be said that the history of Protestantism has been marked by intense debate over the specific role of natural law. Natural law was taken over at least marginally because of several biblical references to a law "written in man's heart" and because the history of Christian philosophical ethics impelled people to take it seriously. St. Paul said that even those who had never been confronted by the Word of God in the prophets' language were responsible before God because He had not left himself without witness. Law seemed somehow to be built into the universe and was accessible through reason, patterned behavior, and conscience.[241]

The Christian man, in ethics based on natural law, was able to build upon this foundation. There simply were certain rights and wrongs structured into reality. Problems have arisen whenever the question of the content of this somehow existent natural law has been addressed. Roman Catholics, for example, said that artificial birth control was against natural law, but most Protestants came to disagree.

The content of a natural moral law was always a problem because exceptions to what was regarded as normative in one culture could almost always be found in others. Not all societies had placed so much stress on proscriptions against murder or on support of the monogamous family, both of which were topics regularly incorporated in Western talk about the substance of natural law. If it was impossible to agree at all upon the content of such a law, what good was it?

A second line of argument against it came from those who were ready to argue that natural law was unnecessary since God's revealed Word had made His demands clear. Why should people have to depend on a vague universal principle of reason or law to determine what was right or wrong? Other Protestants from Martin Luther to Karl Barth decried the use of natural-law categories because they believed that the fall of man had obscured its presence, or because men would seek to be made just on the basis of what they took it to be, apart from the work of Christ. For Barth, God had no point of contact in man through something like natural law. The natural-law tradition has lived on most prominently in moderate Anglican moral theology, which sees itself at war with various "ethics of decisions" or "contextual ethics."[242]

Of much more importance than natural law as a foundation of Protestant moral language has been the inheritance from the Hebrew Scriptures. This appropriation it shares with Roman Catholicism and the rest of Christianity. Most Protestants conceived that they made a somewhat different use of the Old Testament, since they regarded some Catholic rites and laws to be based on ceremonial and ritual laws of the Old Testament, which evangelicals believed Christ had done away with when He fulfilled the whole old law.

For them the law taken over from the ancient people of God was condensed and codified in the Decalogue, or Ten Commandments, which Yahweh had given through Moses on Sinai. The Protestants who believed that Jesus' fulfillment of the law meant the destruction of the Ten Commandments or the denial of their weight on the Christian have been few in number. Some saw the Decalogue to be congruent with natural law. The Ten Commandments spoke for the permanent will of God and were seen as His revealed stipulations for the way relations between man and God and between man and man were to be worked out. Those Protestants who stressed obedience tended to say that the Christian life depended on a liberal carrying out of the Ten Commandments.[243]

The first "table" of that law called for acknowledgment that Yahweh alone was Lord and God, for proper use of His name and reverence for His holiness. The second table called for honoring of parents and it proscribed murder, adultery, stealing, bearing false witness, and coveting. Yahweh had spoken thus in order to ensure proper personal and societal life out of regard for all men. Thus this law was ultimately grounded in His preserving love.

The Ten Commandments could be literal laws, pictures of the ideal life, general guidelines or descriptions. They were not the path to salvation, since Christ's atoning work was the only way. Nor should they be used by men who through obedience to them would seek to make claims that they merited God's favor. Other Old Testament concepts taken over into Protestant ideas of morality were that of the covenant between God and His people and the belief that His prophetic Word is to judge all human ventures. The result would be a realm of justice and righteousness.

Protestantism has had some Marcionite voices, people who argued that the Old Testament had to be forgotten or even repudiated. But even those who regarded all the Scriptures as canonical and as participant in God's saving work have tended to concentrate more on the New Testament in the discussion of ethics. Here the figure of Jesus himself has been central. While the theologians have wrestled with the questions of Jesus' absolute and uncompromising ethics, as captured in the synoptic Gospels in the Sermon on the Mount, popular Protestantism usually defines itself as responsive to Jesus' way and words. The medieval idea of the imitation of Christ lived on in the eras when there was real confidence that the Gospel records were sufficiently reliable historically to build a clear picture of Jesus' character and intentions, so that he could be set forth as an example.[244]

Jesus' ethics combined concern for justice with a call for love. The problem came when His completely uncompromising prescriptions were to be applied in real life. Did he really mean that all men who ever lusted after a woman should cut out their offending eye? Did he really mean that men must always love their enemies and turn the other cheek? If so, what happens in self-defense and in military activity? Protestant sectarians often argued that men must be willing victims for the sake of Jesus' truth. So some became complete pacifists. Most Protestants have been ready to take up arms. How could they be utterly serious about Jesus' commands against adultery and generally casual about His equally strenuous injunctions against retaliating against evil? It was easy to give assent to His criticism of pride, His injunctions to love, His pictures of free response. But what about the impossibility of His demands in the spheres of politics, which are built on compromise?[245]

Cynics often remark that outside radical sectarian Protestantism no one even tries to live up to Jesus' words, "Be ye therefore perfect, even as your heavenly Father is perfect"! In that reading, all other Protestants are involved in some sort of exegesis that makes it possible for them to accept *and* reject the Sermon on the Mount or to interpret it in such a way that its force is blunted to mean the opposite of what it clearly says. It could be that the Sermon on the Mount should be taken merely as a description of the perfect life that occurs when the Kingdom of God appears. Or it could be an ideal which, even though not lived up to, could be a guide. It might be the base from which conscientious compromise could be measured or the transcendent norm which is used to call under judgment all the compromises that have been made. All these options have found many followers in the circles of Protestant ethicists, most of whom want to build on the Gospel portrait of Jesus but few of whom find ways to be consistent and literal.

St. Paul is often ranged at the side of Jesus in discussions of New Testament ethics. Whereas Jesus said that He had not come to destroy but to fulfill the law and while He actually raised the law's demands, Paul kept his eye on the question of how man is justified by grace through faith. In that pattern the concentration seemed to fall on what seemed to be the virtual antithesis of Jesus' concern. Paul, brought up under the Jewish law, could at times speak appreciatively of it, but his final theological judgment was personal: "I died under the law." The law had been designed to be a schoolmaster who would accompany the learner on the way to Christ, but in the matter of justification it worked out that the law only served to accuse man, to point out sins that had not previously been reckoned as sins. But Christ had kept the law, and God's acceptance of Christ's reconciling work meant that the Christian who was found to be in Christ was now free of the law. He might do what the old law had asked him to do, but he would do it for a different reason.[246]

Love and liberty were, then, the keystones of what Paul took from Jesus' proclamation and the Church's recall of Christ. The Christian man was no longer at war with God. His faith so identified him with Christ that God no longer looked at him from the viewpoint of one who was failing to keep the law. In fact, attempts to keep the law in the old sense might lead to boasting and thus to exclusion from the realm of the justified. Now it was the love of Christ which constrained and controlled men who were in the Spirit. They would act out of spontaneous Christ-like love to serve others even to the point of giving their lives for others. Agape, God's kind of love, could be discerned in their self-giving, a giving which did not strive for recognition. This pattern of ethics was also eschatological: it did not set out principles or laws for all kinds of human conduct but was designed to prepare people for ready response to what God called men to in various situations in the light of the urgency of the times.[247]

Love-centered and freedom-directed ethics of decision in Protestantism pick up these Pauline motifs. Sometimes they have been radicalized by reference to St. Augustine's word, "Love God and then do as you please." That dictum was designed to stress how the man whose life was completely taken up with God could be depended upon to know and to do the right. Enemies of modern "situation ethics" have seen in it, not the truth for perfected life, but merely license for the errant in the modern world. Yet something of the Augustinian line survives in most Protestant ethical teaching. The conservative moral theologian would say that loving God would mean incorporating His natural law and philosophical principles into a way of life based also on the Decalogue, Christ's words and ways, and Paul's descriptions of the reconciled life. The radical contextualist would say that loving God frees man from concern about petty rules and regulations and liberates him for a neighbor-centered ethic.[248]

A classic statement of freedom-centered ethics came from Martin Luther, who accepted the apparent contradictions in Christian ethics and heightened the paradox. "A Christian is a perfectly free lord of all, subject to none. A Christian is a perfectly dutiful servant of all, subject to all." Luther could take seriously the Decalogue, but the accent fell on loving decision. The ethics of freedom directs all to the neighbor. The Christian must look first at the neighbor's need, and then be a Christ to the neighbor. What impels one against love ceases to be and should no longer be a law. Yet law could be relied upon to give a picture of what God had in mind for the care of the earth, the community, the neighbor.[249]

The dangers in Lutheran ethics have centered in antinomianism. The sinner can say that he likes to commit sin, God likes to forgive it, all is well arranged. He can say that he loves God and is thus free to do what he will. The law is no longer to dominate his life, so he can live apart from what it reveals or demands. It hardly seems necessary to say that Luther opposed such distortion, and concentrated on the whole message of God for norms of the Christ-like life. But he refused to ground ethics in the following of God's laws.

The generally Lutheran pattern of ethics is an ethics of faith, for it relies not on the question of rewards and merits but on living out the life consequent upon the act of being justified. It has been an ethics of love, for reasons stated above. And it is an ethics of hope or promise, to bring up the eschatological point of view borrowed from St. Paul. Faith is forward-looking, related to man's *vivificatio*, his living with Christ. It is easiest to spell out what this pattern never can be: it can never suggest that the Christian life based on law, whether the Decalogue or the Sermon on the Mount, can please God. Only faith in Christ's saving act is related to God's initiative in grace.[250]

While the radical sectarians saw Lutheran ethics with its regard for "the orders of creation" including the state and the family to be too ready for compromise, Anglicans and Calvinists felt that it did too little justice to the claims of the law. Neither would be ready to stress the creative power of law at the expense of justification by grace through faith, but both were willing to see the ways in which the law could inform, enlarge, give structure to, and prop up the Christian life. Through these lineages both moral law and scriptural law were given new hearings; natural law and ethics based on principles have been more regularly defended in Reformed Protestantism than in radical or Lutheran evangelical movements. An ethics of obedience as opposed to an ethics of decision has been the result.[251]

Recent Protestantism, as it has wrestled with the complexity of issues in a world of compromise and as it has related to existentialist philosophies, has engaged in a rereading of Christian ethics. It begins with Jesus' radical command to love and to place all reliance on love in human relations. On this basis it adds Paul and Augustine, Luther and the antinomians. The goodness of an act depends upon man's relationship to God in Christ and his ability to respond in free self-giving love to the neighbor in need. Advocates of a resultant contextual ethics or situation ethics like to condense their point of view into a few slogans. Love is always good. Love is the only norm. Love equals justice. Love justifies its own means. Love forces man to decide on the spot, often between apparent bad choices. Critics of contextualism say that agape is not enough, that love can be too easily sentimentalized, and that the Christian cannot take law so lightly.[252]

Despite novel terminologies, the debates between situationists and advocates of principled ethics are as old as Christianity itself. They are far from being settled. To some extent, they can be seen as complementary and not contradictory assertions in the mouths of all except a few extremists on both sides. The tensions seem to be built into history, into law and love, into the gap between ideal and reality. Protestant ethics does have certain consistent marks, however. It is theocentric and monotheistic. The good Protestant sets out to please God, not man. The Protestant moral path is to be guided chiefly by love of God in Christ and not by observance of law. It is to be worked out in the vocations of forgiven people, whose forgiveness liberates them to face each day free for the other, and for whom the prospect of forgiveness is a sustaining force in the face of inevitable future failures to live the good life.

14. PEOPLE AND THE PEOPLE OF GOD: RACE AND NATION

One of the favored metaphors describing the Christian Church is "the People of God." The biblical picture of the Church as a people has been taken up with enthusiasm by Protestants, who find in it a continuity with ideas they have always sought to express. The Church is the communion of saints, the gathering of the faithful, the congregation of pilgrims. Most of evangelical Christianity would join with the Lutheran confessional writings in asserting that the Church is not a Platonic ideal in the mind of God but is made up of people. That assertion is both theologically apt, they would say, as well as empirically verifiable. The Protestant churches, then, are people. The historical question that goes with the assertion is: "Which people?" Who makes up the constituency of a fellowship that describes itself as catholic and universal, devoted to the One who gave himself to reconcile all men, to bring saving life to all? And if, as it happens, not all peoples are part of Protestantism, how are they regarded—not as individuals, but as classes, nations, and races?[253]

For two-thirds of its history, Protestantism had been almost exclusively white, of European and, derivatively, American stock. Its racial theorists made much of the presumed Aryan, Nordic, and Teutonic roots of the kinds of people who were predisposed to be Protestant, people who were by nature lovers of freedom, a special class of men who were particularly innovative and productive. Not until the missionary movement converted substantial numbers of Asians and Africans around the middle of the nineteenth century were there many yellow or black Protestants. Not until toward the middle of the twentieth century, when they began to be thought of as representatives not of missionary outposts but of indigenous and autonomous Younger Churches, was there wide recognition that to be Protestant could mean other than being white. And not until blacks in America became assertive and the consciousness of Third World definitions was prevalent in the West, was nonwhite Protestantism regarded as a force with which to reckon.

189

Two realities, then, stand out as hidden but dominating non-theological factors in the makeup of Protestantism; without them the entity cannot be comprehended. The first of these is racial: Protestantism for over three centuries was a white man's religion, and even today it remains statistically overwhelming so. It went wherever northern European white men went, and other people who were drawn to it were drawn more or less on European white men's terms. They had to acquire the ethos and outlook of people in a white history, nuanced in styles of piety, family life, hymns, ways of stating doctrines, and patterns of etiquette. White was the measure; all else was derivative, dependent, exceptional, and mutational.

Within this racial configuration another subtlety had devastating implications for the Protestant people of God, namely, Protestantism's proclivity for giving birth to, favoring, or drawing much of its life from nationalism within the European-American sphere. Nationalism might have existed apart from Protestantism, and Protestantism could have come to birth and could have survived without nationalism, but the fact is that the two grew symbiotically. Few factors served to divide Protestantism so radically as did the adherence of its various churches to the goals of the nations in which they found themselves. They provided much of the sanction and some of the ceremonial support for the ideals and programs of modern nationalists. After a discussion of Protestantism and race it will be worthwhile to pursue the question of nationalism as a subdividing and defining force.

Any discussion of Protestantism and race properly begins with the special problem of Judaism. Protestantism has been not only white but Gentile white, a reality which most Europeans and Americans have taken for granted. The Jew was excluded because he wanted to be; as the only substantial minority group in Europe at the time of the Reformation, the Jewish community had to struggle to hold onto its identity, and it resisted the few sporadic attempts of Protestantism to convert. If a Jew did convert, this was done at the expense of Jewish community: the fact of becoming a Protestant meant for almost all Jews a complete wrenching from their own past, from synagogue and family and even neighborhood. There was only one set of terms by which one could become a Protestant: by turning Gentile in every aspect except blood inheritance.[254]

Jewish history is full of complaints that Jews were regarded fully as men only if they would convert. Even as late as the Nazi period in Germany many of the best friends the Jews had in the Protestant community, people who have since come to be thought of as heroes for their self-sacrifice in the Jewish cause, based much of their support for Jewish people on the theological prospect that they might become Protestant Christians and, hence, fully deserving men. The same Jewish history is full of resentments against Protestants for the many efforts at conversion that were made. Why did you not leave the Jewish community alone, respecting the integrity of the Jews' faith? That is the question that is asked as part of this expression of resentment.[255]

The complaint has more historical justification than the resentment. It is demonstrably true that Protestants had almost never tried to look at the faith of Judaism empathically. They almost never regarded the Jew as a complete and worthy human so long as he remained in his condemned religious community.

The second charge, that Protestants made too many attempts to convert Jews, has less historical basis. There has been some rhetoric about efforts that had to be made, particularly after the awakening of a missionary consciousness. After all, did not the New Testament command that the Gospel be preached to all people? And did it not promise that Christ's coming again would occur only after God's ancient people would embrace the New Covenant? It is also true that here and there individual conversions occurred and converts were welcomed into some congregations.[256]

Awareness of these exceptions persists in the recall of famous men: Karl Marx's parents had found it advisable to take on at least external observances of Protestant forms; Felix Mendelssohn-Bartholdy, of Jewish background, was a Christian composer; a Jew became a Christian church historian and took on the name Neander, the new man. These German examples can be duplicated here and there in other national cultures.

Overall, however, the Protestants took over and sometimes intensified medieval Christian views of Jews. They did what they could to exclude them from larger communities, segregating them in ghettos and passing what laws they could to inhibit their activities. They perpetuated stereotypes about ugly racial features: the Jews were miserly, greedy usurers, and cheating merchants. Protestants supported these views with theological opinions derived from the reading of the New Testament record: these were the Christ-killers. They had shouted down God's curses upon themselves and their descendants, the contemporary Jews. The Gospels said so. The curse had not been removed. The Jew still did not accept Christ. Protestantism both politically and theologically was overwhelmingly anti-Semitic at worst and casually condescending in some rare, exceptional better moments.[257]

The extreme case of the divorce between God's ancient people and His new Protestant people occurs on the first pages of main-line Protestant history. Probably never since the beginnings has there been such virulent theological anti-Semitism as there was in the later writings of Martin Luther. Even in the Nazi period German anti-Semites were still reproducing Luther's violent and often scatological writings against the Jews to support anti-Jewish tendencies. Luther had set out to convert the Jew. Shortly after the beginning of the Reformation he expressed the faith that now, with the papist's yoke off, the Jew would be free for the first time in centuries to look at the Gospel in fresh and freeing terms. He was visited by a couple of Jews at the time of the Diet of Worms and seemed to take encouragement from the conversation. But he was soon disappointed; Jews did not come over to his side.[258]

Then issued a stream of writings whose tone was, to put it simply, murderous. Apologists have tried to explain it away as being theological, not personal; it was the writing of a genius who was complex and who no longer had control of himself. Whatever the rationalizations, the writings did reveal an almost pathological hatred of nonconverting Jews. People who stood in Luther's tradition without actually turning to their spiritual ancestor for reinforcement of anti-Jewish views, at the very least could have found no motive for changing attitudes if they had consulted him.

Anglican, Reformed, and radical Protestantism have little comparable literature. While there were rare expressions of congeniality, there were few genuine attempts to take an inner view of the life of Judaism, to say anything positive about the shape of Jewish community, or to pay positive regard to Jews who remained Jews. This is not the place, however, to write another chapter in the painful history of Protestant anti-Semitism. At this point it is necessary only to note that even in the case of the single "other" racial presence in Europe through Protestant history it rarely occurred to anyone to regard the Jew as part of the people of God or to consider him a full partner in the human story.[259]

The first locale in which it is possible to see the whiteness of Protestant people as an obsession on a large scale is in North America. There, first, Protestant majorities lived with large minorities of other races. And there, again, it is easy to see that nonwhite meant second-class status. The first exposure was to be the native

American, mistakenly called Indian by Columbus and thus named by the Protestant people ever after.

Whatever part Roman Catholicism played in colonizing the southern two-thirds of the hemisphere or that portion of North America which became Canada, the thirteen colonies were settled by nominal Protestants. By 1776, at the birth of the nation, only about 20,000 Catholics thrived in a population of almost 4,500,-000. Only a small percentage of the remainder of the population were active in Protestant churches—American colonists were not very faithful churchgoers.

Protestants had the spiritual field virtually to themselves; they were legally established in nine of the thirteen colonies. Almost all the elites and oligarchies who set the tone and mood and ethos in the colonies were Protestant, and they set out to create an evangelical empire. So a study of American religious racial attitudes almost until the middle of the nineteenth century permits concentration on Protestantism.[260]

Some of the original colonists listed the conversion of the natives as one of their purposes, and these statements at times seem to have been based in genuine sentiments. The Indian was not yet known, and there were romantic pictures of his possibilities. The devil had decoyed these fine creatures to this part of the world, but now that the Church had been reformed and North America was being providentially settled by Protestants, they would come to the Gospel.

By 1622 in Virginia, however, the Indian had shown forceful resistance and missionary efforts virtually broke down there. In New England matters were not much better. By the end of the colonial period only about twelve men were still carrying on missionary endeavors. While the missions had been staffed by some of the finest colonial ministers: John Eliot, David Brainerd, and, briefly, Jonathan Edwards, they knew very little success and lost most of their backing in the once supportive white congregations.

Meanwhile, as a result of wars and treacheries from both sides, only a negative imagery survived and the Noble Savage was seen only as savage. Whereas Western hemispheric Catholicism, in the form of men like Bartolemé de Las Casas, had some apologists and protectors of Indians, Protestant colonists either found their clerics to be aloof or busy reinforcing negative pictures and licensing repressive policies.

The United States Constitution regarded the Indian as a foreigner and most Protestant people did the same. Throughout the century various policies were tried; intermarriage (as at least an eschatological dream), coexistence, removal to reservations, and finally virtual extermination. A few Protestants carried on missionary activities. There were gestures of care and love on the part of individuals. But these were almost always made in the manner of the superior to the inferior, the normative people to the abnormal, the conqueror to the conquered. By the late twentieth century there were almost no Indians in any kind of leadership positions in Protestantism and the native Americans remained a neglected minority, generally perceived as an outsider.[261]

While the Indian represented a dwindling minority, blacks were an ever growing minority as a result of slave trade from Africa and then of reproduction in North America. Throughout most of American history the equation protestant/white was consciously and unconsciously operative in the minds and actions of the American majority.

In the seventeenth and much of the eighteenth centuries the racial attitudes of Protestants who tolerated the slave trade are not always easily defined and clarified. Of course, there was never a sense of equality of races, but at that time at least Protestant biblicists were doing what they could to retain the belief that God had made all men of one blood.[262]

As decades passed, however, at least in the American south where slavery seemed to remain more economically advantageous longer than in the north, even this last tenet affirming the blacks' full humanity came to be called into question. Not only was much more made of Yahweh's cursing Ham, the son of Noah (and in American mythology Ham was the ancestor of the blacks), but some people ingeniously tried to suggest that blacks came from a separate race, tracing their ancestry to the story of Cain.

What is impressive is the degree to which a population generally apathetic about churchgoing turned to the Bible and the clergy for explanations of a bewildering racial situation. Not only slavery as an institution but also the identity and status of the black race itself had to be explained in biblical terms.

Since many Protestant rites implied or confirmed men's legal status (marriage; baptism), evangelical churchmen often adapted their view of the scheme of salvation and licensed black procreation without benefit of marriage and even excused themselves for reluctance to baptize. More often they simply redrafted the theology or laws about rights and did permit marriage and baptism, but without the conferring of other human rights.[263]

All the while there were missionary activities among slaves. And as the number of northern freed men grew, American blacks developed autonomous and, in every instance, Protestant denominations. In their externals these churches paralleled the white groups: they were Baptist or Methodist. They followed the same ordinances, read the same Bible, had similar polity, organized on familiar lines, developed a parallel professional clergy. The degree to which they were able to bring to their denominations some residues of African religious style is a much debated point.[264]

What is to be noted here is the ironic fact that in the later years of slavery and through most of the ensuing century of segregated church life, blacks had formed some of the nation's largest Protestant churches. These were strong, multimillion-member denominations of generally faithful church people. There are some indications that church meant more in the lives of many black communities than in the lives of their white counterparts—if only because many other institutions were denied blacks. But the black Protestant churches were to the nation at large "invisible institutions."

Men can show invisible love to invisible Christians in invisible institutions, and some Protestant theology in the century after the Civil War did express the reality of spiritual bonds. But in the visible, practical realm, there was very little contact. Almost never was there an expression of the reality that blacks were fully part of the Protestant "people of God." Well into the twentieth century the president of the largest Protestant denomination, the Southern Baptist Convention, felt called upon to apologize to his followers for the fact that by accident he was at a banquet in the north attended by one black Protestant.

While attitudes excluding blacks from consideration were most obvious in the rural south for some decades, by World War I enough descendants of slaves had moved north to create new problems for white northerners. They also systematically segregated themselves and excluded blacks, and there was little spiritual intercourse at least before the 1950s. By the time the reactive black separationist movements were formed in the 1960s, only a very small minority of America's black and white Protestants shared life together in congregations or even in denominations. To white Protestants, Protestantism still meant white.[265]

The extreme cases of German evangelical anti-Semitism and American Protestant anti-Indian, antiblack definition can be paralleled in the experience of the rest of Protestantism. The difference in most other cases lies in the fact that the test came in the matter of attitudes toward nonwhite, non-Gentile races far from home, at some distance from the missionary sending centers. For an understanding of the instinctive way in which majority Protestants continued to think of their faith as being related normatively to the white world, it is necessary to survey opinions about culture contacts made by missionaries during the period of colonial expansion and imperialism.

We shall exempt from this survey reference to attitudes toward "the Turk." Many early missions from Europe and America were briefly directed to the Near East and North African Muslim territories. But the missionaries encountered such massive resistance to Christian endeavor in the world of Islam that the racial picture is complicated by the uniform religious and military attitudes. The Turk, as he had been centuries before when Christians and Muslims fought for the Near East, North Africa, Spain, and even into France, continued to be regarded as beyond the scope of potential inclusion in the world of Protestant people. Needless to say, with such a history no new racial attitudes had to be developed: each side saw the other as conniving, treacherous, barbaric, and hopeless—an enemy to be conquered. The attempt to see Arab people or other Islamic groups as any part of the people of God was soon given up.

More positive culture contacts remained possibilities when the Protestant nations of Holland, England, Germany, and the United States after the late eighteenth century expanded their political and economic spheres into the parts of the world where there had previously been less exposure. This capitalist and colonial expansion occurred, it should be noted, soon after the Enlightenment, a period or movement—if we may call it that—in which more positive attitudes toward non-Christian non-Westerners had begun to develop. Rousseau's picture of the Noble Savage inspired some to look for a romantic innocence among primitives. Gotthold Ephraim Lessing had extricated himself enough from Protestant prejudices to write *Nathan the Wise*, a drama implying spiritual equality among Christian, Muslim, and Jew. An anticipation of interest in comparative religion was present in the natural theology of the Enlightenment, when men of generally deistic tendencies played down the idea of special revelation and argued that divinity was spread through natural reason among all men of good will. The Enlightenment had prepared elites at least to see something worthwhile in other races and religions.[266]

When contacts were developed, however, these positive approaches remained theoretical or were quickly forgotten. India provides one of the better case studies. There had been some continental efforts to missionize India, but the more significant endeavors, significant because they were to be tied in with the successful imperial outreach of Great Britain, began with the arrival of shoemaker William Carey at the end of the eighteenth century.

Carey, like the first missionaries to North American Indians and blacks, held a higher view of the racial potential of the people he had come to convert and serve. He saw them as "the most mild and inoffensive people in the world," who were merely captive to religious superstition. Change the religion and you would have no problem with the race or nationality. But Carey was an exception, and after him much of the story is one of regression. The English, for one thing, had not been so missionary in their intentions as the Spanish and Portuguese had been. They were often nettled by the presence of missionaries. For every positive vision by a Carey there were thousands of reports back from commercial-minded Englishmen who found reasons to despise the people of India.

Missionaries persisted, however. Through the years many broke out of the elitist enclaves that were shaped by the greatest modern imperial power. Unfortunately for the perpetuation of Carey's kind of positive view, they did not meet with the anticipated success and often had to explain away their failures in the language of racial inferiority. Henry Martyn, Carey's most notable and equally self-sacrificing successor, looked out at a crowd of holy men who had disfigured themselves and saw that their appearance was "but a faint emblem of their inward depravity and moral vileness."

The negative pictures of Indian religionists combined with increasing deepening of stereotypes about the "black" Indians. The aristocratic sense of the British colonialists often lived on in the Protestant missionaries who came with them. The missionary efforts seemed eventually to stimulate a long-overdue revitalization of Indian religions, Hindu, Muslim, and Buddhist, and the new spiritual energies there brought more resistance and more negative attitudes. The idea that the converts in India deserved to be a Younger Church with full parity came late to most Protestants sent from England or remaining home to hear the accounts.[267]

The yellow man might also be converted in China during the nineteenth century, but conversion did not mean that he was to be regarded as an equal. Religion was worn as a mark of superiority by the British and Americans in China. The most positive portrayals of the resistant Chinese made of them children, and children, the Protestant Bible readers knew, needed discipline for their own good. At best paternalistic, always condescending, and at worst exclusive, these attitudes perpetuated a missionary mentality that retarded a sense of partnership on the part of Chinese Protestants. When Communists took over in mid-twentieth century it was not difficult for them to repay in kind the white people who had regarded themselves as culturally and religiously superior.

The story was similar in Japan, though some features of the Japanese character struck Westerners as admirable. When Orientals made their way to the American west coast, Protestants joined their neighbors in developing anti-Asian racial stereotypes and exclusionist policies.[268]

The Westerners in India had first contact with darker people and thought of these Caucasians as "black." The term "black," because of its biblical associations with sin, carried with it almost metaphysical connotations of evil. Therefore, one would not expect Euro-Americans to regard true blacks in Africa as equals or brothers. By the time of the missionary period almost three centuries of slave trade had complicated the picture, and American domestic policies further prevented the possible development of the thought that African converts were truly part of the same people of God.

Just as William Carey in India could sustain some reasonably positive sense, so a man like the famed David Livingstone did what he could to speak favorably of the African character and way. He came to know the Makololo and reported that "they perform actions sometimes remarkably good, and sometimes equally the reverse. . . . On the whole, I think they exhibit just the same strange mixture of good and evil as men do elsewhere." Such an assertion would have provided a good base for a Protestant doctrine of man. But even the loving Livingstone thought of the Africans as children, and most of his colleagues held more hostile or frustrated views of black possibility.[269]

In the nineteenth century biblically based distortions concerning the nature of man and race were scientifically reinforced by pseudo-Darwinian views of human development. In Africa in particular it was possible to explain black inferiority in the terms of retarded evolution and thus to justify exploitative policies. The conservative evangelicals needed only the Bible and their own eyes. The liberals and the secularizers, to whom Darwin was a more congenial figure, had a new and more respectable "scientific" basis. Despite all the sacrifices of Protestant missionaries, then, there were few reserves in Protestant theology or action on which to draw to prevent the development of colonial and imperial rationales for subjugating and mistreating blacks.

Nowhere were antiblack attitudes more successfully sustained on a Protestant base than in those southern African nations where very small clusters of whites formed governmental elites to keep the black's majorities from self-determination. Among these are Rhodesia and the Republic of South Africa. South Africa is regarded as the world's most notorious case study of ecclesiastical support for racist policy. The policy called apartheid seeks virtually complete segregation of races and prevents the native majority from attaining freedom or dignity.

The Dutch Reformed Church, the church of the majority within the governing minority, is constantly called upon to justify these policies to the rest of the Protestant world, where there has been at least some awakening of conscience on the matter. As late as 1954 at a conference of Protestant theologians the Anglican bishops agreed that apartheid, which creates two "peoples of God" on racial lines, was not contrary to Christ's teachings. And the Dutch Reformed leaders said that if whites and natives worked together it would be sinful. Equal rights "is a misinterpretation of scripture and therefore a defiance of the will of God." God was "Hammabdil, the Maker of Separations" of "light from darkness." It was the intention of the Lord that mankind should live in separate nations.[270]

If one is happy to report that these situations have changed in much of official Protestantism, the reporting can be done only in full recognition that when tested, most Protestants do not open their doors to each other across racial lines and that many of them continue to use their faith to reinforce their separatist attitudes. The awakening that finally did come, came often only because of the new aggressive consciousness of blacks and other nonwhites, or because of the efforts of government or commercial self-interests, or because of the exposure of public media of communication.

Even the liberal Protestant was slow to overcome his sense of white superiority. It is always unfair to judge men of previous ages by standards of a later one, though it should not be against the rules to measure Protestants by their own charter documents, including especially the New Testament. And it is a matter of regret that Protestant leaders who were forward-looking on other issues were unable to transcend racism.

Thus the American Social Gospel movement, which did some pioneering in the field of social justice early in the twentieth century, was if anything a retarding agency in the matter of foreseeing a full brotherhood in world Protestantism. Its liberal theologians often fused personal observation with Social Darwinian theory to justify a pattern of racial condescension. The white Anglo-Saxon was considered the normative or standard race, against which others were to be measured and graded.

Josiah Strong, one of the more effective publicizers of the movement, argued that in the whole order of creation the inferior is to make way for the superior. "Thus the Finns were supplanted by the Aryan races in Europe and Asia, the Tartars by the Russians, and thus the aborigines of North America, Australia and New Zealand are now disappearing before the all-conquering Anglo-Saxons. It would seem as if these inferior tribes were only precursors of a superior race, voices in the wilderness crying 'Prepare ye the way of the Lord!' " Meanwhile, Anglo-Saxon Protestant religiosity was "more vigorous, more spiritual, more Christian than that of any other." Yet Strong considered himself to be the enemy of racial prejudice.[271]

Racial stereotypes were even carried over among Caucasians to explain the superiority of Anglo-Saxons, Nordics, or Teutons, who chose Protestantism as opposed to the lazier, slovenly, more self-indulgent southern Europeans and South Americans, who remained in Catholic bondage by their own choice. Madison Grant, a racist with fewer redeeming features than Josiah Strong displayed, in his *Races of Europe* (1899) pointed out that the Nordic race as opposed to the Mediterranean race was made up of people who were "domineering, individualistic, self-reliant and jealous of their personal freedom both in political and religious systems and as a result they are usually Protestants." It was significant to him that most artists showed Christ to be blond. "This is something more than a convention, as such quasi-authentic traditions as we have of our Lord strongly suggest his Nordic, possibly Greek, physical and moral attributes."[272]

The racial theories of Protestant cultures up to the recent past might suggest that a pan-white religion devoted to its blond Christ might have united all men. But the Protestant people of God were more seriously divided from within than might have been expected, and these internal divisions were felt more acutely than those across racial lines, since racial separation often implied physical distances continents apart. The Protestant world was torn over the issue of the nationhood of its adherents, and equally explicit doctrines of national superiority and support of local patriotisms developed on Protestant soil with clerical sanction.

Late twentieth century resurgent nationalism throughout the Third World or among the developing nations displays many bonds to reawakening religions. In Japan, a highly developed non-Western land, revived Shinto, Buddhism, and other ancient faiths are joined by fresh value-creating agencies like *Soka gakkai* to support a new sense of national identity. China's cultural revolution had at least a quasi-religious cast, even where it opposed the traditional religions of China. The African nations as they have come to assert themselves are reexploring historic symbols of African religion and the Arab world cultivates ties with Islam to sustain new nationalism. Connections between religion and nationalism, then, are not surprising or new or few.

Students of modern religious nationalism, however, regularly point to the Protestant contributions as being early and intense. Hans Kohn attributes the particular strength of the Protestant-nationalist nexus (in comparison to the religious development in Catholic countries, where anticlericalism is often a part of nationalist movements) to the tendency, at least in continental Protestantism, to speak of a radical disjunction between civil and religious realms. Thus Martin Luther spoke of ruling the church by the Gospel and the state by the law, and not permitting the two spheres to have much to do with each other. This, in Kohn's eye, licensed the autonomous and encroaching state and left servile and patriotic Lutherans with little to do but to support the civil rulers whether they were good or bad—and to prop their support with biblical passages. It may well be that Lutheran Protestantism in Scandinavia and Germany has supported existing regimes and made such patriotic demands on these grounds.

The same argument does not hold true for the equally nationalistic British, Scots, Netherlanders, Swiss, and Americans. The nations that rose under the sphere of Calvinist and Reformed dominance did not accept Luther's version of a theory of two disengaged kingdoms. Every detail of civil life in Calvin's Geneva was to come under the scrutiny of religious authorities. In most of these nations the church was established and found few problems with establishment in its theology. No vacuum was left, as in Lutheran lands. Nationalism however, was supported there also by

Protestant theology and power. It must be said that not all the reasons for the gravitational pull of Protestantism to nationalism and vice versa have yet been understood. Perhaps the question of the connection is too historically complex to admit of explanation. Suffice it to say that nationalism has been a competitor to historic Protestantism in its quest for men's allegiance, even religiously speaking—and yet, paradoxically, has also been supported by the church's leadership, who should have perceived in it a threat to their own witness and message or power.[273]

Carlton J. H. Hayes, a foremost student of the religious dimensions of nationalism, argued that all the preconditions for modern versions of that faith were first present in England. Among these were the rise of vernacular literatures accompanied by the waning of cosmopolitanism; the decline of a sense of an *oikoumene;* the emergence of the monarchical national state over against feudalism, city states, or the warmed-over Holy Roman Empire; the transformation of guild or manorial local economy into a national-state economy; the disruption of Catholic Christendom and the establishment of national churches. All these were happening in the England of Henry VIII through Elizabeth I. Add to this the religious ideology infused by gifted Protestant spokesmen, and modern nationalism is on the scene. In England, for example, John Milton in the *Areopagitica* could speak of God-fearing Puritan Englishmen as God's chosen people, as Israelites had been long ago.

Milton's theoretical "apple-of-God's-eye" sense of chosenness was effected in the world of *Realpolitik* in the career of Oliver Cromwell and his attempt to produce a Protestant commonwealth. Even after the restoration of monarchy, England was never to forget this religious impulse to assert its chosenness in relation to other peoples. These people had learned that they were "a people that have had a stamp upon them from God; God having, as it were, summed up all our former honor and glory in the things that are of glory to nations, in an epitomy, within these ten or twelve years last past." Milton's or Cromwell's vision was not uncritical: there was to be a regenerate England that would conquer or serve the other nations as an example. In Scotland, the nationalism of the post-Reformation period was similarly reinforced by the sense of a set-apart *Ecclesia Scoticana.*[274]

Both sides of the channel and of the Atlantic evidenced a sense of chosenness, mission, and destiny. If the British version produced ambiguous consequences during the imperial period, the German counterpart was more ominous and, in the twentieth century, more destructive. Ernst Troeltsch underplayed the role of religion in the development of nationalism, but most other scholars have seen the rise of national churches in Protestantism to be contributors not only to Protestant weakness but also to national strength. Luther was no simple nationalist, though he did make use of early nationalist sentiments to bring German territorialists into harmony against the trans-Alpine tyranny of Rome. The Hussite movement in Bohemia was a tremendous stimulant to and exploiter of nationalist sentiment there, even before Luther.

Effective continental nationalism had to wait for the latter years of the Enlightenment and the years of romantic awakening. In Germany, for example, the philosopher Hegel gave metaphysical and religious reasons for seeing the divine plan come to a consummation in the rise of Prussia. Pro-Protestant thinkers like Johann Gottlieb Fichte and Gottfried Herder and the theologian Friedrich Schleiermacher were employing amazing rhetorical skills to stimulate German nationalism many decades before Prussia had risen to such prominence that it could provide armies to turn the sentiment into bloody aggression. Schleiermacher despised cosmopolitanism and considered it a vagrancy. "Christianity demands attachment to the nation"; whoever was not a nationalist was "an alien in his house of God."[275]

French Protestants, in the minority but also often in power, could join François Guizot in his lavish praise of national aspiration. Cannon were blessed on both sides in 1870 in the Franco-Prussian War. The German Kaiser could count on Protestant support just as Bismarck had before him, for court preachers stood by the sanction the German sense of chosenness. The account of the Nazi leadership's appropriation of Protestant machinery and ideology for the Reich is a familiar, sad chapter in the unfolding story.[276]

Particularly instructive is the case of Protestantism's formative role in American nationalism. Here was an instance where people of many different European backgrounds, English, Scotch-Irish, Scandinavian, German, Dutch, and French, could not unite on traditional grounds of common language or tradition. Yet they did have common territory and interest, and with little difficulty formed a relatively homogeneous nation in a short period of time.

There had been little sense of incipient nationalism until the middle decades of the eighteenth century. The symbols of unity had followed at first the lines of each colony or expressed bonds with the mother country. But the Great Awakening of the 1730s and 1740s found revivalists traveling from colony to colony developing a sense of intercolonial destiny. Reaction to the rumors that the Anglicans intended to place a bishop in the colonies was another stimulus. Ministers of many theological stripes, except for most Anglicans (who were sworn to support the crown) used their pulpits to call for the formation of an American nation after separation from England.[277]

A quarter century after the war and after the most difficult constitution-making efforts to create unity, it was Protestant churchmen who began to invoke the most extravagant claims for American destiny. They used, in many cases, postmillennial language, a terminology that envisaged optimistic and progressive men preparing a place and a time for Christ's second coming—in America. They developed missionary societies to carry the Gospel into the world and benevolent humanitarian agencies to transform semimoral America into a fitting place for the millennial rule.

The Mexican War, which many of them did not support, was seen by others as the opportunity to expand into Catholic territories in the hemisphere and to enlarge Christ's true Kingdom. The Civil War found the Protestant clergy to be the chief supporters of the south's morale, but northern clergymen were no laggards either, and liberals like Horace Bushnell and Theodore Parker joined their conservative colleagues in blessing their version of America's causes. At the end of the century, the Spanish-American War permitted a new burst of Protestant progressive patriotism, and the sense of mission or manifest destiny was reinforced in the churches, which had been growing throughout the century.[278]

What of the new nations, the developing countries, the Third World? It has been the experience at ecumenical conferences that for a variety of reasons the Protestants from the Younger Churches no less than their tired older parents tend to support their particularist and often warring regimes on religious grounds. There is little transcendence of the claims of the state on the part of evangelical churchmen, even when its ventures are morally compromising. At the end of the colonial and imperialist eras Protestant leaders in the expansive countries often seem to be more free than are Third World churchmen to engage in criticism of their government or to call for some detachment or disengagement from patriotic and military ventures in the name of a supranational Christ and an ecumenical people of God.

We have given attention to Protestant nationalism not because Protestantism alone has ordinarily supported whatever regimes have come to power. Most religions do. What is impressive or ironic in the Protestant picture is the fact that the prophetic Protestant principle specifically calls people to be most critical of the entities of which they are a part. They are to be skeptical about the claims of their own family, tribe, locale, community, church, and state. Many religions (like Shinto) explicitly call for an ideological bond between the religious and civil realms.

Protestantism responds to a Scripture which in the one half of its dialectic asks men to support the "powers that be." The other half calls for men to obey God rather than men; to speak God's testimonies before rulers and not to be ashamed; to call for righteousness and justice at any expense. Protestants have found it easier or more profitable to listen to the first half of its message than to the second, at the expense of the realization of a single people of God.

15. LIFE IN THE CITY OF MAN

Protestantism took form in a period when political secularization had begun. By political secularization is meant that the reality of a single empire that was intended to be coextensive with the *corpus Christianum* had begun to be challenged. Statesmen like Machiavelli appeared, to argue for a political order largely independent of ecclesiastical control or of historic theological foundation. Leaders of particular territories or what were to become nation-states, while remaining Christian, began to contend for positions at the expense of the papacy. In doing so they began to weaken the concept of a single Christendom in which empire and pope interacted in positive ways. More and more elements of society were coming to the point at which they no longer needed or desired theological symbols for interpretation. Renaissance art is an example. Protestantism found that relation to the new secular situation called for different theological resources and different practical strategies in the various areas where it began to spread. Working out the relations to the political order became an urgent task.[279]

The evangelical leaders had basically two models with which to work, and most of them finally adhered to one of these. The inheritance which came instinctively to the conservative reformers derived from Constantinian Christianity. For over a millennium the Western church operated in a pattern of mutual benefit to civil and ecclesiastical rulers. Documents (e.g., "The Edict of Milan") from the early fourth century symbolized the general end of the persecution of Christians while making Christianity the official religion of the Roman state. This heritage was affirmed by conservative reformers even as it was recognized as the beginning of the fall of the church by the left-wing reformers.

As a result of the Constantinian settlement, Christianity in the West lived in a single symbolic order which really permitted no dissent. Medieval sectarians had to become refugees. At various times heresy was proscribed and heretics were hunted down. To most Christians of that era no alternative to officially sanctioned or supported religion would have been conceivable. To rulers in the period, the need for civil powers to come to terms with religious leadership and symbols was essential, instinctive, a pragamatic necessity.

This is not to say that through these ages popes and emperors never disputed about power or jurisdiction. Nor should it imply that lesser mortals in the two hierarchies, religious and civil, were never at odds. Bishops and priests were constantly in conflict with the petty rulers, kings, and feudal lords across the Western European map. At times the pope succeeded in convincing European subjects that the spiritual realm was supreme and that the imperial powers had to do obeisance to it. In other periods the emperor came to ascendancy and a politically weakened pope did him service.

What was significant about the relationships was that it would not have occurred to antagonists to suggest that the two did not have to be part of a single reality. What later came to be called the separation of civil and religious realms would have been unimaginably remote from their minds even as they struggled for position and influence within a single cohering order. Many reformers were to inherit that medieval approach to political life, even though they rejected the pope as head of one sphere or the emperor as leader in the other.

The other model came from pre-Constantinian Christianity. Originally reconstructed by the more primitive sects and by leaders who advocated a return to the pristine and pure early apostolic Christianity, enough of it survived in later separationist Protestantism and in the consequent secular state to give warrant to the idea that this always had been the *only* Protestant intention. As remembered by these reformers, the early Christians appeared to be concerned to keep their distance from Caesar and all that the emperor symbolized. Christ's Kingdom was not of this world. While he permitted minimal recognition of the world's power to the point of suggesting that Jews should give Caesar's money back to Caesar, he was most concerned that men's lives be dedicated to giving back to God all that was due Him—which was everything except Caesar's mammon. Since Caesars regularly made anti-God demands it was clear that one could not always honor the emperor and support the civil rulers because Christians were to obey God rather than men.[280]

These reformers knew that the early Christians were often persecuted for a variety of reasons. While most of the new religions of the Mediterranean area were tolerated, Christians refused to make the minimum compromises with the religious cult of the emperor. Some of them were fanatics who evidently wanted to be persecuted. They appeared to be politically subversive. Communication of intentions and activities between imperial and Christian sides was often quite poor and this led to misunderstandings of the kind that lay at the basis of the political murder of early Christians.

Whatever the reasons, the new sectarians saw in their suffering an example of what Christ had expected of His people in a hostile world. As the reforming parties began to live out the logic of separation from many political demands, they began to suffer at the hands of both civil and religious powers. Before long they read themselves into the situation of the early Christian pilgrims, refugees, and exiles. Their experience was confirmed by a rereading of the New Testament and the fathers. Some of them did minimal obeisance and may have regarded the state as ordained by God. But they refused to take oaths, serve in armies, or provide theological support for the state's claims.[281]

The vast majority of sixteenth century Protestants adopted the more convenient and conventional Constantinian model. The whole Church of England, the Presbyterian Church of Scotland, all of the new state churches of emerging Scandinavia, the churches of the Netherlands, Switzerland, and many territories of Germany retained the tie between ecclesiastical and civil spheres of authority. The political battles and even military engagements of the era found conservative reformers basically content with such a situation.

The Peace of Augsburg of 1555 saw Protestant and Catholic leaders alike ready to accept the principle and practice *cuius regio, eius religio.* Whoever assumed political control of an area, Protestant of whatever variety or Catholic, was in a position to name the religion of that region or jurisdiction. Dissenters were in effect to be removed, exiled, suppressed, or converted; at best they might be tolerated. A hundred years later after the complex religious-military events of the Thirty Years' War, the Peace of Westphalia once more implied terms similar to those of Augsburg.[282]

Despite acceptance of the Constantinian paradigm, there were now differences from the earlier situation. Many of these were practical. It was one thing to see interpenetrating civil and religious realms when a single pope and emperor had stood at the top of the hierarchies. But the Holy Roman Empire was on the point of breaking up. The nationalism of most northern and western European territories induced intense rivalry against the pope and, increasingly, against the emperor, who often retained only figurehead importance. But these territories were in competition with each other, and different brands of Protestantism were at war with each other because of the political differences. It was difficult for this reason for a political Protestantdom to replace Christendom. And in many areas dissent acquired the allegiance of enough people to be a problem for uniformitarians. While Protestants joined Catholics in persecuting English and continental sectarians, their hearts were not always in it. In any case, they found it impossible to suppress or exile all dissenters the way medieval powers had isolated and banished Waldensians, Albigensians, and Cathari.

One other factor was important in the preparation of the situation whch was to lead to the breakup of Constantinianism two centuries later. Many of the mainline reformers, Luther not least of all, placed a new theological element into the political situation by their employment of language separating two spheres, the civil and the religious. In effect they set forth a charter for political autonomy. Rulers of secular states could with considerable plausibility reach back to men like Luther for legitimacy. So frequently and so effectively did they do so, and so prevalent has the separationist ideal become that these conservative reformers have often been given more credit than they deserve for the modern political arrangement.[283]

The seed may have been present in these reformers, but it was not to sprout for two centuries. The logic of a division between ecclesiastical and political regiments may have been implicit in their theologies and their own sense of statesmanship. But if the seed and the logic were there, they were not developed or acted upon until dissent had considerably more voice and until the secular orbit had been much more free to be enlarged, as it was in early America, where "separation between church and state" in the late eighteenth and early nineteenth centuries represented an innovation in the administrative side of church life.[284]

Some sort of nominal or minimally effective religious establishment has lived on into the late twentieth century in many Protestant nations, among them England, Scandinavia, and in a more compromised way, Germany. Yet this has become a minority situation. It is little believed in even by some archbishops who stand at the head of the religious forces. To most observers, religion supported by the state, whether in the form of tax subsidy or implicit recognition of its superior claims, is living on borrowed times. Almost everywhere else the autonomy of the state and the independence of the churches has become normative.

Since disestablishment, the voluntary system in church life and the relative separation between civil and religious authorities have become so widespread and have been advocated so frequently and strenuously by virtually all breeds and brands of Protestants that many have been led to believe that the later situation was promoted by all early Protestants. Since radicals and sectarians stood alone in anticipating and helping to bring about the modern situation, attention should turn to them first.

Radicalism and sectarianism have meant different things even within the first generation of Protestantism. Many of the sects were born in the context of militancy and sometimes even as part of a program for the violent overthrow of the existing order. Some of the radical prophets infused their followers with a revolutionary and iconoclastic spirit. As a consequence these followers began to storm the churches and topple images or smash the windows as marks of their opposition to the existing church.

Nor was that all. They would depict various apocalyptic futures in which the saints would rule if only they would take history into their own hands. By the middle of the 1520s, at the time of an aborted peasant uprising in Germany, some of the prophets allied with the revolutionary forces and took the sword into their own hands against Catholic and Protestant leaders alike. But it would be misleading to portray all sectarians as militants. The majority soon were advocating the path of nonresistance and peace. Many of the earlier militants later turned pacifist and adopted the strategy of letting themselves be victimized for the sake of Christ.[285]

Both the militant and the nonresistant antiestablishment patterns were present almost from the first in Protestantism. They did not rise as reactions to complacent evangelical leadership or compromises. By 1523 in Switzerland and by the mid-1530s in Germany they were present in great variety and with considerable sense of presence. While their eschatological promises varied from suggestions that the world was ending to the idea that they and their followers would rule, and while their styles differed from the idea of accepting to that of rejecting the sword, they united in one position. They refused to be satisfied with the existing political order and its ties with Catholic or Protestant religious powers. They wanted the two spheres separated, not merely because they feared that establishment granted illegitimate power and favored position to their ecclesiastical enemies. Instead, they believed that the pure and primitive apostolic church could be restored and the freedom of the Christian sustained only if they were able to develop religious life without the support or interference of the political rulers.

Separation for the sake of the purity of the church came easily in the political realm to people who had already resolved to be separate in the ecclesiastical realm. These sectarians were fighting against the idea of Christendom, whether Catholic or Protestant. They believed that the church had fallen as it had moved into Constantinianism. They thought that the more prominent reformers showed neither the intention nor the will to transcend that situation. The sectarians rejected what they saw to be a kind of automatic, nominal, and halfhearted church membership as a birthright. Instead they demanded discipleship, commitment, believer's baptism, and a self-conscious turning of one's back upon the world. Often they were literalists and in their reading of the Sermon on the Mount as the basic text from the career of Jesus they found it necessary to repudiate the idea of taking oaths. His injunction to love one's enemies and to turn the other cheek and his description of a Kingdom "not of this world" moved them into sincere positions of noncompliance with the demands of courts, military leaders, lawmakers, and civil rulers.

Such a view of a regenerate church separate from the state, with noncooperating members of the former standing at some distance from the leaders of the latter, did not always rise from a simply negative view of the state. Many Anabaptists allowed that the state was indeed the creation of God; they agreed with the established reformers that it belonged to the divine order of creation and that it could even do good among men. But this did not mean Christians could take political office.

These radicals knew that the state was built on the problem of channeling or suppressing violence, and the police or military power necessary for its perpetuation implied a coercion and other kinds of violence which they felt could not be executed by the regenerate, who lived in a realm of perfection and freedom. Ask them what would happen when a state would run out of nonregenerates to coerce submission, when all would be regenerates, and they would answer that the civil power as now known would no longer be needed when men reached perfection and lived in a realm governed by the love of Christ. That stage had not yet arrived, so the state was legitimate as an instrument for the nonregenerate. The true believers could not lift themselves out of the world of political orders entirely.

Government was to be affirmed in its sphere. But affirmation of government did not necessarily mean contentment with all existing governors or acquiescence in all that they demanded of Christ's people, including the taking of oaths or military service. Thus the radicals often appeared to be revolutionary.

While government was legitimate in its sphere, that sphere was to be limited to include noninterference in the life of the true Church. The radicals were also more ready than were the conservatives to invoke the sanctions of the biblical passage that Christians ought to obey God rather than men. They refused the kinds of compromises on this point which political Christians have always known they have had to make in the face of ambivalences in the political world. They have sometimes been described as New Testament monists who turned their back on the theocratic models and violent practices of God's ancient people as described in the Old Testament. They adhered more to the eschatological, politics-transcending language of Christ's Kingdom in the New Testament.

Some of the sectarian movements did come to power in certain isolated instances. Best known of these were the Quakers, who while they looked like separationists because of their opposition to the English church, actually had a theocratic picture in mind. They believed in the perfectibility of the Christian. During the decade or two of their rise to prominence in mid-seventeenth century England and in Pennsylvania in the American colonies, they were quite clear in their belief that nothing could now stop the free spread of the Spirit among the people of "the friendly persuasion." At last a political order could be built on free acceptance and love and not on the threat of the sword. They permitted men to hold governmental office.[286]

When the Spirit did not immediately bring about the Kingdom of peace and love and when Quakers saw that they would have to live in the face of a still evil government, most of them moved away from office-holding and into a kind of passivity or quietism. When Quaker William Penn was given title to a huge American territory, Quakers did come into rule. But their quietism and pacifism did not serve them well in the face of Franco-British and Indian military challenges and by the 1740s they yielded power as the result of the compromises of some and—as the world counted such things—the political irrelevance and ineffectiveness of the others. Quakerism remained a kind of brief theocratic exception to the sectarian separationist rule.

Eventually more influential than the left-wing reformers or the

Quaker theocrats were the clusters of dissenting Puritans, Brownist, Congregationalists, Separationists, and Baptists who grew to prominence in seventeenth century England and the Netherlands and who were to find in the American colonies a theater for experiment. Out of them has grown the peculiar modern Protestant position regarded by many in America at least as the inclusive or exhaustive Protestant statement.[287]

The peculiarity of the position lay in the separationists' intention and ability to live with a complicated stance. On one hand, they wanted church and state to be separate, both to permit the development of a free state and to prevent interference by the civil power in the churches. On the other hand, they took very positive views of government, believed that the Christian should involve himself with political office and process, and urged that Christianity, once it was disestablished and freed of legal bonds, should be permitted to have an impact on the civil affairs of men.

A brief glance at the American resolution and at the part this style of dissent played will illumine a broadly accepted modern version of the Protestant position. Many of the earliest colonists had been theocrats. The kinds of Puritans who came to power in the Massachusetts Bay Colony did not have the separation of civil and religious spheres in mind. Nor did the more moderate and latitudinarian Anglicans in Virginia picture disestablishment as a desirable circumstance. But the American equivalent of a believers' church grew up in a variety of schisms in New England's Congregational churches as the separatist and Baptist factions came to prominence. In the middle colonies, Baptists, Mennonites, and other dissenters were welcomed, and from this base they spread both north and southward. New England's Baptists made their way down into Virginia. Presbyterians and Lutherans, congenial to establishment in Scotland and in Germany and Scandinavia, sided with dissenters when they came to America. Quakers, no longer theocratic in outlook, sided with all these.

Meanwhile, out of some Protestant and some Enlightenment backgrounds, a number of statesmen began to advocate disestablishment in the various colonies and to support a separation of the political and ecclesiastical realms. Thomas Jefferson, Benjamin Franklin, James Madison, and others joined forces with dissenting clerics. In the face of all this, established church leaders made an increasing number of concessions and compromises and found that, if anything, the churches did as well without governmental support and in a situation of voluntary acceptance and freedom.[288]

The practical necessity of building a nation out of colonies with differing establishments or no legal provisions for religion at all forced the situation. Between the 1770s in the southern colonies and the 1820s and 1830s in the northern, the last legal ties were broken. The struggle had taken no lives and led to the imprisonment or inconveniencing of few; the votes were present in legislatures and in the populace; therefore, the change seemed inevitable. But its consequences were dramatic and its implications epochal. At last the Constantinian pattern had been decisively broken. Anglicans, Lutherans, and Calvinists who had chosen the Constantinian pattern in Europe found the new mode congenial and often claimed it to be a working out of their own theological logic—as, in some cases, it may have been.[289]

Most of the Americans happily adjusted to disestablishment. The evangelicals remained the strongest religious force and were often able to mobilize votes for legislative programs they favored. They were free to infuse the new republic with evangelical ideals and interpret it with Protestant symbols. However, when millions of Catholics came on the scene, they feared that the end of evangelical republicanism was at hand. Many of them intensified their support of separationism, no longer for the sake of the freedom of the church but because they feared that the vestiges of establishment in national practice could be exploited by the Catholic leaders and masses and would lead to support of Catholic institutions.

While Protestants continued to accept tax exemption for their institutions and through the subsequent century made many compromises with the idea of "absolute separation," they worked almost unanimously through the middle of the twentieth century to see to it that no tax funds reached the peculiar institution of Catholic parochial schools. An ideological separationism was the result of this practical situation, and many Protestants became vigilantes along what Jefferson had called the wall of "the separation of church and state."[290]

Most separationists advocated the autonomous state and the voluntary church, but they did not believe that such a distinction need lead to passivity. From their tradition came much of the impetus for modern political Protestantism. Congregationalists, Presbyterians, Baptists, and others who did not welcome ties between civil and religious realms did believe that Christians should invoke symbols of Christ's coming Kingdom to transform the social order. They worked for what Walter Rauschenbusch called the Christianization of the industrial, economic, educational, familial, social, and even political orders in movements of social reform and eventually through the Social Gospel. They were joined in this by Episcopalian Christian Socialists, even as most Lutherans, despite their old Erastian or theocratic views, believed that modern separation meant that the Church as Church should not involve itself with social transformation. Decisions about politics and the state in modern Protestantism, it can be seen, do not consistently grow out of the sixteenth century positions so much as out of other kinds of theological emphases or historical contingencies.[291]

The heirs of the conservative and established Protestants of England, Scandinavia, and Germany, and the Reformed nexus of the Netherlands, parts of Germany, Switzerland, and parts of France, vastly outnumber the descendants of sectarian Protestantism in most parts of the Protestant world. They have been given the task of adapting their own Erastian or theocratic lineages so that they could come to terms with the autonomous, secular modern political states that their fathers unwittingly helped spawn.

The Church of England developed without any desire for separation between civil and religious realms on the part of the reformers. Just before the Reformation the monarch had been named Defender of the Faith, a title he was to keep after the schism with the papacy. Parliament for four and a half centuries has played its part in governing the Anglican Church, including regulation of the Book of Common Prayer, and relations between crown and mitre have always been close. Dissent rose only through bloodshed at the time of the Puritan revolt and on toward the time of the Glorious Revolution of 1688.

From 1689 on through the next two centuries British churchmen engaged in long, gradual, moderate compromises and adaptations. As they yielded power to secular authorities and space to Nonconformity and dissent, they did not lose interest in political and social influence. The Christian Socialists and a distinguished lineage of activist bishops, priests, and laymen and laywomen signified the Anglican heirs' intentions to bring the worlds of Christ and Caesar together on a new set of terms as the old legal pattern changed.[292]

Except for a complicated situation in Scotland, Calvinism had fewer of the problems and possibilities associated with monarchy to deal with during its rise. Calvinist leaders, particularly in Switzerland and parts of Germany, were really free to help establish government on models of their choice. But John Calvin and his associates on the Continent and John Knox in Scotland were anything but separationist in their logic. Every detail of Genevan life, including most notably those in the legal sphere, was scrutinized by ecclesiastical leaders. Heretics were persecuted on Calvinist soil as they had been on Catholic territory. Calvin was a legally trained man and possessed a sophisticated knowledge of government, as did many French and Dutch Calvinist leaders.

While the Genevan and Massachusetts Bay theocracies were eventually to disintegrate, Calvinism's heirs did take over into the secular political era their leader's positive view of government and his mandate to Christians to have regard for the civil welfare of men. Calvinism in its established heritage joined forces with the sons of dissenters in the Social Gospel movement and in other attempts to bring Protestant theology into relation with public life. The transition from theocracy to democracy never meant for Calvinists an abdication from responsibility for the political ordering of life, and they have distinguished themselves in that sphere.[293]

The record of Lutheranism has been much different. Luther said enough about the distinction between the civil and religious "regiments" to make it possible for moderns to draw on him for elements of a separationist ideology. It is true that he conceived of the two realms very distinctly. The church was ruled by the Gospel, and the law had no place in the life of the justified man. The state was ruled by the law, where the grace and mercy of the Gospel would have led to sentimentalization and disorder. To rule the church by the law and the state by the Gospel would, in his formula, mean to enthrone the devil and to exile God. Such language, accompanied as it was by often negative references to the state's role makes Luther sound like a dualist. Yet the Gospel and the law of God were, finally, both parts of the Word of God and in that transcendent sphere were seen to be united. Luther rejected the sectarian identification with the peasants' revolt and sided with the princes (whom he also regularly scolded), partly out of his fear of anarchy and disorder. He accepted the government of the churches by prince-bishops in a settlement that may be characterized as Erastian.

Luther did not succeed, then, in fulfilling the radicals' dream of keeping the churches free of civil government and interference. Nor was he successful at providing a rationale for Christians' disobedience to the state beyond some support of what today would be called selective conscientious objection, the need to refuse to fight in unjust wars along with some occasional reference to the reminder that "we ought to obey God rather than man."

In the matter of Romans, chapter 13, Luther sounded much more authoritarian, asking for unquestioned obedience to "the powers that be." The Christian citizen should take part in the political processes, could hold governmental offices, and as a Christian prince, should rule equitably and with even temper. But the Church as such could hardly serve as a check against the unjust civil order or ruler. The Sermon on the Mount was interpreted to fit into the prior acceptance of Romans, chapter 13, as the basic biblical word on the matters of politics. The Lutherans revealed a Constantinian state of mind in their acceptance of the terms of the Peace of Augsburg. The tradition of Lutheranism in Germany, Scandinavia, and America through the period of the rise of modern nationalism has been toward passivity, uncritical acceptance, and acquiescence in the face of the demands of the state.

The virtually complete secularization of the modern state, the scope of problems not capable of resolution without political involvement, and the shock of Lutheran complicity in the rise of the totalitarian state in Nazi Germany shocked people of the Lutheran tradition into reexamination. In an ecumenical age they have been free to go shopping at Calvinist or sectarian counters and to incorporate elements of other Christian traditions. But through the examples of Bishop Eivind Berggrav in Norway or Martin Niemöller and Dietrich Bonhoeffer in Germany they have taken a new look at Luther's doctrine of two regiments.

The move from acquiescence toward resistance and political involvement has come out of two Lutheran resources in particular. On the one hand, there has been a new appreciation that in Luther, too, the law is also God's law and is a *dynamis* or power for working out human relations, although it is not a saving agency. And in Luther's endorsement of *justitia civilis*, the civic righteousness of citizen or ruler even if he is not a believer, there has been found the germ of a positive view which calls the Church to relate to the world not through the Gospel but through the law. Luther's direct contributions to modern political democracy have been called into question but his indirect aid for Christians who recognize the importance of politics has been studied and acknowledged in fresh ways.[294]

Protestantism brought to modernity, then, two basically conflicting approaches to civil and political order. In this case as in few others the sectarians' minority position eventually was accepted by the majority and established Protestantism came to recognize in it both a means of keeping religion free of state intervention and of permitting the civil powers to extend religious liberty and to be neutral in things of the spirit, without abdicating all responsibility for making a Christian witness and to engage in creative activity in politics and government.

16. PROTESTANTISM AND THE WORLD OF PRODUCTION

The student of world history who studies the atlas of the Protestant and non-Protestant worlds should soon notice something remarkable. Where Protestantism has been active for some time in history, there industrial and technological progress, or "modernization," seems to have taken place earlier and at a more rapid rate than elsewhere. The connection between Protestantism and productivity has therefore produced much discussion and remains a controversial topic.

Not only is it the case that the North Atlantic nations, once under Protestant dominance, outstripped the areas that make up what now is called the Third World or the underdeveloped or developing nations, or that these nations developed more readily where the Western influence was strong. In a subtler measure, these lands of Protestant ethos also earlier outproduced the other European and Western hemispheric nations, where Catholicism was and remained dominant. When one speaks on such a world-historical subject, exceptions are apparent, but the connection has been so obvious that it has evoked curiosity. A number of theories are possible.

The first of these would speak of simple and complete coincidence. In such an interpretation, it would be noted that virtually all factors leading to a certain kind of development were present in lands that happened also to be Protestant, and that Protestantism was largely irrelevant to the subsequent history. It could be that central Europe and England, where a new kind of capitalism appeared in the sixteenth century, would have proceeded on the same course had there been no Luther or Calvin or Puritan leaders. For the onset of the industrial revolution, similarly, it could be that England, and then the United States, with Germany in a parallel development, just happened to have the combination of resources, population, native inventiveness, and opportunity to trigger a "take-off in economic growth" and that it would have made no difference had the whole populations of these remained Catholic.

Such coincidences are possible in history, and it is impossible to refute to everyone's complete satisfaction the critics of alternatives. After all, something happened. We do not know why matters did not develop on the same schedule everywhere and we have no way of repealing history to learn the exact complex causes at the start of such a phenomenon. Yet the coincidental theory is not too attractive. Too many suspicions that a clue is present have emerged in the mind of the person who observes the lines of congruence between areas of Protestant dominance and places where productivity was early, rapid, and intense. Therefore, whether they chose to credit Protestantism for bringing the world into a new era or blame it for permitting exploitation of the earth and the alienation of men in a capitalist-industrialist society, most of them have gone on to suggest that somehow the culture of evangelical faith and the world of production were bonded, causally connected.

A second view, much easier to defend, would suggest that almost all factors for development were present in north central Europe and Anglo-America. Protestantism was a trigger or a constant nudging mechanism, to start and hurry along what would have happened anyway. Technology or investing have their own logic and their own kinds of attractiveness, and men responded. But the Protestant had special reasons for doing so, and his ardor helped the cause along. This approach is attractive in that it does not make extravagant claims, does justice to natural and secular factors in history, and still allows for a specific kind of spiritual agency. We shall return to an elaboration of it later.

The most widely accepted yet the most controversial attitude has been one which sees Protestantism providing a real initiative and continuing impetus in the world of productivity. Much economic analysis that relates religion to production in modern times has followed Marxian lines. These suggest, in effect, that in class struggles or in economic management a certain course of action is desirable for people who have acquired power. Their status, situation, and class predispose them to act predictably. But they are uneasy about some of the bases for or consequences of their activity. So they reach for a self-justifying rationale, an ideology which legitimates their course.

An alternative view arose in the case of Protestantism. What if people acted on certain views of life, death, and destiny, views which they held even when these were inconveniencing? What if it turned out that these particular views were what were needed to set the modern economic and industrial productive process in motion? Beliefs have consequences, and these beliefs were sufficiently sustaining to support people through development.

Variants of such a view have been widely propagated and adhered to in the twentieth century and anticipated long before that. Development went through several stages. First, before modern industrialization occurred, there was something called capitalism, and people at Geneva under Calvin's influence, or in England at the time of the Puritans gave it a great push. They were willing to risk capital for investment and learned how to have money work for them.

Then, in a more dramatic stage, the world saw a change which had to be called a revolution even though few guns were fired. It signified a transformation of the landscape from green villages to huge smoky cities connected by railroads and filled with modern inventions, all within a second of cosmic history, a seventy- or eighty-year period. This industrial revolution has not ended, but has gone into second and third stages. Meanwhile, evangelical Protestants who were experiencing revival helped people interpret the new age and make use of its opportunities.[295]

If we suspend judgment for the moment and forget about subtle variations on the historical factors, we can do justice to some of the features in Protestantism which have been cited as explanatory of the connections. The first of these is the fact that Protestantism was a religion of seriousness at the moment when the world demanded great dedication to progress. Whereas Catholicism had allowed for moral lapses with a convenient sacramental system permitting people to come under grace and into good graces, the Protestant approach to forgiveness, however theologically celebrative, was psychologically sobering.

One had to show forth the fruits of forgiveness. A kind of asceticism had moved from the monastery out into the world, and most Protestants took a dim view of cavorting and orgies, of the residues of the medieval feast of fools or the sixteenth century equivalent of fiestas and siestas in the warmer climates. Protestantism was often opposed to fun, even good clean fun—and fun was a distraction from production. It wasted time and could lead to purposelessness, dissipation, and drift.[296]

Not only was Protestantism serious; it had a peculiar doctrine of man's place in the divine scheme. Particularly in the Calvinist lineage it was believed that man was predestined for salvation or condemnation. What did this doctrine have to do with production in the world? Many critics of the theories that there were ties are befuddled on this front. Would not people have been expected to be simple libertines in such a system, since it had already been determined whether or not they were saved? Or if not libertines, would they not at least have been passive, letting God do all things? Men were respondents, not agents in such a plan.

Such a theory would make sense if the Calvinists had shown passivity in other fields. But they were industrious. They tried to anticipate every aspect of civic and governmental life; they were busy rearranging familial life and personal ethics. Somehow, whether it made logical sense to non-Calvinists or not, they found it important to say that men should take over agency in history. They should act in such a way that they could prove their election and demonstrate that they were part of the predestined community. If that was the case, it so happened that this proving had to go on largely in the world of the market or the farm or the workshop, since these believers had already turned their back on ecclesiastical asceticism and had left the monastery doors and the convent's cloistered walls behind. One demonstrates that he is among God's called by the way he makes use of his time and proves himself in the world.

To the idea of a religion of seriousness and the need to prove one's election, add another element. While this was all to be enacted in the world, the divine-human transaction was beginning to turn more mundane. The result has been called a worldly asceticism. Students of the complex subject of secularization credit Protestantism with being an agent of the move that caused men, who had their eyes only on heaven above, to turn also to the earth below. In the Catholic system, some insecurity was built into all of life. The quest for forgiveness then involved some constant appeasement of God through participation in the obligations of the church. But in Protestantism there was less constant devotion to the question of one's merits before God and a certain freedom to pursue the things of the world that stood before man—even though man was not to lose sight of the realm where moth did not corrupt nor treasures rust.

Now our Protestant, still believing and pious though he may be, was taking a new look at the resources of earth. But he was sufficiently troubled lest he should lose himself in them. He was not sufficiently conscience-free to avoid asking how he could best make use of the resources. So Protestantism developed a view of the stewardship of the goods of the earth and the hours of the day.

Since man's life was being measured as a fulfillment of his response to the divine, he should not waste his moments or his days. He must make good use of his time and shun the frivolous. He must notice that generations will follow him and that he must therefore be a steward of the minerals and products of the world. He was to be worldly but not too worldly. In John Wesley's familiar formula, he was to earn all he could, save all he could, and give all he could of the world's things—and yet not turn simply worldly. His Christian doctrine of stewardship was a kind of subtle control or check. This view of stewardship later helped make possible the rise of a middle class, as it led people away from views in which they accepted their status as being all that God intended for them.[297]

Enter another factor: the system of government. If government turned out to be hostile toward the enlargement of the circle of the affluent; if it chose to inhibit the gathering of wealth; if it insisted on a static view of who was to rule and be ruled, there was little opportunity for everyone to take part in capitalist or industrial change—or at least not in the late medieval or early modern context. (Marxian and other socialisms produced variants of the Christian transformation later on; we are here talking only about liberation from a medieval society.)

Now it happens, say some theorists, that the same Protestantism which favored production was also instrumental in propagating doctrines of man that helped prepare the way for modern democracy. The case for this point does not have to be overdone. Not all of Protestantism was freeing, and the world's modern liberators have by no means always been Protestant. Some democratizing trends occurred apart from and in spite of the churches of Protestantism. But there was some opening in the sphere in which men were governed, and Protestantism made some contribution to it.[298]

Finally, Protestantism offered a doctrine of one's vocation or calling which allowed for a new sense of the meaning of production. In a somewhat overstated case, linguistic studies suggested that the Latin or Catholic nations did not even have a term which meant quite what "calling" or *Beruf* or *Kallelse* meant in northern Europe. This was the case because the true vocation had been purportedly confined to the convent or monastery, to clerics who were called to serve God through a spe-

cial ministry—while everyone else simply followed his pursuits
without special divine sanction.[299]

This theory suggests that the closing of the monasteries meant
that the concept of vocation could move outdoors. The forgiven
Christian tried to please God not on his knees but at his desk. He
was free to work out the consequences of the guiltless life by
making shoes or investing capital and not only by following rou-
tines of prayer. This concept of a calling in the middle of one's
world was a major impetus for effecting change in a developing
world.

The theorists who thus link Protestantism and production in the
capitalist and industrial-technological transformation of the world
find plenty of historical moments for reexamination, and recognize
the complexity of the problems that come with the details. The
case is familiarly made in the instance of Puritans in earlier
England. They were pilgrims working their way through a hostile
world. But they were also enterprising lawyers and importers, people who sought the world's improvement and their own advancement.

In the Wesleyan era the new evangelical came along to justify
man's climbing in the industrial and economic system just at the
moment when climbing was possible and, in a way, necessary. Not
everyone grasped the ethic or profited from it. A whole working
class emerged in an industrial nation like England without ever
really coming under the care of the church. There seemed to be
no necessary Protestant interpretation that helped him account for
his world or make his life bearable. But for some decades, middle-
class entrepreneurs found in their evangelical beliefs a base for
expansive action.[300]

In England the need for ecclesiastical interpretation or sanction
seemed to disappear very rapidly, and pragmatic views of production soon predominated while the churches lost out. Secularization
followed a somewhat different trend in America. People not only
did not fall away from the old churches; they built and filled new
ones. They did not turn their back on the preachers who had
earlier told them to shun riches and be content with poverty.

Now they welcomed the words of the same preachers or their
sons who reread their Protestant Gospel and announced that god-
liness was in league with riches; that God wanted men to make,
save, and give money; that poverty was not simply a state given by
God but a situation gained by evil or errant men who were being
punished for their sloth. Significantly, in the United States even

those who were not a part of the churches kept something of this ethic. William Graham Sumner and others added a scientific frill, turning the competitive productive code into Social Darwinism, and Andrew Carnegie called his ethic the Gospel of Wealth.[301]

The classical formulator of the view which tied Protestantism to capitalism was the German sociologist Max Weber. He has not been mentioned to this point for two reasons. First, because he is not responsible for all the kinds of associations suggested here. He stated his case in a rather precise fashion, concentrating on a couple of Protestant moments. The other reason: evocation of his name points to one of the most vehement controversies in twentieth century sociology of religion, if not of all sociology in the West, the debate over "the Protestant Ethic." In that debate Weber has been overcredited and overblamed for some creative and still quite modest interpretations of history. So dramatic, so beguiling, and so apparently self-explanatory did his essay seem to his disciples that their enthusiasm evoked criticisms which ranged all the way from those that necessitated slight details of revision to those that dismissed him wholesale.[302]

Just as it is unprofitable here to detail the "Weber thesis" controversy, so it is impossible to avoid some discussion of the topic to which it related. Why has there been so much controversy? There are many reasons. Weber and his school may have been simply wrong. They were certainly wrong in detail, and historians who scrutinize almost any of the instances he cited can find reason to fault him. Further, a secular age mistrusts frankly religious explanations for phenomena so encompassing as capitalism or, later, industrial development.

There are other good reasons. It can be shown that there was capitalism before there was Protestantism and that in fact many Genevans or Netherlanders who were Calvinist either dragged their feet in the matter of Calvinism, or were capitalists but did not seek or seem to employ their religious interpretations to explain and legitimate their course. A number of students have carefully looked at development in parts of the world where Protestant influence was minimal and found that other religions or ideologies could also coexist with capitalism. What was unique about Protestantism's commitment to it?

What can be said? It is hard to challenge the observation that Protestantism and the ethos of productivity developed side by side; there is something to the view presented by the Protestant atlas. Without trying to determine whether or not developments would have come "purely secularly," one can say that they did come with the benefit of Protestant rationales and energies, and they probably look or sound somehow different because of the endorsements they received.

The student of the phenomenology of Protestantism is committed to seeing what particular flavor evangelical Christianity contributed to a process that may have come without its aegis or accompaniment even as he keeps his eye on the obvious effects capitalism and industrialization had on Protestantism. It seems incontrovertible to say that these disrupted both traditional community and parish life. They placed a different kind of valuation on the roles men played in production. They did help force man to look at inventiveness and creative processes in a new way. And they no doubt contributed to the altered view in which man had increasing dominion over creation—even to the point that he may have lived under the illusion that whatever was made was made by man.[303]

The connections between the world of production and the world of Protestantism left the reflective believer with dilemmas and ambiguities. He was not to give himself completely to the world, but he was to be at home with it in new ways. He did not want to give up his belief in a transcendent order, but the mundane became ever more distracting or attractive. Whether he was the great agent of change or not because of his creed, he did find clerics and theologians at hand who could reinterpret and transform his creeds so they at least allowed and encouraged him to participate in production and development. After all, did not his Bible tell him to "have dominion" and "subdue" the creation? What the earnest Protestant set out to do at all, he did with a vengeance. He could prove his election or, when he failed, could find forgiveness at hand. Somehow he remained thirsty for an otherworldly Gospel if he adhered to the church at all even as he embraced the world afresh.

17. EXPRESSION IN THE ARTS

Religion and the arts have long been seen to have common roots and common appeals. The ecstasy of the prophet and the inspiration of the poet bear some common characteristics. The pictorial artist has been able to render concrete that which otherwise would have been diffuse, vague, or abstract, and thus has helped focus the imagination of worshipers. Worshipers have often danced before their gods, sung praises, or acted out dramas which paralleled stories of divine judgment or rescue. Religionists build altars, shrines, or temples, and the impulse to adorn them is strong. So great has been the appeal of the arts that many religions have also found reason to limit or prohibit the use of graven images which might distract from spiritual realities. Christianity through the years has experienced all these connections and its leaders periodically have encouraged the arts or been ambivalent or hostile in their presence.[304]

For numerous reasons, Protestantism has been seen chiefly in the latter category. Protestant champions of the arts like to recall their great creative geniuses: can a faith which has attracted a painter like Rembrandt van Rijn, a poet like John Milton, or a composer like Johann Sebastian Bach legitimately be seen as a discourager or inhibitor of the artistic impulse? It is argued that the Reformation itself swept Europe in part because its first generation gave people songs and hymns to sing. The northern Europeans, the Americans, and their missionaries—no less than the Catholics—built houses of God. Religious educators have consistently decorated their lesson materials with illustrations of biblical scenes; these may vary greatly in quality and rarely are high art, but, it is reasoned, they give evidence of the fact that Protestants do not always fear representation in images.

Despite the occasional outbursts of genius and the more frequent encouragement of talent, the record of Protestantism in relation to the arts is mixed. When estheticians or art historians reach for adjectives to characterize this faith's expressions, they usually content themselves with words like "realistic," "full of simplicity," "straightforward," or "iconoclastic." The first three of these are admirable qualities in the arts, but if they are overemphasized, the limits placed on consistent artistic development are obvious. And the fourth, iconoclastic or image-breaking, is, of course, a destructive impulse. Protestantism is a religion of the Word, uneasy about objectification of the divine drama in images which might themselves draw the devotion of the supplicant from the invisible God beyond the gods. It has often and maybe even usually been uneasy about unrestricted bodily attention, and has rather consistently feared the ecstasy of the dance through most of the years of its history. Despite Rembrandt, Milton, and Bach, and a host of lesser figures, it can be seen that Protestantism had reasons to be uneasy with arts.

The Protestant eye has not always been closed to beauty, even when images were prohibited. The rigorous Shaker sect in America restricted most forms of art, but it encouraged communal dances while discouraging overt erotic expression. Its devotees found ways to depict elements of the divine drama. The tools and furniture of this simple people are widely regarded as esthetic achievements in the practical field. The Community of True Inspiration at Amana, Iowa, may have forbidden the painting of houses as an ostentatious luxury, but it did not prohibit its adherents from building trellises completely covering houses so that vines and flowers might grow to beautify them. Protestant movements which prohibited visual arts often saw their followers produce magnificent song. The drama of the theater might have been proscribed, but subtly transformed dramatic elements survived in the stately processions and movements of the liturgy.[305]

At times beauty has even served as one of the highest metaphysical categories. Jonathan Edwards, perhaps America's most noted theologian and revivalist, placed "consent to being" at the center of his system as a description of divine order or the fitness of things in a universe governed by the living God. The Puritan preachers were critical of florid rhetoric, but they strove for a direct and ordered pulpit style which gave shape to their generation's striving for beauty. Arts incorporating use of the word were seen to be least threatening, and music was often encouraged. Even when the visual arts have been employed, Protestant decisions were often based less on fear of all representation than on concern lest "papist" approaches be perpetuated, to the confusion of the faithful.[306]

When freed of these polemical concerns, the evangelicals have not, Muslim style, eschewed images for abstract and geometrical decoration. They permitted frankly anthropomorphic portraits of the invisible Father or Spirit and did not shrink from the theologically scandalous aspects of the humanity of Jesus Christ, the incarnate one.[307]

The roots of Protestant ambiguity on these subjects are tangled and complex. Among them is the historical case. Protestantism emerged at a moment when what might be called the secularization of the arts had already proceeded far. Whereas most of the artistic endeavor of the Middle Ages had been filled with biblical or church historical content or had been created under the patronage of the church and for its use, by the time of the Reformation the Renaissance revealed artists to be preoccupied with thisworldly and even frankly pagan themes. Even when the church was sponsor of the arts as it often was in the Italian Renaissance, it tolerated or enjoyed lavish and sensual imagery which offended the Protestant sensibility.[308]

The religious roots of the dance had been largely lost and the world-denying Protestant saw only erotic or other distracting vestiges in the dance of its day, a dance which could not easily be incorporated into worship. The medieval mystery and morality plays had begun to give way to drama which was a competitor to and not a servant of the church's worship. Protestantism, involved with the grim business of survival, developed doctrines of stewardship which saw most artistic production to be frivolous, trivial, or demonic.

Protestants knew well enough that the arts had served religion in the past. Concerned as they were to ratify or certify all the experiences which the Bible had offered, the divines were forced to recognize that David had danced naked before the altar, an act that was not disapproved of in the biblical documents though it was certainly offensive to the emerging modern mentality of Europeans. They knew that art signified the appropriation of the world of nature and human creativity into the divine order of things or it symbolized the divine penetration of the natural—ideas that should reinforce such an incarnational religion as early Protestantism claimed to be. They knew of the aid that myth and ritual, artistically adorned, gave to the straying imaginations of worshipers. But they also remembered that these could overpower, that the prophets scorned solemn assemblies where graven images prevailed. Theologically they had no choice but to be ambivalent.

To the historical phenomenon of the secularization of the arts and the theological necessity to deal paradoxically with a human endeavor so potent there must be added a third reason for Protestant difficulties with the arts. In a sense this afflicted Catholic artists as well, but not in the acute form. Catholics, with their agreements upon liturgical calendars, their well-established lore about martyrs and saints, and their long traditions in architecture, were able to evoke a common imagery based on an accepted pool of symbols.

Protestantism was born at a time when this lore was being dissipated, when there was a breakdown of the world of symbolic communication. No longer was the visible world so easily seen to be transparent to another invisible order of things, with symbolic connections that could be agreed upon by all. The bread and wine no longer "became" the body and blood of Christ; they tended merely to represent these. The connection between the symbol and the symbolized was now arbitrary, casual, and random. Each artist tended to have to create his own symbolic universe. The result was a decline in the communicative qualities of art and the development of private skeins of meaning. The case of William Blake demonstrates that such a trend is not always debilitating to the creation of great art, but it also shows how it complicates public and liturgical comprehension. Each artist seemed to be on his own; he could not rely upon a tradition as a base for recognition of what he wished to say.[309]

A final major inhibitor of Protestant expression was the intense moral preoccupation of the adherents of this version of Christianity. Those who stand in the Protestant tradition take for granted the bonds between religion and morality and have difficulty being empathic with those who have professed religions in which morality is secondary. Other faiths have been content to provide an interpretation of meaning in the universe or to suggest esthetic delight without pressing at all points for the moral consequences of the interpretation of the delight.

Protestant Christianity, however, came on the scene in part as a morally reforming agency. It attracted people who often wanted to discipline themselves for participation in their movement and for building a better world. An obsession with biblical and other Christian moral claims resulted. The artist was not always so preoccupied with the moral implications of what he did. In a sense, his art was to exist for its own sake or for the viewer's or listener's delight. The addition of moralizing features often meant the death of art.

A survey of Protestantism's varied relations with the arts begins with a recall of its attitude toward dance. A chapter on the subject would be very brief; a library on it would be rather bare. There has been, until recently, almost no Protestant encouragement of the dance except among marginal groups like the Skakers. Gerardus van der Leeuw, a student of the subject, went so far as to say that "the idea of a religious dance is inconceivable" to Protestants, who tended to frown even on innocent dances outside the religious circle. A religion that did not dance or that could not conceive of dancing is certainly an exception in history, and it breaks ties with most of its ancestors.

The dance was one of the most elemental art forms. It seemed to be universal as exhibitor of the play elements that were so closely related to the rise of the religious impulse. Dance helped the faithful channel their eroticism, symbolize the religious aspects of fertility, ward off lightning or war or judgment, or call attention to the beauty of bodily movement. Never in Protestantism![310]

The dance and its type of theater survived only in barely recognizable routinized and stately forms in liturgical movement. Not all Protestants did away with processions; there were ordered and graceful movements on the part of the minister and sometimes his attendants even in the most austere of Reformed churches. The Anglicans could "beat the bounds of their parish" on Rogate Sunday, when clerics and laymen alike processed around the borders of the parish. Regal Protestants allowed for banners and trumpets and flags to tie their liturgies to the monarchical enterprises which they endorsed. Many of the motions connected with the river baptism of radical Protestants or the accession to the altar in the Lord's Supper on the part of the more ceremonial retain elements of the dance. But one way to assure the minimization of these features would be to call attention of Protestants to the "dance" aspects of these. They would either refute the charge or purge the element itself. Dance and theater have had almost no place in Protestant worship until the recent past, and they have even been discouraged in most cultures surrounding Protestantism.

The case of music, so closely related to the dance or theater, is vastly more complicated. Almost every Protestant leader or movement has been called upon to take a stand in relation to the musical arts. Sometimes there has been frank and open endorsement and encouragement, and music has been incorporated into the most sacred moments of celebration of the Christian drama. At the opposite extreme, there have been occasional and usually unsuccessful efforts to prohibit all music. More frequently, music was at once encouraged and discouraged: vocal music would be supported and instrumental music outlawed; or choral music which simply expanded on biblical texts would be permitted but the creations of contemporary poets would be forbidden. All these are evidences of the musical impulses combined with a nervousness about them in Protestantism.

Why has there been a generally more open attitude to music than to dance or the visual and plastic arts? Many reasons have been offered. For one thing, musical expression is hard to prevent. Almost all people are equipped with vocal cords which can give voice to song, and it is difficult to suppress song. The communal character of choral music was recognized. It served to unite a congregation or a movement, whereas the painting of an altarpiece might give rise to individualistic and private expression. Music is kinetic, it moves on; there are fewer temptations to see it as an objectification of the divine invisible order. Music cannot remain around as a symbol to be idolized. Most of all, music can be supportive of words and a religion of words gravitated naturally toward an art form which would add mnemonic power or memorability to psalms, other scriptural passages, or the works of men who elaborated on these.[311]

Luther, it is well known, openly endorsed the use of musical arts in worship and in daily life, and insofar as Protestantism derives from his revolt it has seldom had difficulty with music. Luther himself played the lute, made song central to his family life, saw the need to provide songs snatched from the devil for his godly movement, and wrote notable hymns. One hymn, translated as "A Mighty Fortress Is Our God," a free elaboration on the words of Psalm 46, became known as the battle hymn of the Reformation. Luther composed hymns of various liturgical elements for his revised mass: *Kyrie, Gloria, Sanctus,* and other parts of worship were rhymed settings of biblical themes. Luther once said that he placed music second only to theology as an expression that could be used in the service of God, an endorsement that could not help but find support among a music-hungry people.[312]

The German Reformation gave birth to a characteristic form of the hymn called the chorale. Numerous poets and composers contributed to this medium from the Reformation era down through the pietist era, when men like Paul Gerhardt personalized the divine drama in very soulful and intimate hymns which were almost Christ-mystical in character. It was this tradition of people's music that the greatest musical pietest of all, Johann Sebastian Bach, took over and made the foundation of his great masses, cantatas, and passions. However complicated Bach's counterpoint may have been, his choice of biblical themes and hymnodic motifs were unsophisticated and direct reflections of the dialogue between a gracious God and the responding soul. In Bach's era, not only choral music but also and especially the organ was elevated to new prominence in worship, and some of the noblest Protestant art was produced.[313]

While later Anglican hymnody is also a major contribution to music, the Reformation in England was not similarly born in song. Thomas Cranmer and his colleagues were not poets, nor were they as concerned to provide people with song. But they were not antimusical, and much of the chant of pre-Reformation times survived. The Anglican tradition of music was enriched by continental contacts, particularly from those sources where psalms were set to simple chants. The Swiss Reformation under John Calvin became the source for many of these, and the Geneva Psalter is one of the better-remembered shapers of the Protestant hymnodic tradition. The accent in this song was on the vernacular expression of faith, on uncorrupted and uncorruptible simplicity, and on vocal, not instrumental music. Some of the reworked psalms of that derivation, subtly transformed, are still sung in Protestant worship.[314]

The great era of English church music began in the eighteenth century, where it rose out of Nonconformity. Isaac Watts was one of the founders of this lineage, in a series of well-remembered personal elaborations of biblical themes. The Wesleyan movement was another outburst of song, particularly because John Wesley's brother Charles was the gifted author of hundreds of hymns. In the nineteenth century the evangelical movement in the Church of England saw a rebirth of hymn-writing, and the benevolent and missionary movements of that century were inspired by countless songs which stressed the gifts of God's grace in Christ and man's joyful fulfillment of consequent obligations of gratitude and love to Him.

The hymns of these various pietist and evangelical moments at their best delicately avoided the problems that often beset their traditions: sentimentality, subjectivity, and banality. Those who sneer at the tradition of Victorian church music remember most of all the moments of such lapses into mediocrity and the maudlin. At worst and at best pious hymnody shows that not all Protestants have always been suspicious of rhythm, rhyme, melody, and accompaniment, and many of them have advertised their movements as being given over to and nurtured by song.

The story is much more complicated insofar as pictorial and plastic arts are concerned. Long before Protestantism was on the scene there had been iconoclastic movements, as in the Eastern church, where reformers saw people's devotion to iconic representations of deity and saints as being so engrossing that human objects became talismans. Numerous medieval Catholic reforms, not least of all spiritual Franciscanism nor last of all Savonarola's scourgings, concentrated on the dangers of symbolization of the divine. When people regarded relics, craft objects, icons, or crucifixes as themselves endowed with miraculous power they evoked prophetic criticism.

For the most part, however, the Christians of the Middle Ages were thoroughly at home with visual arts, as the eloquent silent testimony of sculpture, painting, and stained glass in European cathedrals suggests. In a preliterate age, when books were in the possession of a few learned elites, two- and three-dimensional representations of the divine-human drama was a most effective way of propagating and deepening faith and devotion.

The Protestant attitudes toward this tradition are so varied that they defy attempts to reduce all of Protestantism to a few simple generalizations. For the most part, conservative reformers retained all but the more offensive images, while cautioning people against devotion to the symbol at the expense of the reality. The extreme reformers were simple iconoclasts, setting out to destroy stained glass and whitewash the walls of churches they took over. Between them was a wide range of people with varying attitudes. Folk art was most readily accepted, and the first printed Bibles were often illustrated with simple woodcuts. Polemical arts were welcomed and anti-Catholic cartoons became a popular form of invective. Instruction books for the young were illustrated, evidently without fear lest the portrayal of biblical events or moral situations produce a new family of distracting icons.[315]

On the other hand, few first-generation reformers were themselves as gifted at painting as some of them were at music, nor were they notably expressive about their responses to it. Luther was a friend of Lucas Cranach, no minor figure in the German art of his day. Cranach gave support to the Lutheran movement in numbers of his paintings. But Luther's writings are short on comment concerning his appreciation of such art. Albrecht Dürer, the most highly regarded German artist of his day, found the Protestant movement congenial and altered some themes in his art as he moved away from Western Catholicism, but little is known of the reformers' attitudes toward his work. In England the Reformation saw the destruction of many monasteries and other Catholic cultural centers, and decoration in church buildings was often destroyed or neglected, but few reformers left a record of either vehement appreciation or violent rejection of painting and sculpture.[316]

Reformed Protestantism that derives from Switzerland and the Low Countries is most often singled out as the great inhibitor of visual artistic production in service of the church or devoted to Christian themes. It is true that Calvin was closer to Thomas Müntzer than he was to Luther in his view of the danger of imagery, and Calvinism was almost proverbially iconoclastic in its appropriation of the biblical command which forbids graven images. This attitude has persisted down into the twentieth century, when the profound Reformed theologian Karl Barth could write simply that images have no place at all in Protestant worship: they bring about inattention to the preaching of the Word and individualize what should be a simple communal gathering. Zwingli's attitudes toward the arts was more complicated, but he, too, was anything but a patron.[317]

Given such a background, it seems paradoxical or ironic that Reformed Christianity provided the setting for the man who is conventionally regarded as the Protestant artist par excellence— and, in the eyes of certain critics, the only truly great artist informed by Protestant approaches to reality, Rembrandt van Rijn. Too much can be made of his ecclesiastical context. If one wishes to contrast him to Bach in music, it must be said that he did not stand in a tradition of expression. He alone among the great Dutch and Flemish painters of his century is remembered for Protestant painting on biblical themes. Most of his contemporaries were seen to be more thisworldly and interested in materialistic themes and rewards. Rembrandt seems, in that sense, to be a mutation. Nor did a school of biblical painters of note follow him.[318]

Having said this and then having moved on to note the general neglect of Rembrandt among the Protestant faithful, who have often been content to leave him in the galleries while they adorn their Sunday school literature with fifth-rate art, it is equally necessary to point to the plausibility of the case for Rembrandt as Protestant artist. He repudiated the pagan themes of the Italian Renaissance in service of the church, and left behind theatrics or the histrionic, seeking to find drama in the commonplace settings of life. It is there that he located the biblical narrative; there is in his work a startling recognition of the simple full humanity of Jesus Christ, who is seen in humble and conventional settings. Christ is no Pantocrator, no elongated iconic figure, no transcendent and spatially remote being, no wearer of a crown other than one of thorns. Here, instead, is a man who visits hovels, shares quiet meals with disciples, and identifies with sufferers. Rembrandt reflects on biblical narratives, not on the grandeur of the Mass. This was religious art that was neither partisan nor ecclesiastical.

If the first great era of Protestant music which culminated in Bach in the pietist era was followed by at least a respectable hymnody, hardly anything comparable appeared post-Rembrandt in Protestant painting. The secularization of subject matter was proceeding apace; the churches rarely offered patronage to the first-rate artists; the pious seemed timid about the better art of their day. Were one to make a list based on a poll of art critics who were willing to list the greatest artists of the past couple of centuries, almost none of them could be listed as expressers of a Protestant tradition in Christianity.

William Blake was a biblically based Protestant, but his mystical private vision was so eccentric and out of context that his fellow believers in his time did not learn how to locate it in their tradition. Vincent van Gogh had been shaped by a social Christian approach and his early work had biblical themes, but however religious his later art may have been, it simply was not recognized as part of a Protestant tradition. Something in the violence of Emil Nolde's twentieth century expressionism has led many to locate him in the tradition; but men like these are rare exceptions. Graham Sutherland in England was called upon to help create the new Coventry cathedral. Here, again, the act seems isolated and not part of a general and consistent Protestant support of visual arts comparable to the churches' taste for music.[319]

Sculpture represented its special problems, perhaps because many of the biblical injunctions about images derived from three-dimensional representations of golden calves, fertility goddesses, and baalim. Sculpturesque portrayals of the deity were explicitly forbidden. In medieval Catholicism, it was often the three-dimensional object that had been treated with most magical regard. Some Protestant traditions always and everywhere opposed images of every sort so far as worship was concerned. The crucifix with a corpus was replaced by a bare wooden cross, and sometimes even the cross was prohibited. Many Protestant churches wanted the Catholic cross with its connotations of medieval suffering piety replaced by the more secular weathercock, herald of a new dawn.

When Protestants list their sculptors, they sometimes note the work of the Scandinavian Bertel Thorvaldsen, whose Christ figure has been reproduced in thousands of evangelical sanctuaries. Or they may mention moments in the career of British sculptor Henry Moore, when he worked in the service of the church or chose religious themes. Such instances are rare in Protestant history.[320]

All the foregoing attitudes seem to be changing in contemporary ecumenical Protestantism. Recent Protestantism has been influenced by a liturgical revival, an openness to Catholicism, a reexamination of tradition, a reexploration of the meaning of myth or symbol or ritual in the life of man, and a new affirmation of the secular and the material aspects of existence. As a consequence there seems to be considerable new experiment with folk music in the Mass, a freedom to bring the dance back into the sanctuary, an explosion of color in a world of banners. The younger and more experimental in particular seem at home with these. At the same time, reaction is also present. The Protestant mistrust of body and arts has not disappeared; it is constantly taking new forms. The great exception has been the almost universal acceptance of the idea of employing the architect's art in building houses of God.

Four and a half centuries of Protestantism have given rise to not one but many traditions of artful church building. Ordinarily these traditions parallel Catholic and secular developments in each age and place, for architecture of all arts seems to be born in a context. This context is provided by practical necessities of climate, pragmatic opportunities based on new inventions in building, environmental factors like available materials, and a common ethos based on the fact that few architects or schools of architects have worked only for the church. Thus they carry with them many expressive nuances from their secular art.

Protestants opposed to images have seldom recognized that the realization of the idea of a house of God is one of the most powerful images of all. It may recall the realities of cave or tent or home —all images based on the idea that God needs or welcomes a house, and so does man. Deep psychological needs are met through the creation of houses or sanctuaries where the divine presence is to be appropriated or perceived in a particular way. There should be no reasons why iconoclastic Protestants should not have remained consistent field preachers, with no place to find shelter in their pilgrimage; or they could always have used homes or profane public buildings. Few of them did, and if they were born in a movement of radical rejection of sanctuaries, usually within a generation or two they were under a special kind of roof.

The first generation or even century in Protestantism saw little new architectural activity. Ordinarily the existing Catholic churches were taken over and adapted. In England the tendency was to remove the rood-screen and other elements designed to conjure a sense of mystery at the expense of communication and communion among all the gathered people. In Reformed areas, there was usually considerable white painting and removal of statuary. In radical Protestantism all but the stained glass had to go, and sometimes even it was destroyed and replaced. Lutheranism largely took over the churches as they were, removing only what appeared to it to be egregiously supportive of offenses in the Mass. The result was that Protestant buildings looked like their ancestors, but had begun to be more simple and less adorned.

So it was in the seventeenth and eighteenth centuries that as old churches disintegrated and had to be replaced or new ones had to be built in areas of new and enlarged populations, Protestants began to fashion churches of their own. An example of a Protestant type of this era was the New England congregational meeting-house. Ordinarily wooden, white, with plain glass and accenting pulpit and pew at the expense of table and font, these buildings were usually perfectly adapted to their use to provide undistracting surroundings for their central purpose, the gathering of people for hearing of the preached Word.[322]

Similarly simple auditoriums were erected in the Netherlands, though these were often of brick and stone and other more durable materials. The English artistic genius of the era was Sir Christopher Wren who, after the London fire, built about fifty churches. Except for the best known, St. Paul's Cathedral, most of these churches were able to exemplify his Protestant ideal: to make churches settings for intimacy, for seeing and hearing. The mystery of the Mass was to be replaced by open communicative settings.[323]

From the 1640s to the 1840s the English-speaking Protestant world favored such simple styles. In the middle of the nineteenth century a Gothic revival, associated with the romantic notions of the Oxford and Cambridge movements swept England. This coincided with an era of new building, for England was growing very rapidly and as a result of the industrial revolution the new population was shifting away from old parish centers. Unfortunately, the complex tracery of the Gothic form was expensive and funds were not always easy to acquire. Therefore in many cases the result was a dreary stereotyping of the older Gothic forms. The same was true in mission fields and in America, where the Gothic style came to be favored by so many that when people later were to ask for a church that looked like a church they usually meant that they wanted an adaptation of Gothic.[324]

The Gothic intrusion in the nineteenth and twentieth centuries has been the source of concern to architectural and religious purists. It was not, said the architectural critics, an authentic expression of the building possibilities of the age. Even more, said Protestant reflectors on the phenomenon, the Gothic and the Protestant impulses had little in common with each other.

The Gothic had been devised to enhance the mystery and remoteness of the transcendent drama of the Mass. Its long, narrow, high styling provided acoustical problems for listeners to sermons.

Peter Taylor Forsyth, noted British Congregationalist thinker, once said with tongue only halfway in cheek, that Gothic architecture was the invention of the devil to keep people from hearing the Gospel. Its arrangement of fixed pews at a distance from the altar was a departure from earlier Protestant arrangements that had favored the circular, the rectangular, or the fan-shaped, where worshipers could face each other for a sense of community and the uplifting of one another. Liberal and modernistic American preachers whose theology had nothing in common with the medieval often tried to provide their adherents with some sense of tradition, security, and continuity, by housing them in lavish and un-Protestant Gothic houses of God.

The middle of the twentieth century saw a new flowering of church building. In Germany new houses of God to replace those lost in the devastations of bombing and shelling attracted noteworthy architects. England was a bit less experimental and less productive but there were some impressive achievements. An affluent America, experiencing a revival of support for religion, dotted the landscape with buildings good, bad, and mostly mediocre. After several decades of revival, however, it was possible to note that almost all architectural geniuses of the secular age had taken their turn at building: Le Corbusier (though not for Protestants), Frank Lloyd Wright, Mies van der Rohe, Eero Saarinen, Rudolf Schwarz, and others.[325]

It is difficult for observers to stand in the middle of the pluralism of styles in what seems to be a disordered century and generalize about what was Protestant in these expressions. A certain modesty and simplicity of line, an expression of what Paul Tillich called "holy emptiness," did characterize many of these. At the same time, perhaps because of the liturgical revival, there was more accent on the altar or table than there had been, and the arrangement of seating regularly tried to break away from the impersonal Gothic toward more communal, face-to-face patterns.

The Protestant house of worship, when its builders have been thoughtful about the theology of the congregation, will have certain predictable features. The more consciously it stands in the Catholic liturgical tradition, as many Anglican and Lutheran churches anywhere in the world do, the more likely they are to make much of altar and font along with the pulpit. Where the continental or American Reformed traditions are perpetuated, the pulpit will be accented—as in old and new Dutch churches, where it receives tremendous architectural emphasis in both size and position. The Protestants most distrustful of images will continue to build something like lecture halls, settings for preaching and prayer. To point to these varieties is to reinforce the theme that the artful building of houses of God has been an evidence that Protestantism is not consistent in its rejection of images.[326]

A survey of Protestant relations to the arts should include some reference to literature. It is virtually impossible to write of this without making it a complete history of Protestantism, for the evangelical churches have been most at home with verbal communication and have often worked to render it esthetically appropriate. Luther's translation of the Bible was accompanied by his act of contributing to the modern literary German, and the King James Version of the Bible achieved something similar for the English-speaking world. The Protestant poets often wrote hymns; at their best, they reached the heights that Milton found. John Bunyan was Protestant in all his impulses and themes. In the United States, at a time when the old evangelical empire was breaking up, novelists like Nathaniel Hawthorne and Herman Melville, who were not at all at home with the churches of their day, still elaborated on the inherited motifs of New England Puritanism, with its drama of good and evil.

The old uneasinesses were there, too. In most ages of religious revival, Protestants have favored pious evangelical injunctions about art, and until the twentieth century frequently opposed the novel as being the devil's distraction. Or they would try to appropriate the fictional form to present ungainly allegories of the faith.

Seldom has genius been encouraged in the churches. Goethe, himself of a divided mind about the Protestant culture which had helped shape him, spoke in the mood of many bewildered geniuses when he remarked, "I've done so many kinds of things, and yet there is not one of my poems which could stand in the Lutheran hymnal."[327]

The twentieth century revivals of Catholic literature were seldom accompanied by similar Protestant movements. Something in the moralizing, pro-orthodox, serious Protestant genius has tended to prevent even writers who were church members from taking up themes or modes that reflect Protestant life. Thus, while Protestant publishers are constantly producing books of fiction and poetry, the history of twentieth century literature is not impoverished if it neglects to include a chapter on Protestant expression.[328]

From the foregoing it can be seen that dance, drama, sculpture, and to a lesser degree, painting, have not often fared well in Protestantism. Its preachers, prophets, revivalists, and theologians provide considerable reinforcement for those who see Protestantism as a dour, moralizing, image-shattering faith. But this record is balanced somewhat by the examples of music and architecture, where there has been less uneasiness and more freedom.

18. FAMILY AND SEXUAL LIFE

Anthropologists have found the family to be the most intimate and smallest of social institutions. Some version or other of the family seems to be present in every culture. Historians and sociologists of religion at the same time have found that religion has served as a means for interpreting and integrating family life, sexual matters, and the rites of the various stages along life's way. Pregnancy, childbirth, puberty, marriage, and death all regularly come under the aegis of the shamans or priests, and religious ceremonies and meanings are attached to each. Protestantism is no exception to what appears to be a virtually universal impulse. Its teachings and practices are concentrated with great intensity on the family unit, and the family has been conditioned by the cultures of Protestantism. Few elements of evangelical teaching reach more deeply into personal life than do those which concern sexuality and family.[329]

The family is a bearer of tradition, and is also the product of tradition. For that reason no one need be told that Protestants were not able to start from the beginning and innovate as if nothing had occurred previously in the West. For the most part, they were free only to work out variations on long-established themes. Before the adjustments and innovations are noted, then, one should look at what the inheritances of Protestants were when in the sixteenth century they brought their reforms to bear on the intimacy of the family circle and the role of sexuality in the life of man. The legacy included biblical teaching derived from both Testaments along with many accretions of later Western traditional teaching and experience.

From the Hebrew Scriptures, or the Old Testament, Protestants carried over the idea that the family was a gift of creation, an order provided by a loving Creator. While modern ethologists and anthropologists may suggest that the family was a creation in response to certain biological necessities or was an inevitable precondition for the extension of the species, Protestant teaching began at a different point, by regarding the family as a shaping act of Yahweh, "who settest the solitary in families."

If the family was a creation of God, then its every detail was supported by His governance and preserving acts. Protestant preaching was often devoted to the biblical analogies and parables which picture Yahweh and Israel related as are husband and wife —as in the prophecies of Hosea and Jeremiah. Even the erotic Canaanite poem called the Song of Songs in the biblical canon was often allegorized to suggest theological relations between God and man, between Christ and His Church.

At the root of this Old Testament teaching was what might be called a covenantal and not a sacramental view of marriage, and it was this covenantal view that most Protestants were to carry over, develop, and continue to stress. This covenantal base was given a profound interpretation because throughout the Scriptures God's revelation was constantly tied to the genealogical factor. Through "the seed" of Abraham all the peoples of the earth would be blessed.

Since the New Testament saw this revelation to be fulfilled in the coming of Jesus, of the seed of Abraham and Jesse and David, Protestant teaching on the incarnation only reinforced the emphasis on the sacredness and importance of the sexual bond and the family. While the Old Testament often portrayed polygamous marriage as being common among the patriarchs and kings, Protestantism almost never picked up this model and found various ways to explain away the presence of polygamous relations in those Scriptures. For the rest, the sermons of Protestants referred so frequently to Old Testament models that one may safely suggest that Protestant leadership thought it was largely picking up and affirming age-old Hebraic patterns.[330]

To this Old Testament base was added distinctive New Testament interpretations, and Protestantism built on centuries of Christian elaboration on New Testament themes. Once again, divine revelation had been linked to the marital parable in Pauline teaching, where Christ was frequently pictured as the bridegroom, and the Church was His bride. With such a metaphor in mind, it was inevitable that Protestants would find their views of the sacral character of marriage reinforced: the Holy Spirit would not have guided the biblical writers to speak thus of Christ and Church were God not favorably disposed to regard marriage as a good condition for man—this in reference to Catholicism, which was seen to have downgraded marriage through its teachings on virginity and the desirability of celibacy.

The inheritance of New Testament teaching did build a certain ambivalence into Protestant teaching, particularly in those circles where a biblical literalism was to prevail. On one hand, the New Testament heightened the pressure put upon marriage. Polygamy was done away with and monogamous marriages were permanent. Whereas the Mosaic code provided some room for dissolution of marriage, in Jesus' teaching as recorded in the Gospels, only adultery provided an occasion for divorce.

On the other hand, Jesus could speak of people who had to disrupt even marriage and the family for the sake of His Kingdom, and could regularly scold those who put wife, children, or parents ahead of God's saving rule—a rule which sometimes seemed to disrupt normal relationships. Jesus could honor the family and yet speak critically of sexual tendencies. He was known to have dealt favorably with people in familial relations, yet He could also observe that those who did not marry and who abstained from sexual relations were more free to be disciples or messengers of the Kingdom.

The tensions built into marriage by literalists who dealt with Jesus' teachings were reinforced in the circle of those who gave equal weight to the work of St. Paul. The apostle's name was associated with letters that asked husbands to regard their wives with the most profound love, since their marriage was patterned after the relationship of Christ to His Church. Yet Paul seems often to have been negative toward the sexual motif in human life, and he gave many Protestants a more or less negative view of marriage when he seemed to base it chiefly in the need for man to rein in his desires through a single, socially controllable bond. "It is better to marry than to burn" was not necessarily the most positive charter for human coupling. And Paul's bonding of current cultural practices with his interpretation of the order or sequence of creation (Adam first, Eve secondarily and derivatively) was taken over into most Protestant culture as a warrant for androcentric religion, full of male superiority and male dominance.[331]

Whether Protestantism chose to work out Pauline motifs in the culture or whether it merely found biblical reinforcement for what it would have said or done anyway, as matters turned out the evangelical leadership helped provide some models. In these, woman was regarded as inferior, marriage was confined either to the need for procreation or to the disciplining of man's otherwise uncontrollable desires, and man was the governing head of the family. Much of Protestant history, then, has seen woman restricted to *"Kinder, Kirche, Küche,"* three German "k's" which confined her scope to the raising of children, the generally passive attendance at church, and a home in the kitchen and in devotion to undramatic houschold activities.

If the New Testament's two central figures helped contribute to ambivalence in Christian marriage, the practices of Western believers between the first and the sixteenth centuries reduced the tension by concentrating on the occasional high views of virginity and the negative views of marriage in the Bible. With the exception of occasional medieval sects, Catholic Christianity had retained marriage, and the celebrations of wedded union are many and varied in both liturgical and private language throughout the centuries before the Protestant movement took shape. The monastic and celibate orders, however, were rated more highly and special sanctions were attached to the lives of those who abstained from sexual and family life for the sake of Christ and the Church. Protestants almost everywhere set out to reverse this order of values as part of their basic reform, and often rejected clerical celibacy and monastic ideals as a central part of their protest—even if they could not accompany this rejection with fully positive views of the sexual dimensions of human existence.

The Protestant movement also contributed to a certain secularization of marriage. While in the Church of England the clerics were the recorders of marriages until the second half of the nineteenth century, elsewhere Protestants often stressed the civil and contractual character of marriage and turned over most jurisdictional matters concerning wedding and divorcing to civil, not ecclesiastical, courts. Human law was to govern most aspects of marriage, a teaching that the reformers thought they were taking from the Levitical code in the Hebrew Scriptures. This did not mean that ecclesiastical teachers and teachings were not to have any bearing on marriage and sexual practices. Instead, churchly blessing was ordinarily given to the wedding service and Christian interpretations were used to reinforce the covenantal and civil aspects of family life.[332]

The first Protestant innovation was a de-sacramentalizing of marriage, a beginning of a secular or civil rendering of nuptiality. The Western Catholic Church had regarded marriage as a sacrament. This meant that in Catholic definition, marriage was instituted by Christ (in the form recognized by the church) and it conferred grace as a spiritual benefit. This the evangelicals refused to acknowledge.

Protestants stressed the continuity between non-Christian and Christian family life. Both were of "the order of creation." They stressed a tie between pre-Christian and Christian forms. To biblical literalists, then, this meant clearly that Christ had not instituted marriage. And while Protestant spiritual literature is full of sometimes earnest and sometimes rhapsodic reinforcements of the idea that mutual confirmation of faith between marital partners could lead to growth in grace and holiness, it equally rejected the idea that it could impart the grace of God. For all of these reasons, marriage could not be called or regarded as a sacrament. The Council of Trent isolated this innovation as having special significance and pointedly condemned Protestants for not speaking of marriage in sacramental terms.[333]

The removal of a sacramental character and the location of marriage records in the civil courts and tradition, while it may have meant a secularization of sorts, was not seen by Protestants to be a downgrading of marriage. Indeed, they saw that they were taking a new approach to both the spiritual and the mundane elements in marriage.

In the Church of England, as a matter of fact, a quasi-sacramental view of marriage remained, and this was not pointedly condemned by many other Protestants, who found in it an inoffensive way of regarding marriage as well as another legitimate way of reinforcing the seriousness with which it should be treated. By quasi-sacramental we mean that many Anglican teachers were reluctant to use the word "sacramental" because they did not believe that Christ instituted the act or that grace came through it, yet they retained many service books and liturgies which used sacramental language and at least wanted to associate many of the symbols of sacramental life with marriage. This led Anglicans to take a more wary view of remarriage even after approved divorces (because of adultery) and permitted them to speak more favorably of virginity than did many of the continental Protestants. As a result, in the nineteenth century some Anglicans reinstituted the celibate and monastic ideals.[334]

Anglicans were among the few Protestant groups to carry on extensive debates about remarriage after divorce, but they were by no means the only Protestants who disapproved of the breaking of the marriage bond. The seriousness with which they regarded the Bible has led Protestants almost always and everywhere to condemn divorce or to take extremely negative views of it. At the same time, their regard for the Bible did not always lead them to take absolutely literally Jesus' recorded reference to adultery as the only legitimate reason for dissolving marriage. Luther—who despised divorce so much that he favored bigamy over it and counseled Philip of Hesse to take a second wife rather than to reject the first—did allow for extended desertion as a second reason for divorce. His coworker Philipp Melanchthon and many other early reformers extended this even further to include physical brutality and attempted murder as grounds for severance. From these extreme occasions it can be seen that Protestants were no more ready to favor simple divorce than were Catholics, who did speak of marriage in sacramental terms.[335]

The second Protestant innovation has also been implied in what has preceded. The evangelical leaders virtually unanimously rejected the Catholic elevation of celibacy as an ideal and a norm. Reasons for this rejection were obvious. The reformers' views of both merits and vocation committed them to such a position. The monastic and celibate states had been depicted as bringing their followers into a closer relationship to God and as earning them more merits as the occasion for God's issuance of more grace. This was all rejected because of Protestants' teachings that men were made just by grace through faith, and not by merits.

As a corollary of the teaching on merits, it was insisted that men could fulfill their calling equally well whether in clerical or lay states and that the humblest housewife could be doing God's will as well as the contemplative or cloistered monastic. There seemed to be few clearer or more consistent ways to underscore these teachings than to attack the ideals of celibacy and virginity and to elevate marriage and family living.[336]

So vehement was the rejection of celibacy that many Roman Catholic polemicists for over 400 years have tried to minimize the spiritual motives for the Reformation by arguing that the real reasons for Protestantism's rise lay in the unwillingness or inability of reformers to keep their vows of celibacy. It is true that the first generation of Protestant clergy had to be made up of people who had been ordained in Catholicism and who thus had taken vows of celibacy—vows which they now had to break. But the biographies of most of these men show that they made the theological or religious break long before they took a second step toward marriage.

Some reformers, including John Calvin, continued to have good things to say about virginity and were concerned about breaking vows lightly. Luther, on the other hand, while a tardy and half-reluctant marrier himself, rather heartily urged clerics to break their vows of celibacy and take wives as they moved into the Protes-

tant sphere. Even in Luther some vestiges of procelibate ideology
endured, however, as can be seen from his general views on sexuality and his repose of marriage in the bodily demands of the male.
Coitus was to be accompanied by some sense of shame and sexual
intercourse was somehow blighted by sin. In this respect the Lutheran reformers stood in an Augustinian line. It could reasonably
be inferred, then, that abstention from sexual activities should be
highly regarded. But Luther was too concerned to make his point
about merits and vocation to permit people to draw that conclusion.[337]

A third Protestant innovation, then, can be seen as the positive
counterpart to the rejection of celibacy. By permitting and enjoin-
ing evangelical clerics to marry, Protestants inevitably and unwittingly created a new institution, the parsonage family. This unit
was destined to have unimaginably extensive consequences in the
churches and the culture. While Protestants saw themselves as
declericalizing the church, matters did not turn out that way and
in countless parishes the role of the clergyman remained at least
as notable and visible as it had in the celibate tradition of Roman
Catholicism.

This visibility of the cleric was extended to his wife and children,
and the parsonage was to serve as a model for parochial family life.
The wife was often referred to in the sermons. The moral record
of the children was regarded as a kind of certification of the effectiveness or a mark of the ineffectiveness of the minister-father.
Since the parsonage has been a center of at least minimal literacy
in barely literate culture and of high intellectual standards in more
literate societies, the children of the minister and his wife often
were bearers of cultural tradition. Impressed as they were with
moral and theological themes, they were also often poised to ago-
nize over life's basic issues. Both in what they accepted and in what
they rejected these children often turned out to be influential and
the parsonage has had many side effects in society.

Not only did the parsonage provide a model or a workshop. It
served as the locale in which sexual symbolism in the church was
refashioned. Protestantism rejected many of the richer sexual symbols associated with Catholicism. The rite of baptism was purged
of some of the associations with phallus and womb which it had
acquired or perpetuated in some Catholic ceremonies. It is a different matter for a sexually active married Protestant minister to give
devotion to Mary than for one whose celibate imagery conjures
different associations in the minds of people he serves. As a result,

Protestantism often repressed some sexual dimensions that had been more positively regarded in the Catholic cults of the Virgin, male and female saints, and in many sacramental activities.

If there has been a downgrading or a complicating of sexual symbolism, the presence of a married clergy did also bring changes into the concepts of pastoral roles and counseling. Throughout the centuries of Protestantism there has been some advertisement of the suggestion that the minister, because he is a sexually active being in the legitimate forms provided by marriage and because he is dominant in familial roles which imply the raising of children, will have different and special insights into the problems and joys of his parishioners. As a result, his counsel on latter-day issues such as abortion, birth control, mixed marriages, and intimate sexual life was described as being more credible than would be the word of the Catholic clergy, for whom no such legitimate and free outlets for sexual activity and family impulses are provided.

Despite the attention given to marriage in Protestant theology and pastoral counsel and despite the ratification given high views of marriage by a wedded clergy, few historians of the West have been able to conclude that Protestant history as a whole has been characterized by very positive views of sexuality. One can concoct from the writings of most Protestant leaders extensive anthologies of very negative views of marriage and sexuality.

First of all, all overt sexual activity was to be channeled through marriage or carried on only between people who were betrothed —if even between them. Many Protestants have feared or decried the dance because of its erotic overtones and implied sexual character. They have been uneasy about other kinds of routinized noncoital sexual expression outside marriage and have almost unanimously repudiated sexual intercourse outside the marriage bond. There has been great attention to dress and custom, gesture and word, and anything else that could relate to sexual stimulation.

Some of these attitudes were taken over from Catholicism. Yet if one wanted to write a history of romantic and ribald forms of Christianity, he would be better advised to visit Latin Catholicism's culture than he would to attend to Protestant expressions. Perhaps personality traits developed in the northern European climates had their part to play, as amateur anthropologists through several centuries have contended. Perhaps very subtle adjustments in sexual symbolism as a result of Protestant teachings on marriage played their part. A biblical literalism has reinforced these, for Protestants often overlooked the Old Testament's earthy realism and its occasionally lavish eroticism as they hurried to the New Testament where Jesus' and Paul's sterner views prevailed. And this biblical determination was reinforced by the Augustinian and other influential Western traditional teachings.

So it was that Martin Luther, for example, while he was himself a lusty and robust advocate of many conjugal joys, turned somber when he was theologically reflective and spoke of marriage as a "hospital for the sick" and the medicine for those ill with lust. This kind of expression was based on a widespread medieval view of the male sexual capacity and of the implied view that men had no choice but to routinize sexual activity in marriage or artificially restrain themselves in celibacy. The wife was then often spoken of, also by Luther, in the biblical category of "the vessel" who contains the man's seed and is passive in the face of his sexual aggressions. One engages in intercourse repentantly, for even this natural act, which is necessary for procreation and the survival of the species, is not only God-endowed but also blighted by sin.

Luther's dialectical view was hard to sustain. Something in man leads him to regard sexuality numinously and his fear of sexuality led many to stress only the sinful side of eroticism. Calvin, it must be said, had a more affirmative view of marriage, just as he had a slightly more positive view of celibacy than did Luther. Much of Protestantism has been a variation on the themes these pioneers and their earliest associates set forth.

If historians have had to note Protestant negativism and dour attitudes toward marriage and sexuality, they have also often been ready to note more positive contributions. While some of the reformers were reluctant to do away with brothels, since they saw sexual activity to be inevitable for most males, they did gradually work for reforms. They rather consistently attacked the double standard in sexuality which had often permitted the man to roam while forcing the woman to be faithful only to him. They continued to accent the procreative role in marriage, but just as often accompanied this by stresses on companionship and communion among wedded partners, and were thus more free than were Catholics to take more positive views of birth control when modern devices and means for limiting births were developed.[338]

The spectrum of Protestant teachings on the subject of planned parenthood is broad; although the first reaction of most Protestants had been to oppose birth control, in modern times these attitudes have been transformed by most evangelicals, and other teachings—among them, care and stewardship of the earth—have been adduced alongside the biblical injunctions to "be fruitful and multiply." Almost everywhere in recent times Protestants have taken positive attitudes toward birth control, in the face of Eastern Orthodox and Roman Catholic opposition to these teachings and the latter's stress on procreation as being the only goal for sexual activity in marriage.

Modern advocates of sexual freedom have rather consistently attacked Protestant cultures for their negativity, implied asceticism, joylessness, and contributions to repression. Sigmund Freud and a generation of psychoanalysts who saw in sexuality the root of most behavioral explanation found in Protestant self-denial and sternness a perfect foil. Documentation for their attacks is not hard to come by, and by the standards of a later generation much Protestant teaching on marriage and sexuality is not only nonbiblical but expressive of warped personalities or of undialectical theological positions. Yet the use of Protestantism as a foil has led to many exaggerations and distortions of types that historians must address and correct, both for the sake of accuracy and of fairness.

The supreme example of such stereotyping has come to be associated with the term "Puritanism," which is virtually synonymous with antisexuality in the vocabulary of most modern sexual liberationists. A glance at Puritanism will reveal something of the dangers of overgeneralization. The stereotype would not have grown up if there had been no basis at all for its rise. Puritan literature and practice do reveal many kinds of negative teachings on human impulses. The Puritan did believe that all details of life came under divine sovereignty and were to provide opportunities for exemplifying one's elect status and working out the canons of holiness.

With that as a starting point, Puritanism paid sexuality the compliment of taking it very seriously and seeing it in these contexts. At the same time, Puritans were not the simple ascetics moderns picture them to be. In both England and America they partook heartily of food and drink. While many frowned on dancing, they favored a joyful marriage feast. They were highly aware of sexual dimensions in marriage, and cultivated warm personal bonds among partners, even though their affections were finally to be set on things above. True Protestants, they feared idolization of the beloved or adoration between parent and child, but little in their way of life conforms to the caricatures Puritanism's enemies have created.[339]

Much the same could be said for a second hedonists' *bête noire*,

continental pietism, which took equally seriously the interpretation of all of life by biblical-Protestant canons, and therefore reproduced some of the negative language on this subject. At the
same time Protestant pietism produced an "above-ground" expression in hymnody and poetry in which erotic imagery was
frankly celebrated. The family life of many pietists was characterized by a sense of marital equality, warm parent-child relations,
manifest love, and even a measure of earthy devotion to sexual
themes.

The more negative language should probably be reserved for a
third stereotype, Victorianism, which could be abstracted from the
complex life lived by latter-day Puritan-evangelicals in England
and America. There sexual repression did often dominate at the
expense of the development of honest or authentic personalities.
At the same time what has been called a pornotopia, or a porno-
graphic underground, developed as a counterpart and perhaps as
a result of the Protestant society's artificial suppression of sexual
expression and impulse.[340]

Ambiguous and then negative views of sexuality have not carried
over into later Protestantism's overall view of the family. Not a few
internal critics have suggested that Protestant practice has been
too familial in direction. In the nineteenth century the aspirant
bourgeois monogamous unit, culturally conditioned as it was,
came to be regarded as a kind of timeless repristination or reproduction of the original and only pure unit of Christian life. There
was less theological or homiletic counsel available to the sexually
inactive, single (by choice or chance), widowed, or divorced Protestant than there was for the good burgher who filled a pew with
wife and children. Such an approach has made Protestantism particularly vulnerable to cultural changes which it has not always
recognized. From the authoritarian, male-centered family, there
has been a modern movement toward matriarchy and filiarchy,
with women and children now being asked to carry more burdens
of family life than historic Christian teaching or natural situations
would presuppose.

Many Protestants were late to realize that the modern nuclear
monogamous family in middle-class culture was a much different
creation from what was meant by the family in biblical times. There
the tribal or clan contexts and the multigenerational setting did
much to alleviate some pressures which make life in families in the
modern world often unbearable and certainly not feasible. The
Protestant rhetoric still enjoins the family to be the basic unit also

for education of the young even though modern education, mass media, and casual friendships outside the circle of the family assault the value system theoretically propagated in the pressured and torn-apart family. Recent Protestantism, therefore, has been marked by attempts to begin to break out of the "normative" views of family life that have limited it and to take on a realistic view of the family in culture—even as it seeks to preserve what has been good in family living.[341]

The accompanying change in marital mores and the associated strain on church teaching has been called the modern sexual revolution. This phenomenon has been occasioned by complex factors; frequently cited among them have been secularization, a relativism based on the contact of people from many cultures inside pluralism, a response to a modern technological and impersonal society, a decline in the authoritarian reading of God's law in the Bible, and —to the sterner prophets—just plain human perversity of the kind that was to mark living in the last days. More positively, some Protestants have seen in the sexual revolution an effort to separate authentic from inauthentic demands, to extricate people from a repressive situation, to free them from fears (as Christians are to be freed from fears and made guiltless), and a positive recognition of some boons in human arrangement as a result of modern scientific discovery—including inventions that have cast premarital or extramarital intercourse into a different light.

At the heart of these adaptations have been certain emphases that do not come easily to many Protestants. Among these is a frank celebration of the body, a new personalism which devotes itself more to the "thou" than to the "it" of laws, however favorable to the man these laws may have been, and includes an ethic that looks at people in various contexts and situations rather than descending on them with universally applicable absolutes. Because of the natural curiosity people have about sexuality, such new looks are inevitably controversial, and Protestant teachers are anything but of one mind concerning what is sometimes called a new morality or a situation ethic in sexual and familial matters.[342]

Whatever the outcome, the assault on traditional morality has shown how culturally conditioned it has been, and many Protestants have found that there were more options available to them within a biblical context than among those they had inherited from their fathers. At the very least, many cultural accretions which had no biblical basis have been called into question and sexual ethics will be altered somewhat even among those who resist theologies that embrace the sexual revolution. The experience of missionaries among polygamous but religiously faithful Protestants in Africa has forced reappraisal on those who made the Western family normative.

The historian William E. Lecky was not alone when in the nineteenth century, while discussing Puritanism, he pointed to the masculine character of Protestantism. In fact, he saw Protestantism to be "the most masculine form that Christianity has yet assumed." He went on to say that "in the great religious convulsions of the sixteenth century the feminine type followed Catholicism, while Protestantism inclined more to the masculine type. Catholicism alone retained the Virgin worship, which at once reflected and sustained the first." Such observations can lead to considerable subjective judgment; what, after all, is "masculine" and "feminine"?[343]

It is safer to say that Protestantism has been largely androcentric and uneasy about sex while affirmative about the family, and it has been so on the basis of its biblical and theological interpretation. Meanwhile, it has contributed to masculine cultures even as it has lived off them; not until the middle of the nineteenth century did women begin to raise an attack against such creations. The step-up in women's attempt at a full liberation of consciousness and position will almost certainly color the future of Protestant interpretations of family and sexual life, and will cause reappraisal of all its symbols, terms, models, and ideals.

AFTERWORD

In 1937, Paul Tillich asked whether the end of the Protestant era had come. Mass disintegration in society had led people to look for mass collectivisms, and they seemed to be turning to three authorities: Christian Catholicism, nationalistic paganism, and communistic humanism.[344]

One of these three has gone through much travail since Tillich wrote. Catholicism has experienced disintegration, and almost nowhere in the world threatens to satisfy men's hunger for authoritarianism and their yearning to escape into collectivism. This disintegration has even led to the point where some bishops and even more notable theologians have begun to question Catholic authority as symbolized in the doctrine of papal infallibility. Should their questioning spread and become effective within the church, one aspect of the Protestant attack would begin to be obsolete. Stated more positively, some ecumenical stirrings suggest that one day convergences between Catholicism and Protestantism may be possible, even though they were not dreamed of for four and one-half centuries. Protestantism as a consistent force would no longer be necessary on its own terms in the Western Christian church if its principle could also be embodied in what had been Roman Catholicism.

Nationalistic paganism and communistic humanism are both alive and well and they are frequently in partnership. Nationalism is often the real religion of majorities in once Protestant lands, and Protestant symbols are employed to legitimate the claims for the ultimacy of the nation. Authentic protest against such employment on the part of evangelicals has been rare but remains necessary if the Protestant principle and any of its ecclesiastical or cultural embodiments are to survive and be of service to men.

Communistic humanism as often as not is swallowed up in nationalistic paganisms, but on many occasions it thrives on its own and provides Christians with opportunities for dialogue, just as it has long threatened their existence. Protestants attracted to that dialogue or to the socialist or revolutionary causes have also not given much evidence of their ability to disengage themselves from those causes and to utter the prophetic word against their new identifications.

Neither the institutional nor the cultural prospects for Protestantism seem very bright to an observer in the late twentieth century. Readers of this book can see how readily Protestantism became established, authoritarian, and un-self-critical. Though several hundred millions remain, even the number of Protestant church members has been in relative decline in many nations where once it was high. The Protestant era may, indeed, be coming or have come to its end. Perhaps the spirit of prophecy will then need new embodiments, and the witness to a transcendent God will find new incarnations as Protestantism joins other religions that, as Tillich noted, are "threatened by secularism and paganism." On the other hand, Protestantism has passed through trial and experienced decline frequently in the past and has followed such phases with renewal. It is possible that surprising forms of new life could present themselves at this century's end.

BIBLIOGRAPHICAL REFERENCE MATERIAL

In order to be of the greatest aid to the greatest number of readers of this book, the author has let availability and accessibility of materials be among the major criteria for selection in this list. For that reason the virtually boundless literature in the form of periodical articles, privately printed monographs, and doctoral dissertations has been excluded. Most of the books cited here can be found in libraries of reasonable size. Whenever possible, preference has been given to titles which are in print, though in hundreds of cases it has not been possible to provide such current and popular books.

On the same principle of selection I have restricted myself almost entirely to English-language writings—either translations of continental scholarship or the products of Anglo-American research. The readers who are able to use foreign languages can gain access to German, French, and other books by pursuing leads provided by bibliographies in many of the books cited in this list. I have tried to recommend books with good bibliographies whenever possible.

Also for reasons of space it has not been possible to provide here all data concerning publication; names of publishers and translators have been omitted. Nor is attention always called to the matter of revisions or numbered editions. In some cases the date of the earliest edition has been supplied; at other times revised versions have been referred to without full explanations for the choice. The reader will appreciate the reasons for this approach: it makes possible citation of a larger number of titles and, since this is also an essay, it makes the "reading flow" easier on the eye.

In many but by no means all instances the publishers' cities have been provided on an international basis. Canadian, Australian, and other readers may often find that local branches of international publishing houses might have been mentioned, but inclusion of all these would also have added inordinately to the length of the essay.

It seems unfortunate that one must stress in an introduction like this what has to be left out; on the other hand, the critical test of reading lists in books that cover such a wide variety of topics seems to be the question of what has been left out. It is my hope that despite the arguments over taste, the inevitable subjectivity of choice, and the natural limits of any single author's acquaintance-ship with books, the titles which follow represent much of the best literature on their subjects.

FOREWORD

1. These definitions come from the argument developed in Os-car Cullmann, *Catholics and Protestants, a Proposal for Realizing Christian Solidarity* (London 1960), a book whose purpose was to suggest mutual collections of gifts for Catholic and Protestant poor as a step toward furthering Christian unity.

CHAPTER 1

2. For a discussion of the parallel development of Anglo-American evangelical religion and colonial expansion, E. J. Hobsbawm, *The Age of Revolution 1789–1848* (Cleveland and New York 1962), pp. 217 ff.

A convenient reference book on the whole scope of recent missionary activity is Burton L. Goddard, *The Encyclopedia of Modern Christian Missions* (Camden, New Jersey, London, and Toronto 1967). A publication of the faculty of the Gordon Divinity School, the work reflects a generally conservative-evangelical point of view. It is reliable and accurate in its portrayal of the activities of over 1,400 agencies, almost all of them Protestant. While this bibliography is generally restricted to English-language works, mention here must also be made of Franklin H. Littell and Hans Hermann Walz, *Weltkirchen Lexikon* (Stuttgart 1960), which brings together much material not easily accessible elsewhere on the current situation of churches throughout the world.

Any introduction to the topic of missionary activity involves some reflection on the theological assumptions behind it. An intro-duction to the thought of significant contemporary scholars is condensed in a work edited by Gerald H. Anderson, *The Theology of the Christian Mission* (New York, Toronto, London 1961). The book's excellent bibliography will introduce the reader to biblio-graphies, journals, and the names of representative authors, among them notably Emil Brunner, Walter Freytag, Bengt Sundkler, Max Warren, Ernst Benz, Gustav Warneck, A. C. Bouquet, Kenneth Cragg, William Ernest Hocking, Hendrik Kraemer, D. T. Niles, Edmund Perry, Arnold Toynbee, Joachim Wach, R. Pierce Beaver, Donald A. McGavran, John A. Mackay, Lesslie Newbigin, Julius Richter, Georg F. Vicedom, and Samuel M. Zwemer, men who devoted much of their career to inquiry on this and similar topics.

A chapter describing an atlas of Protestantism should make bibliographical reference to atlases, but the store of these is relatively meager. Robert S. Dell, *An Atlas of Christian History* (London 1960) is an ambitious but spotty effort that could be described as necessary but inadequate for comprehensive study. An older work, Harlen P. Beach and Charles H. Fahs, *World Missionary Atlas* (New York 1925) is actually the most recent work concentrating on missionary materials; it includes a listing of missionary societies, some statistics, maps, and narrative accounts.

For statistics, the series of *World Christian Handbook*s (London 1949–) serve best, though the quality varies from edition to edition and the degree of reliability in a field which borders on pseudo-scientific reckoning is uncertain. Each January the *International Review of Missions* (Edinburgh 1912–) reviews events in missionary areas around the world.

General surveys: the best work is R. H. Glover and J. H. Kane, *The Progress of World-Wide Missions* (New York 1960). This work has been revised from editions dating back to 1924 and includes a twenty-page bibliography. A survey which accents the conservative evangelical effort and point of view and which includes useful tables is John Caldwell Thiessen, *A Survey of World Missions* (Chicago 1955).

Three authors who have written many books on the history of missions are Kenneth Scott Latourette, Stephen C. Neill, and R. Pierce Beaver. Latourette's inclusive and summary work is a *History of the Expansion of Christianity* (New York and London 1939–1945); volumes 3–7 cover the modern period. The work is divided into chapters dealing with various geographic areas and includes an extensive and valuable bibliography. Neill's comprehensive book is more brief, *Christian Missions* (Harmondsworth, Middlesex, England and Baltimore, Maryland 1964). Neill argues that as the result of missionary expansion Christianity has become the world's first universal religion. Out of the Beaver corpus, see at this point *Ecumenical Beginnings in Protestant World Mission: A History of Comity*

(New York, Edinburgh, and Toronto 1962), a study of the concept and practice of territorial responsibility for evangelization.

3. Most of the studies of colonialism or imperialism either overlap with missionary and political writings or concentrate on individual areas. An exception is Stephen Neill's general history of *Colonialism and Christian Missions* (New York, Toronto, London, and Sydney 1960), a book that is more sympathetic to Christian problems than most recent books have been. A brief bibliography is appended.

4. Kenneth Scott Latourette began his career as a Sinologist and as an historian of missions specialized in work on China. Therefore his book first published in 1929, *A History of Christian Missions in China* (New York 1967) still holds interest; it is a very fair-minded treatment of a complex history; for the period after 1928 see pp. 431–45 in his *Christianity in a Revolutionary Age* (New York 1961), volume III. A period piece that still holds interest is Donald Mac-Gillivray, ed., *A Century of Protestant Missions in China: Being the Centenary Conference Historical Volume* (Shanghai 1907). Edmund S. Wehrle, *Britain, China, and the Antimissionary Riots 1891–1900* (Minneapolis 1966) is representative of the recent literature dealing with cultural conflict as a result of missions. For recent China, see Francis Price Jones, *The Church in Communist China: A Protestant Appraisal* (New York 1962), which includes annotated suggestions for further reading, and a book which includes non-Protestant materials, Richard C. Bush, Jr., *Religion in Communist China* (Nashville, Tennessee and New York 1970), written just before China began to give signs of new openness to the West.

5. Works in English on Taiwan, or Formosa, are generally rather specialized, but see William Campbell, *Formosa under the Dutch: Described from Contemporary Records* (London 1903) and Lillian Dickson, *These My People* (Grand Rapids, Michigan 1958).

6. Korea has received more attention, as is evidenced by the following: L. George Paik, *The History of Protestant Missions in Korea 1832–1910* (Pyeng Yang 1929); T. S. Soltun, *Korea, the Hermit Nation and Its Response to Christianity* (London 1932) and H. H. Underwood, *Tragedy and Faith in Korea* (New York 1952).

7. On the roots of Japanese Christianity in the sixteenth and seventeenth centuries, a period of Catholic activity which must be understood as a background for later Protestant work, see the substantial book by C. R. Boxer, *The Christian Century in Japan 1549–1650* (Berkeley and Los Angeles 1951 and 1967). An older work that includes Protestantism along with Orthodoxy and Ro-

man Catholicism is the standard two-volume Otis Cary, *A History of Christianity in Japan* (New York 1909). Charles Iglehart in *A Century of Protestant Christianity in Japan* (Tokyo and Rutland, Vermont 1959) was occasioned by a centennial of activity. Winburn T. Thomas also concentrated on *Protestant Beginnings in Japan: The First Decades, 1859–89* (Rutland, Vermont 1959); the more recent turmoil is covered in Raymond G. Hammer, *Japan's Religious Ferment* (London 1961). Writings by and about Kagawa are easily accessible; see William Axling, *Kagawa* (London and New York 1932) and Jessie M. Trout, *Kagawa, Japanese Prophet* (London 1959). The latter includes excerpts from Kagawa's writings. Another sample of biographical literature is Norimichi Ebizawa, ed., *Japanese Witness for Christ* (London 1957), five studies by Japanese writers. On theological interplay, Carl Michalson, *Japanese Contributions to Christian Theology* (Philadelphia 1960) holds much of interest.

8. The literature on India is at least as extensive as that on Japan. From a large selection, the following might be noted: Stephen Neill, *The Story of the Christian Church in India and Pakistan* (Grand Rapids, Michigan 1970), a work new enough to be able to include a chapter on the formation of the ecumenical united churches of India. The more developed of these is in South India; its history has been written by Bengt G. M. Sundkler, *The Church of South India* (London 1954). One of the earlier volumes that is still cited is Julius Richter, *A History of Missions in India* (New York and Chicago 1908); it is marred by the author's neglect of Catholicism and his anti-British statements. A brief and readable work is Catherine B. Firth, *An Introduction to Indian Church History* (Madras 1961).

9. The literature on Southeast Asia is less satisfactory. Thailand is treated in Kenneth E. Wells, *History of Protestant Work in Thailand 1828–1958* (Bangkok 1958) and, earlier, in G. B. McFarland, ed., *Historical Sketch of Protestant Missions in Siam, 1828–1958* (Bangkok 1928). William C. B. Purser, *Christian Missions in Burma* (London 1911) concentrates on Anglicanism; excellent up to 1911, it needs supplementation. Students of Burma have characteristically concentrated on the pioneer Adoniram Judson, beginning with Francis Wayland, *Memoir of the Life and Labours of the Rev. Adoniram Judson, D.D.* (Boston 1853), a two-volume work and continuing with Courtney Anderson, *To the Golden Shore: The Life of Adoniram Judson* (Boston 1956). An interesting work describing confusion of communications is Helen G. Trager, *Burma Through Alien Eyes* (New York and Washington 1966).

Three general works on Southeast Asia are Kenneth P. Landon,

Southeast Asia, Crossroads of Religion (Chicago 1949); Rajah Mani-kam, *Christianity and the Asian Revolution* (New York 1954); and the same author's work in tandem with Winburn T. Thomas, *The Church in Southeast Asia* (New York 1956).

10. A curious work on Oceania is Louis B. Wright and Mary Fry, *Puritans in the South Seas* (New York 1936), a highly antimissionary volume but a rare book in that it pays the island world the compliment of Western attention. See also Harrison M. Wright on *New Zealand 1769–1840: Early Years of Western Contact* (Cambridge, Massachusetts 1959), a study of Western impact on Maori. Paul B. Pedersen, *Batak Blood and Protestant Soil: The Development of National Batak Churches in North Sumatra* (Grand Rapids, Michigan 1970) brings those important churches to the attention of Western scholars. Hendrik Kraemer, *From Mission Field to Independent Church: Report on a Decisive Decade in the Growth of Indigenous Churches in Indonesia* (London 1958) is another rare English book in a field dominated by works in Dutch and German; it deals with 1926 to 1935 and is often pointed to as an exemplary work for its treatment of a transition in missionary understandings. On New Guinea, see Georg F. Vicedom, *Church and People in New Guinea* (London 1961). Most missionary literature dealing with the Philippines is, naturally, Roman Catholic; Protestant works are largely denominational, but see Dwight E. Stevenson, *Christianity in the Philippines* (Lexington, Kentucky 1955). One critical and one favorable work balance each other in discussion of an interesting development in Philippines history. A Catholic and critical work is Pedro S. de Achutegni and Miguel A. Bernard, *Religious Revolution in the Philippines* (Manila 1969); a favorable Anglican study of the same subject, the Aglipayan "Philippine Independent Church" is Lewis B. Whittemore, *Struggle for Freedom, History of the Philippine Independent Church* (Greenwich, Connecticut 1961).

11. Most of the literature encompassing all of Africa is brief, overgeneralized, denominational, or apologetic in character. The great exception is the four-volume work by Charles R. Groves, *The Planting of Christianity in Africa* (London 1948–1958); much of the work deals with the pre-Protestant era, but the treatment of Protestantism in the later volumes is generous. Excellent bibliographical clues can be found in the footnotes. Thomas A. Beetham, *Christianity and the New Africa* (New York, Washington, and London 1967) deals with the present and the future prospects in the face of Islamic expansion and anticolonialism; there are maps, graphs, and a bibliography. Ram Desai, *Christianity in Africa as Seen by Afri-*

cans (Denver, Colorado 1962) includes anticolonial criticisms of Christianity. An interesting sociological work is David B. Barrett, *Schism and Renewal in Africa: An Analysis of Six Thousand Contemporary Religious Movements* (London, New York, Nairobi, Addis Ababa, and Lusaka 1968), a study of the new groups, many of them derived from Protestant missionary activities.

12. On racial consciousness and tension, with frequent references to religion, see Thomas Patrick Melady, *The Revolution of Color* (New York 1966), which includes a bibliography, and the more strident Ronald Segal, *The Race War* (New York 1966), whose second chapter deals with Africa.

13. Two works on North Africa merit brief notice: T. J. P. Warren, *North Africa Today* (Tunis 1947) and W. T. T. Millham, ed., *North Africa, Lands of the Vanished Church* (London 1949?). J. Spencer Trimingham, *The Christian Church and Missions in Ethiopia* (London and New York 1950) includes a short chapter on modern missions; there is a popular account of the Sudan Interior Mission's work in Ethiopia in an undocumented work, Raymond J. Davis, *Fire on the Mountain* (Grand Rapids, Michigan 1966). Ethiopia and the Sudan are often, of course, included in East Africa in geographical and political works, but in missionary history they have more in common with North Africa.

14. On lower East Africa the standard religio-political work is Roland Oliver, *The Missionary Factor in East Africa* (London and New York 1952). More concentrated geographically is a fine case study which brings together missiological and sociological concerns, John V. Taylor, *The Growth of the Church in Buganda* (London 1958). Kenya is treated in Keith Cole, *Kenya: Hanging in the Middle Way* (London 1959). See also Gustaf Bernander, *The Rising Tide: Christianity Challenged in East Africa* (Rock Island, Illinois 1957).

15. W. T. T. Millham, *West Africa: A Babel of Tongues* (London 1949?) and S. G. Williamson and J. Bardsley, *The Gold Coast—What of the Church?* (London 1953) are general introductions that can best be described as barely adequate. Of more interest is J. Spence Trimingham, *The Christian Church and Islam in West Africa* (London 1955), a contribution to a series of pamphlets sponsored by the International Missionary Council. Ghana is treated in Hans W. Debrunner, *A History of Christianity in Ghana* (Accra 1967), described as the first attempt at tying together the denominational histories of Ghana; there is a good bibliography. Sidney George Williamson, *Akan Religion and the Christian Faith* (Accra 1965) is an excellent study of the interaction between denominationalized

Christianity and a people which has accepted elements of it yet fused it with their traditional view of the world. Hans W. Debrunner, *A Church between Colonial Powers* (London 1965) is a sophisticated study of the Evangelical Church in Togo; it contains a bibliography. For a general survey see Joseph C. Wold, *God's Impatience in Liberia* (Grand Rapids, Michigan 1968); it deals with a nation whose leadership is Christian; again, there is a good bibliography. A former missionary, Gilbert W. Olson, has written of *Church Growth in Sierra Leone* (Grand Rapids, Michigan 1969); he brings together various denominational histories; well documented with suggestions for further reading.

Samples of some of the literature on Nigeria are: J. F. Ade Ajayi, *Christian Missions in Nigeria 1841–1891: The Making of a New Elite* (London 1965), a scholarly work on Protestant accomplishments in the formation of an educated middle class; Emmanuel A. Ayandele, *The Missionary Impact on Modern Nigeria 1842–1914* (London 1966), which discusses reactions of the sectors of Nigerian communities to Protestant missionary work; John B. Grimley and Gordon E. Robinson, *Church Growth in Central and Southern Nigeria* (Grand Rapids, Michigan 1966), with accent on Christian successes in the face of Islam; James B. Webster, *The African Churches among the Yoruba 1888–1922* (Oxford 1964), which relies in part on oral sources. All four have bibliographical appendices.

16. George M. Theal, *The History of South Africa* (London, 1892–1919), an eleven-volume work, and George Cory, *The Rise of South Africa* (London 1910–1930), five volumes, are often seen in continuity; so far as religion is concerned, they share the thesis that the missionaries of the London Missionary Society who evangelized much of the area betrayed the white South Africans because they sided with the Colored against the white farmer interests; Monica Wilson and Leonard Thompson, eds., *The Oxford History of South Africa* (New York 1969) in its first volume covers the period to 1870 and includes excellent material on the component racial groups. The only general study of the nineteenth century in South African church history is Johannes Du Plessis, *History of Christian Missions in South Africa* (London, Bombay, and Calcutta 1911), a denominational work that deals more with missionaries than with the evangelized people. See also Horton Davies and R. H. W. Shepherd, *South African Missions 1800–1950* (London 1954), and for more modern developments, G. B. A. Gerdener, *Recent Developments in the South Africa Mission Field* (London 1958).

Four worthwhile samples of regional or national studies are:

John V. Taylor and Dorothea A. Lehmann, *Christians of the Copperbelt* (London 1961), on Northern Rhodesia (Zambia); William M. Macmillan, *Bantu, Boer and Briton* (London 1929), which responded to the Theal-Cory argument and favored the London Missionary Society; Desmond Clinton, *The South African Melting Pot: A Vindication of Missionary Policy 1799–1836* (London and New York 1937), which parallels Macmillan's concern; Bengt G. M. Sundkler, *Bantu Prophets in South Africa* (London, New York, Toronto 1961), treating integration and segregation and the consequence of segregation: a synthetic version of Christianity plus tribal religion.

17. The Middle East and Near East are treated in J. T. Addison, *The Christian Approach to the Moslem: A Historical Study* (New York 1942); the later chapters deal with the period in which Protestants also were active; the second volume of Donald Attwater, *The Christian Churches of the East* (Milwaukee, Wisconsin 1935 and 1947) discusses chiefly the Orthodox churches of the area; an understanding of these is essential for any comprehension of the Protestant fate in the East; the only general history and one which again reflects the author's anti-British outlook is Julius Richter, *A History of Protestant Missions in the Near East* (Edinburgh, New York, and Chicago 1910). Two general, issue-centered works are Denis Baly, *Multitudes in the Valley: Church and Crisis in the Middle East* (Greenwich, Connecticut 1957) and C. W. Milford, *The Middle East: Bridge or Barrier* (London 1956). There are some topics of interest in Leon Arpee, *A Century of Armenian Protestantism 1846–1946* (New York 1946).

18. While this essay concentrates on Protestantism, some introduction to Orthodoxy is necessary for anyone who wishes to explore Protestant ventures in areas where the Orthodox dominate. For present purposes a number of modern, popular works should serve, especially since some of them include bibliographies: a convert from Anglicanism to Orthodoxy who knows what questions non-Orthodox would have on their minds, Timothy Ware, has written *The Orthodox Church* (Harmondsworth, Middlesex, England and Baltimore, Maryland 1963); consult also Ernst Benz, *The Eastern Orthodox Church: Its Thought and Life* (Garden City, New York 1963), a little book by an amiable outsider; apologetic expositions by John Meyendorff, *The Orthodox Church* (New York 1962) and Alexander Schmemann, *Eastern Orthodoxy* (New York 1963); Carnegie Samuel Calian, *Icon and Pulpit: The Protestant-Orthodox Encounter* (Philadelphia 1968) brings to focus the issues implied in the subject of this book on Prot-

estantism; Calian includes a reading list of materials which bear on the encounter.

19. Because of Russia's prominence and the complex character of the evangelical churches' situation in Russia, the topic of Protestantism in the Soviet has evoked considerable interest in the Christian community. Nikita Struve, *Christians in Contemporary Russia* (New York 1967) includes extensive well-intended references to the evangelicals. So does Constantin de Grunwald, *The Churches and the Soviet Union* (London and New York 1961 and 1962). An account highly favorable to the conservatives is J. C. Pollock, *The Faith of the Russian Evangelicals* (New York and Toronto 1964); its British title is *The Christians from Siberia* (London 1964). Michael Bourdeaux, *Opium of the People: The Christian Religion in the U.S.S.R.* (London and Indianapolis, Indiana, 1965) refers to Baptists and evangelicals at some length, and the same author develops Protestant themes at book length in *Religious Ferment in Russia: Protestant Opposition to Soviet Religious Policy* (New York, London, Toronto, and Melbourne 1968). A general view of the situation of Christians in Russia and elsewhere "behind the Iron Curtain" is Kurt Hutten, *Iron Curtain Christians: The Church in Communist Countries Today* (Minneapolis, Minnesota 1967). It is casually documented and there is no bibliography.

20. There is no adequate English-language work which segregates the story of Protestantism in predominantly Catholic European nations. The works of Kenneth Scott Latourette deal most generously with the topic, particularly in *The Twentieth Century in Europe* (New York 1961). Two ecumenical books are Stewart Herman, *Report from Christian Europe* (New York 1953) and Adolf Keller, *Christian Europe Today* (London 1942). Most other works are tendentious and often biased. Paul Blanshard concentrated on Iberia in *Freedom and Catholic Power in Spain and Portugal* (Boston 1962), a story of Catholic abuses; the same author also wrote an anti-Catholic work on Ireland, *The Irish and Catholic Power* (London 1954). The report by John D. Hughey, Jr., *Religious Freedom in Spain* (Nashville, Tennessee 1955) is typical of the tales of woe suffered by Protestants in Spain.

21. Very valuable as a comprehensive work on Latin America and its evangelicals is William R. Read, Victor M. Monterroso, and Harmon A. Johnson, *Latin American Church Growth* (Grand Rapids, Michigan 1969); this is in a series on Church Growth, one which includes works on Mexico, Korea, Brazil, Nigeria, Liberia, and Tabasco (Mexico) in other volumes. It would be difficult to find a

more useful or well-edited bibliography on the subject than the one included by the authors; students of Latin American Protestantism would be well advised to begin with that list. A tract of considerable interest is Sante Uberto Barbieri, *Land of Eldorado* (New York 1961), which explores Protestant history and possibilities in Latin America. There is a useful chapter on Protestant Pentecostalists in Prudencio Damboriena, *Tongues as of Fire: Pentecostalism in Contemporary Christianity* (Washington 1969). Clyde W. Taylor and Wade T. Coggins, *Protestant Mission in Latin America* (Washington 1961) is a two-volume assessment from the conservative evangelical angle of vision. A sociological and theological view of Pentecostals in Brazil and Chile is Emilio Willems, *Followers of the New Faith* (Nashville, Tennessee 1967).

CHAPTER 2

22. The historian who has worked most consistently with the concept of Christendom is Christopher Dawson. His *The Dividing of Christendom* (New York, 1965) reflects his Catholic view of the rise of Protestantism.

23. A number of general discussions of Protestantism as an entity have appeared in recent decades; many of them include special pleading and few have general historical or phenomenological significance. However, a few can be singled out as deserving readers' attention for background or to locate issues. Among these are: Louis Bouyer, *The Spirit and Forms of Protestantism* (Cleveland, Ohio 1964), a Calvinist-turned-Catholic priest reflects on the faith he left behind; R. Newton Flew and Rupert E. Davies, *The Catholicity of Protestantism* (Philadelphia 1954) argues that the free churches also perpetuate Catholic Christian ideals; Hugh Thompson Kerr, *Positive Protestantism* (Philadelphia 1950) looks back to the Reformation to call Protestants forward into prophetic ministry; Wilhelm Pauck, *The Heritage of the Reformation* (Glencoe, Illinois 1961) is a master teacher's exposition of random Protestant themes.

General histories of the Reformation vastly outnumber those devoted to the whole development of Protestantism as a single phenomenon. Émile G. Léonard, *A History of Protestantism* (Indianapolis 1968) is valuable chiefly because its first volume—the only one translated to date—includes an enormous bibliography that will introduce readers to non-English (chiefly French and German) titles; none of those titles will appear in this bibliography.

One of the most convenient bibliographies in English appears in a comprehensive, balanced, if not particularly exciting coverage of the whole age, Harold J. Grimm, *The Reformation Era, 1500–1650* (New York and London 1967). Professor Grimm begins his bibliography with a listing of reference materials and other scholars' bibliographies; that collation is indispensable for students of the period. Less detailed than Grimm but perhaps capable of holding interest of newcomers more readily are: Roland H. Bainton, *The Reformation of the Sixteenth Century* (Boston 1952); the same author's *The Age of the Reformation* (Princeton, New Jersey 1956) which includes documents; Owen Chadwick, *The Reformation* (Harmondsworth, Middlesex, England and Baltimore, Maryland 1964); E. Harris Harbison, *The Age of the Reformation* (Ithaca, New York 1955) and Hans J. Hillerbrand, *The Reformation in Its Own Words* (New York 1964), a collection of primary sources. An earlier English-language work that still holds interest is Preserved Smith, *The Age of the Reformation* (New York 1920); much debated in recent years has been the partly speculative sociological account, Guy E. Swanson, *Religion and Regime* (Ann Arbor, Michigan 1967). J. Leslie Dunstan, *Protestantism* (New York 1961) blends historical narrative with documents, while Roland H. Bainton in the second volume of *Christendom* (New York 1966) deals with the whole church, with special reference to Protestantism, in modern centuries.

24. Out of the wide literature concerning "pre-reformers," note the following: Roberto Ridolfi, *The Life of Girolamo Savonarola* (New York 1959); George M. Trevelyan, *England in the Age of Wycliffe* (London 1899 and New York 1963); Matthew Spinka, ed., *Advocates of Reform, from Wyclif to Erasmus* (Philadelphia 1953); (Spinka has written extensively on Huss elsewhere).

25. The Whitehead reference is to Alfred North Whitehead, *Science and the Modern World* (New York 1948), p. 1.

26. The most extensive lists of Protestant varieties frequently occur in Catholic works; as an example, pp. 322 ff. in John A. Hardon, S.J., *The Protestant Churches of America* (Westminster, Maryland 1956).

27. The modern Lutheran churches are listed and described in Carl E. Lundquist, *Lutheran Churches of the World* (Minneapolis, Minnesota 1957). A technical discussion of their essence, from the viewpoint of a conservative German theologian, appears in Werner Elert, *The Structure of Lutheranism* (St. Louis, Missouri 1962).

28. To begin on Reformed-Presbyterian churchmanship: John

T. McNeill, *The History and Character of Calvinism* (New York 1954), a classic account with a bibliography; the informal John A. Mackay, *The Presbyterian Way of Life* (Englewood Cliffs, New Jersey 1960); James Moffatt, *The Presbyterian Churches* (London 1928); J. N. Ogilvie, *The Presbyterian Churches of Christendom* (London 1925); Arthur Dakin, *Calvinism* (London and Philadelphia, Pennsylvania 1946); C. L. Warr, *The Presbyterian Tradition* (London 1933).

29. J. W. C. Wand, *Anglicanism in History and Today* (New York and Toronto 1962) is regarded as a contemporary classic. Anglicanism is an "idea" that finds embodiment in the life of the churches. G. K. A. Bell, *A Brief Sketch of the Church of England* (London 1929) still merits reading; G. F. S. Gray, *The Anglican Communion* (London 1958) is of general interest, as is P. E. Fore and F. L. Cross, *Anglicanism* (London 1935). Stephen Neill also has summarized the Anglican complex in *Anglicanism* (Harmondsworth, Middlesex, England and Baltimore, Maryland 1960). The bibliography in Neill is sufficiently annotated and accessible to guide interested readers further into Anglican writing.

30. A modest introduction to world Methodism can be found in Rupert E. Davies, *Methodism* (Harmondsworth, Middlesex, England and Baltimore, Maryland 1963). Most of the other Methodist works are issue-centered, biographical, or geographically localized, but one might take note also of C. J. Davey, *The March of Methodism* (London 1951) and E. Gordon Rupp, *Methodism in Relation to the Protestant Tradition* (London 1952), the latter by a British Methodist historian who has distinguished himself also in the study of the continental Reformation.

31. A British Congregationalist, Daniel Jenkins, has tried to capture the free-church genius in his *Congregationalism: A Restatement* (London and New York 1954). A. Peel and D. Horton discuss *International Congregationalism* (London 1952); Williston Walker, *The Creeds and Platforms of Congregationalism* (New York 1893) remains useful. For the Baptist churches, see E. A. Payne, *The Fellowship of Believers: Baptist Thought and Practice Yesterday and To-Day* (London 1952). Payne was an ecumenical leader and apologist for Baptist principles. Earlier, H. Wheeler Robinson explained the faith in *Baptist Principles* (London 1926) and *The Life and Faith of the Baptists* (London 1927). F. T. Lord, *Baptist World Fellowship* (London 1955) deals with the international setting. A readable chronicle is Robert G. Torbet, *A History of the Baptists* (Philadelphia 1952).

32. While there are numerous histories of most phases of the Anabaptist movements, the contemporary complex of Mennonite-

Brethren-churches has been less adequately treated. William R. Estep, *The Anabaptist Story* (Nashville, Tennessee 1963) attempts an inclusive history; Franklin H. Littell, *The Free Church* (Boston 1957) collates the life of various believers' churches. Donald F. Durnbaugh, *The Believers' Church: The History and Character of Radical Protestantism* (New York 1969) is the best general introduction.

33. Surprisingly few attempts have been made to gather the strands of American Protestantism into a single story. Among the noteworthy attempts are Jerald C. Brauer, *Protestantism in America: A Narrative History* (Philadelphia 1965); the author wrote for young people and laymen, not for specialists; Winthrop S. Hudson, *American Protestantism* (Chicago 1961) is a pithy and pointed account; see also Martin E. Marty, *Righteous Empire: The Protestant Experience in America* (New York 1970). Authors within various traditions contributed to Vergilius Ferm, ed., *The American Church of the Protestant Heritage* (New York 1953).

Protestantism is generously treated in the following books whose titles suggest that all religion in America is under consideration: Sidney E. Mead, *The Lively Experiment: The Shaping of Christianity in America* (New York 1963), masterful interpretive essays; William Warren Sweet, *The Story of Religion in America* (New York 1950) is the standard history; Clifton E. Olmstead, *Religion in America, Past and Present* (Englewood Cliffs, New Jersey 1961) is crowded with details; Edwin S. Gaustad, *A Religious History of America* (New York 1966) is, like Brauer, a work which young people will find attractive. Willard L. Sperry, *Religion in America* (Boston 1963) is an interpretation of the religious scene.

Also of general value for plotting American Protestantism are several reference works: Edwin S. Gaustad, *Historical Atlas of Religion in America* (New York 1962); Frank S. Mead, *Handbook of Denominations in the United States* (Nashville, Tennessee 1970), an official-sounding digest of details about churches; Elmer T. Clark, *The Small Sects in America* (Nashville, Tennessee 1965), the most used reference work in its field; Frederick E. Mayer, *The Religious Bodies of America* (St. Louis 1954), useful despite its systematic Lutheran bias.

34. The whole of Christian history from the Adventist point of view has been set down in four volumes by LeRoy Edwin Froom, in *The Prophetic Faith of Our Fathers* (Washington 1950 ff.). Arthur W. Spalding, *Origin and History of the Seventh-Day Adventists* (Washington 1961) has general interest; Clara Endicott Sears, *Days of Delusion* (Boston 1924) and Richard H. Utt, *A Century of Miracles*

(Mountain View, California 1963) tell the story from vastly differing viewpoints.

35. Literature on Pentecostalism and holiness churches is growing rapidly. John T. Nichol, *Pentecostalism* (New York and London 1966) briefly tells the story of the rise of the movement and catalogs its various subgroups. It is a pioneering work, not a last word. Nichol's bibliography is of special value, since so many sources of the movement are hard to find. For a critical review, see Nils Bloch-Hoell, *The Pentecostal Movement* (New York 1964). A history of the Assemblies of God appears in Carl Brumback, *Suddenly . . . From Heaven* (Springfield, Missouri 1961), an insider's version. Timothy Smith, *Called unto Holiness* (Kansas City, Missouri 1962) is the story of the Nazarenes, a group of independent origins sometimes too casually classified with the Assemblies of God.

36. Since the heirs of the radical Reformation tend to be worldwide fellowships, an introduction to their literature appears above in note 32, but several specifically American mutations should be recognized. Most valuable is Donald F. Durnbaugh and L. W. Shultz, *A Brethren Bibliography 1713–1963* (Elgin, Illinois 1964). Harold S. Bender has performed a similar service for another group in *Two Centuries of American Mennonite Literature . . . 1727–1928* (Goshen, Indiana 1929). John Christian Wenger, *The Mennonite Church in America* (Scottdale, Pennsylvania 1966) incorporates both history and theology in its discussion. An extreme subgroup in the Mennonite family that has attracted much attention is the Amish; John Andrew Hostetler, *Annotated Bibliography on the Amish* (Scottdale, Pennsylvania 1951) introduces its literature.

As native American growths, the heirs of nineteenth century primitive Gospel movements, the Disciples of Christ and the Christian Church, have attracted many historians and other writers to the story of their causes. An informal interpretation of the former is Byrdine Akers Abbott, *The Disciples: An Interpretation* (St. Louis 1964); a militant conservative in the divided movement, James DeForest Murch, is author of *Christians Only: A History of the Restoration Movement* (Cincinnati, Ohio 1962). Howard E. Short, *Doctrine and Thought of the Disciples of Christ* (St. Louis 1951) is a standard, easy-to-read guide; the best-accepted history is Winfred E. Garrison and Alfred T. DeGroot, *The Disciples of Christ: A History* (St. Louis 1948).

37. The Evangelical United Brethren, since merged with Methodism, are described by Paul Himmel Eller, *These Evangelical United Brethren* (Dayton, Ohio 1950).

The Quakers have been studied on an international scale, but they also lived an independent life in nineteenth and twentieth century America. For the American side, the collection edited by Edwin B. Bronner, *American Quakers Today* (Philadelphia 1966) provides an introduction; D. Elton Trueblood has been the best-known modern propagator of the Quaker vision in America, as in his *The People Called Quakers* (New York 1966).

38. The temptation to detail Mormon literature is very strong, but to keep matters in proportion we shall refer to only a few characteristic titles. Thomas F. O'Dea, *The Mormons* (Chicago 1957) is the best general sociological analysis by a non-Mormon. A critical work is Wallace Turner, *The Mormon Establishment* (Boston 1966); it discusses community and personal strains resulting from application of Mormon tenets; favorable treatment appears in William Muelder, *The Mormons in American History* (Salt Lake City 1957), wherein the author claims that Mormonism is a kind of fulfillment of many American themes. In a similar vein is Milton Vaughn Backman, *American Religions and the Rise of Mormonism* (Salt Lake City 1965).

39. Universalism's story is told in Richard Eddy, *Universalism in America: A History* (Boston 1884–1886), a two-volume contribution to a series; it is often described as the only comprehensive work on the subject. There is a good bibliography in Elmo A. Robinson, *American Universalism* (New York 1970). Universalism and Unitarianism have now merged into one denomination; a pictorial attempt to inform the memberships concerning the separate histories was Henry H. Cheetham, *Unitarianism and Universalism: An Illustrated History* (Boston 1962). A thorough work, Earl Morse Wilbur, *A History of Unitarianism* (Cambridge, Massachusetts 1945–1952) in two volumes threads together the story of that faith in America and in Europe.

References to American groups only casually referred to in this essay (Christian Scientists, Jehovah's Witnesses, Shakers, and others) along with hundreds of other citations of volumes dealing with denominations mentioned in this chapter will be found in Nelson R. Burr, *A Critical Bibliography of Religion in America* (Princeton, New Jersey 1961), two volumes, an invaluable guide to all aspects of American religion; a condensed and updated version is Nelson R. Burr, *Religion in American Life* (New York 1971).

40. For the later (post-Reformation era) career of Lutheranism in Germany see Andrew Drummond, *German Protestantism since Luther* (London 1951), an unsatisfying book but one of the few in

English dealing with the subject; sorely out of date and also never more than adequate is K. D. Macmillan, *Protestantism in Germany* (Princeton, New Jersey 1917).

41. It is not possible to provide a bibliography on the Reformation in Sweden; the literature is too extensive. Too meager is the list of books on the character of the subsequent Scandinavian churches, but note the collection by distinguished scholars (Einar Molland, Regin Prenter and others) in Leslie Stannard Hunter, *Scandinavian Churches* (London and Minneapolis 1965). The editor appends a two-page bibliography of works in English, devoted chiefly to works on the churches in the separate Scandinavian nations.

42. Harold J. Grimm's book (note 23) in its bibliography, pp. 643–45, provides ample material on the further spread of the Reformation, particularly to Baltic areas, Bohemia and Moravia, and Austria. Students of Reformation history should consult these references. Imre Revesz, *History of the Hungarian Reformed Church* (Washington 1956) is one of the rare books which carries the story beyond the sixteenth century.

43. For Reformation histories, see again the bibliography in John T. McNeill (note 28). Something of the spirit of the lineage of Calvinism is found in M. Eugene Osterhaven, *The Spirit of the Reformed Tradition* (Grand Rapids, Michigan 1971).

44. Otto Zoff, *The Huguenots* (New York 1942) is a lively book written by a Catholic; I know of no modern work in English on French Protestant development.

45. The writings of Pieter Geyl, especially *The Revolt of the Netherlands 1555–1609* and *The Netherlands Divided 1609–1648* (London 1937 and 1936), have done much to locate the role of religion (it was minor) in the Dutch revolt. Unfortunately, there are no worthwhile works in English on the later Low Countries Protestant churches.

46. There is, fortunately, an excellent history of post-Reformation transitions in Scotland; it is J. H. S. Burleigh, *A Church History of Scotland* (London, Toronto, New York 1960). Well over the last third of the book deals with post-Reformation events and forms. See also J. R. Fleming, *A History of the Church in Scotland 1834–1929* (Edinburgh 1927 and 1933), a two-volume standard work treating the modern period. Of considerable interest is the opinion-filled R. Stuart Louden, *The True Face of the Kirk: An Examination of the Ethos and Traditions of the Church of Scotland* (London, Glasgow, Toronto, and New York 1963). The reader will gain some under-

standing as to why *Ecclesia Scoticana* is such a live concept in Scottish churches.

47. A. G. Dickens, *The English Reformation* (New York 1964), Geoffrey R. Elton, *England under the Tudors* (London 1955), and Thomas M. Parker, *The English Reformation to 1558* set the stage for subsequent developments; see note 29 for materials on later Church of England trends.

48. Succinct essays on the meaning of Puritanism appear in Alan Simpson, *Puritanism in Old and New England* (Chicago 1955); for the story of the beginnings, see William Haller, *The Rise of Puritanism* (New York 1938) and Marshall Knappen, *Tudor Puritanism* (London and Chicago 1939). Arthur S. P. Woodhouse, *Puritanism and Liberty* (London 1938) reveals the varieties of Puritanism on decisive subjects. William Haller, *Liberty and Reformation in the Puritan Revolution* (New York and London 1955) carries the story into the debates at the time of the Revolution.

49. Horton Davies, *The English Free Churches* (London, New York, and Toronto 1963) is a rich miniature dealing with Puritans, Presbyterians, Congregationalists, Baptists, and their heirs in England. Ernest A. Payne, *The Free Church Tradition in the Life of England* (London 1944) covers similar ground, with a stronger apologetic sense.

50. The one volume on radical Protestant origins that is basic in any library is George Hunston Williams, *The Radical Reformation* (Philadelphia 1962); while there is no bibliography, the footnoted documentation is excellent.

CHAPTER 3

51. A number of excellent histories of Christian thought have been produced under Protestant auspicies. The most ambitious twentieth century work in English promises to be a multivolume book, the first of which has appeared: Jaroslav Pelikan, *The Emergence of the Catholic Tradition 100–600* (London and Chicago 1971); it is a demonstration of the catholic spirit in modern Protestant writing and will be a landmark series. The whole set will be called "The Christian Tradition: A History of the Development of Doctrine." It will parallel the magisterial work of Adolf Harnack, *History of Dogma* (New York 1961), a seven-volume work which appeared through five editions up to 1931–1932 in German. Harnack's is termed by Pelikan "after more than eighty years, the one

interpretation of early Christian doctrine with which every other scholar in the field must contend." Harnack is critical of the Greek spirit and dogmatizing tendencies; Pelikan offers a balancing Protestant appreciation.

A shorter book which is convenient though far less significant is the two-volume textbook produced by a Lutheran, Otto W. Heick, *A History of Christian Thought* (Philadelphia 1965–1966). On early Christian history, one of the better works is John N. D. Kelly, *Early Christian Doctrines* (New York 1958), a modest counterpart to Pelikan's first volume. More dated is Arthur Cushman McGiffert, *A History of Christian Thought* in its modern reissue (New York 1947). A valid contribution but one dwarfed by Harnack is Reinhold Seeberg, *Text-book of the History of Doctrines* (Grand Rapids, Michigan 1952), which began to appear in Germany in 1895 and was revised through a fourth German edition in 1953–1954. Of special interest because of the author's philosophical point of view is Paul Tillich, *A History of Christian Thought* (New York 1968).

52. Typical of the better recent efforts at writing a comparative symbolic or dogmatic study is Einar Molland, *Christendom: The Christian Churches, Their Doctrines, Constitutional Forms and Ways of Worship* (New York 1959). The Protestant section should also be consulted in the following works: Alexander Stewart, *Creeds and Churches* (London 1916), which concentrates on doctrine; William A. Curtis, *A History of Creeds and Confessions of Faith in Christendom and Beyond* (Edinburgh 1911); Charles A. Briggs, *Theological Symbolics* (Edinburgh 1914). More recently there appeared J. L. Neve, *Churches and Sects of Christendom* (Blair, Nebraska 1952) and a Reformed-partisan work, Wilhelm Niesel, *The Gospel and the Churches* (Philadelphia 1962). While most of these volumes compare Roman Catholicism, Protestantism, and Orthodoxy, they all sort out the various Protestant confessions. The approach attracts less interest in the ecumenical age and in a period when churches are more reluctant to devise doctrinal statements and often more uncertain about their relation to historic ones.

53. A number of books make available edited versions of the Protestant confessions, almost always along with earlier and other Christian creedal statements. Most extensive and useful despite its age is the three-volume work, Philip Schaff, *The Creeds of Christendom, with a History and Critical Notes* (New York 1905). Shorter enterprises of considerable worth are Brian A. Gerrish, *The Faith of Christendom* (Cleveland 1963), more than half of which is given over to Protestant statements, and John H. Leith, *Creeds of the*

Churches (New York 1963), which treats the modern and largely Protestant materials in a similar proportion of his volume. See also Henry S. Bettenson, *Documents of the Christian Church* (New York and London 1956).

Protestantism lacks a modern English history of heresy, but there are provocative chapters in Walter Nigg, *The Heretics* (New York 1962).

54. An extensive exposition of the Barmen Declaration appears in Arthur C. Cochrane, *The Church's Confession under Hitler* (Philadelphia 1962).

55. References to the history of Protestant thought appear in a number of general histories, most of which accent institutional change. Standard volumes are James H. Nichols, *History of Christianity 1650–1950* (New York 1956), a careful work written for textbook purposes from a decisively Protestant point of view; John W. C. Wand, *A History of the Modern Church from 1500 to the Present Day* (London and New York 1946 and 1930), by a distinguished Anglican; Kenneth Scott Latourette, *Christianity in a Revolutionary Age* (London and New York 1958–1962), whose five volumes reflect the author's interest in missionary expansion, but which try to deal fairly with theological construction.

Three works which combine some historical reference, some systematic effort, and considerable personal commitment are James H. Nichols, *Primer for Protestants* (New York 1947); John Von Rohr, *Profile of Protestantism* (Belmont, California 1969); John Dillenberger and Claude Welch, *Protestant Christianity* (New York 1955). The third has the most historical interest.

A number of contemporary scholars have incorporated much history of theology into their treatments of specific aspects of Protestant development. A very informal but attractive work is Robert McAfee Brown, *The Spirit of Protestantism* (New York 1961), which attempts in brief compass to suggest the dimensions of ongoing Protestantism. George W. Forell, *The Protestant Faith* (Englewood Cliffs, New Jersey 1960) is more formal but not more technical. A major German theologian, Karl Heim, in *The Nature of Protestantism* (Philadelphia 1963), wrestled with the question of Protestant thought in relation to Catholicism.

Heinrich Bornkamm, *The Heart of Reformation Faith* (New York 1965) is another sober German attempt to find a kind of Protestant essence; he concentrates on Lutheranism. More ecumenical is Gustaf Aulén, *Reformation and Catholicity* (Philadelphia 1961), which sees continuities between earlier Christianity and Protestantism.

Hermann Diem, *Dogmatics* (Philadelphia 1959) takes up the problems of Christian thought in the light of modern hermeneutical challenges, while editor Daniel T. Jenkins has brought together a number of thinkers to discuss *The Scope of Theology* (Cleveland 1965).

Three works which discuss the mid-twentieth century situation of Christian thought on various topics, all of them in rather simple language, are William Hordern, *A Layman's Guide to Protestant Theology* (New York 1955); John B. Cobb, Jr., *Varieties of Protestantism* (Philadelphia 1960), and a group of conservative authors brought together by Carl F. H. Henry, ed., *Basic Christian Doctrines: Contemporary Evangelical Thought* (New York 1962).

Personal visions, some of them of major and enduring value, appear in some books which collate Protestant (and, sometimes, other Christian) ideas. For example, Ernst Troeltsch, *Christian Thought: Its History and Application* (London 1923) in very brief compass raises most of the great questions introduced by modern relativism. Arthur C. McGiffert, *The Rise of Modern Religious Ideas* (New York 1915) was written from an American liberal's point of view, as was William Adams Brown, *Christian Theology in Outline* (New York 1906).

Four similar efforts of British provenance are Leonard Hodgson, *Christian Faith and Practice* (Oxford 1951); John Macquarrie, *Principles of Christian Theology* (New York 1966), which fuses Anglican and Heideggerian visions; J. S. Whale, *Christian Doctrine* (Cambridge, England 1941), an ecumenical Congregationalist statement of considerable clarity; Thomas E. Jessop, *An Introduction to Christian Doctrine* (London, Melbourne, Johannesburg, Toronto, and New York 1960), of general interest.

Representative of a catholic Lutheran point of view is Gustaf Aulén, *The Faith of the Christian Church* (Philadelphia 1948). In these works the historic dimensions are secondary.

56. An excellent collection of writings, many of them Protestant, providing personal approaches to theological problems, has been made by A. Roy Eckardt, *The Theologian at Work* (New York 1968).

57. A number of reformers, their movements, and their styles are capably presented and analyzed in Brian A. Gerrish, ed., *Reformers in Profile* (Philadelphia 1967) and Ernest G. Rupp, *Patterns of Reformation* (London 1969), which focuses on secondary characters of the Reformation's first generation.

58. There has been considerable recovery of interest in the "left wing of the Reformation" and an extensive body of literature is

beginning to appear. Leonard Verduin, *The Reformers and Their Stepchildren* (Grand Rapids, Michigan 1964) is sympathetic in its treatment of this wing, while harsh in his judgments on the mainline reformers. Hans J. Hillerbrand, *A Fellowship of Discontent* (New York 1967) includes some radical reformers in his study of restless temperaments throughout modern Christian history. Guy F. Hershberger, ed., *The Recovery of the Anabaptist Vision* (Scottdale, Pennsylvania 1957) is a favorable discussion of the radicals. John C. Wenger, ed., *The Complete Writings of Menno Simons* (Scottdale, Pennsylvania 1956) introduces modern readers to the thought of an outstanding representative of this portion of the movement.

59. Helmut T. Lehmann and Jaroslav Pelikan, eds., *Luther's Works* (St. Louis and Philadelphia 1955–) is to be a fifty-five-volume edition, most of which has appeared at this writing. Translations are excellent, editing is meticulous; it should be the standard English source series on Luther for a long time to come. A few highlights of Luther's career are available in a generous paperback book, John Dillenberger, ed., *Martin Luther: Selections* (Garden City, New York 1961) and should be consulted by newcomers to the subject.

A number of lives of Luther try to do justice to his contributions to the history of Christian thought. The most popular (deservedly so) among English-language works has been Roland H. Bainton, *Here I Stand: The Life of Martin Luther* (Nashville, Tennessee 1950), written in excellent style by a catholic-minded Quaker. Gerhard Ritter, *Luther: His Life and Work* (New York 1963) has also attracted wide attention; more brief is Franz Lau, *Luther* (Philadelphia 1963). Ernest G. Schwiebert, *Luther and His Times* (St. Louis 1950) excellently locates Luther in his academic setting. The early development of his thought appears in Heinrich Boehmer, *Road to Reformation* (Philadelphia 1946).

Among the notable English-language works on Luther's thought are Henrich Bornkamm, *Luther's World of Thought* (St. Louis 1958), which argues that that thought remains important; an equally moderate summary, Paul Althaus, *The Theology of Martin Luther* (Philadelphia 1966); Ernest G. Rupp, *The Righteousness of God* (London 1953), which gets to the heart of matters, as does another work by a British Methodist, Philip G. Watson, *Let God Be God* (Philadelphia and London 1947) on Luther's theocratic emphasis; a collection of contemporary-based essays, Heino O. Kadai, ed., *Accents in Luther's Theology* (St. Louis 1967); a positive reading by a Roman Catholic, Harry J. McSorley, *Luther: Right or Wrong* (New York and Minneapolis 1969), concentrating on Luther's debates over man's will.

Jaroslav Pelikan, *Obedient Rebels* (London and New York 1964) employs Paul Tillich's themes of "Catholic substance and Protestant principle" in Luther's Reformation; the author's earlier work, *From Luther to Kierkegaard* (St. Louis 1950) traces the consequences of Luther's thought. Of some interest is a work exploring the Swedish Luther-renaissance, Edgar M. Carlson, *The Reinterpretation of Luther* (Philadelphia 1948).

60. Zwingli has been receiving scholarly attention after midcentury. The best introduction to his thought is in G. W. Bromiley, ed., *Zwingli and Bullinger* (Philadelphia 1953), a fine translation of the major works of the Swiss reformer in "The Library of Christian Classics." Henry Bullinger received notice over a century ago in T. Harding, ed., *The Decades of Henry Bullinger* (Cambridge England 1949–1952), a dated four-volume edition.

Still referred to is Samuel M. Jackson, *Huldreich Zwingli* (New York and London 1901), a biography, but a brief and popular recent work, Oskar Farner, *Zwingli the Reformer* (New York 1957), has subsequently attracted notice; for present purposes, the allusion of Zwingli's thought, see the useful Jacques Courvoisier, *Zwingli: A Reformed Theologian* (Richmond, Virginia 1963).

61. Clyde L. Manschreck has edited the writings of *Melanchthon on Christian Doctrine* (New York 1965) out of the twenty-eight-volume German edition, and has presented, also in English, a life, *Melanchthon, the Quiet Reformer* (Nashville, Tennessee 1958). Melanchthon is a much debated figure; some of the controversies are summarized in Franz Hildebrandt, *Melanchthon: Alien or Ally* (New York 1946).

Calvin, like Luther, has been treated at library length and one can only hint at some clues which give access to his thought. English-speaking readers should all begin with the major source, John T. McNeill, ed., *John Calvin: Institutes of the Christian Religion* (Philadelphia 1960), two more volumes in the "Library of Christian Classics." For those interested in his biblical thought there is the reprint of *Commentaries of John Calvin* (Grand Rapids, Michigan 1947–) in forty-six volumes. R. N. Carew Hunt, *Calvin* (London 1933) is a brief and worthwhile life.

The accent in this chapter falls, however, on Calvin's thought; fortunately, there are excellent English translations or original works on this subject, beginning with François Wendel, *Calvin: The Origins and Development of His Religious Thought* (New York and London 1963) and Wilhelm Niesel, *The Theology of Calvin* (Philadelphia

1956). Of interest also are Edward A. Dowey, *The Knowledge of God in Calvin's Theology* (New York 1952) and Thomas F. Torrance, *Calvin's Doctrine of Man* (London 1949).

62. There are no twentieth century works to match editions of Cranmer brought out in the first half of the nineteenth century; see J. E. Cox, ed., *The Works of Thomas Cranmer* (Oxford 1844–1846), two volumes. A modern appraisal is Geoffrey W. Bromiley, *Thomas Cranmer Theologian* (New York 1956) and another brief work, Francis E. Hutchinson, *Cranmer and the English Reformation* (London and New York 1951); Jasper Ridley, *Thomas Cranmer* (Oxford 1962) is excellent. Some of the genius of the formulation in the Church of England is apparent in D. Hague, *The Story of the English Prayer Book* (New York and London 1926). Other leaders of the British change are discussed in Marcus L. Loane, *Masters of the English Reformation* (London 1954) and E. G. Rupp, *Six Makers of English Religion, 1500–1700* (New York 1957). Additional histories of the English Reformation include some materials on the development of theology. Among these are T. M. Parker, *The English Reformation* (New York 1950) and F. M. Powicke, *The Reformation in England* (New York 1941). Charles Cremeans, *The Reception of Calvinist Thought in England* (Urbana, Illinois 1949) holds interest on a particular topic having to do with the transmission of Protestant thought. See, finally, Charles and Catherine George, *The Protestant Mind of the English Reformation* (Princeton, New Jersey 1961).

63. The standard English translation of the Lutheran Confessions is Theodore G. Tappert, ed., *The Book of Concord* (Philadelphia 1959), though much material of abiding interest from a very conservative point of view is incorporated in introductions to *Concordia Triglotta* (St. Louis 1921). Discussions of these documents are carefully treated in Edmund Schlink, *Theology of the Lutheran Confessions* (Philadelphia 1961) and Willard Dow Allbeck, *Studies in the Lutheran Confessions* (Philadelphia 1968).

64. An advocate of a return to scholasticism in Lutheran circles has written an historical overview of the period which produced it, Robert Preus, *The Theology of Post-Reformation Lutheranism* (St. Louis 1970). The same author produced a conscientious work, *The Inspiration of Scripture: A Study of the Theology of the Seventeenth Century Lutheran Dogmaticians* (Mankato, Minnesota 1955). There are selections from writers of this period in the dated Heinrich Schmid, *The Doctrinal Theology of the Evangelical Lutheran Church* (Minneapolis 1961). Auguste Lecerf, *An Introduction to Reformed Dogmatics* (London 1949) is a Calvinist counterpart to some of these works. Selec-

tions of writings in this tradition appear in the well-edited work by John W. Beardslee, *Reformed Dogmatics* (New York 1965).

65. While an enormous, rambling, antipietist history appeared long ago in Germany, Albrecht Ritschl's work (1880–1886), no adequate treatment exists in English. A beginning can be made through John T. McNeill, *Modern Christian Movements* (Philadelphia 1954) and there is at last an edition of Spener's *Pia Desideria*, edited by Theodore G. Tappert (Philadelphia 1964), but there is not even an adequate life of Spener in English. For a representative pietist activist's life, John R. Weinlick, *Count Zinzendorf* (Nashville, Tennessee 1956).

66. The literature on Puritan thought is extensive; some of it was introduced in note 48. Leonard J. Trinterud, ed., *Elizabethan Puritanism* (New York 1971) is a noteworthy collection, well introduced, of early Puritan documents, while Horton Davies, *The Worship of the English Puritans* (London 1948) presents liturgical thought and practices.

67. The implications of the era of Enlightenment for religion have been extensively explored. Readers interested in following many trails through the material are well advised to consult the superb bibliographical essays in Peter Gay, *The Enlightenment: An Interpretation* (New York 1966 and 1969), a two-volume work with about 250 pages of suggestions for further reading, along with critical comment—critical of religion, too! A convenient narrative work is G. R. Cragg, *The Church and the Age of Reason* (Harmondsworth, Middlesex, England and Baltimore, Maryland 1960) and the same author's *Reason and Authority in the Eighteenth Century* (Cambridge, England 1964); Cragg has also written on the period to and through Enlightenment in *From Puritanism to the age of Reason* (Cambridge 1966). Norman Sykes's masterful *Church and State in England in the Eighteenth Century* (Cambridge, England 1934) qualifies stereotypes concerning the monopoly of deist thought in that time and place. Carl L. Becker, *The Heavenly City of the Eighteenth Century Philosophers* (New Haven, Connecticut 1932) is a provocative essay on the quasi-religious aspects of apparently nonreligious *philosophes*. R. L. Stromberg, *Religious Liberalism in Eighteenth Century England* (Oxford 1954) merits notice, as does Basil Willey, *The Eighteenth Century Background* (New York 1941), a comprehensive, perceptive interpretation. A sample of deist writings is conveniently available in E. Graham Waring, *Deism and Natural Religion* (New York 1967).

American manifestations of the Enlightenment religious spirit have been discussed by G. Adolf Koch in *Religion of the American Enlightenment* (New York 1968), a reprint of *Republican Religion* (1933). Equally interesting is Herbert M. Morais, *Deism in Eighteenth Century America* (New York 1960). A sourcebook, Adrienne Koch, *The American Enlightenment* (New York 1965) includes some material on the religious views of the national founding fathers.

The continental Enlightenment and the German *Aufklärung* are capably treated in Ernst Cassirer, *The Philosophy of the Enlightenment* (Boston 1951) and Paul Hazard, *European Thought in the Eighteenth Century*. For the challenges to religion following the Enlightenment, Franklin L. Baumer, *Religion and the Rise of Scepticism* (New York 1960) serves as a lively introduction. The latter chapters of Arthur C. McGiffert, *Protestant Thought before Kant* (New York and London 1911) deal with this period.

68. The place to begin on Wesleyan sources is Albert C. Outler, ed., *John Wesley* (New York 1964), which includes an authoritative introduction by a Wesleyan scholar capable of setting his work against the larger Christian background. An uncritical edition from 1829–1831 has been reprinted: Thomas Jackson, ed., *The Works of the Rev. John Wesley, A.M.* (Grand Rapids, Michigan 1958–1959) in fourteen volumes. Lives of Wesley are numerous; a few elaborate on his contributions to Protestant theology. See Martin Schmidt, *John Wesley: A Theological Biography* (New York 1963) and, for public impact, Maldwyn L. Edwards, *John Wesley and the Eighteenth Century: A Study of His Social and Political Influence* (London and New York 1933).

For the general background to British awakenings, John H. Overton and Frederic Relton, *The English Church 1714–1800* (London and New York 1906) remains a standard; more controversial is Elie Halévy, *History of the English People in 1815* (London 1937), because he restores a thesis that Methodism helped England avoid French Revolutionary-style upheaval. The writings of E. G. Rupp deal with Methodism in this setting; see *Methodism in Relation to the Protestant Tradition* (London 1952).

American awakenings in the eighteenth century receive sourcebook treatment in Richard L. Bushman, ed., *The Great Awakening: Documents on the Revival of Religion 1740–1745* (New York 1970). More extensive is Alan Heimert and Perry Miller, *The Great Awakening: Documents Illustrating the Crisis and Its Consequences* (Indianapolis, Indiana 1967). A well-received brief book about the northern revivals is Edwin Scott Gaustad, *The Great Awakening in New England* (New York 1957) and on the southern, Wesley M. Gewehr, *The*

Great Awakening in Virginia, 1740–1790 (Durham, North Carolina 1930).

The high church version of the romantic awakenings was best symbolized by the Oxford Movement. Eugene R. Fairweather, ed., *The Oxford Movement* (New York 1964) is a collection of documents from the movement which has been almost overstudied in comparison with similar Protestant trends. The first edition (1891) of an important work by a participant has been reprinted: R. W. Church, *The Oxford Movement: Twelve Years, 1833–1845* (Chicago and London 1970). Owen Chadwick, *The Mind of the Oxford Movement* merits attention, as does a character study of the participants, Geoffrey Faber, *Oxford Apostles* (London 1954). The best review of Oxford theology comes from Sweden: Yngve Brilioth, *The Anglican Revival: Studies in the Oxford Movement* (London 1925).

69. Inevitably but regrettably there are fewer materials on the continental awakenings, but materials on them are integrated into the pro-evangelical Paul Scharpff, *History of Evangelism* (Grand Rapids, Michigan 1966), and there are frequent references in the first volume, "The Conservative Phase 1815–1871" of William O. Shanahan, *German Protestants Face the Social Question* (Notre Dame, Indiana 1954).

70. The Whitehead reference is to Alfred North Whitehead, *Adventures of Ideas* (New York 1955), pp. 30 f. James F. White, *The Cambridge Movement: The Ecclesiologists and the Gothic Revival* (Cambridge, England 1962) demonstrates the importance of the Gothic revival in English religious thought.

71. For nineteenth century historical and theological developments there is a growing literature in English. "The crisis of historical consciousness" is implied in numbers of works on the philosophy and theology of history as these relate to faith. In part because of their bibliographies, it is useful to turn first to the general theological discussion, Eric C. Rust, *Towards a Theological Understanding of History* (New York 1963) and, even more, to Alan Richardson, *History Sacred and Profane* (Philadelphia 1964). R. G. Collingwood, *The Idea of History* (New York and London 1946) is a philosophically profound work that touches on the century's developments in religious thought. Several chapters in Karl Löwith, *Meaning in History: The Theological Implications of the Philosophy of History* (Chicago 1949) are devoted to the impact on Christianity of devastating reappraisals of the meaning of history.

A brief general church history of the nineteenth century is Alec R. Vidler, *The Church in an Age of Revolution* (Harmondsworth, Middlesex, England and Baltimore, Maryland 1961). Equally sketchy because of its brevity is Josef L. Altholz, *The Churches in the Nineteenth Century* (Indianapolis 1967). A durable and trustworthy introduction to the thought of the era is H. R. Mackintosh, *Types of Modern Theology: Schleiermacher to Barth* (London 1937). A badly translated portion of a longer work by Karl Barth provides that gifted theologian's viewpoint on the era: Karl Barth, *Protestant Thought from Rousseau to Ritschl* (London and New York 1959); less useful is E. C. Moore, *An Outline of Christian Thought since Kant* (London 1909). Organized around his own philosophical ideas and not without interest, though by no means a conventional history, is Paul Tillich, *Perspectives on 19th and 20th Century Protestant Theology* (New York 1967). Valuable sources not always easy to find appear in Bernard M. G. Reardon, *Religious Thought in the Nineteenth Century* (Cambridge, England 1966).

While the more drastic metaphysical aspects of the crisis developed on the Continent, England also experienced intellectual assaults, and these have been well covered by historians. The two volumes by Owen Chadwick, *The Victorian Church* (New York and London 1966 and 1970), present a broad sweep of ecclesiastical matters, including the crises of faith and theological renewal. C. C. Gillispie, *Genesis and Geology: A Study in the Relations of Scientific Thought, Natural Theology, and Social Opinion in Great Britain* (New York 1959) reliably covers the period before Darwin, while Herbert G. Wood, *Belief and Unbelief since 1850* (Cambridge, England 1955) includes science among the assaults on religion. Two deserving and enduring works on theological reconstruction are Clement C. J. Webb, *A Study of Religious Thought in England from 1850* (Oxford 1933) and Leonard E. Elliott-Binns, *Religion in the Victorian Era* (London 1936).

72. Terrence N. Tice leaves Schleiermacher students in his debt as a result of his publication of a reference work with 1,928 items, *Schleiermacher Bibliography* (Princeton, New Jersey 1966). Since it is annotated, readers are directed to it for a comprehensive guide.

73. Sidney Hook, *From Hegel to Marx* (Ann Arbor, Michigan 1962) presents adequate, succinct summaries of the thought of David Friedrich Strauss, Bruno Bauer, Arnold Ruge, Max Stirner, and Moses Hess as precursors of Marx on the Hegelian left. Ludwig Feuerbach was the most influential figure in this succession. His *Lectures on the Essence of Christianity* (New York and London 1967) and *The Essence of Christianity* (New York: Harper 1957) are representative. One of the best, though at some times confusing,

reviews of radical thought is Karl Löwith, *From Hegel to Nietzsche* (New York 1964); he concentrates properly on Nietzsche and some of the others who were treated more briefly by Hook. Most of them operate outside the orbit of Protestant theology and belong only indirectly in this history.

74. Two studies of Ritschl, who translates poorly (and wrote poorly) and thus is seldom reprinted, are David L. Mueller, *An Introduction to the Theology of Albrecht Ritschl* (Philadelphia, 1969) and, with much more of the author's own theology intertwined, Philip Hefner, *Faith and the Vitalities of History* (New York 1966). Ritschl's successor was church historian Adolf Harnack, whose works are available in a number of English translations; his *History of Dogma* has been cited in note 51; see also *What Is Christianity?* (New York 1923), his most popular work.

Out of this neo-Kantian school came much of the impetus for later liberalism and modernism in England, America, and Germany. For English developments see the documents in A. O. J. Cockshut, *Religious Controversies of the Nineteenth Century* (Lincoln, Nebraska 1966) and the collection of lectures in Anthony Symondson, ed., *The Victorian Crisis of Faith* (London 1970), which deal with Anglican backgrounds to later controversy. Another book in this area is M. A. Crowther, *Church Embattled: Religious Controversy in Mid-Victorian England* (Devon, England, 1970). J. K. Mozley, *Some Tendencies in British Theology from the Publication of "Lux Mundi" to the Present Day* (London 1951) surveys the impact of liberal thought in Anglicanism in particular. A. M. Ramsey, *From Gore to Temple* (London 1960) covers the same general sphere; theology plus churchmanship are covered in a collection, G. S. Spinks, ed., *Religion in Britain since 1900* (London 1952). Leonard E. Elliott-Binns, *English Thought 1860–1900: The Theological Aspect* (London and New York 1956) should also be consulted.

American liberal theology still awaits critical review; a beginning was made in Frank H. Foster, *The Modern Movement in American Theology* (New York 1939); some main themes reappear in Kenneth Cauthen, *The Impact of American Liberalism* (New York 1962) and, in a much more slight volume by Lloyd J. Averill, *American Theology in the Liberal Tradition* (Philadelphia 1967). William R. Hutchinson, ed., *American Protestant Thought: The Liberal Era* (New York 1968) is a short sourcebook of writings by liberals; writings from the same period are also included in Sydney E. Ahlstrom, *Theology in America* (Indianapolis, Indiana 1967), a book valuable for Ahlstrom's introduction. The second volume of Shelton H. Smith, Robert T.

Handy and Lefferts A. Loetscher, *American Christianity* (New York 1963) also contains many liberal essays. Shelton H. Smith, *Changing Conceptions of Original Sin* (New York 1955) concludes with chapter on modernist anthropological doctrines.

Bernard M. G. Reardon, ed., *Liberal Protestantism* (Stanford, California 1968) makes available short writings of Hermann Lotze, Albrecht Ritschl, Wilhelm Herrmann, and other Protestant liberals. There are few worthwhile book-length secondary writings on the whole sweep of continental theology in the period.

75. It is not possible here to provide a detailed introduction to contemporary theology, nor is it necessary since the works are so easily available and there are numerous guides into the material. Beginners should turn first to Daniel Day Williams, *What Present-Day Theologians Are Thinking* (New York 1963) and then proceed to John B. Cobb, Jr., *Living Options in Protestant Theology* (Philadelphia 1962) or William Nicholls, *The Pelican Guide to Modern Theology* (Harmondsworth, Middlesex, England and Baltimore, Maryland 1969). A pioneer in introducing continental thought to America was Walter Marshall Horton, and his *Contemporary Continental Theology* (London and New York 1938) has stood up well. A number of significant essays appear in Arnold Nash, ed., *Protestant Thought in the Twentieth Century* (New York 1951). John Macquarrie includes ample coverage of Protestants in his well-packed *Twentieth-Century Religious Thought* (New York 1963). Advanced students will find a complex, confusing, yet worthwhile discussion of the topics in Paul Ramsey, ed., *Faith and Ethics: The Theology of H. Richard Niebuhr* (New York 1957), particularly in the essay by Hans W. Frei.

The works of contemporaries will be cited in the topical chapters that follow, and so are not cited in this historical chapter.

CHAPTER 4

76. For extensive bibliographies of the unitive movements, see excellent appendices in Ruth Rouse and Stephen Charles Neill, eds., *A History of the Ecumenical Movement 1517–1948* (Philadelphia and London 1967) and a second volume, edited by Harold E. Fey, *A History of the Ecumenical Movement 1948–1968* (Philadelphia and London 1970). Also of use are Paul A. Crow, Jr., *The Ecumenical Movement in Bibliographical Outline* (New York 1965) and Henry R. T. Brandreth, *Unity and Reunion: A Bibliography* (London 1948) for earlier materials.

It should be noted that most modern ecumenical works include Orthodox and Roman Catholic materials along with Protestantism, but it is the Protestant element in these books that receives attention here.

First, a list of general histories or interpretations: John A. Mackay, *Ecumenics: The Science of the Church Universal* (Englewood Cliffs, New Jersey 1964) is an effort by a senior statesman of the church to provide some method and system for discussions of unity as a theological science; Walter Marshall Horton, *Christian Theology: An Ecumenical Approach* (New York 1955) is a pioneering attempt by a moderate liberal to incorporate international and interdenominational accents into systematic thought; Robert McAfee Brown, *The Ecumenical Revolution* (Garden City, New York 1967) is an historical report and theological appreciation by an involved churchman; it might be the best first work for a layman on the whole subject.

Of approximately equal merit are two British works, Norman Goodall, *The Ecumenical Movement* (London and New York 1961) and Leonard Hodgson, *The Ecumenical Movement* (Sewanee, Tennessee 1951), a much shorter work; both speak positively of the efforts at Christian union. Otto A. Piper, *Protestantism in an Ecumenical Age* (Philadelphia 1965) sorts out evangelical responsibilities as a consequence of ecumenism. An attempt to see modern efforts in the light of long development in the early church is Albert C. Outler, *The Christian Tradition and the Unity We Seek* (New York 1957), outstanding for its attempt to give Protestants a more-than-biblicist understanding of the issues. Samuel McCrea Cavert, *On the Road to Christian Unity* (New York 1961) systematically appraises the whole unity movement. Charles Clayton Morrison, *The Unfinished Reformation* (New York 1953) speaks for the end of an era: he was ready for virtually complete and inclusive Protestant unity, but remained wary of Orthodoxy and opposed to Roman Catholicism in their present forms; yet it is a dramatic polemic and call to action.

Outstandingly useful for the period before Vatican Council II are the four series of *Documents on Christian Unity* edited by Bishop G. K. A. Bell (London 1924, 1930, 1948, and 1958).

Because of the extraordinary sweep of the subject, we cite several additional works on aspects of the history or interpretation: Geoffrey F. Nuttall and Owen Chadwick, eds., *From Uniformity to Unity, 1662–1962* (London 1962); the very compact Norman V. Hope, *One Christ, One World, One Church* (Philadelphia 1953); Robert S. Bilheimer, *The Quest for Christian Unity* (New York 1952); two antiecumenical works, or at least works critical of the main trends, Geoffrey W. Bromiley, *The Unity and Disunity of the Church* (Grand Rapids, Michigan 1958) and Ian Henderson, *Power without Glory: An Appraisal of the Ecumenical Movement* (New York 1961); an idealistic philosophical theologian's alternative, Eric L. Mascall, *The Recovery of Unity: A Theological Approach* (New York 1958) and two works exceptional because they grow out of a modern Reformed monastic community, Max Thurian, *Visible Unity and Tradition* (London 1964) and Roger Schutz, *Unity: Man's Tomorrow* (London 1962).

Orthodox-Protestant relations have not been isolated in many books, but note Joseph Gill, *The Orthodox and the Ecumenical Movements* (London 1962) and George Every, *Misunderstandings between East and West* (London and Richmond, Virginia, 1966). The Commission on Ecumenical Mission and Relations has prepared a 23-page document of resources, *Toward a Protestant Understanding of Orthodoxy* (New York 1966).

Roman Catholic-Protestant relations are, of course, much more regularly addressed. Only a sample of the literature can be discussed here. Hans Asmussen and Thomas Sartory, *Lutheran-Catholic Dialogue* (Baltimore, Maryland 1960) is extremely reconciliatory, just as Robert McAfee Brown and Gustave Weigel, *An American Dialogue* (Garden City, New York 1960) is an irenic proposal setting ground rules for Catholic-Protestant discussion; three French Christians relate across confessional boundaries in Jean Bosc, Jean Guitton, and Jean Danielou, *The Catholic-Protestant Dialogue* (Baltimore, Maryland 1960). A Catholic layman, Daniel Callahan, edited *Christianity Divided: Protestant and Roman Catholic Theological Issues* (New York 1961); an American Anglican treatment is Frederick C. Grant, *Rome and Reunion* (New York 1965). Critical of Catholicism before the Council, Gerrit C. Berkouwer, a Dutch leader, set forth his position in *The Conflict with Rome* (Philadelphia 1958) and then reported on the Council in *The Second Vatican Council and the New Catholicism* (Grand Rapids, Michigan 1965). A continental view appears in Edmund Schlink, *After the Council: The Meaning of Vatican II for Protestantism and the Ecumenical Dialogue* (Philadelphia 1968), while an American Congregationalist's and Lutheran's notes can be compared in Douglas Horton, *Vatican Diary: A Protestant Observes the Vatican Council II* (Boston 1966) and George A. Lindbeck, ed., *Dialogue on the Way: Protestants Report from Rome on the Vatican Council* (Minneapolis 1965).

On the theological issues, K. E. Skysgaard, *One in Christ* (Philadelphia 1957) was a pre-Vatican II "catholic" Protestant essay; even more conciliatory was Max Lackmann, *The Augsburg Confession and Catholic Unity* (New York 1963), a contrast to Franz J. Leenhardt, *Two Biblical Faiths: Protestant and Catholic* (Philadelphia 1964). From the Catholic side, an ex-Protestant focuses on sacraments in Louis Bouyer, *The Word, the Church and the Sacraments in Catholicism* (New York 1961).

77. The better works on the Marburg Colloquy from the historical point of view are in German, but a conservative Lutheran's surgical theological analysis has been translated: Hermann Sasse, *This Is My Body: Luther's Contention for the Real Presence in the Sacrament of the Altar* (Minneapolis 1959).

78. Henry Eyster Jacobs, *The Lutheran Movement in England* (Philadelphia 1894) is a dated sketch of British developments; Herbert M. Smith, *Henry VIII and the Reformation* (London and New York 1948) is an Anglican review; the polemics are noted in Ersin Doernberg, *Henry VIII and Luther* (Stanford, California 1961).

79. Hardon, note 26.

80. John T. McNeill, *Unitive Protestantism* (Richmond, Virginia 1964), a reprint of an earlier work, remains one of the better overall surveys of Protestantism's travails on the matter of unity through history; McNeill was able to insert an additional short paragraph bringing his account up to 1963.

81. This argument is developed in Denis de Rougemont, *The Christian Opportunity* (New York 1963).

82. Consult the source books in notes 53 and 63 for examples of these documents.

83. Ernst F. Winter, ed., *Erasmus–Luther: Discourse on Free Will* (New York 1961) reprints the two figures' debates on the nature of the will and illustrates how nonecumenical sixteenth century churchmen could sound. While he never became Protestant, Erasmus' work did parallel many Protestant concerns and he should be thought of in this context; see P. S. Allen, *The Age of Erasmus* (Oxford 1924), Johan Huizinga, *Erasmus of Rotterdam* (New York 1953) and, especially, Roland H. Bainton *Erasmus of Christendom* (New York 1969). Bainton best demonstrates Erasmus' proto-ecumenical spirit and tendencies.

84. Ecumenical relations have always been most complicated in pluralistic America. A number of earlier works reveal some efforts at facing the problem of disunity there: Samuel S. Schmucker, *Fraternal Appeal to the American Churches: With a Plan for Catholic Union on Apostolic Principles* (New York 1839) for the Lutherans; William

Reed Huntingdon, *The Church Idea: An Essay Towards Unity* (New York 1884), an Anglican approach; Philip Schaff, *The Principle of Protestantism* (Philadelphia 1964), which reprints Schaff's reformed appeal for Christian harmony from 1845; Josiah Strong, *Our Country: Its Possible Future and Its Present Crisis* (New York 1885), a white Protestant expression of Manifest Destiny, anti-Catholicism, and anti-secularism by a Congregationalist; Alexander Campbell, *Christianity Restored* (Bethany, Virginia 1835), a founder of the Disciples of Christ seeking to transcend denominations, and Robert Baird, *Religion in America* (New York 1844), in which a Presbyterian promoter of the Evangelical Alliance reported on America in "Evangelical"-unitive terms.

H. Richard Niebuhr, *The Social Sources of Denominationalism* (New York 1929) is considered a classic, though the author himself later corrected its onesided sociological depiction; H. Paul Douglass, *Church Unity Movements in the United States* (New York 1934) reviewed the alternatives to denominationalism in the same period.

85. James Hastings Nichols, ed., *The Mercersburg Theology* (New York 1966) brings together writings of Philip Schaff and John Williamson Nevin on the subject of unity and similar themes; both were "high church" Reformed theologians of note. Nichols wrote an excellent history of their ecumenical experiment, *Romanticism in American Theology: Nevin and Schaff at Mercersburg* (Chicago 1961).

86. Charles I. Foster, *An Errand of Mercy: The Evangelical United Front 1790–1837* (Chapel Hill, North Carolina 1960) unites the British and American evangelical cooperative efforts in a single story, told with some condescension; useful bibliography.

87. The major work on earlier English ecumenical tendencies, well documented, is Norman Sykes, *The Church of England and Nonepiscopal Churches in the Sixteenth and Seventeenth Centuries* (London 1948). An outstanding pioneer was John Dury; J. Minton Batten, *John Dury, Advocate of Christian Reunion* (Chicago 1944). Nineteenth and early twentieth century writings having a bearing on this theme are: Charles Lindley Wood Halifax, *The Reunion of Christendom* (London 1895), by a well-intended if naïve irenicist; Horatio Nelson, *Home Reunion: Reflections on the Present Position of Nonconformists and an Appeal for a Better Mutual Understanding* (London 1905); Arthur C. Headlam, *The Doctrine of the Church and Christian Reunion* (London 1920); James Cooper, *Reunion: A Voice from Scotland* (London 1918). One of the outstanding theologians of the nineteenth century threaded reunitive themes throughout his writings, as in Frederick Denison Maurice, *The Kingdom of Christ* (London 1837–

1838), in three volumes. Of course, the Oxford Movement was full of ecumenical expression; for an example, Edward Bouverie Pusey, *The Church of England a Portion of Christ's One Holy Catholic Church, Etc.* (London 1865, but these writings usually were concerned more with the situation vis-à-vis Rome than toward Nonconformity. See also A. Chandler, *The English Church and Reunion* (London 1916) and, for Scottish developments, J. R. Fleming, *The Story of Church Union in Scotland: Its Origins and Progress, 1560–1929* (London 1929).

88. Not many of the continental ecumenical documents or secondary sources have been translated, though their story is well told in the general histories introduced above, especially John T. McNeill, *Unitive Protestantism* (note 80). Studies of several figures or writings by them include: John Amos Comenius, *The Labyrinth of the World and the Paradise of the Heart*, translated for the first time in the twentieth century (Chicago 1942), and, thanks to the translator, a biography, Matthew Spinka, *John Amos Comenius, That Incomparable Moravian* (Chicago 1943); W. C. Dowding, *The Life and Correspondence of George Calixtus* (Oxford 1863); George J. Jordan, *The Reunion of the Churches: A Study of G. W. Leibnitz and His Great Attempt* (London 1927); Norman Sykes, *Daniel Ernst Jablonski and the Church of England: A Study of an Essay Towards Protestant Union* (London 1950).

89. On the history of the Y.M.C.A., Clarence Prouty Shedd, *History of the World's Alliance of Young Men's Christian Associations* (London 1955). The World Student Christian Federation is treated by Ruth Rouse, *The World's Student Christian Federation: A History of the First Thirty Years* (London 1948). Before it was integrated into the World Council of Churches, the story of the I.M.C. was well told by William Richey Hogg, *Ecumenical Foundations: A History of the International Missionary Council and Its Nineteenth-Century Background* (New York 1952). Hogg also wrote a more popular work, *One World, One Mission* (New York 1960), a once-over-lightly dealing with the connection between Protestant missions and ecumenism. In the same vein are R. Pierce Beaver's history of comity, *Ecumenical Beginnings in Protestant World Mission* (Note 2); Stephen Neill, *The Unfinished Task* (London 1957); and Henry Pitney Van Dusen, *One Great Ground of Hope: Christian Missions and Christian Unity* (Philadelphia 1961).

For a reasonably widespread range of reports on or from various national Councils of Churches or Protestant church mergers, see the volumes by Rouse-Neill and Fey (note 76), whose bibliographies try to log the everchanging record. Of special importance are Samuel McCrea Cavert, *The American Churches in the Ecumenical Movement* (New York 1968); Robert McAfee Brown, *The Challenge to Reunion: The Blake Proposal under Scrutiny* (New York 1963), on American Protestantism's most ambitious scheme to overcome its most divided condition; J. Webster Grant, *The Canadian Experience of Church Union* (London and Richmond, Virginia 1967); James Edward Lesslie Newbigin, *The Reunion of the Church: A Defence of the South India Scheme* (London 1960); and James Kellock, *Breakthrough for Church Union in North India and Pakistan* (Madras 1965). For denominational attempts to set their houses in order (Lutheran with Lutheran, Presbyterian with Presbyterian, etc.) the denominational histories can be consulted.

90. The various assemblies of the World Council of Churches provide glimpses of Protestant developments; reports on these are in: James W. Kennedy, *Venture of Faith: The Birth of the World Council of Churches* (New York 1948); James H. Nichols, *Evanston: An Interpretation* (New York 1954), which reflects a strongly Protestant point of view; James W. Kennedy, *No Darkness at All* (St. Louis 1962); Kenneth Slack, *Uppsala Report: The Story of the World Council of Churches Fourth Assembly, etc.* (London 1968); each of these is more interesting than the lengthy council memorials and proceedings or project papers.

Overall interpretations of the W.C.C.'s life are to be found in the gigantic work by David P. Gaines, *The World Council of Churches: A Study of Its Background and History* (Peterborough 1966); in the early but useful miniature by Bishop G. K. A. Bell, *The Kingship of Christ: The Story of the World Council of Churches* (Harmondsworth, Middlesex, England and Baltimore, Maryland 1954) and a tract by Paul Griswold Macy, *If It Be of God: The Story of the World Council of Churches* (St. Louis 1960).

Records or narratives of a number of major conferences or organizations which led up to the World Council of Churches are illuminating. While only scholars will be interested in the nine-volume report of the World Missionary Conference of 1910, John R. Mott, *The Decisive Hour of Christian Missions* (New York 1910 remains worth reading for the way it conveys the enthusiasm and urgency of missionary life that year. E. S. Woods interpreted the Faith and Order meeting of 1927 in *Lausanne 1927: An Interpretation of the World Conference on Faith and Order etc.* (London 1927), while Hugh Martin, *Edinburgh 1937: the Story of the Second World Conference on Faith and Order* (London 1937) expounds the meaning of that subsequent meeting. John E. Skoglund, *Fifty Years of Faith and Order: An Interpretation of the Faith and Order Movement* (St. Louis 1964) and Lukas Vischer, ed., *A Documentary History of the Faith and Order Movement* (St. Louis 1963) are standard volumes on the movement which survives even after the W.C.C. was formed.

91. Most of the anticcumenical writing is either moderate in its theology or pamphlet-style; an extremely conservative interpretation is J. Marcellus Kik, *Ecumenism and the Evangelical* (Philadelphia 1958), while James DeForest Murch, *Cooperation without Compromise* (Grand Rapids, Michigan 1956) tells the story of the National Association of Evangelicals, an organization of conservative opponents of the National and World Council of Churches.

92. While he is friendly to the movement, Robert Lee in *The Social Sources of Church Unity: An Interpretation of Unitive Movements in American Protestantism* (Nashville, Tennessee 1960) shows how in one nation at least not all drives toward unity have purely theological roots. The author designed it to be a counterpart to H. Richard Niebuhr's thesis about denominationalism's social sources.

CHAPTER 5

93. Much of the literature having to do with theodicy, "the problem of God," "God-talk," and the like, is classified under the category of Christian Apologetics—a defense or presentation of the faith on some grounds or other. An excellent, moderate introduction to the subject, though it was written before the twentieth century discussion of Christian atheism had occurred, is Alan Richardson, *Christian Apologetics* (New York 1947). Reflective of more traditional Reform conservatism influenced by the scholastic tradition is Edward J. Carnell, *An Introduction to Christian Apologetics* (Grand Rapids, Michigan 1948). Popular apologetics was for some years in the hands of an Oxford don, a lay convert to Christianity whose literary style and ingenuity attracted many people: Clive Staples Lewis, whose *Mere Christianity* (London 1953) is entertaining and, to many unmoved by more formal philosophical talk, compelling. Written during the decade of a new outbreak of talk about the problem of God is a balanced view by a British Congregationalist, Daniel Jenkins, *The Christian Belief in God* (Philadelphia 1963). Because much of the current version of the problem relates to the use of language, Diogenes Allen, *The Reasonableness of Faith* (Washington 1968) holds special interest, since the author explic-

itly sets out to face challenges from that field.

One of the most explicit defenses of monotheism occurs in a brief essay, H. Richard Niebuhr, *Radical Monotheism and Western Culture* (New York 1960). Reflective of subsequent debates about the existence and nature of God is John Macquarrie, *God and Secularity* (Philadelphia 1967). While Macquarrie is influenced by Heideggerian philosophy, his fellow Anglican Eric L. Mascall, in *The Secularization of Christianity* (New York 1966), uses the tools of philosophical idealism to counter those who have argued that Christianity must adopt the guise of the secular order. Carl Michalson, *Worldly Theology* (New York 1967) makes his response on the basis of a carefully worked out existentialist and Heideggerian rationale. Another middle-of-the-road statement which tries to do justice to the radical challenges to belief in God in the secular world yet affirms traditional Christianity is A. Michael Ramsey, *Sacred and Secular* (London 1965). A brief, informal discussion of the problems occasioned by secular developments in relation to Christian belief in God is David Baily Harned, *The Ambiguity of Religion* (Philadelphia 1968).

94. Two polls which show how the overwhelming majority of Protestants (and all Americans) assert belief in God are discussed in Martin E. Marty, Stuart E. Rosenberg, and Andrew M. Greeley, *What Do We Believe? The Stance of Religion in America* (New York 1968). British parallels are reported on in Michael Argyle, *Religious Behaviour* (London 1959).

95. The best discussion of the Arminian-Latitudinarian and near-deist influence in eighteenth century Anglican theology is chapter VIII on Bishops Benjamin Hoadly and Richard Watson in Norman Sykes, *Church and State in England in the XVIIIth Century* (note 67). Conrad Wright, *The Beginnings of Unitarianism in America* (Boston 1955) clearly narrates the rise of similar thought in New England.

96. The philosopher who was most influential in the development of "process theology" in Protestantism was Alfred North Whitehead; see especially his *Process and Reality* (1929); William Christian, *An Interpretation of Whitehead's Metaphysics* (New Haven 1959) and D. M. Emmet, *Whitehead's Philosophy of Organism* (London 1932) expound themes related to the development. A number of essays in Paul A. Schilpp, ed., *The Philosophy of Alfred North Whitehead* (New York 1951) are illuminating. An American philosopher who stands in this tradition but is more explicit than Whitehead in relating his thought to the specific religious question is Charles

Hartshorne; his *The Divine Relativity* (New Haven 1948) is representative of his view of God, sometimes called panentheism. Influenced by Whitehead and Hartshorne, yet doing his work in the context of theological faculties, was Henry Nelson Wieman; *The Source of Human Good* (Carbondale, Illinois 1946) is his climactic systematic address to the question. Bernard E. Meland, author of *The Realities of Faith* (New York 1962) and *Faith and Culture* (New York 1953), while not a cultic devotee of the approach, learned from it and fused it with insights from Rudolf Otto and expressed himself with more esthetic sense and sensitivity. A variety of elaborations on the themes of process appear in Bernard E. Meland, ed., *The Future of Empirical Theology* (Chicago 1969), papers growing out of the University of Chicago, whose Divinity School for many years was influenced by process thought; typical in the volume are the essays by Bernard M. Loomer, John B. Cobb, Jr., Schubert Ogden, and Daniel Day Williams. Williams' own *God's Grace and Man's Hope* (New York 1949) and *The Spirit and the Forms of Love* (New York 1968) show how this philosophy bears on distinctively Christian themes.

Two notable articulators of a version of process thinking are Cobb and Ogden. John B. Cobb, Jr., *A Christian Natural Theology Based on the Thought of Alfred North Whitehead* (Philadelphia 1965) acknowledges its debts to the past and marks new paths, as does Ogden, who has been similarly influenced by Hartshorne; Schubert M. Ogden, *The Reality of God* (New York 1966) includes essays that manifest the problems and possibility of the approach. It represents one of the most serious attempts to propound a metaphysic in Protestant thought in recent years.

Not precisely in this lineage, but sharing the concern for natural theology, have been a number of Anglicans. Archbishop William Temple, *Nature, Man and God* (London 1935) defended natural theology at the height of the antinature "crisis theology" vogue; Lionel Thornton in the same period and, later, Norman W. Pittenger carried these concerns. It should also be noted in the 1970s that some Roman Catholics, often influenced by Pierre Teilhard de Chardin, are working with an approach that for long had been considered Protestant and have turned to process though at a time when the old scholastic synthesis in philosophy no longer seems to be available or effective.

97. Thomas J. J. Altizer probably came closest to the description of Protestant/atheist/near-pantheism; his major works in this spirit are *The Gospel of Christian Atheism* (Philadelphia 1966) and

some contributions to a work coauthored with William Hamilton, *Radical Theology and the Death of God* (Indianapolis 1966); Hamilton does not share the pantheistic coloring of Altizer.

98. Paul Tillich's impressive system, originally appearing in three volumes, has been reprinted as a single volume, *Systematic Theology* (Chicago and New York 1967); volume II brings together his philosophy with the questions of Christ. Less formidable works from the Tillichian corpus on this theme are *Biblical Religion and the Search for Ultimate Reality* (Chicago 1955) on the Bible and the philosophers and *Dynamics of Faith* (New York 1958). A part-time disciple who joined Tillichian approaches to those derived from Rudolf Bultmann and others is John A. T. Robinson who discussed God in *Exploration into God* (Stanford, California 1967).

99. While the discussion of "personality" will be a part of most books on the Trinity (note 104), see at this point Clement C. J. Webb, *God and Personality* (London 1918).

100. For the near-deist illustrations, see note 95.

101. Schleiermacher and Ritschl are introduced in note 74; Friedrich Schleiermacher, *The Christian Faith* (Edinburgh and Naperville, Illinois 1928) provides the best discussion of the topic in Schleiermacher. The left-wing Hegelians can be approached through works detailed in note 73. There is an extensive literature on Troeltsch; see the bibliography in Benjamin A. Reist, *Toward a Theology of Involvement* (Philadelphia 1966), which extrapolates on the basis of Troeltschian themes.

102. In this note we shall introduce some of the neo-orthodox and other moderate expositors of a "doctrine of God" in the middle of the twentieth century. For Aulén, see note 55. John Baillie, *Our Knowledge of God* (New York 1939) was the work in which the view of God as "the Other who is most near" is elaborated upon. Emil Brunner, *The Christian Doctrine of God* (London and Philadelphia, 1950) is part of the multivolume *Dogmatics* by a neo-orthodox thinker who had some appreciation of natural theology. Often eclipsing him was his contemporary, Karl Barth, whose *Church Dogmatics* included a volume (II, 1) on *The Doctrine of God* (1957)

God's transcendence is the theme in Karl Heim, *God Transcendent* (New York and London 1936 and 1935), a work which evidences the struggle with scientific thought; Edward Farley, *The Transcendence of God* (Philadelphia 1960), a reliable exegesis of the thought of Reinhold Niebuhr, Tillich, Heim, Hartshorne, and Wieman on this subject; David Cairns, *God Up There?* a popular defense of transcendence, dependent to a considerable extent on Brunner.

A number of works can be cited as broadly representative of existentialist translations of Christian "God-talk." Notable among these are Friedrich Gogarten, *The Reality of Faith* (Philadelphia 1959) and two works by an American influenced by him, Carl Michalson, *The Rationality of Faith* (London and New York 1964 and 1963) and Carl Michalson, ed., *Christianity and the Existentialists* (New York 1956), though these essays are often twice-removed from the topic under discussion; Otto Piper, *God in History* (New York 1939); Helmut Gollwitzer, *The Existence of God as Confessed by Faith* (Philadelphia 1964); two works by Gerhard Ebeling, *The Nature of Faith* (London and Philadelphia 1966) and *Word and Faith* (Philadelphia 1963); Daniel Jenkins, *Beyond Religion* (Philadelphia 1962). Michalson, Ebeling, and Jenkins deal with the question of talking about God in a time which Dietrich Bonhoeffer had spoken of as being "non-religious."

In this setting one should also mention that classic-style Reformed scholastic dogmatic syntheses are still being assembled; one which discusses the attributes of God is Louis Berkhof, *Systematic Theology* (London 1941).

103. For Luther's view of God's sovereignty see the Luther literature introduced by Watson (note 59); for Calvin, by Edward A. Dowey, *The Knowledge of God in Calvin's Theology* (note 61).

The Holy Spirit provides the conventional category by which Protestant theologians speak of God bridging from His transcendence to the world of man, and the literature is considerable— though it is a truism to say that Protestantism has not worked out coherent witness to the biblical Spirit in connection with philosophical inquiry. Joseph Haroutunian, *God with Us* (Philadelphia 1965) shows the attempt of a theologian originally influenced by Calvin and Barth, who later took up the problem of immanence. More traditional is Regin Prenter, *Spiritus Creator*, (Philadelphia 1953), which contents itself with describing Luther's view on the Holy Spirit. George S. Hendry, *The Holy Spirit in Christian Theology* (London and Philadelphia 1965) and H. Wheeler Robinson, *The Christian Experience of the Holy Spirit* (London 1928) have been well-received as summary statements; and Daniel T. Jenkins, *Tradition and the Spirit* (London 1951) faces up to the way ecclesiastical heritage and the interrupting work of the Spirit come together. Three works more representative of modern theological contexts are Arnold B. Come, *Human Spirit and Holy Spirit* (Philadelphia 1959); Lindsay Dewar, *The Holy Spirit and Modern Thought* (New

York 1959); and Henry Pitney Van Dusen, *Spirit, Son and Father* (New York 1958).

104. The Trinity is usually discussed routinely and in context in full-ranging works of systematic theology; only occasionally in modern times have Protestants written treatises on the subject. Among the better of these are R. S. Franks, *The Doctrine of the Trinity* (London 1953); Leonard Hodgson, *The Doctrine of the Trinity* (London 1946); Cyril C. Richardson, *The Doctrine of the Trinity* (Nashville, Tennessee 1958); and in a sometimes confusing but always engrossing work of literary excellence, an esthetic appreciation, *The Mind of the Maker* by Dorothy Sayers (New York 1956).

105. John Osborne, *Luther* (New York, 1961).

106. Herman Sasse, *Here We Stand* (Minneapolis 1946), is a traditionalist Lutheran's discussion of differences between Lutheran and Reformed theology with an accent on this subject of the finite and the infinite.

107. While the scientific challenges reach into all aspects of Christian faith and teachings (for example, biblical authority), it is the doctrine of God that is most directly implied. A pioneer survey of the issue, which is read as a period piece, is Andrew D. White, *A History of the Warfare of Science with Theology in Christendom* (New York 1955), a reprint of a two-volume work from 1896. One dimension of the "warfare," the aspect of natural science, is treated in John Dillenberger, *Protestant Thought and Natural Science* (Nashville, Tennessee 1960). John C. Greene, *Darwin and the Modern World View* (Baton Rouge, Louisiana 1963) refers to the present topic, as do Harold K. Schilling, *Science and Religion* (New York 1962) and Ian G. Barbour, *Issues in Science and Religion* (Englewood Cliffs, New Jersey 1966). More recently the doctrine of God has been thrown into a new set of contexts by the development of technology and cybernetics; a discussion of these topics from a more or less Barthian point of view is to be found in Kenneth Vaux, *Subduing the Cosmos* (Richmond, Virginia 1970); note the bibliography.

108. A discussion of the cultural implications of postmodernity for the doctrine and experience of God is to be found in Gabriel Vahanian, *The Death of God* (New York 1961).

109. The phrase concerning the experience of the absence of God is from Hamilton-Altizer, *op. cit.* (note 97) p. 28.

The obsession with language replaced a dialogue with existentialism in Christian circles, particularly in England and America, shortly after the middle of the twentieth century; while this way of posing the question may have had little effect on the laity, it preoccupied philosophical theologians. Antony Flew and Alasdair C. MacIntyre, eds., *New Essays in Philosophical Theology* (London 1955) collected some of the earlier religious responses to the challenge of analytic language; in *God and Philosophy* (London 1966) Antony Flew took up the issues philosophy posed to theism. Basil Mitchell, ed., *Faith and Logic: Oxford Essays in Philosophical Theology* (London 1957) brought together a number of other essays from what was often called the Oxford school. Other British language philosophers who took up the question of theism were John Wilson, *Language and the Pursuit of Truth* (Cambridge, England 1956) and *Language and Christian Belief* (New York 1958); John Wisdom, *Paradox and Discovery* (Oxford 1965); and, most notably in ecclesiastical circles, Ian Ramsey, *Christian Discourse: Some Logical Explorations* (London 1965) and *Religious Language: An Empirical Placing of Theological Phrases* (London 1957). While not formally of the "language schools," John Macquarrie contributed through *God-Talk* (New York and London 1967). The Canadian Donald D. Evans authored a tightly reasoned book, *The Logic of Self-Involvement: A Philosophical Study of Everyday Language about God as Creator* (London 1963).

William F. Zuurdeeg, *An Analytical Philosophy of Religion* (Nashville, Tennessee 1958) and Jules Moreau, *Language and Religious Language* (Philadelphia 1961) helped alert the American Protestant community to the issues, but a more inclusive constructive statement on "the manifold logic of theism" was made by Frederick Ferré, *Language, Logic and God* (New York 1961). The most publicized book concerned with these issues, Paul van Buren, *The Secular Meaning of the Gospel* (New York 1963), dealt programmatically with major Christian theological themes but concentrated on the problem of speaking about God in modern philosophy; the author was identified by the press with the sensational death-of-God school, but he has continued more quietly to pursue his linguistic inquiries.

After the death-of-God stage there have been a number of reconstructive attempts, including Sten H. Stenson, *Sense and Nonsense in Religion* (Nashville, Tennessee 1969) and Jerry H. Gill, *The Possibility of Religious Knowledge* (Grand Rapids, Michigan 1971). Through the years John Hick has made notable contributions to Protestant systematic theology in its struggle with language, as in *Faith and Knowledge* (Ithaca, New York 1957).

110. The death-of-God controversy has already been alluded to. While much of it was carried on in ephemeral periodicals, some

books do illumine the event. Thomas W. Ogletree, *The Death of God Controversy* (Nashville, Tennessee 1966) is very brief, but adequately sets forth the positions of the more celebrated spokesmen, especially Thomas J. J. Altizer and William Hamilton. A devastating reply by a conservative is Kenneth Hamilton, *Revolt against Heaven* (Grand Rapids, Michigan 1965). C. W. Christian and Glenn R. Wittig, eds., *Radical Theology: Phase Two: Essays in a Continuing Discussion* (Philadelphia 1967) incorporates work by numbers of Protestants who identified with the death-of-God motif.

Radical theology and the death-of-God voice grew out of a decade-long attempt by Protestants to relate their thought to the realities of secularization. William Hamilton, *The New Essence of Christianity* (New York 1961) represented an early attempt, but a more moderate stage in that thinker's career; Ronald Gregor Smith, *The New Man* (London 1956) is sometimes credited with being the first book of its kind, though Smith's debt to the German Dietrich Bonhoeffer was openly acknowledged. Later Smith produced *Secular Christianity* (New York 1966). Dorothee Sölle, *Christ the Representative: An Essay in Theology after the "Death of God"* (Philadelphia 1967) is a German response, typical of the movement in radical theology in that it attempted to hold to Jesus Christ even though metaphysical bases for conceiving and speaking of God had become problematic. An American theologian, Frederick Herzog, in *Understanding God* (New York 1966) has tried to review the whole "God problem" and to address it by reference to "the new hermeneutic," a school of interpretation indebted to German philosopher Martin Heidegger.

111. Through the whole controversy about God, Protestant philosophers and sociologists have on occasion attempted to provide a new basis for discussion by relocating the question in the issue of the experience of transcendence. These efforts go back as far as William James, *The Varieties of Religious Experience* (New York and London 1902) and Rudolf Otto, *The Idea of the Holy* (London 1923), and extend to efforts like one which sees "signs of transcendence" in the modern world, Peter L. Berger, *Rumor of Angels* (Garden City, New York 1969).

On almost all the issues discussed in chapter 5, the reader should consult Langdon Gilkey, *Naming the Whirlwind: The Renewal of God-Lanugage* (Indianapolis, Indiana 1969), which after a review of the situation presents an exploratory constructive theological effort.

CHAPTER 6

112. Fortunately for readers in the area of faith's relation to history, two of twentieth century Protestantism's most important thinkers addressed themselves to the subject, and their works provide a profound introduction to the complex theme: Paul J. Tillich, *The Interpretation of History* (New York and London 1936) and Reinhold Niebuhr, *Faith and History* (New York 1949), which compares Christian and modern views of history.

113. Certain earlier views, particularly those of Augustine and medieval sectarianism, are so important for Protestant development that some suggestions for introductory reading on the pre-Protestant period are in order at this point. Robert A. Nisbet, *Social Change and History* (New York 1969) surveys the whole "Western Theory of Development"; a long chapter on "The Christians" is almost entirely an extrapolation on Augustinian themes. G. L. Keyes, *Christian Faith and the Interpretation of History* (Lincoln, Nebraska 1966) is a study of St. Augustine's philosophy of history. A convenient edition of Augustine is *The City of God* (New York 1950), but many are available. An extensive bibliography in Keyes will lead readers further into the literature, but several additional titles are relevant to the present theme: Joseph John Rickaby, *St. Augustine's City of God* (London 1925), a Roman Catholic interpretation; John Neville Figgis, *The Political Aspects of St. Augustine's "City of God"* (London 1921); and Roy W. Battenhouse, *A Companion to the Study of Augustine* (Oxford 1955). R. A. Markus, *Saeculum: History and Society in the Theology of St. Augustine* (Cambridge, England 1970) is to the point of this subject; I cannot resist citing Peter Brown, *Augustine of Hippo: A Biography* (London 1967) even though it does not restrict itself to Augustine's view of history—it is a superb biography. R. H. Barrow, *Introduction to Saint Augustine "The City of God"* (London 1950) and H. A. Deane, *The Political and Social Ideas of Saint Augustine* (New York and London 1963) should also be consulted.

Three other works have reference to pre-Reformation millennialism: Sylvia L. Thrupp, ed., *Millennial Dreams in Action* (New York 1970) brings together papers from a conference on the subject; a few of these deal with the period in question while others carry the topic to the modern and non-Christian world; Ernest Lee Tuveson, *Millennium and Utopia: A Study in the Background of the Idea of Progress* (Berkeley, California 1949) complements Norman Cohn,

The Pursuit of the Millennium (New York 1970), a revised edition with a first-rate bibliography.

114. Alan Richardson, *Sacred and Profane* (note 71) is a general discussion of the Christian views of history and includes a reading list; Karl Löwith, *Meaning in History* (note 71) concentrates largely on Christian approaches; Herbert Butterfield, *Christianity and History* (New York 1950) is a Christ-centered statement by a distinguished British historian; some of the chapters in E. Harris Harbison, *Christianity and History* (Princeton, New Jersey 1964) reflect on philosophy of history; Eric C. Rust, *Towards a Theological Understanding of History* (note 71) makes some contribution, as does Roger L. Shinn, *Christianity and the Problem of History* (New York 1953); Ralph G. Wilburn, *The Historical Shape of Faith* (Philadelphia 1966) competently traces the fate of Augustinian and other earlier Christian ideas in the Protestant and secular worlds, while Carl Michalson brings an existentialist Christian point of view to *The Hinge of History* (New York 1959). Two European noteworthy works are Hendrikus Berkhof, *Christ the Meaning of History* (Richmond, Virginia 1966) and numerous essays in Paul Ricoeur, *History and Truth* (Evanston, Illinois 1965).

Eugen Rosenstock-Huessy, *The Christian Future* (New York 1946) is a sometimes eccentric, often prophetic, always profound personal view of how Christian views of history relate to the secular order; more secular-minded in its embrace of modern trends but grounded in biblical views is Arend Th. Van Leeuwen, *Christianity in World History* (New York and London 1966 and 1964). The classic on *The Idea of Progress* is by J. B. Bury (New York 1932), but it discusses the Protestant world only marginally; therefore, as a counterpart, John Baillie, *The Belief in Progress* (London 1950) should be consulted.

115. On biblical views of time and the suggestion that the whole of history has Christian meaning, see the works of Oscar Cullmann, notably *Christ and Time* (Philadelphia 1950), which sees the deed of Christ as the center of history, and *Salvation in History* (New York and London 1967), a summary of Cullmann's life work. More existentialist in outlook is Rudolf Bultmann, *History and Eschatology* (Edinburgh 1957), whose American title is *The Presence of Eternity* (New York 1957); Isaac C. Rottenberg, *Redemption and Historical Reality* (Philadelphia 1964) also reflects from a Protestant point of view on the meaning of Christ for history.

Two modern Protestant views of creation are Karl Heim, *The World: Its Creation and Consummation* (Edinburgh 1962), influenced by existentialist themes, and Langdon Gilkey, *Maker of Heaven and Earth* (Garden City, New York 1959), which is open to "process" views.

Theologies of the future or centered in hope came to be stressed in the 1960s; anticipating these was a popular work, Howard C. Kee, *The Renewal of Hope* (New York 1959). Ernst Benz, *Evolution and the Christian Hope* (Garden City, New York 1966) runs parallel to such theologies, synthesizing the thought of Teilhard de Chardin and earlier Anglo-American Protestant evolutionary theology; Taito A. Kantonen, *The Christian Hope* (Philadelphia 1954) also antedates the "future and hope" school.

The thought of that school or emphasis was best summarized in a memorable book, Jürgen Moltmann, *Theology of Hope* (New York and London 1967), while the same author's *Hope and Planning* (New York and London 1971) extends the dimensions of thought into various problem areas. Carl E. Braaten, *The Future of God* (New York and London 1969) is an American comprehension of the subject.

Two contemporary discussions of "the last things" are John Baillie, *And the Life Everlasting* (New York 1933) and the more radical John A. T. Robinson, *In the End God: A Study of the Last Things* (London and New York 1968).

116. A sophisticated juxtaposition of religious themes with secular views of the meaning of history is to be found in John T. Marcus, *Heaven, Hell, and History* (London and New York 1967). The accent falls consistently on the secular attempts to move beyond inherited religious views. Not much remains of the biblical heaven or hell in these versions.

117. Sidney H. Rooy, *The Theology of Missions in the Puritan Tradition* (Grand Rapids, Michigan 1965) brings together some views on history held by outstanding English and American Puritans, and Peter Gay, *A Loss of Mastery* (University of California 1966) reflects sourly on the decline of the quality of historical thinking as William Bradford, Cotton Mather, and Jonathan Edwards spoke for a dying theological world. Gay likes neither their old world nor the new, but his chapter on Edwards in particular shows how millennial thinking began to dominate. Ernest Lee Tuveson, *The Redeemer Nation* (Chicago and London 1968) traces millennial-messianic-missionary views derived from Protestantism through later American history.

On Dwight Moody and later American premillennialism one should consult a major biography, James F. Findlay, Jr., *Dwight L.*

Moody: American Evangelist, 1837–1899 (Chicago 1969) and, for the world around him, the best book on the revivalist implications of such views of history, William G. McLoughlin, *Modern Revivalism* (New York 1959). On the history of premillennialism in nineteenth century England and America nothing surpasses Ernest R. Sandeen, *The Roots of Fundamentalism: British and American Millenarianism 1800–1930* (Chicago and London 1970). His bibliography is so original and detailed that one is tempted simply to direct readers to it, but several titles on the subject should be cited for special mention. C. Norman Kraus, *Dispensationalism in America* (Richmond, Virginia 1958) discusses one element in some premillennial thought; on the earlier history of revivalism and its approach to history, Timothy L. Smith, *Revivalism and Social Reform* (New York 1957). Beyond these suggestions: back to Sandeen.

"Demythologized" postmillennial thinking continues to be employed in rather secular versions in Harvey Cox, *The Secular City* (New York 1965) and Gibson Winter, *The New Creation as Metropolis* (London 1963).

118. H. Richard Niebuhr, *Christ and Culture* (New York 1951) is essential reading for anyone who wishes to canvass the range of Protestant and other Christian views of this subject. Its typological approach may not always do justice to subtle details of history, but it is provocative and coherent and has had much influence.

119. On British Christian socialist progressive thought: Charles E. Raven, *Christian Socialism, 1848–54* (London 1920) broke ground and is still useful, accompanied by Gilbert C. Binyon, *The Christian Socialist Movement in England: An Introduction to the Study of Its History* (New York 1932). Less accessible but of much merit is Torben Christensen, *Origin and History of Christian Socialism 1848–54* (Copenhagen 1962). More theoretical is C. K. Gloyn, *The Church in the Social Order: A Study of Anglican Social Theory from Coleridge to Maurice* (Forest Grove, Oregon 1942). The story is extended beyond the high period of Christian socialism in Peter d'Alroy Jones, *The Christian Socialist Revival, 1877–1914* (Princeton, New Jersey 1968) and Maurice B. Reckitt, *Maurice to Temple: A Century of the Social Movement in the Church of England* (London 1947).

The American Social Gospel and its views of purpose has been well covered by historians. Everyone should begin by reading sources garnered from the writings of Washington Gladden, Richard T. Ely, and Walter Rauschenbusch in Robert T. Handy, *The Social Gospel in America 1870–1920* (New York 1966). One can trace the pre- and post-history along with the main years in James Dombrowski, *The Early Days of Christian Socialism in America* (New York 1936); Charles Howard Hopkins, *The Rise of the Social Gospel in American Protestantism* (New Haven 1940); and Paul A. Carter, *The Decline and Revival of the Social Gospel: Social and Political Liberalism in American Protestant Churches, 1920–1940* (Ithaca, New York 1954). Because of historical naïveté and a neo-orthodox bias, W. A. Visser 't Hooft, *The Background of the Social Gospel in America* (Haarlem 1928) should be used with care. Some reference to social experimental theory appears in Henry F. May, *Protestant Churches and Industrial America* (New York 1949) and Aaron I. Abell, *The Urban Impact on American Protestantism, 1865–1900* (Cambridge, Massachusetts 1943). See also David Noble, *The Paradox of Progressive Thought* (Minneapolis 1958) and H. Richard Niebuhr's relevant chapters in *The Kingdom of God in America* (New York 1935). Some parallels in German Protestantism are discussed in William O. Shanahan, *op. cit.* (note 69).

120. While the two Niebuhrs are the best-known "Christian realists," and their writings should be consulted on the topic, much of value can be found in John C. Bennett, *Christian Realism* (New York 1941), an attempt to transcend both liberal optimism and neo-orthodox pessimism and passivity. A narrative of Protestant attempts to work out such theories is the pro-Niebuhr history, Donald B. Meyer, *The Protestant Search for Political Realism, 1919–1941* (Berkeley, California 1961).

121. Herbert Lüthy, *From Calvin to Rousseau* (New York and London 1970) traces the working out of certain ideas of Reformed Protestantism into the Enlightenment era, concentrating on the themes of "tradition and modernity." While more will be made of the "Weber Thesis" connecting Calvinist Protestant views of history and purpose with the rise of modern capitalism, some readers may wish to begin to explore the theme at this point. Contemporary essays on the subject have been gathered in S. N. Eisenstadt, ed., *The Protestant Ethic and Modernization* (New York 1968), which includes a bibliography. H. R. Trevor-Roper, *Religion, the Reformation and Social Change* (London 1964) has some bearing on the topic, as does A. Davies, *John Calvin and the Influence of Protestantism on National Life and Character* (London 1946).

122. The reference to Tillich is from Paul Tillich, *On the Boundary* (New York 1966), p. 75. For Lutheran historical views and their cultural impact, see Karl Holl, *The Cultural Significance of the Reformation* (New York 1959).

123. Most modern Protestant works on Providence are written

to connect that theme with the problems of evil and pain. Note-worthy among many efforts are John Hick, *Evil and the God of Love* (New York 1966), the work of a theologian equipped to deal with language analysis; the popular apologist C. S. Lewis, *The Problem of Pain* (London and Glasgow 1940); William G. Pollard, *Chance and Providence* (New York 1958) by a scientist turned theologian; Herbert H. Farmer, *The World and God* (London and New York 1935), a systematic theological approach, as is John S. Whale, *The Christian Answer to the Problem of Evil* (London and New York 1936). Of a much different character is the work of a French Protestant phenomenologist who deals with symbolism in a number of religious traditions: Paul Ricoeur, *The Symbolism of Evil* (New York 1967).

Reference has been made to the thought of American Puritans on purpose, Providence, and destiny. The Puritan tradition on these themes has been expounded in great detail and with authority by Perry Miller in *The New England Mind: The Seventeenth Century* (New York 1939); *Orthodoxy in Massachusetts, 1630–1650* (Cambridge, Massachusetts 1933); *Errand into the Wilderness* (Cambridge, Massachusetts 1958) and in a source book, Perry Miller and Thomas H. Johnson, eds., *The Puritans* (New York 1938), in two volumes.

124. On Arminius and Arminians: Carl Bangs, *Arminius* (Nashville, Tennessee 1971) is by far the best access in English; A. W. Harrison, *The Beginnings of Arminianism* (London 1926) is helpful; for the international influence, consult Rosalie Littell Colie, *Light and Enlightenment: A Study of the Cambridge Platonists and the Dutch Arminians* (New York 1957).

125. The allusion is to the title of Carl L. Becker, *op. cit.* (note 67).

126. Some Protestant discussions of Marxian philosophies of history include: John C. Raines and Thomas Dean, eds., *Marxism and Radical Religion* (Philadelphia 1970), essays relating Marxism to modern Protestant trends; some of the articles in Paul Oestreicher, ed., *The Christian Marxist Dialogue* (New York and London 1969); Helmut Gollwitzer, *The Christian Faith and the Marxist Criticism of Religion* (New York and London 1969 and 1970), by an on-the-scene man in Germany; John C. Bennett, *Christianity and Communism Today* (New York 1960), from the viewpoint of "Christian realism"; Donald Mackinnon, ed., *Christian Faith and Communist Faith* (London 1963); Charles C. West, *Communism and the Theologians: Study of an Encounter* (Philadelphia 1958); Matthew Spinka, *Church in*

Communist Society: A Study in J. L. Hromadka's Theological Politics (Hartford, Connecticut 1954), a work on the earlier positions of a Czech existentialist theologian; the popular Alexander Miller, *The Christian Significance of Karl Marx* (London 1946); Emil Brunner, *Communism, Capitalism, and Christianity* (London 1949); Eduard Heimann, *Reason and Faith in Modern Society: Liberalism, Marxism, and Democracy* (Middletown, Connecticut 1961); another popular work, William Hordern, *Christianity, Communism, and History* (Nashville, Tennessee 1954); Hans-Gerhard Koch, *The Abolition of God: Materialistic Atheism and Christian Religion* (Philadelphia 1963). None of these is expressive of militant anti-Communist thought of the kind that characterized much Protestant writing in the first quarter century of the Cold War, though almost all authors express criticism of Marxian philosophy of history and its political consequences. Because of the volatility of the issue, the stance of Christians and Marxists is changing constantly and it is difficult to assemble a bibliography truly representative of world Protestantism on this matter.

127. More will be supplied later on nationalism; at this point consult Carlton J. H. Hayes, *Nationalism: A Religion* (New York 1960); written by a Catholic historian, the book notes the rise of nationalism especially on British Protestant soil.

128. Early in the twentieth century Frederick R. Tennant published two enduring books on the topic of sin: *Origin and Propagation of Sin* (Cambridge, England 1902) and *The Concept of Sin* (Cambridge, England 1912). Neo-orthodoxy was much preoccupied with the topic; the classic from this general orbit is Reinhold Niebuhr's Gifford Lectures, *The Nature and Destiny of Man* (New York 1941 and 1943), two volumes; the same author's *The Self and the Dramas of History* (New York 1955) was another elaboration of the doctrine of man; Emil Brunner, *Man in Revolt* (New York 1939) stressed human responsibility before God despite sin, and contended that God's grace enhanced man's responsibility. It is often regarded as the best of Brunner's books.

Eric L. Mascall, *The Importance of Being Human* (New York 1958) is an Anglican philosophical theologian's attempt to depict "eucharistic man" as an alternative to other models. Similarly positive is Alexander Miller, *The Man in the Mirror* (New York 1958). Two conservative Protestant contributions of note are J. Gresham Machen, *The Christian View of Man* (New York 1937) and Gerrit C. Berkouwer, *Man: The Image of God* (Grand Rapids, Michigan 1962). For the views of Luther, Calvin, Wesley, and others mentioned or implied in this chapter one should consult the previously recommended books on the theology of each; many of the books in this footnote also discuss the prime Protestant figures' views on man, sin, selfhood.

129. Einar Billing, *Our Calling* (Philadelphia 1964) creatively condenses materials on vocation from the viewpoint of a leader of Sweden's Luther renaissance; taking issue with Billing on some points is Gustaf Wingren, *Luther on Vocation* (Philadelphia 1957). Alexander Miller, *The Renewal of Man* (New York 1955) offers excellent comment on vocation; John Oliver Nelson, ed., *Work and Vocation* (New York 1954) has some articles of merit on the question.

130. Arthur G. Gish, *The New Left and Christian Radicalism* (Grand Rapids, Michigan 1970) contends that there are parallels between strands in the thought of the radical Reformation and some contemporary socio-political leftist movements. Martin E. Marty and Dean G. Peerman, eds., *New Theology No. 6* (New York 1969) collected essays, many of them by Protestants, on similar connections. There is a bibliography in Gish.

131. A Protestant lay poet, Chad Walsh, in *From Utopia to Nightmare* (New York 1962) brought together many literary materials on the subject of disenchantment with utopia and, from a Christian point of view, urged that some measure of utopian thought remain alive. The bibliography in Gish (note 130) includes numerous books of utopian tendency, a mark that was observable in much "Christian radicalism" and "theology of the future and hope."

CHAPTER 7

132. An introduction to all the major themes of this chapter can be found in E. M. B. Green, *The Meaning of Salvation* (Philadelphia and London 1966 and 1965). Writing from a moderately conservative point of view he collates biblical, historical, and contemporary materials. While there is no bibliography, the footnotes will introduce students to a large body of literature.

133. Chapters 1 and 2 in Green (note 132) discuss Old Testament concepts of salvation. See also the articles on "Save" and "Salvation" in Alan Richardson, ed., *Theological Word Book of the Bible* (Philadelphia 1950); the sections on salvation in various works of Old Testament theology will also be illuminating. Among these are Ludwig Köhler, *Old Testament Theology* (London and Phil-

adelphia 1957 and 1958); Edmond Jacob, *Theology of the Old Testament* (London and New York 1958); Gerhard von Rad, *Old Testament Theology,* volume I (New York and London 1962).

134. Because the teachings on grace, salvation, and faith are usually considered central for Protestantism, it is advisable here to bring together materials on these subjects as they relate particularly to the work of Jesus Christ. The theological background can be surveyed in John M. McIntyre, *On the Love of God* (New York 1962), which describes the whole movement of God toward man. This is consolidated in the Incarnation, the taking on of flesh in Jesus Christ. Bjarne Skard, *The Incarnation* (Minneapolis 1960) is a typical Protestant representation of that doctrine.

Classic views of the God-man relation in Christ have been reworked by several modern Protestants. Donald M. Baillie, *God Was in Christ* (New York and London 1948) is an excellent guide, particularly to Pauline teaching. Emil Brunner, *The Mediator* (London 1934) is that neo-orthodox theologian's interpretation of Christology; Oscar Cullmann, *The Christology of the New Testament* (London and New York 1959) shows how biblical theology can be restated in the light of contemporary situations. He concentrates on the names and titles of Christ.

Many recent theologians have written books reappraising the meaning of Christ, the acknowledgment of His Lordship. Wolfhart Pannenberg, *Jesus—God and Man* (Philadelphia 1968) is an extremely demanding version; John Knox, *Christ the Lord* (New York 1945) is a moderately liberal American biblical scholar's summary; Karl Heim, *Jesus the Lord* (Edinburgh 1959) and *Jesus the World's Perfecter* (Edinburgh 1959) relate the figure of Jesus to cosmic views of history. So do the works of Lionel S. Thornton; these are erudite, almost idiosyncratic volumes by a man who could be described as an Anglican-Augustinian process theologian. See *The Incarnate Lord* (London and New York 1928); *The Form of the Servant: The Dominion of Christ* (Westminster 1952), which sees Christ's act as restoring original creation; *The Form of the Servant: Christ and the Church* (Westminster 1956), which is not so much a fullblown ecclesiology as it is a connection between Christ and church seen as a divine-human mystery.

Two "secular" analyses, attempting to portray Jesus as a figure at the center of the modern world and at home with the modern expectation, are Erik Routley, *The Man for Others* (New York 1964) and John J. Vincent, *Secular Christ* (Nashville 1968).

Beyond the discussion of meaning and Lordship come questions of the words and works of Jesus. Vincent Taylor, *The Life and Ministry of Jesus* (London 1954) is a well-regarded account by a biblical theologian, as is the more popular Archibald M. Hunter, *The Work and Words of Jesus* (London and Philadelphia 1950). Robert S. Franks, *The Work of Christ* (London and New York 1962) is an historical understanding; Ernest J. Tinsley, *The Imitation of God in Christ* (London and Philadelphia 1960) argues that the old model *imitatio Christ* has contemporary possibility.

The best-known, though overly typological, modern discussion of the atonement is Gustaf Aulén, *Christus Victor* (London 1970), which has gone through several editions. Thomas H. Hughes, *The Atonement: Modern Theories of the Doctrine* (London 1949) is a more balanced, less provocative approach. William J. Wolf, *No Cross, No Crown* (New York 1957) reads easily, as does John S. Whale, *Victor and Victim* (Cambridge, England 1960). Frederick W. Dillistone, *The Significance of the Cross* (Philadelphia 1964) ponders symbol and reality. Two authors who have just been introduced also have written on the atonement: Vincent Taylor, *The Atonement in New Testament Teaching* (London 1941) and *Jesus and His Sacrifice* (London 1937), and Lionel S. Thornton, *The Doctrine of the Atonement* (London 1937).

A number of writers have accented the Resurrection as a fulfillment of the working out of God-man relations in Christ. Markus Barth and Verne H. Fletcher, *Acquittal by Resurrection* (New York 1964) leads this list. Daniel P. Fuller, *Easter Faith and History* (Grand Rapids, Michigan 1965) approaches the subject from a conservative angle, and gives readings of liberal idealism, dialectical theology, and modern hermeneutics on the subject. Richard R. Niebuhr, *Resurrection and Historical Reason* (New York 1957) is one of countless works which ponder problems of faith and history as connected with the resurrection. A popular work is Thomas S. Kepler, *The Meaning and Mystery of the Resurrection* (New York 1963), whereas Floyd V. Filson, *Jesus Christ the Risen Lord* (Nashville, Tennessee 1956) grows out of biblical theology. Three works which concern themselves little with historical problems and much with theology are a conservative German work, Walter Künneth, *The Theology of the Resurrection* (London and St. Louis 1965) and two British works, Greville D. Yarnold, *Risen Indeed* (New York, London, and Toronto 1959) and A. Michael Ramsey, *The Resurrection of Christ* (Philadelphia 1946).

135. William Telfer, *The Forgiveness of Sins* (Philadelphia and London 1960 and 1959) is a guide to some of the historical Pro-

testant-Catholic issues; a Catholic writer, Stephen Pfürtner, O.P., contrasts *Luther and Aquinas on Salvation* (New York and London 1964); Jacques de Senarclens, *Heirs of the Reformation* (Philadelphia 1963) contrasts evangelical and Roman Catholic views, particularly on christological implications.

136. On grace, justification, and the forgiveness of sins, the literature in the reformers' writings is extensive; here the accent falls on modern interpretations. A classic but complex and inelegant work is Albrecht Ritschl, *The Christian Doctrine of Justification and Reconciliation* (Edinburgh and New York 1902 and 1900). One of the most helpful books on grace is William T Whitley, ed., *The Doctrine of Grace* (London and New York 1932), while John S. Whale, *The Protestant Tradition* (Cambridge, England 1955) also concentrates on grace. Philip S. Watson, *The Concept of Grace* (London and Philadelphia 1959) is informed by studies of Luther. James G. Emerson, Jr., *The Dynamics of Forgiveness* (Philadelphia 1964) reflects on the place of this teaching in the context of Christian community. Lesslie Newbigin, *Sin and Salvation* (Philadelphia and London 1957 and 1956) and Vincent Taylor, *Forgiveness and Reconciliation* (London 1941) both turn on the sin-grace nexus.

137. Samples of the way in which the liberation theme is reflected in an emerging "black theology" are to be found in James J. Gardiner and J. Deotis Roberts, Sr., eds., *Quest for a Black Theology* (Philadelphia 1971) and James H. Cone, *Liberation: A Black Theology of Liberation* (Philadelphia 1970).

138. Robert T. Osborn, *Freedom in Modern Theology* (Philadelphia 1967) concentrates particularly on Rudolf Bultmann ("Freedom as Existence"), Paul Tillich ("Freedom to Be") and Karl Barth ("Freedom in Christ"), and guides the reader into the appropriate materials by these theologians.

139. Dietrich Bonhoeffer, *The Cost of Discipleship* (New York and London 1959) develops the concept of "cheap grace"; see especially pp. 35–47.

140. For a discussion by a Catholic of Protestantism's focus on narrow elements in salvational doctrine, see Erich Przywara, S.J., "St. Augustine and the Modern World" in M. C. D'Arcy, S.J., *et al.*, *Saint Augustine* (New York 1957).

141. Much modern Protestant thought on the changed experience and metaphors of human need derive from Dietrich Bonhoeffer's discussion, particularly in his *Letters and Papers from Prison* (New York and London 1967), pp. 177 ff. The literature on Bonhoeffer is enormous; a bibliography of his English translations is

available in most of the major works on the martyred German thinker, but the most convenient of these is in Peter Vorking, II, ed., *Bonhoeffer in a World Come of Age* (Philadelphia 1968). See John D. Godsey, *The Theology of Dietrich Bonhoeffer* (Philadelphia 1960) for a representative earlier work and John A. Phillips, *Christ for Us in the Theology of Dietrich Bonhoeffer* (New York 1967), both because it is typical of radical theology's interpretation and because it concentrates on themes explored in this chapter.

142. Gustaf Aulén, *Christus Victor* (note 134), discusses the corruption of Luther's teachings on God's wrath as enemy in his chapter on Luther. Both Roland Bainton, *Here I Stand* (note 59) and Heinrich Boehmer, *Road to Reformation* (note 59) include important discussions of Luther's struggle for faith in biographical and theological contexts.

143. Thomas M. McDonough, *The Law and the Gospel in Luther* (New York 1963) stresses Luther's radical view of faith and the disjunction between law and Gospel in his writings. See also the typological considerations in Anders Nygren, *Eros and Agape*, two volumes (London 1932–1939) and the fine review in Heinrich Bornkamm, *Luther's World of Thought* (note 54). Hermann Sasse, *Here We Stand* (note 106) is a stanch and unreconstructed Lutheran attack on Calvinist views of law and Gospel and predestination (III, 3).

144. W. E. Stuermann, *A Critical Study of Calvin's Concept of Faith* (Tulsa, Oklahoma 1952); Wilhelm Niesel, *The Theology of Calvin* (Philadelphia 1956); H. Kuiper, *Calvin on Common Grace* (Grand Rapids, Michigan 1930) and Lorraine Boettner, *The Reformed Doctrine of Predestination* (Grand Rapids, Michigan 1932) are the appropriate works on this subject; see the other introductions to Calvin recommended in note 61.

145. See G. C. Berkouwer, *The Triumph of Grace in the Theology of Karl Barth* (Grand Rapids, Michigan and London 1955) and Karl Barth, *The Knowledge of God and the Service of God* (London 1938).

146. Joachim H. Seyppel, *Schwenckfeld, Knight of Faith* (Pennsburg, Pennsylvania 1961) and Paul L. Maier, *Caspar Schwenckfeld on the Person and Work of Christ* (Assen, the Netherlands 1959) bear on this subject.

147. Harald Lindström, *Wesley and Sanctification* (Stockholm 1946) deals with themes of justification, grace, sanctification, and perfection.

148. On perfection and conversion: John K. A. Reid, *Our Life in Christ* (Philadelphia and London 1963), a general review of pos-

sibilities for spiritual development; R. Newton Flew, *The Idea of Perfection in Christian Theology* (London 1934); O. R. Jones, *The Concept of Holiness* (London and New York 1961); Adolf Köberle, *The Quest for Holiness* (Minneapolis 1936) all deal with the question of growth in grace. Bernhard Citron, *New Birth: A Study of the Evangelical Doctrine of Conversion in the Protestant Fathers* (Edinburgh 1951) provides historical introduction; recent works are Erik Routley, *The Gift of Conversion* (London 1957), which includes references to Augustine, Luther, and Wesley, and Owen Brandon, *The Battle for the Soul* (Philadelphia 1959).

149. The latter portions of Aulén (note 134) deal adequately with modern liberal trends.

150. Ritschl is discussed in Aulén (note 149); chapter 5 in Richard R. Niebuhr, *Schleiermacher on Christ and Religion* (New York 1964) introduces the Schleiermacher literature.

151. Note 138, Osborn, *op. cit.*, provides access to several modern theologians; see also Karl Barth, *Christ and Adam* (New York 1957) for a novel treatment; John Oman, *Grace and Personality* (New York 1925) merits continued reference; Peter T. Forsyth, *The Person and Place of Jesus Christ* (Boston 1909) is a noteworthy work by the British Congregationalist, who is discussed in John H. Rodgers, *The Theology of P. T. Forsyth: The Cross of Christ and the Revelation of God* (London 1965).

152. The reference here is to Robert N. Bellah, *Beyond Belief* (New York 1969).

CHAPTER 8

153. The concept of revelation has been much developed and debated in modern Protestant theology. John Baillie, *The Idea of Revelation in Recent Thought* (New York 1956) is the best introduction to the attitudes of Karl Barth, Paul Tillich, Emil Brunner, and others. Brunner speaks of himself in *Revelation and Reason* (Philadelphia 1946) and in *The Divine-Human Encounter* (Philadelphia 1943). Lionel S. Thornton, *The Form of the Servant: Revelation and the Modern World* (Westminster, Maryland 1950) combines interest in biblical themes of revelation and modern organismic philosophical approaches. H. Richard Niebuhr, *The Meaning of Revelation* (New York 1941) has been highly influential for the way it tackles the question of divine authority and the relativity of the human situation.

154. An attractive access to the problems associated with canonical questions is provided by Floyd V. Filson, *Which Books Belong in the Bible?* (Philadelphia 1957); its bibliographical appendix calls attention to works which trace the history of the canon.

A number of general histories of the fate of the Bible in Protestantism and in the church at large have implications for the argument of this chapter. One could begin with Robert M. Grant, *A Short History of the Interpretation of the Bible* (New York and London 1963). Much more extended treatment is given by a number of authors in S. L. Greenslade, *The Cambridge History of the Bible: The West from the Reformation to the Present Day* (Cambridge, England 1963); see particularly the chapter by Norman Sykes, "The Religion of Protestants," which refers to a saying by William Chillingsworth from which the title to this chapter was taken. Its bibliography is outstanding. An earlier liberal survey is by Ernest C. Colwell, *The Study of the Bible* (Chicago 1937). Long before, F. W. Farrar, *History of Interpretation* (London 1886) had become a standard work. Two other recent discussions are James D. Smart, *The Interpretation of Scripture* (Philadelphia 1961) and C. W. Dugmore, ed., *The Interpretation of the Bible* (London 1944).

155. For "primitive" views see Alfred T. DeGroot, *The Restoration Principle* (St. Louis 1960).

156. Albert C. Outler discusses the question of Protestant varieties and their relation to Scripture and tradition in his book that was mentioned in note 76.

157. The issues of biblical authority are well summarized in Raymond Abba, *The Nature and Authority of the Bible* (Philadelphia 1958). A similar study, but one which emphasizes Reformation and post-Reformation understandings is John K. S. Reid, *The Authority of Scripture* (New York 1957). Daniel Jenkins, *Tradition and the Spirit* (London and Philadelphia 1951) is a Congregationalist's effort to reintroduce the topic of tradition into Protestant biblical thought. C. H. Dodd, *The Authority of the Bible* (London 1928) is an authoritative, often referred to work. Representative responses from the "neo-evangelical camp" have been collected in John F. Walvoord, ed., *Inspiration and Interpretation* (Grand Rapids, Michigan 1957).

158. A Lutheran historian and theologian, Robert L. Wilken, in *The Myth of Christian Beginnings: History's Impact on Belief* (Garden City, New York 1971) includes intense argument against those who see scriptures untouched by the contingencies of history; Wilken sees no possibility for isolating biblical tradition from tradition.

159. Some reference to Anabaptist views of Scripture will be

found in Roland H. Bainton, *Castellio Concerning Heretics* (New York 1935); Franklin H. Littell, *The Anabaptist View of the Church* (Chicago 1958); George H. Williams, *op. cit.* (note 50). An annotated bibliography appears in a book which includes some reference to Quaker views of revelation, D. Elton Trueblood, *The People Called Quakers* (note 37).

160. Sykes, *op. cit.* (note 154).

161. Gerhard Ebeling elaborates on his views of the Bible in relation to criticism and history in numerous essays, especially chapter I, "The Significance of the Critical Historical Method for Church and Theology in Protestantism," in Gerhard Ebeling, *Word and Faith* (note 102).

162. Marshall McLuhan, *Understanding Media* (New York, Toronto, and London 1964) was the book in which McLuhan presented his views of the passing of linearity and sequentialism as codified on the printed page. Discussions of his controversial sayings appear in Raymond Rosenthal, ed., *McLuhan: Pro and Con* (New York 1968) and Gerald Emanuel Stearn, *McLuhan: Hot and Cool* (New York 1967). Many critics point out that McLuhan's views were shaped in the setting of Catholic higher education and often subtly reflect it.

163. Niebuhr, *op. cit.* (note 153).

164. Willem Jan Kooiman, *Luther and the Bible* (Philadelphia 1961) expounds Luther's doctrine of Scripture and argues that he did not employ doctrines of inerrancy, these came later, with orthodoxy. On the other hand, Michael Reu, *Luther's German Bible* (Columbus, Ohio 1934) virtually identifies Luther's view with orthodoxy's. See also Jaroslav J. Pelikan, *Luther the Expositor* (St. Louis 1959).

165. Roland Bainton, *Hunted Heretic: The Life and Death of Servetus* (Boston 1953) elaborates on the theological views of the proto-Unitarian.

166. E. A. Dowey, *op. cit.* (note 61) incorporates comment on John Calvin's view of Scripture; more directly topical is R. S. Wallace, *Calvin's Doctrine of the Word and Sacrament* (Edinburgh 1954). Calvin and Calvinism are also treated in Robert Clyde Johnson, *Authority in Protestant Theology* (Philadelphia 1959). Barth's modern Calvinistic revisions can be discerned in Karl Barth, *The Doctrine of the Word of God* (Edinburgh and New York 1956).

Much of the defense of modern neo-evangelicalism and fundamentalism centers on views of the Scripture which, the proponents claim, derive from the Calvinistic lineage. Many of these are repetitive; few new notes are sounded in the arguments. The reader, then, may take his choice from among the following: Benjamin B. Warfield, *The Inspiration and Authority of the Bible* (Philadelphia 1948), a nineteenth century American work; Bernard Ramm, *Special Revelation and the Word of God* (Grand Rapids, Michigan 1961) or Edward John Carnell, *The Case for Orthodox Theology* (Philadelphia 1959), both mild and well-reasoned; Herman Bavinck, *The Philosophy of Revelation* (London 1909); G. C. Berkouwer, *General Revelation* (Grand Rapids, Michigan 1955); James I. Packer, *"Fundamentalism" and the Word of God* (London 1958); James Orr, *Revelation and Inspiration* (Grand Rapids 1952); Gordon H. Clark, *Religion, Reason and Revelation* (Philadelphia 1961); Louis Gaussen, *The Inspiration of the Holy Scriptures* (Chicago 1949); Carl F. H. Henry, *Revelation and the Bible* (Grand Rapids, Michigan 1958). Almost all of these authors take pains to dissociate themselves from charges that this view of Scripture is based on a "mechanical" or "dictation" view.

167. For Lutheran scholasticism, see Robert D. Preus, *op. cit.* (note 64).

168. Because of the frequent connection between issues of revelation and miracles, several works on miracles should be consulted. John S. Lawton, *Miracles and Revelation* (New York 1960) aims at comprehensiveness, while Clive Staples Lewis, *Miracles* (New York 1947) is a clever apology. More sophisticated if less engrossing is Ian T. Ramsey, *Miracles, an Exercise in Logical Mapwork* (Oxford 1952).

169. An excellent chapter (V) on the career of modern criticism post-Wellhausen is to be found in E. C. Blackman, *Biblical Interpretation* (Philadelphia 1959 and London 1957).

170. The controversial bishop's life story is told in Peter Hinchcliff, *John William Colenso* (London 1964).

Three debates after the middle of the twentieth century perpetuate the internal difficulties within the liberal camp. One of these was occasioned by Rudolf Bultmann's effort to "demythologize" the New Testament. That controversy can be studied in the following: Rudolf Bultmann, *Theology of the New Testament* (New York 1951–1955); Hans W. Bartsch, ed., *Kerygma and Myth: A Theological Debate* (London and New York 1962), a collection of basically sympathetic pieces; Friedrich Gogarten, *Demythologizing and History* (New York 1950); Ian Henderson, *Myth in the New Testament* (London 1952), and two works which try to move beyond impasse by introducing, among other things, alternative philosophical points of view, John Macquarrie, *The Scope of Demythologizing: Bultmann and*

His Critics (London 1960) and Schubert M. Ogden, *Christ without Myth* (New York 1961).

A second school of interpreters, influenced by Martin Heidegger, have concentrated on hermeneutical questions that are competently reviewed in a very difficult book, James M. Robinson and John B. Cobb, Jr., eds., *New Frontiers in Theology: The New Hermeneutic* (New York 1964).

Related to both of the others have been attempts to comment on what biblical criticism in the liberal schools has done to the figure of Jesus. Albert Schweitzer, *The Quest of the Historical Jesus* (London 1954) reviews issues up to Schweitzer's prime while James M. Robinson, *A New Quest of the Historical Jesus* (London and Naperville, Illinois 1959) brings the story up to date "post-Bultmann." Another pioneer work that has often been referred to through the decades, available in reprint, is Martin Kähler, *The So-Called Historical Jesus and the Historic Biblical Christ* (Philadelphia 1964). Heinz Zahrnt, *The Historical Jesus* (New York 1963) is popular, almost journalistic. More thoughtful are Joachim Jeremias, *The Problem of the Historical Jesus* (Philadelphia 1964) and Günther Bornkamm, *Jesus of Nazareth* (New York 1960).

171. An unfriendly observer looks at fundamentalism's doctrine of Scripture in Gabriel Hebert, *Fundamentalism and the Church* (London and Philadelphia 1957).

CHAPTER 9

172. Alfred North Whitehead, *Religion in the Making* (New York 1926), pp. 58–60.

173. Anne Fremantle, ed., *The Protestant Mystics* (New York 1964) is an excellent selection from the writings of sixty-seven people she denominates "Protestant mystics." Perhaps the most influential of these has been Jacob Boehme; his *The Way to Christ* (London 1911) and *The Confessions of Jakob Boehme* (London 1920) are reprints of centuries-old material; so is George Fox, *A Journal or Historical Account of the Life, Travels, Sufferings, Christian Experience and Labour of Love, etc., of George Fox* (Philadelphia, n. d.). William R. Inge, *Mysticism in Religion* (London and Chicago 1948) is a commentary by a controversial modern Anglican.

174. Søren Kierkegaard's writings have often been reprinted; the most important in this context are *Attack upon "Christendom"* (Princeton, New Jersey 1944); *Concluding Unscientific Postscript*

(Princeton, New Jersey 1941); *Philosophical Fragments* (Princeton, New Jersey 1936).

175. The connection between Protestantism and economic or political individualism is often made, but seldom treated systematically. A treatment of its secularized embodiment in one society is Francis X. Sutton *et al.*, ed., *The American Business Creed* (Cambridge, Massachusetts 1956).

176. This point is elaborated in Wilken, *op. cit.* (note 158).

177. Lee, *op. cit.* (note 92) and Niebuhr, *op. cit.* (note 84).

178. The sociology of religion developed in Protestant *and* other contexts—notably, in the study of primitive religions. But some mention of general works in the field is important to provide a means of seeing Protestant forms in significant settings. To that end, this collection of titles has been brought together.

On the discipline as such: Max Weber, *The Sociology of Religion* (Boston and Toronto 1963); Emile Durkheim, *The Elementary Forms of the Religious Life* (London 1915), which has almost no reference to Western forms; Bryan Wilson, *Religion in Secular Society* (London 1966), which overstates the case for secularization but is provocative; Joachim Wach, *Sociology of Religion* (Chicago 1944), a marvelously compact and systematic volume; Thomas Luckmann, *The Invisible Religion: The Problem of Religion in Modern Society* (New York 1967), a turgid, difficult, yet seminal work on theory; David Moberg, *Religion as a Social Institution* (Englewood Cliffs, New Jersey 1962), which is studded with footnote references to literature growing out of the American context; a variety of approaches are apparent in the collection, Louis Schneider, ed., *Religion, Culture and Society* (New York, London, and Sydney 1964). Roland Robertson, *The Sociological Interpretation of Religion* (New York and London 1970) is inclusive in intention and scope, but has many Protestant references.

One line in my paragraph alludes to the title of a book by Peter Berger and Thomas Luckmann, *The Social Construction of Reality* (Garden City, New York 1966); mention should be made here of other contributions by Berger, who has often trained his sights on Protestantism, as in *The Noise of Solemn Assemblies* (Garden City, New York 1961). Other writers on the American scene include Charles Y. Glock and Rodney Stark, *Religion and Society in Tension* (Chicago 1965); Gerhard Lenski, *The Religious Factor* (Garden City, New York 1961), an essentially Weberian analysis of an American community, in which it is shown how religio-communitarian views influence societal decision; J. Milton Yinger, *Sociology Looks at Religion*

(New York 1963). A British work of note is David Martin, *A Sociology of English Religion* (New York and London 1967) as well as his more theoretical essays, *The Religious and the Secular: Studies in Secularization* (London and New York 1969).

Martin's title refers to secularization; analysis of this process in its relation to Protestantism is a major contribution of religious sociology. Several titles out of a multitude will bring the issues into focus. Arnold Loen, *Secularization* (London 1967) connects it with scientific change and sees the consequences for religion; a theological base is implied in both Bernard E. Meland, *The Secularization of Modern Cultures* (New York 1966), which has much interest in the non-Western world, and Larry Shiner, *The Secularization of History: An Introduction to the Theology of Friedrich Gogarten* (Nashville, Tennessee 1966). Other sociologically informed but basically theological works are David L. Edwards, *Religion and Change* (New York and London 1969), which is preoccupied with the character of community; Stephen Neill, *The Christian Society* (New York 1952), an often overlooked contribution; Martin Jarrett-Kerr, *The Secular Promise* (London and Philadelphia 1966 and 1965); Dennis L. Munby, *The Idea of a Secular Society* (Oxford and New York 1963), which is brief but systematic.

Few books have taken up themes which unite Protestantism, secularization of social forms, and sociology as such; an exception of considerable note is Roger Mehl, *The Sociology of Protestantism* (London and Philadelphia 1970), a solid though not lustrous work.

179. The references in these paragraphs derive from the discussions of Merleau-Ponty, Ludwig Wittgenstein, and Karl Marx in chapter 2, "The End of Secularism," in a book by a British Marxian thinker, Brian Wicker, *Toward a Contemporary Christianity* (London and Notre Dame, Indiana 1966 and 1967).

180. Protestant biblical scholars and theologians have regularly traced the biblical backgrounds to the life of the church, often for purposes suggested by the ecumenical movement. One of the most helpful of these tracings is Paul S. Minear, *Images of the Church in the New Testament* (Philadelphia 1960), which shows that most of some eighty New Testament images are dynamic; the same author's *Horizons of Christian Community* (St. Louis 1959) formally bridges biblical and ecumenical worlds.

John Bright, *The Kingdom of God: The Biblical Concept and Its Meaning for the Church* (Nashville, Tennessee 1953) has been a basic reference for many. R. Newton Flew, *Jesus and His Church* (New York 1938) begins its story in the synoptic Gospels, while the book of Acts provided a base for Floyd V. Filson, *Three Crucial Decades* (Richmond, Virginia 1963). Another Protestant biblical scholar who makes much of the communal experience of the earliest followers of Jesus is John Knox, and two books which detail his findings are *The Early Church and the Coming Great Church* (Nashville, Tennessee and London 1955) and *The Church and the Reality of Christ* (New York 1962).

181. While most Protestants regard the biblical basis of the Church as they read it to be normative, it is important for the student of Protestantism to read works on the subsequent history of the concept and on theological extrapolations. Occasionally church history as a discipline accents the adjective "church"; two examples are Cyril Charles Richardson, *The Church through the Centuries* (London and New York 1938), by an American Anglican, and Martin E. Marty, *A Short History of Christianity* (New York and London 1959) which, despite its title, tells the story not in terms of Christianity but of "one, holy, catholic, and apostolic Church." For Protestants, these histories come to their decisive stage at the time of the Reformation. Luther's view is appraised in Cyril Eastwood, *The Priesthood of All Believers* (Minneapolis 1962); Hermann A. Preus, *The Communion of Saints* (Minneapolis 1948); John M. Headley, *Luther's View of Church History* (New Haven, Connecticut and London 1963); William A. Mueller, *Church and State in Luther and Calvin* (Nashville, Tennessee 1954). All of these works show how Luther developed his teaching over against the papal-hierarchical tradition, and in this sense they are typical of later Protestantism.

At this point a number of theological discussions about the doctrine of the Church should be cited. The Reformation debates continue within Protestantism, as in a Congregationalist-Anglican debate over catholicity, begun by Daniel T. Jenkins, *The Nature of Catholicity* (London 1942), an attack on Anglicanism and replied to by Arthur G. Hebert, *The Form of the Church* (London 1944). A later manifestation came in R. Newton Flew and Rupert E. Davies, eds., *The Catholicity of Protestantism* (Philadelphia and London 1950), a polemical collection.

182. Pius X, *Vehementer*, February 11, 1906, quoted in J. S. Whale, *Christian Doctrine* (note 54), p. 128.

183. The rejection of the Platonic model is found in Articles VII and VIII of the Apology of the Augsburg Confession, in Tappert, *op. cit.* (note 63).

184. For Calvin, see the note on Mueller in note 181; Geddes MacGregor, *Corpus Christi, The Nature of the Church According to the*

Reformed Tradition (Philadelphia 1959); Williston Walker, *John Calvin, the Organizer of Reformed Protestantism* (New York 1906).

185. Anglican views of the nature of the Church can be found in the *Works of Richard Hooker* (London 1890), in two volumes; T. A. Lacey discusses one aspect of ecclesiology in *Authority in the Church* (London 1928) and, similarly, see Gordon Crosse, *Authority in the Church of England* (London 1906); Cyril Garbett, *The Claims of the Church of England* (London 1947); E. J. Bicknell, *A Theological Introduction to the Thirty-nine Articles of the Church of England* (London 1944).

186. The fundamental work on the church-sect typology and, indeed, one of the monumental works of Protestant sociology of religion, is Ernst Troeltsch, *The Social Teaching of the Christian Churches,* two volumes (London and New York 1931).

187. Franklin H. Littell, *op. cit.* (note 159) outlines the radical Reformation's contributions.

188. The most widely accepted thesis about the rise and import of denominationalism is Sidney E. Mead, *The Lively Experiment: The Shaping of Christianity in America* (New York 1963), particularly chapter VII.

189. The record of "out-group" difficulties in a free society is told in Anson Phelps Stokes, *Church and State in the United States,* three volumes (New York 1950); this giant work was condensed and revised with the help of Leo Pfeffer (New York and London 1964). The bibliography in the three-volume work is especially helpful as a guide to the extensive literature on the subject.

190. An adequate work on the polity of the churches is lacking in English; unfortunately Rudolf Sohm, *Kirchenrecht* (Leipzig 1892 and 1923), two volumes, has never been translated and, despite its original value, is out of date. There is a chapter on "Ordo" in Gustaf Aulén, *Reformation and Catholicity* (Philadelphia 1961).

191. Paul M. Harrison, *Authority and Power in the Free Church Tradition* (Princeton, New Jersey 1959) is a welcome analysis of the bureaucracy in an American Baptist denomination; an impressive parallel study of the Church of England in the nineteenth century, Kenneth A. Thompson, *Bureaucracy and Church Reform* (Oxford 1970), well illustrates the dilemma of a complex ecclesiastical institution; it includes a valuable bibliography on a relatively underdeveloped field of study. It refers also to some secular works (K. Boulding, J. Burnham, etc.) which will aid in understanding the organizational and managerial revolutions in the churches.

192. The parish as actual and potential locale for evangelical

community is analyzed and criticized in numerous modern works. Charles Duell Kean, *The Christian Gospel and the Parish Church* (Greenwich, Connecticut 1953) is a forthright essay by an Episcopal parish minister; James E. Dittes, *The Church in the Way* (New York 1967) is a kind of reply to radical critics of the church, an argument that even the banal and humdrum aspects of parish life can have therapeutic effect; Tom Allan, *The Face of My Parish* (New York and London 1957 and 1954) treats evangelism, with a parish in Glasgow as a model; Ernest W. Southcott, *The Parish Comes Alive* (New York 1956) studies renewal in an industrial parish in England, where the house-church concept was tried again; Robert A. Raines, *New Life in the Church* (New York 1961) takes a local church as the locale for renewal; Ross W. Sanderson, *The Church Serves the Changing City* (New York 1955) documents case studies of urban churches in America; Bruce Kenrick, *Come Out the Wilderness* (New York 1962) deals with significant experiments in East Harlem, New York; Roy Blumhorst, *Faithful Rebels* (St. Louis 1967) pushes the limits of parochial definition in high-rise apartments, and Elizabeth O'Connor, *The Call to Commitment* (New York 1963) describes a postparochial covenanted community in Washington D.C.; Robert A. Raines, *The Secular Congregation* (New York 1968) depicts the "worldly" involvements of a Pennsylvania parish. These case studies have to take the place for the present of historical and theoretical materials on the parish; both types of literature are in short supply at the moment.

Meanwhile, a number of theologians and social critics have turned their attention to the larger question of Christian community in the Protestant orbit. Some regard the parish with favor; others look beyond it. Suzanne de Dietrich, *The Witnessing Community* (Philadelphia 1958) uses biblical models; Dietrich Bonhoeffer, *Life Together* (New York 1954) grew out of community in the face of Nazism; William Klassen, *The Forgiving Community* (Philadelphia 1966) makes an effort, largely successful, to connect the doctrine and reality of forgiveness by seeing them in community. James M. Gustafson, *Treasure in Earthen Vessels: The Church as a Human Community* (New York 1961) works with a number of polarities, to great effect; Robert McAfee Brown, *The Significance of the Church* (Philadelphia 1956) examines Christian community past, present, and future; Claude Welch, *The Reality of the Church* (New York 1958) explores "life together" in Christian experience; more personal in orientation is D. Elton Trueblood, *The Company of the Committed* (New York 1961); J. E. Lesslie Newbigin, *The Household of God*

(London 1953) concentrates on the congregation of the faithful, the metaphor of the Body of Christ, and the community of the Holy Spirit; Daniel Jenkins, *The Strangeness of the Church* (Garden City, New York 1955) comments on unique features of Christian common experience; Robert A. Raines, *Reshaping the Christian Life* (New York 1964) expects the common life to be recognized when the Church becomes a redemptive fellowship.

193. David Belgum, *The Church and Its Ministry* (Englewood Cliffs, New Jersey 1963) connects the question of congregational life and the forms of ministry.

194 Dissatisfaction with no longer effective forms of the church has been expressed in countless sociologically and theologically based studies. Johannes C. Hockendijk, *The Church Inside Out* (Philadelphia 1966) has tried to systematize the faults and the possibilities; Colin W. Williams, *Where in the World?* (New York 1963) is similar in tone; George W. Webber, *God's Colony in Man's World* has been a broadly accepted description and prescription; Horst Symanowski raises basic questions in *The Christian Witness in an Industrial Society* (Philadelphia and London 1964 and 1966).

CHAPTER 10

195. The Department of the Laity of the World Council of Churches authorized a study of historical attitudes toward laymen; it appears in Stephen Charles Neill and Hans-Ruedi Weber, eds., *The Layman in Christian History* (Philadelphia and London 1963). Some of the chapters' bibliographical materials are of value for a study of themes in this chapter.

196. For the general subject of the layman in the biblical tradition as perceived by Protestants: Arnold B. Come, *Agents of Reconciliation* (Philadelphia 1960) suggests that laymen are important in the central Christian work; Francis O. Ayres, *The Ministry of the Laity* (Philadelphia 1962) is a biblical exposition; Alden D. Kelley, *The People of God* (Greenwich, Connecticut 1962) is of a general character; Paul Minear, *Jesus and His People* (London 1956) is basic and biblical; the chapter by George Hunston Williams in Neill-Weber, *op. cit.* (note 195) is helpful.

197. Some discussion of books dealing with calling and vocation appears in note 129; Cyril Eastwood, *The Priesthood of All Believers* (London and Augsburg 1960) bases itself in Luther's concept of the church and the laity, but also includes the author's own view

of the role of intercession; Robert L. Calhoun, *God and the Common Life* (New York and London 1935) is a Protestant view of vocation, as is Alexander Miller, *Christian Faith and My Job* (New York 1946).

198. The suggestion that Puritan Reformed churchmanship contributes to political freedom is implicit in James H. Nichols, *Democracy and the Churches* (Philadelphia 1951), which concentrates on contrasts between nineteenth century Roman Catholic and Protestant attitudes. Ralph Henry Gabriel, *The Course of American Democratic Thought* (New York 1940), chapter I, 3, draws parallels between Christianity and democratic attitudes in one nation.

199. The argument of this section relies heavily on Hendrik Kraemer, *A Theology of the Laity* (London and Philadelphia 1959). At midcentury a number of works on the modern role of the laity, often vis-à-vis clerical attitudes, appeared; noteworthy are Frederick K. Wentz, *The Layman's Role Today* (Garden City, New York 1963), which concentrates on America at the end of a religious revival; Howard Grimes, *The Rebirth of the Laity* (Nashville, Tennessee 1962), an optimistic work; Mark Gibbs and T. Ralph Morton, *God's Frozen People: A Book for and about Christian Laymen* (Philadelphia 1965), which is as sprightly as its title implies; Edward R. Wickham, *Church and People in an Industrial City* (London 1957), which concentrates in pioneering fashion on industrialism in Britain.

Preaching set the cleric apart from the layman in many instances. On the role of preaching in modern ministry: Donald Coggan, *Stewards of Grace* (London 1958) concentrates on the implications of preaching for status and definition; Paul E. Scherer, *For We Have This Treasure* (New York 1944) is a high view of preaching, combined with a realistic view of ministerial frailty; Joseph Sittler, *The Ecology of Faith* (Philadelphia 1961) is rich and suggestive; Peter T. Forsyth, *Positive Preaching and the Modern Mind* (Cincinnati 1907) is an original and long-lasting exploration; Dietrich Ritschl, *A Theology of Proclamation* (Richmond, Virginia 1963) is an uncompromising survey of biblical attitudes toward ministry, one which discourages appeals to "relevance"; Henry Grady Davis, *Design for Preaching* (Philadelphia 1958) concentrates on method more than role, as does Richard R. Caemmerer, *Preaching for the Church* (St. Louis 1959).

Less directly related to the question of role, but explanatory of the part preaching and verbal communication play in Protestantism are a number of excellent works: Harry A. De Wire, *The Christian as Communicator* (Philadelphia 1961), which blurs clergy-lay functions; Hendrik Kraemer, *The Communication of the Christian Faith* (Philadelphia 1956), which is consistent with the author's themes in his book on the laity; Theodore O. Wedel, *The Gospel in a Strange, New World* (Philadelphia 1963), by an expert teacher of preachers; James E. Sellers, *The Outsider and the Word of God* (Nashville, Tennessee 1961), which despite a confusing outline has much to say about the history and contemporary situation in communication; Frederick W. Dillistone, *Christianity and Communication* (London 1956), which concerns itself with the Word in evangelization.

200. W. C. Abbott, *A Bibliography of Oliver Cromwell* (Cambridge, Massachusetts 1929) will suggest to the reader the impact of this religio-military leader; C. H. Firth, *Oliver Cromwell* (New York 1906) is often regarded as one of the best biographies; Leo F. Solt, *Saints in Arms: Puritanism and Democracy in Cromwell's Army* (Stanford, California 1957) focuses on religion in the career of some of his associates. Among the numerous biographies of Gustavus Adolphus, note Nils G. Ahnlund, *Gustav Adolf, the Great* (Princeton, New Jersey 1940) and Charles R. L. Fletcher, *Gustavus Adolphus and the Struggle of Protestantism for Existence* (New York 1928). W. S. M. Knight, *The Life and Works of Hugo Grotius* (London 1925) is still valuable in a field where English works are less numerous.

201. Sample biographies of Protestant lay leaders mentioned here: F. Deaville Walker, *William Carey: Missionary Pioneer and Statesman* (Chicago, n.d.) which is uncritical and adulatory; the career of the Tappans is discussed by Charles I. Foster, *op. cit.* (note 86); Standish Meacham, *Henry Thornton of Clapham* (Cambridge, Massachusetts 1964); Oliver Warner, *William Wilberforce and His Times* (New York and London 1963); the biographies of twentieth century ecumenical lay leaders have not yet begun to appear in numbers matching those dealing with nineteenth century heroes.

202. The literature on women as laity and as clerics is belatedly being expanded as a result of worldwide efforts to "liberate" women, also in the churches; much of this writing is in journals and magazines, but pioneer inquiries had occurred in book form before this period. See M. E. Thrall, *The Ordination of Women to the Priesthood* (London 1958); severely proscribing women's role is an arch-conservative androcentric study, Fritz Zerbst, *The Office of Woman in the Church* (St. Louis 1955); Kathleen Bliss, *The Service and Status of Women in the Churches* (London 1952) is helpful on the period she discusses. Anglicans have been particularly preoccupied with the question, in part because of their distinctive views of ministry; note the pamphlet by E. L. Mackenzie, *Women and the*

Liturgical Ministry (London 1934); C. E. Raven, *Women and Holy Orders* (London 1928) which, unlike Mackenzie, favors woman's role; so does B. H. Streeter, *Woman and the Church* (London 1917). These works are all being rendered obsolete by the new stage and type of discussion in the women's liberation movement and with the ordination of women in many more Protestant denominations in the latter third of the twentieth century. On women as ministers' wives, see G. W. Denton, *The Role of the Minister's Wife* (Philadelphia 1962), which compares ministers' wives with those of other professional men. Much pious and hortatory literature exists on this subject, but is worthless for historical or theological purposes.

203. C. J. Davey, *The Methodist Story* (London 1955) includes materials on Methodist women evangelists and Primitive Methodist women preachers. Most of the literature on the German deaconess movement is untranslated. An often overlooked history of "American Protestant Women in World Mission" is R. Pierce Beaver, *All Loves Excelling* (Grand Rapids, Michigan 1968). Beaver provides a brief but well-chosen list of supplementary books, many of them concentrating on individual denominations and agencies; this should be consulted by those who would trace each.

Mention has been made of the suffrage movement in America, a subject which has attracted the attention of many writers. Alan P. Grimes, *The Puritan Ethic and Woman Suffrage* (New York 1967) reveals paradoxical relations between Protestants and others on this subject in the political realm; there are many comments on Protestantism in Aileen S. Kraditor, *The Ideas of the Woman Suffrage Movement 1890–1920* (New York and London 1965), the best book in its field and one which appends a most useful bibliography; a more brief but also more sweeping bibliography, though with less explicit religious reference, is in Aileen S. Kraditor, *Up from the Pedestal: Selected Writings in the History of American Feminism* (Chicago 1968); the list of books for further reading in Ishbel Ross, *Sons of Adam, Daughters of Eve* (New York and London 1969) is helpful on the American scene, though the book is quite jaunty. See also references to evangelicalism in William L. O'Neill, *Everyone Was Brave: The Rise and Fall of Feminism in America* (Chicago 1969).

204. N. C. Masterman, *John Malcolm Ludlow: The Builder of Christian Socialism* (Cambridge, England 1963) is the best on its subject; Richard Ely wrote an autobiography, *Ground Under Our Feet: An Autobiography* (New York 1938).

205. Sociological studies of the clergy-lay gap are rare in most

Protestant societies, but for the United States an excellent beginning has been made in Jeffrey K. Hadden, *The Gathering Storm in the Churches: The Widening Gap between Clergy and Laymen* (Garden City, New York 1969).

206. For the period to 1960, the most convenient volume is Margaret Frakes, *Bridges to Understanding* (Philadelphia 1960), which represents case studies of lay academies in Europe and America; Franklin H. Littell, *The German Phoenix: Men and Movements in the Church in Germany* (Garden City, New York 1960) deals with that nation; John L. Casteel, *Spiritual Renewal through Personal Groups* (New York 1957) is more prescriptive than descriptive.

207. From the library-length list of possibilities for bibliographies on the ministry itself, the following are representative choices: Anthony T. Hanson, *The Pioneer Ministry* (London 1961) is a scholarly biblical view; Robert S. Paul, *Ministry* (Grand Rapids, Michigan 1965) serenely surveys the whole scope of ministry; Thomas W. Manson, *The Church's Ministry* (Philadelphia and London 1948) is an excellent Anglican view; British Congregationalist Daniel Jenkins has two offerings, *The Protestant Ministry* (London and Garden City, New York 1958) and *The Gift of Ministry* (London 1947), the latter a book that must be described as delightful. T. W. Manson, *Ministry and Priesthood: Christ's and Ours* (Richmond, Virginia 1959) also discusses priesthood as an intercessory role; more on this subject will be discussed in note 211.

On the subject of pastoral care, John T. McNeill, *A History of the Cure of Souls* (New York 1951) is indispensable; almost thirty pages of bibliographical reference enhance the value of the volume even more. The best modern Reformed theological extrapolation on the theme is Eduard Thurneysen, *A Theology of Pastoral Care* (Richmond, Virginia 1962), while Martin Thornton, *Feed My Lambs* (Greenwich, Connecticut 1961) and *Pastoral Theology: A Reorientation* (London 1956) are so personal in vision that they must almost be described as idiosyncratic; nevertheless, they are thought-provoking.

208. Discussions of the setting apart of ministry, as in ordination, appear in H. Richard Niebuhr and Daniel D. Williams, *The Ministry in Historical Perspectives* (New York 1956). See particularly chapter VI, "Priestly Ministries in the Modern Church," by Edward Rochie Hardy, Jr. The question of orders is most frequently and strenuously debated in Anglicanism; see the general works on Anglicanism, note 29.

209. George D. Henderson, *Presbyterianism* (Aberdeen, 1954) discusses orders and offices in the Reformed Tradition, as does Harry G. Goodykoontz, *The Minister in the Reformed Tradition* (Richmond, Virginia 1963); Eugene P. Heideman, *Reformed Bishops and Catholic Elders* (Grand Rapids, Michigan 1970) is a controversial contribution to ecumenical discussion; Paul M. Harrison, *Authority and Power in the Free Church Tradition* (Princeton, New Jersey 1959) is a much referred to study of the exercise of office.

210. Roy W. Fairchild and John Charles Wynn, *Families in the Church: A Protestant Survey* (New York 1961) includes interesting material based on interviews and other data, on how ministers and laymen, at least in American Presbyterianism, have different conceptions of their role.

211. The "maceration of the minister" and the confusion concerning the meaning and work of ministry has led to countless modern studies; many of them have psychological dimensions. An extremely valuable bibliography, well annotated, on all dimensions of these role problems in America is to be found in Robert J. Menges and James E. Dittes, eds., *Psychological Studies of Clergymen: Abstracts of Research* (New York, London, and Toronto 1965). Some of the discussion of role has a bearing on ministerial education. James D. Glasse, *Profession: Minister* (Nashville, Tennessee 1968) occasioned much exploration of this topic; earlier Keith R. Bridston and Dwight W. Culver, *Preseminary Education: Report of the Lilly Study* (New York 1964) and *The Making of Ministers: Essays on Clergy Training Today* (Minneapolis 1964) brought together varied views of the subject. The most inclusive work in America at midcentury was H. Richard Niebuhr, Daniel D. Williams, and James M. Gustafson, *The Advancement of Theological Education* (New York 1956), based on a survey. Of worldwide scope is Steven G. Mackie, *Patterns of Ministry: Theological Education in a Changing World* (London 1969).

For the consequent life of ministers, Hans Hofmann, ed., *Making the Ministry Relevant* (New York 1960) has been of help, though it concentrates only on pastoral care. For the Younger Churches, see S. L. Greenslade, *Shepherding the Flock: Problems of Pastoral Discipline in the Early Church and in the Younger Churches Today* (London 1967) and Bengt Sundkler, *The Christian Ministry in Africa* (London 1960). Typical of works on ministerial confusion are John Coburn, *Minister, Man-in-the-Middle* (New York 1963) and E. James, *Odd Man Out? The Shape of the Ministry Today* (London 1962).

212. H. Richard Niebuhr, *The Purpose of the Church and Its Ministry: Reflections on the Aims of Theological Education* (New York 1956).

CHAPTER 11

213. F. W. Dillistone, *Christianity and Symbolism* (London and Philadelphia 1955) is the best introduction to the wider context of sacraments; it also, fortunately, includes a chapter (VII) on "Water Symbolism and Christian Baptism," in which Dillistone throws a different light on the doctrinal discussions surrounding the baptismal act. A standard general work on the sacraments is Oliver C. Quick, *The Christian Sacraments* (London 1928). It should be noted that, for all the historic controversy, baptism is an undernoted subject in recent Protestant books.

214. A discussion of sacramental world-views as they relate to symbolism occurs in a surprising context in Erich Heller, *The Disinherited Mind* (New York 1959), pp. 210 ff. where Luther-Zwingli on the sacraments is referred to as an illuminating moment in the history of discussion of symbols.

215. Gilbert Cope, *Symbolism in the Bible and the Church* (London and New York 1959), especially chapter 4, "Archetypes of Creation," is a rare discussion of psycho-sexual connotations of water rites in Christianity.

216. General discussions of baptism in the Protestant orbit include Oscar Cullmann, *Baptism in the New Testament* (London and Chicago 1950), a careful study of the appropriate texts; John F. Jansen, *The Meaning of Baptism* (Philadelphia 1958), which enlarges on biblical themes; Robert S. Paul, *The Atonement and the Sacraments: The Relation of the Atonement to the Sacraments of Baptism and the Lord's Supper* (Nashville 1960); Karl Barth, *The Teaching of the Church Regarding Baptism* (London 1948), which reveals the author's Zwinglian attitudes and questions infant baptismal practices; A. E. J. Rawlinson, *Christian Initiation* (London 1947), an Anglican contribution; Johannes Schneider, *Baptism and Church in the New Testament* (London 1957), which is congenial to Baptist views; Austin Crouch, *Is Baptism Essential to Salvation?* (Nashville, Tennessee 1953); George Every, *The Baptismal Sacrifice* (London 1959), which partially removes baptism from its sacramental context; G. W. H. Lampe, *The Seal of the Spirit: A Study in the Doctrine of Baptism and Confirmation in the New Testament and the Fathers* (London 1951),

nuanced in its understanding of symbols; Joachim Jeremias, *Infant Baptism in the First Four Centuries* (London and Philadelphia 1960) and Pierre Marcel, *The Biblical Doctrine of Infant Baptism* (London 1953), two continental contributions to the debate about pedobaptism; G. W. Bromiley, *Baptism and the Anglican Reformers* (London 1953), an historical study; Keith Bridston, ed., *One Lord One Baptism* (Minneapolis, Minnesota 1960), a report of the Faith and Order Commission of the World Council of Churches; and W. F. Flemington, *The New Testament Doctrine of Baptism* (London 1948).

217. A number of titles in the previous note (Barth, Schneider, Crouch, Jeremias, Marcel) deal with the controversy over infant and adult baptism; to these may be added R. E. O. White, *The Biblical Doctrine of Initiation: A Theology of Baptism and Evangelism* (Grand Rapids, Michigan 1960), an ambitious defense of believer's baptism. A more popular but no less consistent argument appears in Warren Carr, *Baptism: Conscience and Clue for the Church* (New York 1964).

218. Most architectural discussion in the twentieth century, insofar as it relates to sacramental necessities, concentrates on the Eucharist; thus Gilbert Cope, ed., *Making the Building Serve the Liturgy* (Oxford 1962). An attractive suggestion is the extensive illustrated discussion of the location of the font in chapter 3, "Christ's Sacraments," Donald J. Bruggink and Carl H. Droppers, *Christ and Architecture: Building Presbyterian/Reformed Churches* (Grand Rapids, Michigan 1965).

219. Numbers of Baptist books in note 216 grow out of the historical Anabaptist tradition on baptism; see also Franklin H. Littell, *The Origins of Sectarian Protestantism* (New York and London 1964) and George Hunston Williams, *op. cit.* (note 50).

220. Similarly, Reformed views were implied in references in note 216; but see also, for origins of these views in Calvin, R. S. Wallace, *Calvin's Doctrine of the Word and Sacrament* (Edinburgh 1954).

221. A brief but faithful discussion of baptism in developing Lutheranism appears in chapter IV, 22, "The Sacrament of Baptism," Werner Elert, *op. cit.* (note 27). Elert's bibliographical references are entirely to German and Latin literature.

222. Two works edited by Roman Catholics include much material on Protestant-Catholic relations so far as baptism is concerned: Hans Küng, ed., *The Sacraments: An Ecumenical Dilemma* (New York 1967) and Johannes Wagner, *Adult Baptism and the Catechumenate* (New York 1967), both in the "Concilium" series. The

Küng volume includes a chapter by James McLendon, "Why Baptists Do Not Baptize Infants" and by a Jesuit, Michael Hurley, "What Can Catholics Learn from the Infant Baptism Controversy?"

CHAPTER 12

223. Joachim Jeremias, *The Eucharistic Words of Jesus* (Oxford and New York 1955) is one of the more detailed biblical inquiries on the subject in recent Protestantism; Oscar Cullmann and F. J. Leenhardt, *Essays on the Lord's Supper* (London and Richmond, Virginia 1958) includes essays by Cullmann, "The Meaning of the Lord's Supper in Primitive Christianity" and Leenhardt, "This Is My Body."

224. The Lord's Supper is a predominating theme in the general histories of Christian liturgy and worship; the classic volume is by Dom Gregory Dix, *The Shape of Liturgy* (London 1945), a book full of import also for Protestants. Evelyn Underhill, *Worship* (London and New York 1936 and 1937) reflects that author's more mystico-spiritual approach. Richard M. Spielmann, *History of Christian Worship* (New York 1966) concentrates on historical aspects. Nathaniel Micklem, *Christian Worship* (Oxford 1936); William D. Maxwell, *An Outline of Christian Worship: Its Developments and Forms* (London 1936); and Jean-Jacques von Allmen, *Worship: Its Theology and Practice* (New York 1965) all fuse historical with thematic materials.

225. Much of the discussion of intercommunion has occurred under the auspices of the World Council of Churches; considerable literature has developed, but most of it reflects Protestant-Orthodox concerns, and there is ordinarily little in it revelatory of Protestantism's inner dynamics. But see Donald Baillie, ed., *Intercommunion* (London 1952), a report of a commission appointed by the Faith and Order Conference. Lukas Vischer, ed., *A Documentary History of the Faith and Order Movement 1927–1963* (St. Louis 1963) provides background. Hugh Blenkin, *Immortal Sacrifice: A Study in the Cause of Christian Unity of the Relation between the Sacrifice of Christ and the Holy Communion Service* (London 1964) is a very personal view of the subject; better is Romey P. Marshall, *Liturgy and Christian Unity* (Englewood Cliffs, New Jersey 1965).

226. G. W. H. Lampe, *op. cit.* (note 216) relates baptism to confirmation; see also Lionel S. Thornton, *Confirmation: Its Place in the Baptismal Mystery* (London 1954), an Anglican interpretation.

227. On confession, Max Thurian, *Confession* (London 1958), for a French Reformed monastic's view; and Walter Lüthi and Eduard Thurneysen, *Preaching, Confession, the Lord's Supper* (Richmond, Virginia 1960). Thurneysen wrote the section on "Evangelical Confession."

228. This picture of "the look of the liturgy" was derived chiefly from books referred to in note 224, *q.v.*

229. Yngve Brilioth, *Eucharistic Faith and Practice: Evangelical and Catholic* (London and Philadelphia 1930 and 1958) is by far the best "churchly" view of the sacraments, encompassing in scope, historical and typological in method. Greville D. Yarnold, *The Bread Which We Break* (London, New York, and Toronto 1960) is a fine short survey; Max Thurian, *The Eucharistic Memorial* (London and Richmond, Virginia 1960), in two volumes summarizes the views developed at a French Protestant monastic community. Gustaf Aulén, *Eucharist and Sacrifice* (Philadelphia 1958) is a conciliatory work by a "catholic" Swedish bishop.

230. See again the reference to Erich Heller, *op. cit.* (note 214) on the breakup of the medieval symbolic universe. Cyril C. Richardson, *Zwingli and Cranmer on the Eucharist* (Evanston, Illinois 1949) is an excellent depiction of Zwingli's views. Reformed liturgies are reproduced in Bard Thompson, *Liturgies of the Western Church* (Cleveland, Ohio 1961).

231. The formidable summary of Luther's views of the Lord's Supper is Hermann Sasse, *This Is My Body: Luther's Contention for the Real Presence in the Sacrament of the Altar* (note 77), a conservative Lutheran's informed polemic against Reformed positions. The quotation is from Vilmos J. Vajta, *Luther on Worship* (Philadelphia 1958). Brilioth, *op. cit.* (note 229) presents much analysis of the Lutheran view. Luther D. Reed, *The Lutheran Liturgy* (Philadelphia 1949) is comprehensive and includes bibliographical material.

232. Reformed liturgy and especially eucharistic practice are discussed in Howard G. Hageman, *Pulpit and Table: Some Chapters in the History of Worship in the Reformed Churches* (Richmond, Virginia and London 1962); Charles W. Baird, *The Presbyterian Liturgies* (Grand Rapids, Michigan 1957), a reprint of a nineteenth century work; W. D. Maxwell, *John Knox's Genevan Service Book, 1556* (Edinburgh 1931) reproduces liturgies used by Knox at Geneva, 1556–1559. See also G. J. Van de Poll, *Martin Bucer's Liturgical Ideas* (Assen, the Netherlands 1954); for Calvin, R. S. Wallace, *op. cit.* (note 220).

233. Anglicanism has produced some of the most consistent concern for the Eucharist among non-Roman, non-Orthodox

Christians. Horton Davies, *Worship and Theology in England* (Princeton, New Jersey 1961–1965) is a majestic five-volume work that must be consulted by all who have interests in this subject. C. W. Dugmore, *Eucharistic Doctrine from Hooker to Waterland* (London 1942) throws light on one period covered by Davies. J. C. Bowmer, *The Sacrament of the Lord's Supper in Early Methodism* (Westminster, Maryland 1951) describes an Anglican variant.

234. Paul Tillich, *The Protestant Era* (Chicago 1948), chapter VII on "Nature and Sacrament," speaks of symbol in ways that will inform the understanding of recent Protestant discussions. "Eucharistic Developments in the Evangelical Church," by Wim Luurt Boelens, S.J., in Küng, *op. cit.* (note 222) provides useful data on continental ecumenical developments within the evangelical churches. Massey H. Shepherd, Jr., ed., *The Liturgical Renewal of the Church* (New York 1960) summarized trends in the liturgical movement, which at that time was helping restore the sacraments in the evangelical churches.

CHAPTER 13

235. A bibliography on marriage, family, and sexuality in Protestant perspective is provided in note 341.

236. By far the best lists of books on Protestant education are provided as appendices to chapters in Merton P. Strommen, ed., *Research on Religious Development* (Hawthorn 1971), an encyclopedic work on the contributions of various religious traditions. Robert W. Lynn, *Protestant Strategies in Education* (New York 1964) briefly covers the approaches chiefly of American Protestants. Wesner Fallaw, *The Modern Parent and the Teaching Church* (New York 1946) sees the church to be an extended family for the purpose of education. Robert W. Lynn and Elliott Wright, *The Big Little School* (New York 1971) is a short, overdue introduction to the history of the Sunday school, largely in America.

Several Protestant studies of the effects of religious education are M. G. Ross, *Religious Beliefs of Youth* (New York 1950); Merton P. Strommen, *Profiles of Church Youth* (St. Louis 1963), a Lutheran reckoning; C. W. Stewart, *Adolescent Religion* (Nashville, Tennessee 1967); O. E. Graebner, *Child Concepts of God* (River Forest, Illinois 1960); A. H. MacLean, *The Idea of God in Protestant Religious Education* (New York 1930).

A number of books discuss the modern institutional complex of Protestantism, especially in America. John R. Fry, *A Hard Look at*

Adult Christian Education (Philadelphia 1961) contends that Protestant churchgoers are not casually but willfully ignorant of the Bible, despite lip service to literacy and educational ideals. Bruce Reinhart, *The Institutional Nature of Adult Christian Education* (Philadelphia 1962) demonstrates that much of Christian education is designed to bolster institutions more than to inform or inspire people concerning the Christian way. Wesner Fallaw, *Church Education for Tomorrow* (Philadelphia 1960) criticizes the Sunday school and similar routine forms and seeks alternatives. More positive are Harry C. Munro, *Protestant Nurture* (Englewood Cliffs, New Jersey 1956) and Iris V. Cully, *The Dynamics of Christian Education* (Philadelphia 1958).

237. Most Protestant treatments of death occur in the context of discussions of immortality or resurrection; see references in note 115. Chapter 6, "The Mystery of Death," in Emil Brunner, *The Christian Doctrine of the Church, Faith, and the Consummation* (Philadelphia and London 1962) is a representative discussion.

238. While the pamphlet, or tractarian, literature on giving to the church is unimaginably extensive, it is largely ephemeral and is hortatory in character. A rare exception is Taito A. Kantonen, *A Theology for Christian Stewardship* (Philadelphia 1956). There are useful descriptive chapters in F. Ernest Johnson and J. Emory Ackerman, *The Church as Employer, Money Raiser, and Investor* (New York 1959).

239. Jacques Ellul, *Prayer and Modern Man* (New York 1970) is a characteristically Protestant treatment of prayer; the modern classic is Friedrich Heiler, *Prayer* (London 1932); Gordon S. Wakefield, *The Life of the Spirit in the World of Today* (New York 1969) examines prayer and worship practices; novel treatment appears in D. Z. Phillips, *The Concept of Prayer* (New York 1966), where the author employs tools of language analysis to discuss philosophical groundings of prayer. A liberal Protestant view is Harry Emerson Fosdick, *The Meaning of Prayer* (New York and London 1915).

240. Most modern theologians of note have at some time or other addressed questions of ethics; many of these will appear in subsequent notes, but an introduction to the theme can be found in the following: Paul Tillich, *Love, Power and Justice* (New York 1954), based on the theologian's ontological perception and intricately interweaving its three themes; Dietrich Bonhoeffer, *Ethics* (New York 1955); John C. Bennett, ed., *Christian Ethics in a Changing World* (New York 1966), a collection of calls to social action; Paul Ramsey, ed., *Faith and Ethics* (New York 1957), which contains

numerous essays of value by disciples of H. Richard Niebuhr; Waldo Beach and H. Richard Niebuhr, eds., *Christian Ethics* (New York 1955); Helmut Thielicke, *The Freedom of the Christian Man* (New York 1963) and a two-volume systematic *Theological Ethics* (Philadelphia 1966 and 1967); C. S. Lewis, *Christian Behaviour* (New York 1944), which concentrates on personal ethics; James Sellers, *Theological Ethics* (New York 1966); James A. Pike, *Doing the Truth: A Summary of Christian Ethics* (Garden City, New York 1955), based on a biblical theme but alert to the modern situation; Albert C. Knudson, *The Principles of Christian Ethics* (Nashville, Tennessee 1943) and Austin Farrer, *The Freedom of the Will* (New York and London 1958), which deals with a background subject in the discussion of behavior.

241. Jacques Ellul, *The Theological Foundation of Law* (Garden City, New York 1960) presents a radical Protestant lay jurist criticizing natural-law concepts; a more congenial approach to these concepts is Emil Brunner, *The Divine Imperative* (Philadelphia 1947); Herbert Waddams, *A New Introduction to Moral Theology* (London and New York 1964) is a typically Anglican work in its congeniality to natural principles; for Anglicanism, see also J. V. Langmead Casserley, *Morals and Man in the Social Sciences* (London 1961); William Temple, *Christianity and Social Order* (Harmondsworth, Middlesex, England and Baltimore, Maryland 1956); Oliver C. Quick, *Christianity and Justice* (London 1940); L. Dewar and C. E. Hudson, *Christian Morals* (London 1945).

242. Joseph Sittler, *The Structure of Christian Ethics* (Baton Rouge, Louisiana 1958) creatively bridges ethics of principle and "contextual ethics." Other works on contextual ethics will be introduced in note 252.

243. A Protestant modernist who concerned himself with the description of Old Testament ethics was J. M. P. Smith, whose books *The Moral Life of the Hebrews* (Chicago 1923) and *The Origin and History of Hebrew Law* (Chicago 1931) may still be referred to; more characteristic of more recent thought, however, is R. B. Y. Scott, *The Relevance of the Prophets* (New York 1947) and Walther Eichrodt, *Man in the Old Testament* (Philadelphia 1946).

244. Protestant writings on New Testament ethics include: T. W. Manson, *Ethics and the Gospel* (New York and London 1960), an excellent introduction, as is C. H. Dodd, *Gospel and Law* (London 1951); W. Lillie, *Studies in New Testament Ethics* (Edinburgh 1961); Amos Wilder, *Eschatology and Ethics in the Teaching of Jesus* (London and New York 1954 and 1950); Rudolf Bultmann, *Jesus and the Word*

(New York 1934); Martin Dibelius, *The Sermon on the Mount* (New York 1940); E. F. Scott, *The Ethical Teaching of Jesus* (New York 1924). All share the characteristic modern feature of Protestant books on the subject: they stress the urgency, the decisiveness, the radicality of Jesus' ethical call as recorded in the Gospels.

245. Equally radical in their desire to respond to Jesus' injunctions to love the neighbor and make peace are: Roland H. Bainton, *Christian Attitudes to War and Peace* (London 1961); Cecil J. Cadoux, *Christian Pacifism Re-examined* (Oxford 1940); a French pacifist's tract, Jean Lasserre, *War and the Gospel* (Scottdale, Pennsylvania 1962); Jacques Ellul, *Violence* (New York 1969), which argues that a Christian may have to take part in violence, but his act cannot then be considered Christian; more compromising and more complicated is the writing of a defender of just-war theories, Paul Ramsey, *War and the Christian Conscience* (Durham, North Carolina 1961).

Reinhold Niebuhr has been the great modern delineator of problems relating personal absolutist ethics to political compromise; see his *Moral Man and Immoral Society* (New York and London 1932), the work which brought him to public attention, and *An Interpretation of Christian Ethics* (New York 1935). His brother, H. Richard Niebuhr, in *The Responsible Self* (New York 1963) includes similar themes.

246. For studies of Pauline ethics: C. H. Dodd, *The Meaning of Paul for Today* (London and New York 1949 and 1957) is extremely compressed and revelatory; Morton Scott Enslin, *The Ethics of Paul* (New York 1930) is an American liberal Protestant's view; Rudolf Bultmann devoted himself to the Pauline ethic in *Theology of the New Testament, I,* (New York 1952) and in selected articles collected in his *Essays Philosophical and Theological* (London and New York 1955) and in Schubert M. Ogden, ed., *Existence and Faith: Shorter Writings of Rudolf Bultmann* (New York 1960). Numbers of these develop the theme mentioned in this chapter, that Paul could say, "I died under the law."

247. The much debated modern Protestant isolation of the agape motif through Christian history, Anders Nygren, *Agape and Eros* (London and Philadelphia 1953), in two volumes, provided the impetus for other ethicists to develop that motif.

248. Paul Ramsey, *Basic Christian Ethics* (New York 1950), influenced by H. Richard Niebuhr, revolves around the Augustinian theme concerning love of God and doing what one will.

249. Modern expositions of Luther's ethics appear in George W.

Forell, *Ethics of Decision* (Philadelphia 1955) and, even more, *Faith Active in Love* (New York 1954). Gustaf Aulén, *Church, Law and Society* (New York 1948) places more accent on law in Luther than do most interpreters, but does so consistently with Luther's purposes; see also "Luther on Ethics: Man Slave and Free" by Martin E. Marty in Heino O. Kadai, ed., *Accents in Luther's Theology* (note 59).

250. The rigorist on separating law and Gospel in Luther is Werner Elert; see his *The Christian Ethos* (Philadelphia 1957).

251. Many of the systematic ethical thinkers in the notes in this chapter appear in the Reformed tradition: the Niebuhrs (note 240); Jacques Ellul (note 241); Emil Brunner (note 241); Jean Lasserre (note 245); to these should be added the name of Karl Barth, particularly his *The Knowledge of God and the Service of Man* (New York 1939).

252. Contextual ethics, situation ethics, and "the new morality" have sometimes been clustered and treated sensationalistically. A serious version is Paul L. Lehmann, *Ethics in a Christian Context* (New York 1963), which is full of valuable reflections but somewhat confusingly plotted. The most noticed of the contextualists is Joseph Fletcher, whose *Situation Ethics: The New Morality* (Philadelphia 1966) provoked responses in Harvey Cox, ed., *The Situation Ethics Debate* (Philadelphia 1968). Joseph Fletcher argued his case further in *Moral Responsibility* (Philadelphia 1967).

A textbook summary, *Biblical Faith and Social Ethics* by E. Clinton Gardner (New York 1960) provides convenient summaries of various Protestant, and other Jewish and Christian ethical approaches.

CHAPTER 14

253. On the question of race and racism in general, there is a long bibliography in Ashley Montagu, *Man's Most Dangerous Myth: The Fallacy of Race* (Cleveland 1964); for the myths of Anglo-Saxon superiority in the United States a useful general history is Thomas F. Gossett, *Race: The History of an Idea in America* (Dallas, Texas 1963); Gossett has much comment on religious contributions to the problems.

254. A popular history of Christian attitudes toward the Jews is to be found in Edward H. Flannery, *The Anguish of the Jews* (London and New York 1965). For background, it is important to be aware of Christian theological roots for anti-Semitism; James Parkes, *The*

Conflict of the Church and the Synagogue (New York 1969) is a useful place to begin; see also his *Antisemitism* (London and Chicago 1963). Two documentary histories, both of which include Protestant writings, are Arnold A. Rogow, *The Jew in a Gentile World* (New York 1961) and Leon Poliakov, *The History of Anti-Semitism* (New York 1965).

255. The German anti-Nazi Protestants had a very ambivalent record on the question of the Jews; almost all of them opposed "Aryan clauses" in Nazi-prescribed church constitutions and were critical of persecution of the Jews; however, it has often been pointed out that few of them went so far as to try to understand Judaism on its own terms and usually saw value in the Jew chiefly as a potential convert to Christianity. One of the most controversial instances is Dietrich Bonhoeffer. For some of his statements, see the chapter (III, 1) on "The Aryan Clauses" in Dietrich Bonhoeffer, *No Rusty Swords* (London 1965). The larger setting of the church's confession in this period is told about in Arthur C. Cochrane, *The Church's Confession under Hitler* (note 54).

256. For a summary of nineteenth century views on attempts at conversion, A. E. Thompson, *A Century of Jewish Missions* (New York 1902); John Caldwell Thiessen, *op. cit.* (note 2) in chapter 34, "To the Jew First and Last" reviews evangelical efforts around the world.

257. Bernhard E. Olson, *Faith and Prejudice* (New Haven, Connecticut and London 1963) is a review of four kinds of American Protestant Sunday school literature, an assessment of various forms of theological expression toward Judaism. A sociological study based on some soundings in California is Charles Y. Glock and Rodney Stark, *Christian Beliefs and Anti-Semitism* (New York and London 1966); the authors conclude that Protestant orthodoxy contributes to theological anti-Semitism.

258. Armas K. Holmio, *The Lutheran Reformation and the Jews* (Hancock, Michigan 1949) makes an effort at putting together Luther's complex views of Judaism at various stages of his career; the reformer's writings are available in I. Brandt, ed., *Luther's Works* (Philadelphia 1962), volume XLV. There is an extensive periodical literature on the subject, which has not yet been adequately studied in book-length works.

259. After Auschwitz, in the quarter century after World War II there has been a great increase in Jewish-Christian conversation or "dialogue," without conversion as a goal. Most of the reports on this subject occur in periodical literature; there is no good world-

wide Protestant summary of the subject. A Roman Catholic, John M. Oesterreicher, for some years edited volumes called *The Bridge: A Yearbook of Judeo-Christian Studies* (New York, various dates); Protestant materials and reporting were included.

260. Martin E. Marty, *Righteous Empire* (note 33) makes an effort to tell the story of the formation of an Anglo-Saxon Protestant empire in America, and talks about Protestantism there in ethnic terms.

261. Robert F. Berkhofer, Jr., *Salvation and the Savage* (Lexington, Kentucky 1965) breaks ground on a neglected subject, "Protestant Missions and American Indian Response" from 1787–1862. The author points out that this is the first general history of the subject since 1840. Berkhofer's bibliographical essay is a denomination-by-denomination reference list, of considerable value.

262. The one book which leaves all students of the period before the nineteenth century in its debt on this subject is Winthrop D. Jordan, *White over Black: American Attitudes toward the Negro, 1550–1812* (Chapel Hill, North Carolina 1968). Jordan pays appropriate attention to the Protestant churches in this definitive book, which is based almost entirely on original readings of often obscure sources.

263. The Fund for Theological Education, Princeton, New Jersey, has published *A Bibliography of African and Afro-American Religions* (n.d.). While his name does not appear on the title page, Charles Long was the prime mover in assembling it. Chapter III deals with "Religion during slavery." Students of this subject should consult it as well as Elizabeth W. Miller, *The Negro in America: A Bibliography* (Cambridge, Massachusetts 1970), pp. 32 ff. Two important denominational studies that treat white attitudes toward blacks in this period are Donald G. Mathews, *Slavery and Methodism: A Chapter in American Morality* (Princeton, New Jersey 1965) and Andrew E. Murray, *Presbyterians and the Negro—A History* (Philadelphia 1966).

264. On black churches and black religion, Carter G. Woodson, *The History of the Negro Church* (Washington 1921) was a basic and permanent work; Benjamin E. Mays and Joseph W. Nicholson, *The Negro's Church* (New York 1933) carried on this work and pointed to the community impact. E. Franklin Frazier, *The Negro Church in America* (New York 1963) is a posthumous work of one of the more accomplished black students of the subject; Arthur H. Fauset, *Black Gods of the Metropolis* (Philadelphia 1944) deals more with Negro cults in urban America. Ruby F. Johnson, *The Development of Negro*

Religion (New York 1954) and *The Religion of Negro Protestants* are of mixed value. So are the writings of Joseph R. Washington, Jr., *Black Religion: The Negro and Christianity in the United States* (Boston 1964), rejected by many subsequent, more militant black religionists for its positive views of "white" theology but containing useful comment on the dynamics of black churches under segregation, and his *The Politics of God: The Future of the Black Churches* (Boston 1967), which reflects more of the later postintegrationist mood. By that time more interest had turned to works like Albert B. Cleage, Jr., *The Black Messiah* (New York 1968), which advocated separation of black churches and the proclamation of their independent identity and integrity. Still possessing much interest is W. E. B. Dubois, *The Negro Church* (Atlanta, Georgia 1903). The Fund for Theological Education bibliography (note 263), pp. 18–34, will guide the reader into every aspect of Negro church life. Richard Bardolph, *The Negro Vanguard* (New York 1961) is a story of the earlier black leadership in America; an impressive percentage of this leadership was Protestant clerical in makeup.

265. David M. Reimers, *White Protestantism and the Negro* (New York 1965) is the best history of the developing pattern of white self-segregation after the Civil War. Also on this subject: Ernest Q. Campbell and Thomas F. Pettigrew, *Christians in Racial Crisis* (Washington 1959); Leonard L. Haynes, Jr., *The Negro Community within American Protestantism, 1619–1844* (Boston 1953) which, while it covers the earlier period, reveals something of the mentality that led to postslavery segregation; Frank S. Loescher, *The Protestant Church and the Negro* (New York 1948). There are many references to Protestant churches in I. A. Newby, *Jim Crow's Defense* (Baton Rouge, Louisiana 1965). His chapter on "The Uses of Religion" (chapter 3) introduces most of the preeminent religious white racists of the period.

266. Gossett, *op. cit.* (note 253), chapter III, "Eighteenth-Century Anthropology" has some reference to Enlightenment attitudes on race. Peter Gay, *op. cit.* (note 67), II, 694 ff., enlarges on Rousseauean materials; I, 505 ff. "The Era of Pagan Christianity" is of wider compass; the roots of the study of "The History of Religion" are in this period, but the subject would carry us too far afield.

267. For Carey, see chapter II, "India" in V. G. Kiernan, *The Lords of Human Kind: Black Man, Yellow Man and White Man in an Age of Empire* (Boston and Toronto 1969), a book which has much to say about missionaries and imperialism.

268. Paul A. Varg, *Missionaries, Chinese and Diplomats: The American Protestant Missionary Movement in China 1890–1952* (Princeton, New Jersey 1958) is the best treatment of the Chinese attitudes held by Protestant missionaries. Chapter XII, Gossett (note 253), speaks of anti-immigration attitudes against Orientals in America.

269. Livingstone is quoted by Kiernan, *op. cit.*, pp. 217–218.

270. On South Africa, Kiernan, *op. cit.*, p. 228. See also Ronald Robinson and John Gallagher with Alice Denny, *Africa and the Victorians: The Climax of Imperialism* (Garden City, New York 1968). Stephen Neill, *Colonialism and Christian Missions* (note 3) is, of course, a useful reference on the topics in the previous four notes.

271. Gossett, *op. cit.* (note 253), chapter VIII, "The Social Gospel and Race," introduces the subject.

272. Madison Grant, *The Passing of the Great Race, or the Racial Basis of European History* (New York 1921) and *The Conquest of a Continent, or the Expansion of Races in America* (New York 1933) are typical of this author's approach. Lothrop Stoddard, however, included more religious "documentation" in his similarly racist writings, *The Revolt against Civilization: The Menace of the Under Man* (New York 1923) and *The Rising Tide of Color against White World Supremacy* (New York 1920).

273. Hans Kohn, *The Idea of Nationalism* (New York 1961) is one of the most valuable introductions to the subject, in part because of chapter IV, "Renaissance and Reformation: The Emergence of Nationalism." I recommend a reading of the extensive footnotes in that chapter as one of the best means of making acquaintance with the various reformers' views of nation and nationalism. Salo Baron, *Modern Nationalism and Religion* (New York 1947) is an excellent historical study.

274. Carlton J. H. Hayes, *Nationalism: A Religion* (New York 1960) is a subtle study by a lay Catholic historian who is well aware of Protestantism's impact on nationalistic and patriotic attitudes.

275. The only work in English on this subject includes much more than its title implies, and is invaluable for understanding German patterns: Koppel S. Pinson, *Pietism as a Factor in the Rise of German Nationalism* (New York 1968). Peter Viereck, *Meta-Politics: The Roots of the Nazi Mind* (New York 1961) is biased, but helpful for understanding particularly the romantics' contributions to a mentality eventually attracted to Nazism. Eugene Anderson, *Nationalism and the Cultural Crisis in Prussia 1806–1815* (New York 1939) devotes itself to some crucial years; Robert Ergang, *Herder and the Foundations of German Nationalism* (New York 1931) and Leonard

Krieger, *The German Idea of Freedom* (Boston 1957) make contributions, as does Jerry F. Dawson, *Friedrich Schleiermacher: The Evolution of a Nationalist* (Austin, Texas and London 1965).

276. Koppel S. Pinson, *A Bibliographical Introduction to National Socialism* (New York 1935) is an early compilation which includes many religious titles. The literature on both Protestantism and Catholicism in their relation to Nazism is growing constantly. Most of the books on Protestant support of Hitler are in German; English works on the suffering of the churches or their response are more abundant, and most of these obliquely refer to the problem of support given Nazism by Christians. One of the best of these is J. S. Conway, *The Nazi Persecution of the Churches* (New York 1968). His bibliography refers to numerous books, particularly written by British churchmen, expressing alarm at Protestant-Nazi identifications and interactions in the 1930s. One that remains worth reading is Nathaniel Micklem, *National Socialism and Christianity* (Oxford 1939).

277. Richard L. Merritt, *Symbols of American Community 1735–1775* (New Haven, Connecticut and London 1966) includes a provocative paragraph (p. 173) without documentation on the effects of the Great Awakening on intercolonial communication; not lacking documentation is Alan Heimert, *Religion and the American Mind: From the Great Awakening to the Revolution* (Cambridge, Massachusetts 1966), with its many pages of valuable comment on sources connecting "awakened" Protestantism with emerging nationalism. Carl Bridenbaugh, *Mitre and Sceptre* (New York 1962) reports on reaction to rumors that an Anglican bishop was to be seated in America.

278. Frederick Merk, *Manifest Destiny and Mission in American History* (New York 1963) is of a general character, as is Ernest Tuveson, *op. cit.* (note 117), which deals more with literary-religious materials and less with *Realpolitik*. Religious leadership, notably that of Josiah Strong and missionary imperialists, receive their due in Walter LaFeber, *The New Empire: An Interpretation of American Expansion 1860–1898* (Ithaca, New York 1963). The same is true of Julius W. Pratt, *Expansionists of 1898* (Baltimore, Maryland 1936) and Richard W. Van Alstyne, *The Rising American Empire* (Chicago 1960).

The best guide to American southern nationalism in the Civil War is James W. Silver, *Confederate Morale and Church Propaganda* (Tuscaloosa, Alabama 1957). Hans Kohn, *American Nationalism* (New York 1961) weaves religious themes into its fine exposition throughout. Ray Allen Billington, *The Protestant Crusade* (New York 1938), while speaking of anti-Catholicism, incidentally reveals much concerning Protestant identifications with American nationhood. Edward McNall Burns, *The American Idea of Mission* (New Brunswick, New Jersey 1957) also incidentally treats religion, as does Merle Curti, *The Roots of American Loyalty* (New York 1946). Yehoshua Arieli, *Individualism and Nationalism in American Ideology* (Cambridge, Massachusetts 1964) reveals how religious ideas of nationalism were secularized.

CHAPTER 15

279. Two general works on the background of church and state relations are John A. Hutchison, *The Two Cities: A Study of God and Human Politics* (Garden City, New York 1957) and the more serious T. M. Parker, *Christianity and the State in the Light of History* (New York 1955); the latter, unfortunately, carries the story only through the Reformation.

280. A number of works by Protestants throw light on relations between religion and the civil realm in early Christianity: S. L. Greenslade, *Church and State from Constantine to Theodosius* (London 1954); W. H. C. Frend, *Martyrdom and Persecution in the Early Church* (Garden City, New York 1967), which includes more on the political realm than its title implies; Robert M. Grant, *The Sword and the Cross* (New York 1955) for the narrower aspects and the same author's *Augustus to Constantine* (New York 1970) for the larger sweep of Roman-Christian contacts.

281. Franklin Hamlin Littell, *The Free Church* (Boston 1957) celebrates the contributions of the radical Reformation in the civil realm, as does his *The Anabaptist View of the Church* (note 159). The subject appears frequently in writings reproduced by George H. Williams and Angel M. Mergal, in *Spiritual and Anabaptist Writers* (Philadelphia 1957).

282. For church-state views of Luther and Calvin, William A. Mueller, *op. cit.* (note 181). J. W. Allen, *A History of Political Thought in the Sixteenth Century* (London 1951) is often cited for its breadth; Roland H. Bainton, *The Travail of Religious Liberty* (Philadelphia 1951) discusses the reformers in a memorable fashion. For Luther's theological matrix, Gordon Rupp, *The Righteousness of God* (London 1953) and Aulén, *Church, Law and Society* (note 249).

283. What Hannah Arendt says of secularization's role in revolu-

tion could be said of the whole democratic movement: Christianity contributed to it, but is not really the agent. Hannah Arendt, *On Revolution* (New York 1963), p. 18.

284. Winfred E. Garrison, "Characteristics of American Organized Religion," in *The Annals,* Volume 256, March 1948, pp. 14ff. discusses the church historical significance of American separation of church and state.

285. The nonviolent contribution of sectarians and its contemporary application is the theme of Guy Franklin Hershberger, *War, Peace, and Nonresistance* (Scottdale, Pennsylvania 1944); the same case is made more militantly and with more historic reference in John Horsch, *The Principle of Nonresistance as Held by the Mennonite Church* (Scottdale, Pennsylvania 1940). Appeal to the same tradition appears in a tract for modern times, Guy Franklin Hershberger, *The Way of the Cross in Human Relations* (Scottdale, Pennsylvania 1958), chapter 9, "Anabaptism and the Social Order."

286. Two early twentieth century works still provide excellent materials on Quaker views: William C. Braithwaite, *The Beginnings of Quakerism* (London 1912) and Isaac Sharpless, *Quakerism and Politics* (Philadelphia 1905). Quaker church-state problems come to focus chiefly in wartime, when pacifism is an issue; see Margaret E. Hirst, *The Quakers in Peace and War* (London 1923). Rufus M. Jones, *Quakers in the American Colonies* (London 1923) brings the story to a new continent; a fine historical summary is Edwin B. Bronner, *William Penn's "Holy Experiment"* (Philadelphia 1962).

287. Thomas Cuming Hall, *The Religious Background of American Culture* (Boston 1930) presents an often rejected thesis which suggested that English Nonconformity was largely responsible for American religious liberty. James H. Nichols, *op. cit.* (note 198), crediting Reformed Puritan Protestantism with substantial contributions to democratic life has already been mentioned.

288. By far the best work on the Baptists in America is William G. McLoughlin, *New England Dissent, 1630–1833* (Cambridge, Massachusetts 1971), two volumes. This can be supplemented with localized studies which include Congregationalist history: Jacob C. Meyer, *Church and State in Massachusetts, 1740–1833* (Cleveland 1930); Richard C. Purcell's *Connecticut in Transition 1775–1818* (Washington 1918); and M. Louise Greene, *The Development of Religious Liberty in Connecticut* (Boston 1905). C. C. Goen, *Revivalism and Separatism in New England* (New Haven, Connecticut 1962) will help the reader sort out various strands of Congregational and Baptist witness in the period. Perry Miller, *Roger Williams, His Contribution*

to the American Tradition (Indianapolis 1953) concentrates on one of the more notable theorists. Still worth studying is Sanford H. Cobb, *The Rise of Religious Liberty in America: A History* (New York 1902). Sidney E. Mead, *The Lively Experiment* (note 33) is a fine historical essay on the movement from "coercion to persuasion."

289. This is a major theme of Winthrop Hudson, *The Great Tradition of the American Churches* (New York 1953); see especially Chapter IV on Lyman Beecher.

290. It is impossible here, unless one wants to throw the proportions of this essay into disarray, to follow very far the bypaths Americans have taken after "separation of church and state." However, the turn taken was among the more significant in Christian administrative and political history, and some notice should be taken, even for readers who have no special interest in isolating American Protestant history. In addition to Anson Phelps Stokes's gigantic work, already mentioned (note 189), the following deserve attention: Loren P. Beth, *The American Theory of Church and State* (Gainesville, Florida 1958), with its bibliography; Dallin H. Oaks, ed., *The Wall between Church and State* (Chicago 1963), a collection including some Protestant pieces; Mark DeWolfe Howe, *The Garden and the Wilderness* (Chicago 1965) contrasts two approaches to the subject; Edward R. Norman, *The Conscience of the State in North America* (Cambridge, England 1968), which compares Great Britain and Canada with the United States; John Frederick Wilson, *Church and State in American History* (New York 1965), a collection of sources; Herbert Stroup, *Church and State in Confrontation* (New York 1967), which in the course of a general look at all Christian history has much to say about the United States, and in footnotes (pp. 231 ff.) lists "best books" on church-state relations in various Western nations including the United States. Special notice should be taken of Thomas G. Sanders, *Protestant Concepts of Church and State* (New York 1964), which has been criticized for its attacks on traditional Protestant views in America, but which offers substantial summaries of Lutheran, Anabaptist, Quaker, "separationist," and "transformationist" theories in America.

291. Out of what Sanders (note 290) calls the "transformationist" (moderate-pragmatist) school, largely of Reformed origins, has come much of the most positive Protestant involvement in the secular state's life. A representative thinker in this tradition is John C. Bennett; see his *Christians and the State* (New York 1958), *The Christian as Citizen* (London 1955), and *Christian Ethics and Social Policy* (New York 1946) for the heart of his thought on these mat-

ters. The brothers Niebuhr could also be classified in this category of "transformationist"; they see civil and religious realms as separate but also involved with each other, and perceive the secular order, despite the demonic in it, to be also somehow partly transformable for the working out of divine purposes.

292. Cyril Forster Garbett, *Church and State in England* (London 1907) brings together much of lasting value on the British situation. Related relevant material appears in some essays in Charles Smyth, ed., *The Church and the Nation* (New York 1962) and David Martin, *A Sociology of English Religion* (London and New York 1967), which does not confine itself to Anglicanism.

293. For the ongoing story of the Calvinist tradition, see John T. McNeill, *op. cit.* (note 28).

294. In addition to what has already been said about Lutheranism, the topic of Lutheran resistance to Hitler should be studied; see Conway, *op. cit.* (note 276) and the work of a Norwegian bishop, Eivind Berggrav, *Man and State* (Philadelphia 1951), since these show Lutherans breaking away from static concepts of obedience to the state yet doing so in Lutheran categories.

CHAPTER 16

295. Despite the importance of the study, there is a general paucity of material on the relation of Protestantism to progress, production, industrialization, and technology, though in recent years numbers of scholars are beginning to address themselves to the topics. It is beyond the scope of this book to introduce the general matter from the viewpoint of "secular" coverage, but "Readings and Reference" in the second volume of Melvin Kranzberg and Carroll W. Pursell, Jr., *Technology in Western Civilization* (New York, London, and Toronto 1967) is a well-organized essay on various elements of the culture of industrialization and the world of production, and it should be consulted. One of the gloomiest accounts of the impact of technology on man is by a Protestant lay theologian, Jacques Ellul, *The Technological Society* (New York 1967). Lewis P. Feuer, *The Scientific Intellectual* (New York 1963); Robert K. Merton, *Social Theory and Social Structure* (Glencoe, Illinois 1949); Ernst Benz, *Evolution and Christian Hope* (note 115); and Norman O. Brown, *Life against Death* (Middletown, Connecticut 1959) bring various historical, sociological, and analytic or psychoanalytic bearings to the religious question. See also

John U. Nef, *Cultural Foundations of Industrial Civilization* (Cambridge, England 1958) for the early history; Hannah Arendt, *The Human Condition* (Chicago 1958) for a profound philosophical perception; Herbert Butterfield, *The Origins of Modern Science* (New York 1956) for the scientific element. There is an excellent bibliography and there are references to Protestantism and to religion in Victor C. Ferkiss, *Technological Man: The Myth and the Reality* (New York 1969).

A seminal study, full of clues that have not yet been followed up but are implied in the title, is Ernst Troeltsch, *Protestantism and Progress* (Boston 1958). Denis L. Munby, *Christianity and Economic Problems* (London and New York 1956) and V. A. Demant, *Religion and the Decline of Capitalism* (London 1952) offer two British views. See also two earlier works, A. D. Lindsay, *Christianity and Economics* (London 1930) and J. Stamp, *The Christian Ethic as an Economic Factor* (London 1926), both of which have direct relations to the topic at hand. There is a chapter on the economic views of the Protestant reformers in Albert Hyma, *Renaissance to Reformation* (Grand Rapids, Michigan 1955).

296. The reference to the medieval feast of fools recalls to mind the modern translation of its motifs in Harvey Cox, *The Feast of Fools* (Cambridge, Massachusetts 1969). This book, a charter for a Protestant "Theology of Play," offers a number of back-of-the-book references to religious writing on the subject.

297. For more on Wesley and Wesleyanism, see note 300. A convenient account of the development of the middle class is Charles Morazé, *The Triumph of the Middle Class* (London and Cleveland 1966).

298. This democratic theme appears frequently in the books cited in notes 281 through 288.

299. The discussion of the "calling" derives largely from comment by Max Weber (note 302), and is enlarged upon by Einar Billing, *op. cit.* (note 129); a number of foreign-language references are in a footnote, p. 43, in Kurt Samuelsson, *Religion and Economic Action: A Critique of Max Weber* (New York 1961).

300. Wesley is discussed repeatedly and at some length in Samuelsson (note 299). A seminal essay, often disputed, on the effects of Wesleyanism on English economics and culture, is Elie Halévy, *The Birth of Methodism in England* (Chicago and London 1971). This thesis was "tried out" on a larger public by Halévy, *op. cit.* (note 68). Other historians elaborated on it; J. L. Hammond and Barbara Hammond, *The Town Labourer, 1760–1832* (London 1917) and

Robert F. Wearmouth, *Methodism and the Common People of the Eighteenth Century* (London 1945) discuss various aspects of that thesis and of the Methodist contribution. A Marxian critique of that contribution is E. P. Thompson, *The Making of the English Working Class* (New York 1964), which is full of hostile references to the effects of evangelicalism. More subtle is E. J. Hobsbawm's essay on "Methodism and the Threat of Revolution in Britain," in *Labouring Men: Studies in the History of Labour* (New York 1964). The whole Halévy thesis grew out of remarks in W. E. H. Lecky, *A History of England in the Eighteenth Century* (London 1878–1890), volume 2. Wellman J. Warner, *The Wesleyan Movement in the Industrial Revolution* (London and New York 1930); Robert F. Wearmouth, *Methodism and the Working Class Movements of England 1800–1850* (London 1957); two works by Maldwyn Edwards, *Methodism and England* (London 1943) and *After Wesley* (London 1935) also converge on economic themes.

301. A rather poorly organized book, John R. Bodo, *The Protestant Clergy and Public Issues 1812–1848* (Princeton, New Jersey 1954) and the somewhat better Charles C. Cole, Jr., *The Social Ideas of the Northern Evangelists* (New York 1954) both introduce the leading Protestant American figures during the rise of industrialism and include bibliographies that will help the reader become acquainted with their writings. Incidental comment on Protestantism appears in Joseph Dorfman, *The Economic Mind in American Civilization* (New York 1946–1949), three volumes. For the later period, in Henry May, *op. cit.* and Aaron I. Abell, *op. cit.* there are discussions of Protestant adaptations to industrialization.

Social Darwinism was covered in a model monograph, Richard Hofstadter, *Social Darwinism in American Thought* (Philadelphia 1945). His bibliography lists other works on the subject. Robert Green McCloskey, *American Conservatism in the Age of Enterprise 1865–1910* (Cambridge, Massachusetts 1951) speaks of secularization of the Protestant ethos in the period. There is a reprint of Andrew Carnegie, *The Gospel of Wealth and Other Timely Essays* (Cambridge, Massachusetts 1962).

302. On the Weber thesis, see primarily Max Weber, *The Protestant Ethic and the Spirit of Capitalism* (London and New York 1930), two volumes, and an English extrapolation and application, R. H. Tawney, *Religion and the Rise of Capitalism* (New York 1926). Samuelsson, *op. cit.* (note 296) is a searching criticism. Robert W. Green, *Protestantism and Capitalism: The Weber Thesis and Its Critics* (Boston 1959) is a textbook of source readings. H. M. Robertson,

Aspects of the Rise of Economic Individualism (Cambridge, England 1933) carries on a running debate with Weberians. Julien Freund, *The Sociology of Max Weber* (New York 1968) sets Protestant ethical topics alongside the other contributions of Weber. See especially 4:B.5.

Very valuable are the otherwise not always easily accessible essays collected by S. N. Eisenstadt, *The Protestant Ethic and Modernization: A Comparative View* (New York and London 1968). His bibliography gleans from many cultures.

303. In this note we shall cite a number of works on Protestantism, secularization, industrialization, vocation, and the productive capacity of man as it relates to the care of the earth. Bryan R. Wilson, *Religion in Secular Society* (Harmondsworth, Middlesex, England and Baltimore, Maryland 1969) concentrates on secularization in England and America. Will Herberg, *Protestant, Catholic, Jew* (New York 1955) is an American study of the question of identity, but its comment on the utility of religion relates to the present theme. David O. Moberg, *The Church as a Social Institution* (note 178) in its footnotes will lead readers to various aspects of religion and economic life in America. A British study is H. J. Blackham, *Religion in a Modern Society* (London 1966).

Further on Protestantism and industrialization: E. R. Wickham, *Church and People in an Industrial City* (London 1957) and the historical study, K. S. Inglis, *Churches and the Working Classes in Victorian England* (London 1963); on a worldwide scale, Paul Abrecht, *The Churches and Rapid Social Change* (London 1961); also Horst Symanowski, *The Christian Witness in an Industrial Society* (note 194). H. F. R. Catherwood, *The Christian in Industrial Society* (London 1964) is the view of a theological conservative, open to facing the issues of industrialization.

Marquis W. Childs and Douglas Cater, *Ethics in a Business Society* (New York 1954), with a chapter on "The Church and the Kingdom," has had considerable influence in the United States. William A. Spurrier, *Ethics and Business* (New York 1962) is an extremely informal layman's guide to moral issues; also for laymen is Albert Terrill Rasmussen, *Christian Responsibility in Economic Life* (Philadelphia 1965). Joseph F. Fletcher, *Christianity and Property* (Philadelphia 1947) includes critiques of prevailing Protestant attitudes, as do numbers of essayists in John C. Bennett *et al.*, *Christian Values and Economic Life* (New York 1954).

The care of the earth has only recently begun to be discussed systematically; numbers of attacks have been made on Protestantism because it has encouraged dominion over nature, which has often meant exploitation of nature. Frederick Elder, *Crisis in Eden* (Nashville 1970) is a Protestant's attempt to find resources, but he locates few in Protestantism and celebrates a number of secular ecologists' writings, among them Rachel Carson and Loren Eiseley. Conrad Bonifazi, *A Theology of Things* (Philadelphia 1967) brought together themes of man and nature, as did an exegetical study, C. F. D. Moule, *Man and Nature in the New Testament* (Philadelphia 1967); see also Eric C. Rust, *Nature and Man in Biblical Thought* (London 1953). H. Paul Santmire, *Brother Earth: Nature, God and Ecology in Time of Crisis* (New York 1970) is one of the first systematic attempts to provide a Protestant response to questions of environmental quality.

CHAPTER 17

304. While its scope reaches far beyond Protestantism, Gerardus van der Leeuw, *Sacred and Profane Beauty: The Holy in Art* (New York 1963) is one of the best introductions to the esthetic element and the dimensions of play in religion. See also note 296 and the bibliographical references in Cox's book, note 296.

John W. Dixon, Jr., *Nature and Grace in Art* (Chapel Hill, North Carolina 1964) attempts to provide a modest but comprehensive general esthetic theory for modern religion, and is written by a Protestant theologian; he appends a bibliographical essay of some detail. Curiously, there are few book-length Protestant titles in his list. Perhaps that suggests something of the sparseness of Protestant contributions to the subject. Somewhat similar in intention and also influenced by Paul Tillich is David Baily Harned, *Theology and the Arts* (Philadelphia 1966). Walter L. Nathan, *Art and the Message of the Church* (Philadelphia 1966) is a very limited work, but should be mentioned in a field where major contributions are generally lacking. Nor is Katherine Morrison McClinton, *Christian Church Art through the Ages* (New York 1962) as substantial a work as is needed in the English-speaking world.

305. Shaker visual art is to be seen and studied in John G. Shea, *The American Shakers and Their Furniture* (New York, Toronto, London, and Melbourne 1971); Edward Deming Andrews, *The Gift to Be Simple: Songs, Dances and Rituals of the American Shakers* (London 1940) is the best introduction to that sect's dances.

306. On "consent to being" and its esthetic implications, Roland

Andre Delattre, *Beauty and Sensibility in the Thought of Jonathan Edwards* (New Haven, Connecticut and London 1968); "The Plain Style" is the theme of chapter XII in Perry Miller, *The New England Mind: The Seventeenth Century* (note 123). Kenneth B. Murdock, *Literature and Theology in Colonial New England* (Cambridge, Massachusetts 1949) has informed comment on Puritan poetry; samples of the American Puritan product can be read in Harrison T. Meserole, ed., *Seventeenth-Century American Poetry* (Garden City, New York 1968). Puritan attitudes toward secular music (toward which they showed more tolerance than to church music) are the topic of Percy Scholes, *The Puritans and Music* (London 1934). Leonard Ellinwood, "Religious Music in America" in James Ward Smith and A. Leland Jamison, *Religious Perspectives in American Culture* (Princeton, New Jersey 1961) refers to Puritanism.

307. Examples of Protestant-era portrayals of Jesus are to be found in Joseph Jobé, *Ecce Homo* (New York 1962); Albert Edward Bailey, *Christ and His Gospel in Recent Art* (New York 1948); Marcelle Auclair, *Christ's Image* (New York 1961); none of these deals uniquely with Protestantism, however.

308. Chapter IV, "Renaissance," posed against chapter V:1, "Theatrical art and Protestant Realism," and V:2, "The Reformation Conflict," demonstrates the difference in spirit between Renaissance and Reformation, in Eric Newton and William Neil, *2000 Years of Christian Art* (London and New York 1966), one of the better books on the history of Western religious art.

309. This "breakdown of symbol" has been discussed previously in sacramental context; see Heller, *op. cit.* (note 214).

310. On dance, see note 304; efforts have been made to reintroduce Dionysian motifs to theology. One Protestant who has done so is Sam Keen in *To a Dancing God* (New York 1970), though Mr. Keen himself would be among the first to question what is left of "Protestantism" in his approach to religion.

311. These are numerous references to "the organ controversy" in the Disciples of Christ in America—a typical "primitive Gospel group" in Louis Cochran and Bess White, *Captives of the Word* (Garden City, New York 1969) and other Disciples of Christ histories.

312. Paul Nettl, *Luther and Music* (Philadelphia 1948) and Luther D. Reed, *Luther and Congregational Song* (Philadelphia 1947) introduce the role of music in the Lutheran Reformation.

313. Karl and I. S. Geiringer, *The Bach Family* (New York 1954)

provides access, through its bibliography, to the main themes of Bach research.

314. For Calvin on church music, W. S. Pratt, *The Music of the French Psalter of 1562* (New York 1939); P. A. Scholes, *The Puritans and Music in England and New England* (London 1934) is the standard on its subject. Erik Routley in *Church Music and Theology* (London and Philadelphia 1959), *The Church and Music* (London 1950), and *The Musical Wesleys* (London and New York 1968) devotes himself largely to the English church music tradition. Winfred Douglas, *Church Music in History and Practice* (New York 1962) is largely devoted to English music, too, though there are continental and American references. Other works to consult are: Charles Stanley Phillips, *Hymnody, Past and Present* (New York 1937); Louis F. Benson, *The English Hymn* (New York 1915); Leonard Ellinwood, *The History of American Church Music* (New York 1953); and James Rawlings Sydnor, *The Hymn and Congregational Singing* (Richmond, Virginia 1960). Millar Patrick, *Four Centuries of Scottish Psalmody* (London 1949) is the best introduction to its subject.

315. Little of the literature on adorning of Bibles or the use of cartoons and popular art in the Reformation is available in English or in book-length form. Comment on the subject is scattered through the pages of S. L. Greenslade, *op. cit.* (note 154).

316. A succinct and important discussion of the Reformation and art is to be found in Holl, *op. cit.* (note 122). Alfred Stange, *German Painting: XIV-XVI Centuries* (London and New York, n.d.) introduces Reformation artists. The great work on Dürer is Erwin Panofsky, *Albrecht Dürer* (Princeton, New Jersey and London 1943), in two volumes.

317. The best work in English on Calvin and esthetics is M. P. Ramsay, *Calvin and Art* (Edinburgh 1938); and there is also now a study of Zwingli, Charles Garside, Jr., *Zwingli and the Arts* (New Haven, Connecticut and London 1966). A modern Reformed discussion, dependent in part on the Barthian viewpoint—Barth is quoted in support of its iconoclasm—is André Bieler, *Architecture in Worship: The Christian Place of Worship* (Philadelphia and London 1965).

318. W. A. Visser 't Hooft, *Rembrandt and the Gospel* (Philadelphia 1957) is one of the most relevant books relating Rembrandt to evangelical approaches.

319. Eric Newton and William Neil, *op. cit.* (note 308) in chapters VII and VIII, discusses these and other nineteenth and twentieth century artists and their regard for Christian themes.

320. Moore is also discussed in Newton and Neil (note 308); Thorvaldsen still awaits English studies.

321. Andrew L. Drummond, *The Church Architecture of Protestantism* (Edinburgh 1934) is one of the few attempts to isolate the whole Protestant tradition, though there are, of course, numerous monographs on movements and moments, such as Ronald P. Jones, *Nonconformist Church Architecture* (London 1914); or Martin S. Briggs, *Puritan Architecture and Its Future* (London 1946).

Victor Fiddes, *The Architectural Requirements of Protestant Worship* (Toronto 1961) is a rather dour Canadian book; more catholic is James F. White, *Protestant Worship and Church Architecture* (New York 1964), an attractive reflection on theology and practice. Peter Hammond, *Liturgy and Architecture* (London and New York 1961) is a frequently consulted book wherever liturgy is taken seriously in church building. It includes a fine bibliography on liturgy, architecture, and church architecture. G. W. O. Addleshaw and Frederick Etchells, *The Architectural Setting of Anglican Worship* (London 1948) has historical depth, though it tends to be "denominationally limited."

Protestant buildings are included along with others in Anton Henze and Theodor Filthaut, *Contemporary Church Art* (New York 1956); Edward D. Mills, *The Modern Church* (New York and London 1956), which is mainly British in scope; and G. E. Kidder-Smith, *The New Churches of Europe* (New York 1964)—all of them illustrated extensively.

322. Harold Wickliffe Rose, *The Colonial Houses of Worship in America* (New York 1963) depicts all surviving colonial churches; Edmund W. Sinnott, *Meeting House and Church in New England* (New York, Toronto, and London 1963) provides the reader with many opportunities through pictures to become well acquainted with the New England forms; Marian Card Donnelly, *The New England Meeting Houses of the Seventeenth Century* (Middletown, Connecticut 1968) is the most scholarly recent study, and includes a twelve-page bibliography worth noting.

323. Viktor Fürst, *The Architecture of Sir Christopher Wren* (London 1956) focuses on the work of a genius; on the period, see Basil F. L. Clarke, *The Building of the Eighteenth-Century Church* (London 1963). Gerald Cobb, *The Old Churches of London* (London 1948) is a popular work.

324. On the Cambridge movement, see James F. White, *op. cit.* (note 70) and its American counterpart, Phoebe B. Stanton, *op. cit.* (Baltimore, Maryland 1968). Kenneth Clark, *The Gothic Revival*

(Harmondsworth, Middlesex, England 1964) is a pleasant discussion of Pugin and his contemporaries.

325. See the last three books cited in note 321 for examples of contemporary churches.

326. W. J. G. van Mourik te Velp, *Hervormde Kerkbouw na 1945* (The Hague, the Netherlands 1957) has not been translated, but its fine photographs make the case.

327. Various writers brought together by Greenslade, *op. cit.* (note 154) discuss the impact of the Bible on literary form and vice versa.

328. I can here only point to a few books which introduce the complex of relations between religion and literature in modern culture from Protestant viewpoints. Begin with the work of Nathan A. Scott, Jr., including his earlier works, *Modern Literature and the Religious Frontier* (New York 1958), *Rehearsals of Discomposure: Alienation and Reconciliation in Modern Literature* (New York 1952), *The Tragic Vision and the Christian Faith* (New York 1957), and *The Climate of Faith in Modern Literature* (New York 1964). Amos N. Wilder has also been a consistent student of the subject, with more interest in poetry: *Modern Poetry and the Christian Tradition* (New York 1952), *Theology and Modern Literature* (Cambridge, Massachusetts 1958), and *The Spiritual Aspects of the New Poetry* (New York 1940). Stanley Romaine Hopper, *Spiritual Problems in Contemporary Literature* (New York 1952) ranges widely, as does the British work, Martin Jarrett-Kerr, *Studies in Literature and Belief* (London 1954). On fiction, see William R. Mueller, *The Prophetic Voice in Modern Fiction* (New York 1959). Paul Elmen, *The Restoration of Meaning to Contemporary Life* (Garden City, New York 1958) is studded with quotations, but lacks impact as a whole. Students and other readers who wish to pursue the literature-and-theology topic would do best to see the bibliographies in some of the above-mentioned works, as the topic itself carries us beyond the scope of this book.

CHAPTER 18

329. Norman W. Bell and Ezra F. Vogel, eds., *A Modern Introduction to the Family* (Glencoe, Illinois 1960) brings together a spectrum of modern views about the problems and possibilities of the family. What is significant is the degree of secularization: a book like this can be put together with almost no reference to religion. Those who wish to study the topic of Protestantism, the family, and

sexuality, are advised, however, to introduce themselves through a general work such as Bell-Vogel is.

330, 331, 332, 333. The sections covered by these four notes are highly dependent on the only book which I have found satisfactory on this subject: Derrick Sherwin Bailey, *Sexual Relation in Christian Thought* (New York 1959); chapters I and II cover the biblical materials; V deals with the Reformation and seventeenth century Anglicanism.

334. The Advisory Council on Religious Communities published a *Guide to the Religious Communities of the Anglican Communion* (London 1951); also on this topic: Peter F. Anson, *The Call of the Cloister* (London 1955) and a curious older American work, R. H. Weller, *Religious Orders in the Anglican Communion* (Milwaukee, Wisconsin 1909).

335. Bailey, *op. cit.* (notes 330–333), chapter V.

336. A curious old book, Henry Charles Lea, *History of Sacerdotal Celibacy in the Christian Church* (New York 1966) is one of the more general discussions of celibacy from an ultra-Protestant point of view. Lea did his homework, but his anticlericalism and anticelibacy stands color the entire work. It was first published in 1867. Approximately half the work covers the post-Reformation period, Protestant and Catholic.

337. Once again, these paragraphs on Luther and Calvin are dependent upon Bailey (notes 330–333) and the literature to which he points. But see William H. Lazareth, *Luther on the Christian Home* (Philadelphia 1960).

338. The controversy over birth control in Roman Catholicism has occasioned much new writing on population control from a theological point of view, in Protestantism also. Daniel Callahan, *Abortion: Law, Choice and Morality* (New York 1970) is a comprehensive worldwide survey and should be consulted. Richard M. Fagley, *The Population Explosion and Christian Responsibility* (New York 1960) brought together various Protestant positions on the subject for a commission of the World Council of Churches.

339. The best book on Puritan love, sex, and marriage is Edmund S. Morgan, *The Puritan Family* (New York 1966), though it is confined to New England materials. Emil Oberholzer, Jr., *Delinquent Saints* (New York 1956) is a study of New England Congregational disciplinary actions, and reveals something of the concepts of sexual practice then operative.

340. Steven Marcus, *The Other Victorians* (New York 1966) is "a study of sexuality and pornography in mid-nineteenth-century

England." Much more elaborate and original is Ronald Pearsall, *The Worm in the Bud: The World of Victorian Sexuality* (New York 1969). Both suggest the limits of church control over mores and describe the results of evangelical repression.

341. A number of books on the modern Protestant family model deserve notice here: Roland H. Bainton, *What Christianity Says about Sex, Love and Marriage* (New York 1957) is a modest and moderate, historically grounded exposition. Derrick S. Bailey, *The Mystery of Love and Marriage* (New York 1952) has its intention directed to pastoral counseling. Gibson Winter, *Love and Conflict* (New York 1958) emphasizes the stresses on the contemporary family. James G. Emerson, *Divorce, the Church, and Remarriage* (Philadelphia 1961) takes up controversial topics from a pastoral point of view. Roy W. Fairchild and John C. Wynn, *op. cit.* (note 210) base their work on sociological analyses of understandings of roles. Peter A. Bertocci, *The Human Venture in Sex, Love and Marriage* (New York 1949) is inspirational in character. Arthur W. Calhoun, *Social History of the American Family* (New York 1960) reprints in three volumes a narrative that dates from World War I times; because of the earlier impact of the Protestant churches, this remains a valuable guide.

342. A number of helpful books were prepared shortly before the much publicized "sexual revolution" of the 1960s throughout the Western world, and deserve attention alongside the sexual controversies associated with "the new morality" (note 252). They include: Otto A. Piper, *The Christian Interpretation of Sex* (New York 1941), which is biblical, conservative; William Graham Cole, *Sex in Christianity and Psychoanalysis* (New York 1955), which relates to modern personality sciences; Vigo A. Demant, *Christian Sex Ethics: An Exposition* (London 1963); Seward Hiltner, *Sex and the Christian Life* (New York 1957), which is informed by counseling; and Simon Doniger, *Sex and Religion Today* (New York 1953). These are probably more representative of the counsels of the Protestant churches than are the better-known comments of situation ethicists who are trying to cope with drastic changes in the sex ethos.

343. William E. Lecky, *History of European Morals, from Augustus to Charlemagne* (New York 1879), p. 368.

AFTERWORD

344. Paul Tillich, *The Protestant Era* (note 234), pp. 222 ff.

INDEX

Adventists. *See* Seventh-day Adventists

Afghanistan, Christianity in, 13

Africa
  Christianity in, 10–13, 262–265
  post-Christian sects, 10–11
  See also names of countries

Albania, Christianity in, 16

Algeria, Christianity in, 11

Alsace-Lorraine, Lutheranism in, 17

America
  Protestant division in, 60–61, 62
  separation of church and state, 61

American Bible Society, 63

American Board of Commissioners for Foreign Missions, 63

American Home Missionary Society, 63

Amish, literature on, 271
  See also Mennonites

Anabaptists, 26, 27, 31, 33, 38, 108, 137, 211, 278
  baptism, 160
  church-state relations, 343, 344
  literature on, 269–270
  meaning of name, 158, 160

Anglicanism
  Anglican Communion, 24, 355
  Anglican Orders, 151
  baptism, 162, 163
  Book of Common Prayer, 32, 40–41, 150, 173, 215
  in Burma, 261
  Christian ethics, 187
  and Christian unity, 63
  the Church in, 321
  church-state relations, 346
  and ecumenism, 290–291
  Elizabethan Settlement, 32
  hymnody, 233
  Lambeth Conferences, 64
  literature on, 269, 285, 294
  Lord's Supper, 172, 173–174, 332–333
  natural law, 183
  Ordinal of 1550, 118

Anglicanism (*continued*)
  principle of comprehension, 57
  in Protestant world, 24–25, 26
  Protestantization of England, 31–33
  in Sudan, 12
  Thirty-nine Articles, 35, 173
  in Uganda, 12
  women in, 325–326

Anglo-Catholics, 152, 170, 173, 174

d'Angoulème, Marguerite, 30

Antinomianism, 41, 102

Apologetics, Christian, literature on, 293–300

Aquinas, Thomas, 38, 103
  on salvation, 311

Architecture, 237–240, 353–354
  Gothic revival, 238–239

Arminianism, 25, 41, 294, 306
  central doctrine of, 92–93
  concept of God, 77

Arminius, Jakob, 31, 92

Arnold, Gottfried, 43

Arts, Protestantism and, 227–241, 350–354

Asceticism, 221

Asia
  Protestantism in, 10
  See also names of countries

Assemblies of God, 16, 27, 271

Athanasian Creed, 81

Atonement, 310

Augsburg, Peace of, 22, 208

Augsburg Confession (1530), 35, 41, 57, 320

Augustine of Hippo, 11, 39, 86, 100, 103, 186
  philosophy of history, 301, 302

Aulén, Gustaf, 77

Australia, Protestantism in, 10

Authority
  biblical vs. papal, 117–118, 314
  church/state hierarchy vs. apostolic Christianity, 206–209
  disestablishment and, 210
  tradition as, 118

Azores, Christianity in, 13

357

WESTMAR COLLEGE LIBRARY.

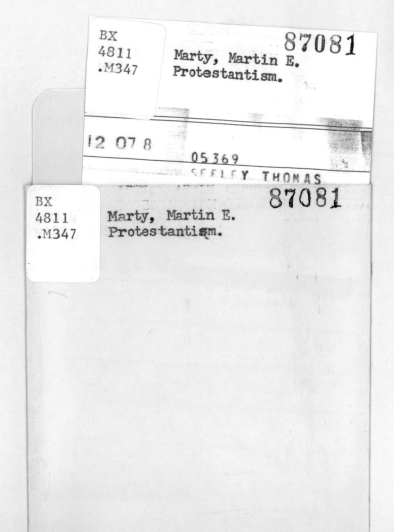

BX
4811
.M347

Marty, Martin E.
Protestantism.

87081

12 07 8

05369

SEELEY THOMAS

87081

BX
4811
.M347

Marty, Martin E.
Protestantism.